Becker Professional Education, a global leader in professional educa[...] [mate]rials for the ACCA for more than 20 years. Thousands of students studyi[ng have] succeeded in their professional examinations studying with its Platin[...] Central and Eastern Europe and Central Asia.

Nearly half a million professionals have advanced their careers through Becker Professional Education's courses. Throughout its 60-year history, Becker has earned a strong track record of student success through world-class teaching, curriculum and learning tools.

Becker Professional Education has been awarded ACCA Approved Content Provider Status for its ACCA materials, as well as materials for the Diploma in International Financial Reporting (DipIFR).

We provide a single solution for individuals and companies in need of global accounting certifications and continuing professional education.

Becker Professional Education's ACCA Study Materials

All of Becker's materials are authored by experienced ACCA lecturers and are used in the delivery of classroom courses.

Study Text: Gives complete coverage of the syllabus with a focus on learning outcomes. It is designed to be used both as a reference text and as part of integrated study. It also includes the ACCA Syllabus and Study Guide, exam advice and commentaries and a Study Question Bank containing practice questions relating to each topic covered.

Revision Question Bank: Exam style and standard questions together with comprehensive answers to support and prepare students for their exams. The Revision Question Bank also includes past examination questions (updated where relevant), model answers and alternative solutions and tutorial notes.

Revision Essentials Handbook*: A condensed, easy-to-use aid to revision containing essential technical content and exam guidance.

*Revision Essentials Handbook are substantially derived from content reviewed by ACCA's examining team.

Becker Professional Education
is an ACCA approved content provider

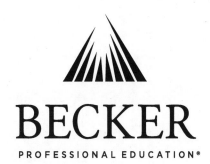

BECKER
PROFESSIONAL EDUCATION®

ACCA
PERFORMANCE MANAGEMENT F5
STUDY TEXT

September 2017 to June 2018 Edition

LICENSE AGREEMENT

DO NOT DOWNLOAD, ACCESS, AND/OR USE ANY OF THESE MATERIALS (AS THAT TERM IS DEFINED BELOW) UNTIL YOU HAVE READ THIS LICENSE AGREEMENT CAREFULLY. IF YOU DOWNLOAD, ACCESS, AND/OR USE ANY OF THESE MATERIALS, YOU ARE AGREEING AND CONSENTING TO BE BOUND BY AND ARE BECOMING A PARTY TO THIS LICENSE AGREEMENT ("AGREEMENT").

The printed Materials provided to you and/or the Materials provided for download to your computer and/or provided via a web application to which you are granted access are NOT for sale and are not being sold to you. You may NOT transfer these Materials to any other person or permit any other person to use these Materials. You may **only** acquire a license to use these Materials and **only** upon the terms and conditions set forth in this Agreement. Read this Agreement carefully **before** downloading, and/or accessing, and/or using these Materials. **Do not** download and/or access, and/or use these Materials **unless** you agree with **all** terms of this Agreement.

NOTE: You may already be a party to this Agreement if you registered for a Becker Professional Education® ACCA Program (the "Program") or placed an order for these Materials online or using a printed form that included this License Agreement. Please review the termination section regarding your rights to terminate this License Agreement and receive a refund of your payment.

Grant: Upon your acceptance of the terms of this Agreement, in a manner set forth above, DeVry/Becker Educational Development Corp. ("Becker") hereby grants to you a non-exclusive, revocable, non-transferable, non-sublicensable, limited license to use (as defined below) the Materials by downloading them onto a computer and/or by accessing them via a web application using a user ID and password (as defined below), and any Materials to which you are granted access as a result of your license to use these Materials and/or in connection with the Program on the following terms:

During the Term of this Agreement, you may:

- use the Materials for preparation for the ACCA examinations (the "Exams"), and/or for your studies relating to the subject matter covered by the Materials and/or the Exams, including taking electronic and/or handwritten notes during the Program, provided that all notes taken that relate to the subject matter of the Materials are and shall remain Materials subject to the terms of this Agreement;

- download the Materials onto any single device;

- download the Materials onto a second device so long as the first device and the second device are not used simultaneously;

- download the Materials onto a third device so long as the first, second, and third device are not used simultaneously; and

- download the Materials onto a fourth device so long as the first, second, third, and fourth device are not used simultaneously.

The number of installations may vary outside of the U.S. Please review your local office policies and procedures to confirm the number of installations granted—your local office's policies and procedures regarding the number of allowable activations of downloads supersedes the limitations contained herein and is controlling.

You may not:

- use the Materials for any purpose other than as expressly permitted above;

- use the downloaded Materials on more than one device, computer terminal, or workstation at the same time;

- make copies of the Materials;

- rent, lease, license, lend, or otherwise transfer or provide (by gift, sale, or otherwise) all or any part of the Materials to anyone;

- permit the use of all or any part of the Materials by anyone other than you; or

- reverse engineer, decompile, disassemble, or create derivate works of the Materials.

Materials: As used in this Agreement, the term "Materials" means and includes any printed materials provided to you by Becker, and/or to which you are granted access by Becker (directly or indirectly) in connection with your license of the Materials and/or the Program, and shall include notes you take (by hand, electronically, digitally, or otherwise) while using the Materials relating to the subject matter of the Materials; any and all electronically-stored/accessed/delivered, and/or digitally-stored/accessed/delivered materials included under this License via download to a computer or via access to a web application, and/or otherwise provided to you and/or to which you are otherwise granted access by Becker (directly or indirectly), including, but not limited to, applications downloadable from a third party, for example Google® or Amazon®, in connection with your license of the Materials.

Title: Becker is and will remain the owner of all title, ownership rights, intellectual property, and all other rights and interests in and to the Materials that are subject to the terms of this Agreement. The Materials are protected by the copyright laws of the United States and international copyright laws and treaties.

Termination: The license granted under this Agreement commences upon your receipt of these Materials. This license shall terminate the earlier of: (i) ten (10) business days after notice to you of non-payment of or default on any payment due Becker which has not been cured within such 10-day period; or (ii) immediately if you fail to comply with any of the limitations described above; or (iii) upon expiration of the examination period for which the Materials are valid as specified on your order confirmation and in the title of the course package. For example, Materials marked, "For Examinations to August 2018," are valid for examinations from September 2017 to August 2018 and the license to these Materials terminates at the end of August 2018. All online packages and Materials will be removed after the relevant examination period and you will no longer have access to the online packages or Materials. In addition, upon termination of this license for any reason, you must delete or otherwise remove from your computer and other device any Materials you downloaded, including, but not limited to, any archival copies you may have made. The Title, Exclusion of Warranties, Exclusion of Damages, Indemnification and Remedies, Severability of Terms and Governing Law provisions, and any amounts due, shall survive termination of the license.

Your Limited Right to Terminate this License and Receive a Refund: You may terminate this license for the in-class, online, and self-study Programs in accordance with Becker's refund policy at https://becker.com/ACCA.

Exclusion of Warranties: YOU EXPRESSLY ASSUME ALL RISK FOR USE OF THE MATERIALS. YOU AGREE THAT THE MATERIALS ARE PROVIDED TO YOU "AS IS" AND "AS AVAILABLE" AND THAT BECKER MAKES NO WARRANTIES, EXPRESS OR IMPLIED, WITH RESPECT TO THE MATERIALS, THEIR MERCHANTABILITY OR FITNESS FOR A PARTICULAR PURPOSE AND NO WARRANTY OF NONINFRINGEMENT OF THIRD PARTIES' RIGHTS. NO DEALER, AGENT OR EMPLOYEE OF BECKER IS AUTHORIZED TO PROVIDE ANY SUCH WARRANTY TO YOU. BECAUSE SOME JURISDICTIONS DO NOT ALLOW THE EXCLUSION OF IMPLIED WARRANTIES, THE ABOVE EXCLUSION OF IMPLIED WARRANTIES MAY NOT APPLY TO YOU. BECKER DOES NOT WARRANT OR GUARANTEE THAT YOU WILL PASS ANY EXAMINATION.

Exclusion of Damages: UNDER NO CIRCUMSTANCES AND UNDER NO LEGAL THEORY, TORT, CONTRACT, OR OTHERWISE, SHALL BECKER OR ITS DIRECTORS, OFFICERS, EMPLOYEES, OR AGENTS BE LIABLE TO YOU OR ANY OTHER PERSON FOR ANY CONSEQUENTIAL, INCIDENTAL, INDIRECT, PUNITIVE, EXEMPLARY OR SPECIAL DAMAGES OF ANY CHARACTER, INCLUDING, WITHOUT LIMITATION, DAMAGES FOR LOSS OF GOODWILL, WORK STOPPAGE, COMPUTER FAILURE OR MALFUNCTION OR ANY AND ALL OTHER DAMAGES OR LOSSES, OR FOR ANY DAMAGES IN EXCESS OF BECKER'S LIST PRICE FOR A LICENSE TO THE MATERIALS, EVEN IF BECKER SHALL HAVE BEEN INFORMED OF THE POSSIBILITY OF SUCH DAMAGES, OR FOR ANY CLAIM BY ANY OTHER PARTY. Some jurisdictions do not allow the limitation or exclusion of liability for incidental or consequential damages, so the above limitation or exclusion may not apply to you.

Indemnification and Remedies: You agree to indemnify and hold Becker and its employees, representatives, agents, attorneys, affiliates, directors, officers, members, managers, and shareholders harmless from and against any and all claims, demands, losses, damages, penalties, costs or expenses (including reasonable attorneys' and expert witnesses' fees and costs) of any kind or nature, arising from or relating to any violation, breach, or nonfulfillment by you of any provision of this license. If you are obligated to provide indemnification pursuant to this provision, Becker may, in its sole and absolute discretion, control the disposition of any indemnified action at your sole cost and expense. Without limiting the foregoing, you may not settle, compromise, or in any other manner dispose of any indemnified action without the consent of Becker. If you breach any material term of this license, Becker shall be entitled to equitable relief by way of temporary and permanent injunction without the need for a bond and such other and further relief as any court with jurisdiction may deem just and proper.

Confidentiality: The Materials are considered confidential and proprietary to Becker. You shall keep the Materials confidential and you shall not publish or disclose the Materials to any third party without the prior written consent of Becker.

Severability of Terms: If any term or provision of this license is held invalid or unenforceable by a court of competent jurisdiction, such invalidity shall not affect the validity or operation of any other term or provision and such invalid term or provision shall be deemed to be severed from the license. This Agreement may only be modified by written agreement signed by both parties.

Governing Law: This Agreement shall be governed and construed according to the laws of the State of Illinois, United States of America, excepting that State's conflicts of laws rules. The parties agree that the jurisdiction and venue of any dispute subject to litigation is proper in any state or federal court in Chicago, Illinois, U.S.A. The parties hereby agree to waive application of the U.N. Convention on the Sale of Goods. If the State of Illinois adopts the current proposed Uniform Computer Information Transactions Act (UCITA, formerly proposed Article 2B to the Uniform Commercial Code), or a version of the proposed UCITA, that part of the laws shall not apply to any transaction under this Agreement.

Contents

Contents

Introduction

ABOUT THIS STUDY TEXT

This Study Text has been specifically written for the Association of Chartered Certified Accountants' fundamentals level examination, F5 *Performance Management.*

It provides comprehensive coverage of the core syllabus areas and is designed to be used both as a reference text and as an integral part of your studies to provide you with the knowledge, skill and confidence to succeed in your ACCA studies.

About the author: Nick Ryan is Becker's lead tutor in performance management and has more than 15 years' experience in delivering ACCA exam-based training.

How to Use This Study Text

You should start by reading through the syllabus, study guide and approach to examining the syllabus provided in this introduction to familiarise yourself with the content of this exam.

The sessions which follow include the following features:

Focus	These are the learning outcomes relevant to the session, as published in the ACCA Study Guide.
Session Guidance	Tutor advice and strategies for approaching each session.
Visual Overview	A diagram of the concepts and the relationships addressed in each session.
Definitions	Terms are defined as they are introduced and larger groupings of terms will be set forth in a Terminology section.
Illustrations	These are to be read as part of the text. Any solutions to numerical Illustrations are provided.
Exhibits	These extracts of external content are presented to reinforce concepts and should be read as part of the text.
Examples	These should be attempted using the pro forma solution provided (where applicable).
Key Points	Attention is drawn to fundamental rules, underlying concepts and principles.
Exam Advice	These tutor comments relate the content to relevance in the examination.
Commentaries	These provide additional information to reinforce content.
Session Summary	A summary of the main points of each session.
Session Quiz	These quick questions are designed to test your knowledge of the technical content. A reference to the answer is provided.
Study Question Bank	A reference to recommended practice questions contained in the Study Question Bank. As a minimum you should work through the priority questions after studying each session. For additional practice you can attempt any remaining questions.
Example Solutions	Answers to the Examples are presented at the end of each session.

SYLLABUS

Aim

To develop knowledge and skills in the application of management accounting techniques to quantitative and qualitative information for planning, decision-making, performance evaluation and control.

Main Capabilities

On successful completion of this text, candidates should be able to:

A. Explain and apply cost accounting techniques.

B. Select and appropriately apply decision-making techniques to evaluate business choices and promote efficient and effective use of scarce business resources, appreciating the risks and uncertainty inherent in business and controlling those risks.

C. Identify and apply appropriate budgeting techniques and methods for planning and control and use standard costing systems to measure and control business performance and to identify remedial action.

D. Identify and discuss performance management information and measurement systems and assess the performance of a business from both a financial and non-financial viewpoint, appreciating the problems of controlling divisionalised businesses and the importance of allowing for external aspects.

Rationale

The syllabus for F5 *Performance Management* builds on the knowledge gained in F2 *Management Accounting* and seeks to examine candidates' understanding of how to manage the performance of a business. It also prepares candidates for more specialist capabilities, which are covered in P5 *Advanced Performance Management*.

The syllabus begins by introducing more specialised management accounting topics. There is some knowledge *assumed* from F2—primarily overhead treatments. The objective here is to ensure candidates have a broader background in management accounting techniques.

The syllabus then considers decision-making. Candidates need to appreciate the problems surrounding scarce resource, pricing and make-or-buy decisions, and how this relates to the assessment of performance. Risk and uncertainty are a factor of real-life decisions and candidates need to understand risk and be able to apply some basic methods to help resolve the risks inherent in decision-making.

Budgeting is an important aspect of many accountants' lives. The syllabus explores different budgeting techniques and the problems inherent in them. The behavioural aspects of budgeting are important for accountants to understand, and the syllabus includes consideration of the way individuals react to a budget. The preparation of fixed, flexible and incremental budgets is *assumed* knowledge from F2.

Standard costing and variances are then built on. All the variances examined in F2 are *assumed* knowledge. Mix and yield variances, and planning and operational variances are explored here and the link is made to performance management. It is important for accountants to be able to interpret the numbers that they calculate and ask what they mean in the context of performance.

The syllabus concludes with performance management systems, measurement and control. This is a **major area** of the syllabus. Accountants need to understand how a business should be managed and controlled and how information systems can be used to facilitate this. They should appreciate the importance of both financial and non-financial performance measures in management.

Accountants should also appreciate the difficulties in assessing performance in divisionalised businesses and the problems caused by failing to consider external influences on performance. This section leads directly to P5.

All of the subject areas covered in this syllabus could be examined in either a public sector or private sector context.

Relational Diagram of Main Capabilities

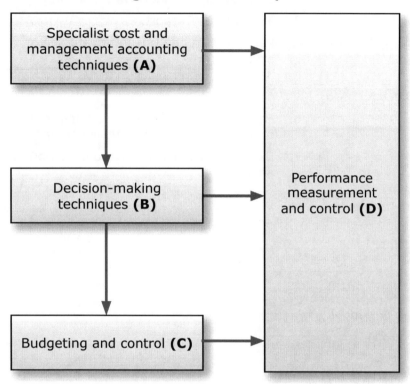

Position in the ACCA Qualification

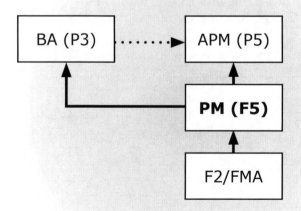

Detailed Syllabus

A. Specialist Cost and Management Accounting Techniques

1. Activity-based costing
2. Target costing
3. Life-cycle costing
4. Throughput accounting
5. Environmental accounting

B. Decision-Making Techniques

1. Relevant cost analysis
2. Cost volume profit analysis
3. Limiting factors
4. Pricing decisions
5. Make-or-buy and other short-term decisions
6. Dealing with risk and uncertainty in decision-making

C. Budgeting and Control

1. Budgetary systems and types of budget
2. Quantitative analysis in budgeting
3. Standard costing
4. Material mix and yield variances
5. Sales mix and quantity variances
6. Planning and operational variances
7. Performance analysis and behavioural aspects

D. Performance Measurement and Control

1. Performance management information systems
2. Sources of management information
3. Management reports
4. Performance analysis in private sector organisation
5. Divisional performance and transfer pricing
6. Performance analysis in not-for-profit organisations and the public sector
7. External considerations and behavioural aspects

ACCA Support

For examiner's reports, guidance and technical articles relevant to this exam see www.accaglobal.com/gb/en/student/acca-qual-student-journey/qual-resource/acca-qualification/f5.html.

The ACCA's Study Guide which follows is referenced to the sessions in this Study Text.

ACCA STUDY GUIDE

A. Specialist Cost and Management Accounting Techniques	**Ref.**
1. Activity-based costing	**1**
a) Identify appropriate cost drivers under ABC.	
b) Calculate costs per driver and per unit using ABC.	
c) Compare ABC and traditional methods of overhead absorption based on production units, labour hours or machine hours.	
2. Target costing	**2**
a) Derive a target cost in manufacturing and service industries.	
b) Explain the difficulties of using target costing in service industries.	
c) Suggest how a target cost gap might be closed.	
3. Life-cycle costing	**2**
a) Identify the costs involved at different stages of the life-cycle.	
b) Derive a life cycle cost in manufacturing and service industries.	
c) Identify the benefits of life cycle costing.	
4. Throughput accounting	**2**
a) Discuss and apply the theory of constraints.	
b) Calculate and interpret a throughput accounting ratio (TPAR).	
c) Suggest how a TPAR could be improved.	
d) Apply throughput accounting to a multi-product decision-making problem.	
5. Environmental accounting	**2**
a) Discuss the issues business face in the management of environmental costs.	
b) Describe the different methods a business may use to account for its environmental costs.	

B. Decision-Making Techniques	**Ref.**
1. Relevant cost analysis	**3**
a) Explain the concept of relevant costing.	
b) Identify and calculate relevant costs for a specific decision situations from given data.	
c) Explain and apply the concept of opportunity costs.	
2. Cost volume profit analysis	**4**
a) Explain the nature of CVP analysis.	
b) Calculate and interpret breakeven point and margin of safety.	
c) Calculate the contribution to sales ratio, in single and multi-product situations, and demonstrate an understanding of its use.	
d) Calculate target profit or revenue in single and multi-product situations, and demonstrate an understanding of its use.	
e) Prepare breakeven charts and profit volume charts and interpret the information contained within each, including multi-product situations.	
f) Discuss the limitations of CVP analysis for planning and decision making.	
3. Limiting factors	**5**
a) Identify limiting factors in a scarce resource situation and select an appropriate technique.	
b) Determine the optimal production plan where an organisation is restricted by a single limiting factor, including within the context of "make" or "buy" decisions.	
c) Formulate and solve multiple scarce resource problem both graphically and using simultaneous equations as appropriate.	
d) Explain and calculate shadow prices (dual prices) and discuss their implications on decision-making and performance management.	
e) Calculate slack and explain the implications of the existence of slack for decision-making and performance management. (Excluding simplex and sensitivity to changes in objective functions.)	

(continued on next page)

Ref.

4. Pricing decisions	**6**

4. **Pricing decisions**

a) Explain the factors that influence the pricing of a product or service.

b) Explain the price elasticity of demand.

c) Derive and manipulate a straight line demand equation. Derive an equation for the total cost function (including volume-based discounts).

d) Calculate the optimum selling price and quantity for an organisation, equating marginal cost and marginal revenue.

e) Evaluate a decision to increase production and sales levels, considering incremental costs, incremental revenues and other factors.

f) Determine prices and output levels for profit maximisation using the demand based approach to pricing (both tabular and algebraic methods).

g) Explain different price strategies, including:

    i) All forms of cost-plus

    ii) Skimming

    iii) Penetration

    iv) Complementary product

    v) Product-line

    vi) Volume discounting

    vii) Discrimination

    viii) Relevant cost

h) Calculate a price from a given strategy using cost-plus and relevant cost.

5. **Make-or-buy and other short-term decisions**   **3**

a) Explain the issues surrounding make v. buy and outsourcing decisions.

b) Calculate and compare "make" costs with "buy-in" costs.

c) Compare in-house costs and outsource costs of completing tasks and consider other issues surrounding this decision.

d) Apply relevant costing principles in situations involving shut down, one-off contracts and the further processing of joint products.

6. **Dealing with risk and uncertainty in decision-making**   **7**

a) Suggest research techniques to reduce uncertainty (e.g. focus groups, market research).

b) Explain the use of simulation, expected values and sensitivity.

c) Apply expected values and sensitivity to decision-making problems.

d) Apply the techniques of maximax, maximin, and minimax regret to decision-making problems including the production of profit tables.

e) Draw a decision tree and use it to solve a multi-stage decision problem.

f) Calculate the value of perfect and imperfect information.

(continued on next page)

C.	Budgeting and Control	Ref.

1. Budgetary systems and types of budget   8

a) Explain how budgetary systems fit within the performance hierarchy.

b) Select and explain appropriate budgetary systems for an organisation, including top-down, bottom-up, rolling, zero-base, activity-base, incremental and feed-forward control.

c) Describe the information used in budget systems and the sources of the information needed.

d) Indicate the usefulness and problems with different budget types (including fixed, flexible, zero-based, activity-based, incremental, rolling, top-down, bottom-up, master, and functional).

e) Prepare flexed budgets, rolling budgets and activity based budgets.

f) Explain the beyond budgeting model, including the benefits and problems that may be faced if it is adopted in an organisation.

g) Discuss the issues surrounding setting the difficulty level for a budget.

h) Explain the benefits and difficulties of the participation of employees in the negotiation of targets.

i) Explain the difficulties of changing a budgetary system or type of budget used.

j) Explain how budget systems can deal with uncertainty in the environment.

2. Quantitative analysis in budgeting   9

a) Analyse fixed and variable cost elements from total cost data using high/low method.

b) Estimate the learning rate and learning effect.

c) Apply the learning curve to a budgetary problem, including calculations on steady states.

d) Discuss the reservations with the learning curve.

e) Apply expected values and explain the problems and benefits.   7

f) Explain the benefits and dangers inherent in using spread sheets in budgeting.   9

3. Standard costing   10

a) Explain the use of standard costs.

b) Outline the methods used to derive standard costs and discuss the different types of cost possible.

c) Explain and illustrate the importance of flexing budgets in performance management.

d) Explain and apply the principle of controllability in the performance management system.

4. Material mix and yield variances   12

a) Calculate, identify the cause of, and explain material mix and yield variances.

b) Explain the wider issues involved in changing material mix (e.g. cost, quality and performance measurement issues).

c) Identify and explain the relationship of the material price variance with the material mix and yield variances.

d) Suggest and justify alternative methods of controlling production processes.

5. Sales mix and quantity variances   12

a) Calculate, identify the cause of, and explain sales mix and quantity variances.

b) Identify and explain the relationship of the sales volume variances with the sales mix and quantity variances.

6. Planning and operational variances   13

a) Calculate a revised budget.

b) Identify and explain those factors that could and could not be allowed to revise an original budget.

c) Calculate, identify the cause of and explain planning and operational variances for:

    i) Sales, including market size and market share

    ii) Materials

    iii) Labour, including the effect of the learning curve.

d) Explain and discuss the manipulation issues involved in revising budgets.

(continued on next page)

Ref.

7. Performance analysis
13
a) Analyse and evaluate past performance using the results of variance analysis.
b) Use variance analysis to assess how future performance of an organisation or business can be improved.
c) Identify the factors which influence behaviour. **8**
d) Discuss the effect that variances have on staff motivation and action. **13**
e) Describe the dysfunctional nature of some variances in the modern environment of JIT and TQM.
f) Discuss the behavioural problems resulting from using standard costs in rapidly changing environments.

D. Performance Measurement and Control | Ref.

1. Performance management information systems
18
a) Identify the accounting information requirements and describe the different types of information systems used for strategic planning, management control and operational control and decision making.
b) Define and identify the main characteristics of transaction processing systems; management information systems; executive information systems; and enterprise resource planning systems.
c) Define and discuss the merits of, and potential problems with, open and closed systems with regards to the needs of performance management.

2. Sources of management information
18
a) Identify the principal internal and external sources of management accounting information.
b) Demonstrate how these principal sources of management information might be used for control purposes.
c) Identify and discuss the direct data capture and process costs of management accounting information.
d) Identify and discuss the indirect costs of producing information.
e) Discuss the limitations of using externally generated information.

3. Management reports
18
a) Discuss the principal controls required in generating and disturbing internal information.
b) Discuss the procedures that may be necessary to ensure the security of highly confidential information that is not for external consumption.

4. Performance analysis in private sector organisations
14
a) Describe, calculate and interpret financial performance indicators (FPIs) for profitability, liquidity and risk in both manufacturing and service businesses. Suggest methods to improve these measures.
b) Describe, calculate and interpret non-financial performance indicators (NFPIs) and suggest method to improve the performance indicated.
c) Analyse past performance and suggest ways for improving financial and non-financial performance.
d) Explain the causes and problems created by short-termism and financial manipulation of results and suggest methods to encourage a long-term view. **15**
e) Explain and interpret the Balanced Scorecard, and the Building Block model proposed by Fitzgerald and Moon. **15**
f) Discuss the difficulties of target setting in qualitative areas. **14**

5. Divisional performance and transfer pricing
a) Explain and illustrate the basis for setting a transfer price using variable cost, full cost and the principles behind allowing for intermediate markets. **17**
b) Explain how transfer prices can distort the performance assessment of divisions and decisions made. **17**
c) Explain the meaning of, and calculate, Return on Investment (ROI) and Residual Income (RI), and discuss their shortcomings. **16**
d) Compare divisional performance and recognise the problems of doing so. **16**

(continued on next page)

FORMULAE

Learning Curve

$Y = ax^b$

Where Y = cumulative average time per unit to produce x units

a = time taken for the first unit of output

x = total number of units produced

b = the index of learning (log LR/log 2)

LR = the learning rate as a decimal

Demand Curve

$P = a - bQ$

$$b = \frac{\text{change in price}}{\text{change in quantity}}$$

a = price when $Q = 0$

$MR = a - 2bQ$

Approach to Examining the Syllabus

The syllabus may be assessed by a paper-based or computer-based examination (CBE). The examination will be structured in three sections and will contain both computational and discursive elements.

All questions are compulsory.

Time allowed: 3 hours

- Section A of the exam comprises 15 objective test (OT) questions of 2 marks each.
- Section B of the exam comprises three 10-mark case-based questions. Each case has five OT questions of 2 marks each.
- Section C of the exam contains two 20-mark scenario-based questions.

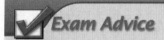 **Exam Advice**

The CBE format introduces many time saving efficiencies compared to the paper-based exam. So to provide an equal assessment, students will have **3 hours 15 minutes** to complete the paper-based exams, compared to 3 hours allowed for session CBEs. For further details see the section *Exam time—providing an equal assessment* at www.accaglobal.com/gb/en/student/changes-to-exams/f5-f9-session-cbe.html

In the CBE there may be instances where extra questions appear for the purpose of quality assurance. In such cases an extra 20 minutes will be allowed.

Section A and B questions will be selected from across the entire syllabus. OT questions in the paper-based examination will contain multiple-choice questions (MCQs) only. OT questions in CBEs will contain a variety of OT types. More detail on the differences between paper-based exams and CBEs can be found in the later Examination Technique section.

Section C questions will mainly focus on the following syllabus areas although a minority of marks can be drawn from any other area of the syllabus:

- Decision-making techniques (syllabus area B)
- Budgeting and control (syllabus area C)
- Performance management and control (syllabus area D)

Questions on topic areas that are also included in F2 *Management Accounting* will be examined at an appropriately greater depth in the F5 exam.

Candidates are provided with a formulae sheet as set out on the previous page.

EXAMINATION TECHNIQUE—PAPER-BASED EXAM

Reading and Planning Time

ACCA recommends that you use the additional 15 minutes allowed for the paper-based exam in reading and planning:

- Decide in which order to do the questions—see the guidance in Exam Strategy below;
- Write a timetable on the front of your question paper, stating at what time you will start each question. You should allocate your time as follows:
  - Section A: 54 minutes
  - 10-mark questions in Section B: 18 minutes each (total 54 minutes).
  - 20-mark questions in Section C: 36 minutes each

Exam Strategy

▨ Do Section C first. It is best to do longer written questions while you are relatively fresh. Start with your best question.

▨ Having completed Section C, do the Section B questions in order of how well you know the topics covered, with your best question first. If you feel that you are very strong on variance analysis, for example, and there is a variance analysis question that you feel comfortable with, do that first. It will build up your confidence.

▨ Start Section A 54 minutes before the end of the exam.

▨ All sections will include easy marks that you should aim to earn. However, Section C questions, in particular, may also contain a discriminator, usually worth three or four marks, that is very difficult. The examiner does not expect most candidates to get that part right. Remember this, and don't get stressed about difficult parts of questions. Unless you are aiming to be a prizewinner you can ignore them, and remind yourself that you need 50% to pass. So why not aim to get the easiest 50 marks instead of the hardest 50 marks?

▨ Do answer all questions. The longer you spend on a question, the fewer marks you generate per minute spent. Always move on to the next question when you have used up the time allocated.

▨ Remember at F5, you cannot pass on calculations alone. You must attempt the written parts of questions.

Section A

▨ These objective test (OT) questions consist of:
  • a "stem" (the question);
  • a "key" (the correct answer); and
  • 3 "distractors" (plausible but incorrect answers).

Illustration 1   Answering an OT Question

A company manufactures two products, C and D, for which the following information is available:

	Product C	Product D	Total
Budgeted production (units)	1,000	4,000	5,000
Labour hours per unit/in total	8	10	48,000
Number of production runs required	13	15	28
Number of inspections during production	5	3	8

Total production set-up costs	$140,000
Total inspection costs	$80,000
Other overhead costs	$96,000

Other overhead costs are absorbed on the basis of labour hours per unit.

Using activity-based costing, what is the budgeted overhead cost per unit of product D?

A $43.84
B $46.25
C $131.00
D $140.64

Illustration 1 Answering an OT Question
(continued)

Solution

Step 1

Start by reading the question in **bold** and interpreting as necessary. This tells you what you have to do. In this case, calculate the budgeted overhead cost per unit of product D.

Step 2

Mentally plan what steps you will take to answer the question. From experience of similar questions on activity-based costing, you will know that you have to do the following:

a. Find the activities and identify their respective driver. In this case set-up costs, inspection costs and other overheads are the activities. The drivers are number of production runs, number of inspections and, by default, number of labour hours.

b. Calculate the cost per unit of driver.

c. Calculate the total costs of each activity that are apportioned to product D based on how many units of driver are used by product D in total.

d. Sum these to get the total overhead costs apportioned.

e. Divide the total sum apportioned by the budgeted number of units of production of D.

Step 3: Solve

a. Cost per unit of driver:
Set-up costs (140,000 ÷ 28) = $5,000 per production run
Inspection costs (80,000 ÷ 8) = $10,000 per inspection
Other overhead costs: (96,000 ÷ 48,000) = $2 per labour hour

b. Apportion costs to product D: $000
Set-up costs (5,000 × 15)   75
Inspection costs (10,000 × 3)   30
Other overhead costs (2 × 10 × 4,000)   80

c. Total overhead costs apportioned to product D   185

d. Overhead cost per unit = $185,000 ÷ 4,000 = $46.25

Step 4

Select the appropriate box on your answer sheet: B

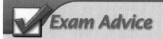

Exam Advice

- Cover up the answers, A, B, C and D, when doing calculations.

- It is not unusual for one of the distractors to be a number that will be calculated before reaching the final solution. Especially under exam pressure you may think that you have the correct answer before you have completed the calculation.

- The majority of questions in Section A (and Section B) are likely to be non-computational. The time pressure for such items is relatively low, allowing more time for computational items.

- If you are getting close to the end of your time allocation for the section and you still have a few questions left to answer—guess! If you have time at the end of the exam you can still come back and check them. Avoid leaving questions unanswered before you move to the remaining sections as you will not be allowed to complete the MCQ answer sheet when the exam time is up.

Section B

- Each set of the five OT questions will be based on a "case" or short scenario.

- Typically three from each set of five OT questions will be computational.

- Although the questions will be scenario-based not all of the questions will rely on the details of the scenario. For example, the scenario is about throughput accounting and one question asks about the theory of constraints.

- As for Section A, ensure that you select an answer for every part of every question; there is no negative marking.

Section C

Numerical Requirements

▦ Before starting a computation, picture your route. Do this by noting down the steps you are going to take and imagining the layout of your answer.

▦ Set up a pro forma structure for your answer before working the numbers. A columnar layout is often appropriate and it helps to avoid mistakes and is easier for the marker to follow. Write clearly and leave space.

▦ Include all your workings and **cross-reference** them to the face of your answer.

▦ A clear approach and workings will help earn marks even if you make an arithmetical mistake.

▦ If you do spot a mistake in your answer, show the correction but it is **not** worthwhile spending time amending the consequent effects of it. The marker will **not** penalise you for errors caused by an earlier mistake.

▦ Don't ignore marks for written recommendations or comments based on your computation. These are easy marks to gain. For example, a linear programme question is likely to have a mark for stating, "It is recommended to make x units of Product A and y units of Product B to maximise contribution".

Written Requirements

Planning

▦ Read the requirements carefully at least twice to identify exactly how many points you are being asked to address. Note the instruction in the requirement, for example, explain, describe, outline. The meaning of these terms is explained in an exam technique article, "Approaching Written Questions", which can be downloaded from the ACCA website.

▦ Jot down *relevant* thoughts on your plan—use the scenario for clues, plus your technical knowledge.

▦ Give your plan a structure which you will follow when you write up the answer. Take into account the marking guide.

Presentation

▦ Use headings and subheadings to give your answer structure and to make it easier to read.

▦ Use short paragraphs for each point that you are making.

▦ Separate paragraphs by leaving at least one line of space between each one.

▦ Use bullet points where this seems appropriate (e.g. for a list of advantages/disadvantages). However, each bullet point *must* read on from an introduction to the list or be complete in itself. You must **not** write in "note form".

▦ In paper-based exams, write legibly using a good-quality **black** pen.

Style

▦ Long, philosophical debate does not impress markers. Concise, easily understood language scores marks.

▦ Imagine that you are a marker; you would like to see a short, concise answer which clearly addresses the requirement.

▦ If you could not complete the calculations required for comment then *assume* an answer to the calculations. As long as your comments are consistent with a sensible assumption (e.g. it must not contradict information in the question) you will be awarded the marks for the comments.

▦ As you write, refer back to the requirement to ensure that you are addressing it. "Knowledge dumping" on a topic will not earn any marks if it does not address the requirement.

EXAMINATION TECHNIQUE—COMPUTER-BASED EXAM

Many of the comments made above regarding paper-based exams also apply to CBEs, in particular the points on time allocation and how generally to approach the questions in each section. However there are some important differences in the OT question types used in CBEs and how responses to long-form questions should be constructed.

OT Types

In addition to single-answer multiple choice question type, the CBE will also contain OT questions drawn from the following types:

- Multiple response—more than one correct answer
- Pull down list—drop down menu
- Fill in the blank—number entry
- Hot area—selecting area(s) in an image
- Hot spot—selecting one point in an image
- Drag and drop—matching

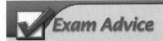

Illustrations of all the types relevant to this exam can be found in Becker's *Objective Test Question Practice* booklet which is also included in Becker's *Revision Question Bank*.

Constructed Response Questions

Although the scenarios and requirements will be the same as for the paper-based exam, candidates must construct their answers using either a:

- blank spreadsheet;
- blank word processing document;
- pre-formatted spreadsheet; or
- template.

The most common forms of input will be a blank spreadsheet or blank word processing document.

Answers to these questions will be marked by subject matter experts and therefore workings for computational requirements must be shown. However, no marks are awarded for formatting and hence a candidate can focus on the content of an answer rather than how it looks.

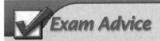

When attempting long-form questions during your revision try out the constructed response workspace referenced at the end of this section to input your answer.

CBE Functionality

During the live exam the following online functionality will include:

- Timer—with a warning when only 15 minutes remain.
- Scratch pad—although the exam centre will also provide physical note paper. The scratch pad/physical notes will **not** be marked.
- Symbols—for selection of currency symbols.
- A calculator with standard and scientific modes—candidates can also bring a physical calculator to the exam.
- Help/Formulae/Tables—which include a guide to the spreadsheet and word processing functions.
- Navigator/Item Review Screen—shows each question's status as:
  - "Complete"—however this does not guarantee that all parts of a question have been completed.
  - "Incomplete"—the question has been viewed but not attempted.
  - "Unseen"—the question has not been viewed.
  - "Flagged for review"—where the candidate has used the flag function.

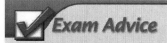
Exam Advice

You are strongly urged to use the following ACCA resources that are available to help candidates familiarise themselves with the CBE style and functionality in preparation for the exam:

- Your Guide to ACCA CBEs (pdf and video);
- Full specimen exam;
- Extra constructed response questions;
- Constructed response workspace.

All are available at www.accaglobal.com/uk/en/student/exam-support-resources/ fundamentals-exams-study-resources/f5/specimen-exams.html

Cost Accounting

FOCUS

This session covers the following content from the ACCA Study Guide.

A. Specialist Cost and Management Accounting Techniques

1. Activity-based costing

a) Identify appropriate cost drivers under ABC.

b) Calculate costs per driver and per unit using ABC.

c) Compare ABC and traditional methods of overhead absorption based on production units, labour hours or machine hours.

Session 1 Guidance

■ **Note** that if you studied F2, sections 1 and 2 of this session should be revision. If not, be sure to work through these sessions carefully; the material here forms the basis of much of what follows later throughout your F5 studies.

(continued on next page)

VISUAL OVERVIEW

Objective: To consider the traditional role of the management accountant and to revise marginal and absorption costing. To learn about activity-based costing.

```
                    ┌─────────────────────────┐
                    │    INTRODUCTION TO      │
                    │  MANAGEMENT AND COST    │
                    │      ACCOUNTING         │
                    └─────────────────────────┘
```

SCOPE OF MANAGEMENT ACCOUNTING

- Management Accounting and Financial Accounting
- Comparison
- Planning, Control and Decision-Making

TRADITIONAL COSTING

- Marginal Costing
- Absorption Costing

ACTIVITY-BASED COSTING

- Introduction
- Cost Drivers
- Steps
- Calculation
- Analysis of ABC

Session 1 Guidance

■ **Understand** the topics that are assumed knowledge (s.2) and be prepared to revise them.

■ **Learn** the steps to apply ABC and understand cost drivers (s.3).

■ **Attempt** *Example 2* to understand the mechanics of calculating ABC. Be prepared to discuss the purpose, advantages and disadvantages of ABC.

1   Scope of Traditional Management Accounting

1.1   Management Accounting and Financial Accounting

Management accounting is concerned with the preparation and presentation of accounting information to management to help them plan, control and make decisions about the operations of the business.

Financial accounting is concerned with the preparation and presentation of accounting information on the performance and financial position of the business.

1.2   Comparison

	Management Accounting	Financial Accounting
Users of information	Management	Shareholders, banks, lenders and suppliers, potential investors, tax authorities and governments
Format of information	Can take any form	Presentation regulated by law and by the profession through Accounting Standards (e.g. IFRS)
Purpose of information	Useful to plan, control and make decisions	Stewardship and investment decisions
Bases of valuation	Relevant costs	Historical costs

1.3   Planning, Control and Decision-Making

Key Point

Encompasses establishing objectives and evaluating policies and actions required to achieve them.

1.3.1   Planning

- **Planning** is the setting of goals and the selection of the means of achieving these goals.
- As businesses become large, these procedures need to be formalised.
- Short-term plans such as an annual budget show in detail the intended results for the forthcoming year.
- Long-term plans, also called "strategic" plans, are usually documents showing the long-term objectives of a business.

1.3.2 Control

■ **Control** means checking that an organisation is on track to meet its long- and short-term objectives, and taking action to correct any deviations from these.

■ Long-term control includes strategic performance evaluation, which aims to measure how an organisation is performing against its strategic objectives.

■ Short-term control focuses on comparing the budgeted results with actual results.

■ This usually takes the form of an operating statement, which breaks down the difference into its component parts (variances).

1.3.3 Decision-Making

■ **Decision-making** usually involves using the information provided by the costing system to make decisions.

2 Traditional Costing

2.1 Marginal Costing

Under marginal costing, fixed overheads are not included in unit costs but are treated as a period cost (i.e. written off in full in the statement of profit or loss in the period in which they occur).

Inventory valuation includes only the variable costs of production.

2.2 Absorption Costing

Under absorption costing, overhead costs must be allocated, apportioned and absorbed.

Exam Advice

These traditional costing methods are **assumed** knowledge from F2.

2.2.1 Allocation

Initially as overhead costs are incurred, they need to be allocated to the cost centres to which they belong. This is where costs which relate to a single cost centre are allocated to that cost centre.

2.2.2 Apportionment

Apportionment is where an overhead is common to more than one cost centre and therefore needs to be shared between the relevant cost centres using an appropriate method of apportionment.

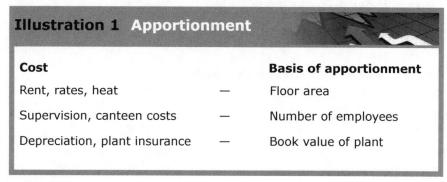

Illustration 1 Apportionment

Cost		Basis of apportionment
Rent, rates, heat	—	Floor area
Supervision, canteen costs	—	Number of employees
Depreciation, plant insurance	—	Book value of plant

2.2.3 Absorption

The total of the overheads in each production department must now be absorbed into the units of production.

This is achieved using one of the following methods:

- direct labour hour rate;
- direct material cost rate;
- direct labour cost rate;
- prime cost percentage rate;
- machine hour rate; or
- unit of output rate.

Example 1 Overhead Absorption

X Co estimates that its factory costs for the coming year will be as follows:

	$
Direct material	40,000
Direct wages	60,000
Prime cost	100,000
Factory overhead	30,000
Total factory cost	130,000

During the year there will be 100,000 direct labour hours, 50,000 machine hours, and 200,000 units will be produced.

Required:

(a) Calculate the overhead absorption rate using each of the following bases:

  (i) direct labour hour;

  (ii) direct materials cost;

  (iii) direct labour cost;

  (iv) prime cost;

  (v) machine hour;

  (vi) unit of output.

(b) Management has decided that the absorption rate per machine hour is the most appropriate method of absorbing overheads. One of the products manufactured by X Co is the Smidget. Each Smidget costs $5 per unit in materials and $10 per unit of direct labour. Making a Smidget requires half an hour of machine time.

  Calculate the full absorption cost of one unit of Smidget.

2.2.4 Summary of Absorption Costing

The diagram below depicts the process describing absorption costing:

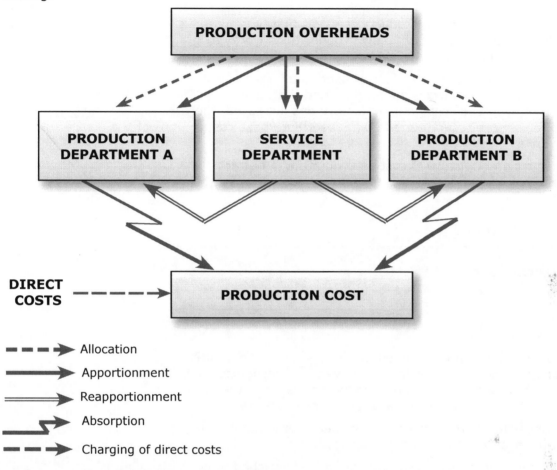

 Allocation

⟶ Apportionment

⟹ Reapportionment

⟿ Absorption

- - -▶ Charging of direct costs

3 Activity-Based Costing

Definition

Activity-based costing (ABC)—an approach to costing and activity monitoring which assigns resources consumed to activities and activities to cost objects (based on estimated consumption). Cost drivers are used to apportion activity costs to output.

3.1 Introduction

Traditional absorption costing uses one method of apportioning all overhead costs between products, typically labour hours or machine hours. This "blanket rate" means that product costs may not accurately reflect the true overhead costs of making a product.

When overhead costs accounted for only a small portion of total factory costs, this inaccuracy was not significant. In modern factories however, due to the reduction in the amount of labour used, and the increase in the amount of high technology, overhead costs are often a significant portion of overall product costs. The inaccuracy of absorption costing is no longer insignificant.

Activity-based costing aims to identify the activities which cause overhead costs to be incurred and to apportion the overhead costs to each product based on the use of the activities by each product.

This approach for calculating product costs was first written about by Cooper and Kaplan, although many organisations were using such methods before this.

ABC recognises that traditional ideas of fixed and variable cost categorisations are not always appropriate and that, as the proportion of overhead costs in manufacture has increased, there is a need for a more accurate method of absorbing these costs into cost units.

It looks for a clearer picture of cost behaviour and a better understanding of what determines the level of costs (i.e. "cost drivers").

3.2 Cost Drivers

> **Definition**
>
> **Cost driver**—a factor which can cause a change in the cost of an activity.

In absorption costing, it is assumed that the volume of output is the factor which determines costs. However, ABC recognises that the amount of cost may be determined by factors other than the volume of output. These factors are called **cost drivers**.

The cost driver for a procurement department, for example, may be the number of purchase orders processed.

An activity can have **more than one** cost driver attached to it. For example, cost drivers associated with a production activity may be:

- machine operator(s);
- floor space occupied;
- power consumed; and
- quantity of waste and/or rejected output.

Therefore, rather than use a single absorption rate, different types of overhead cost are absorbed into units of production using more appropriate rates based on cost drivers. For example, for a particular production department the following rates may be suitable:

- a warehousing cost/kg of material used;
- electricity cost/machine hour;
- production scheduling cost/production order, etc.

These can then be applied and aggregated to calculate an overhead cost per unit as set out in Step 5 of the following section.

3.3   Steps

To find total product costs, overheads are traced to individual production departments, as usual, with common costs being apportioned using suitable bases. Then the steps depicted in Figure 1 are followed.

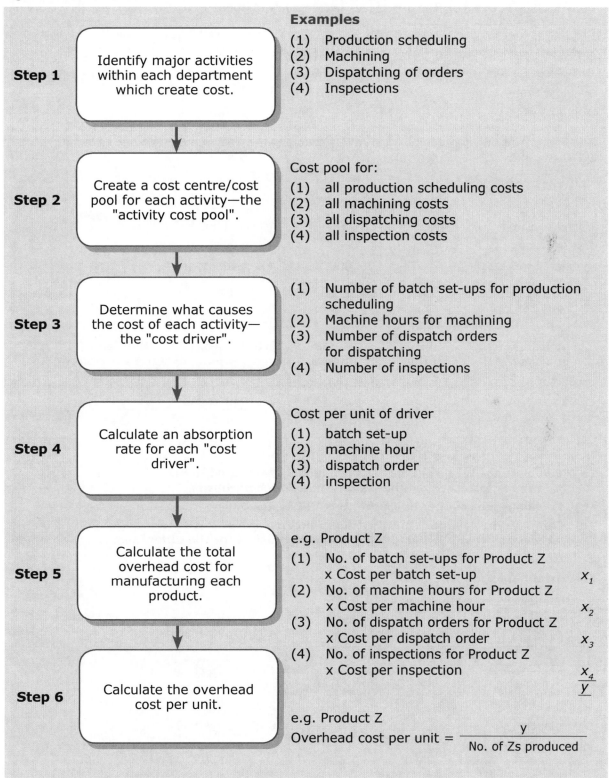

Examples

Step 1 — Identify major activities within each department which create cost.

(1)   Production scheduling
(2)   Machining
(3)   Dispatching of orders
(4)   Inspections

Step 2 — Create a cost centre/cost pool for each activity—the "activity cost pool".

Cost pool for:

(1)   all production scheduling costs
(2)   all machining costs
(3)   all dispatching costs
(4)   all inspection costs

Step 3 — Determine what causes the cost of each activity— the "cost driver".

(1)   Number of batch set-ups for production scheduling
(2)   Machine hours for machining
(3)   Number of dispatch orders for dispatching
(4)   Number of inspections

Step 4 — Calculate an absorption rate for each "cost driver".

Cost per unit of driver

(1)   batch set-up
(2)   machine hour
(3)   dispatch order
(4)   inspection

Step 5 — Calculate the total overhead cost for manufacturing each product.

e.g. Product Z

(1)   No. of batch set-ups for Product Z x Cost per batch set-up x_1
(2)   No. of machine hours for Product Z x Cost per machine hour x_2
(3)   No. of dispatch orders for Product Z x Cost per dispatch order x_3
(4)   No. of inspections for Product Z x Cost per inspection $\dfrac{x_4}{y}$

Step 6 — Calculate the overhead cost per unit.

e.g. Product Z

$$\text{Overhead cost per unit} = \frac{y}{\text{No. of Zs produced}}$$

Having discovered the cost drivers within the business, the original production departments may be reorganised to take advantage of potential cost savings.

3.4 Calculation

Example 2 Activity-Based Costing v Absorption Costing

Total budgeted fixed overheads for a firm are $712,000. These have traditionally been absorbed on a machine hour basis. The firm makes two products, A and B.

	A	B
Direct material cost	$20	$60
Direct labour cost	$50	$40
Machine time	3 hrs	4 hrs
Annual output	6,000	40,000

The firm is considering changing to an ABC system and has analysed the overhead cost into three activities:

Activities /cost pools:		Cost driver:
	$	
Machine related	178,000	Machine hours
Set-up related	230,000	Set-ups
Purchasing related	304,000	Purchase orders
Total overheads	712,000	

	Machine hours/unit	Annual output	Total machine hours	Number of set-ups	Number of purchase orders
Product A	3	6,000	18,000	16	52
Product B	4	40,000	160,000	30	100
		46,000	178,000	46	152

Required:

(a) Calculate the total cost for each product on the assumption that the firm continues to absorb overheads on a machine hour basis.

(b) Calculate the cost per unit using the ABC system.

(c) Compare the cost per unit of each product using ABC with the cost per unit using absorption costing, and identify the main reasons for the difference.

Solution

(a) Traditional

Total overhead   =

Total machine hours   =

Rate per hour   =

	A $	B $
Direct material	20.00	60.00
Direct labour	50.00	40.00
Fixed overhead		
Total		

Example 2   Activity-Based Costing v Absorption Costing (continued)

Solution

(b) ABC

Activities	Machine related	Set-up related	Purchasing related
Overheads	$178,000	$230,000	$304,000
Consumption of activities (cost drivers)	178,000 hrs	46 set-ups	152 orders
Cost per unit of driver			
Cost traced to products			
A			
B			

	A $	B $
Cost per unit		
A		
B		

	A $	B $
Direct material	20.00	60.00
Direct labour	50.00	40.00
Fixed overhead		
Total		

(c) Comparison of costs under ABC and absorption costing

3.5 Analysis of ABC

3.5.1 Advantages

The main advantage of ABC is that the costs per unit are more accurate, as overhead costs are apportioned to products based on their use of the cost drivers rather than using some arbitrary "blanket rate" as used for absorption costing. This leads to the following benefits:

✔ Better decision-making. Companies will have a more accurate knowledge of cost per unit, and therefore profit per unit. They can evaluate whether to stop producing loss-making products.

✔ Where cost plus pricing is used, the use of ABC means that the price will be more likely to achieve the desired margins.

✔ There is a better understanding of what causes costs because of the identification of the cost driver. This enables managers to make more informed decisions on actions to reduce cost.

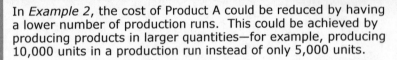

Illustration 2 More Informed Decision

In *Example 2*, the cost of Product A could be reduced by having a lower number of production runs. This could be achieved by producing products in larger quantities—for example, producing 10,000 units in a production run instead of only 5,000 units.

✔ Control of overheads is easier, as responsibility for incoming costs must be established before ABC can be implemented.

✔ More accurate performance measurement leads to better performance management.

3.5.2 Disadvantages

✗ ABC is based on historical data, which may be unsuitable for future strategic decisions.

✗ Selection of cost drivers may not be easy. There may be more than one possible cost driver for a particular overhead, so some judgement is required in selecting an appropriate driver.

✗ Additional time and cost of setting up and administering the system.

✗ Not all costs will be easily identified with particular cost pools, so some allocations will be arbitrary.

3.6　Comparison of ABC and Traditional Methods

The differences between traditional methods of absorbing overheads and ABC methods can be summarised as follows:

Traditional Absorption Costing	Activity-Based Costing
■ Initial allocation and apportionment of overheads is to cost centres.	■ Initial allocation and apportionment of overheads is to cost pools. Each cost pool represents a particular activity.
■ Absorption of overheads of each cost centre is based on volume of output (e.g. number of units or labour hours). As costs may not depend on volume, allocation of some costs may be inappropriate.	■ Absorption of overheads of each cost pool is based on the "driver" that causes the costs to vary. Thus product costs reflect more accurately the activities that cause them.
■ Many different types of costs for a particular cost centre are included in the blanket overhead absorption rate of that department.	■ Costs for a particular activity will include only the costs of performing that activity.
■ Since costs are assumed to depend on volume of output, limited information is provided to management about ways to reduce costs.	■ Identification of cost drivers allows management to understand better the causes of costs and to find more appropriate ways to control them.
■ Absorption costing is relatively straightforward.	■ ABC requires a large project to identify activities and drivers. The accounting system may have to be amended or replaced to provide the information needed.

3.7　Use of ABC in the Public Sector

In many countries, governments are making greater use of management accounting techniques:

■ to allocate government funds more efficiently to areas where they provide the greatest benefits;

■ to reduce the amount of overall government spending;

■ to provide greater transparency, so that taxpayers can see where their money is being spent; and

■ to encourage public sector bodies to become more responsive to their customers.

ABC is useful in helping public sector bodies assess more accurately the costs of the services they provide.

However, the disadvantages of ABC previously mentioned apply also to public sector organisations. Critics also argue that public sector resources would be better spent improving "front line" services than in developing sophisticated accounting techniques such as ABC.

Illustration 3 Hospital Operating Theatre

A hospital needs to monitor the costs per patient; part of this is the cost of surgery.

Under traditional methods, the operating theatre might be treated as a cost centre. An absorption cost per minute could be calculated by dividing the total costs of the theatre by the total number of minutes budgeted to be available. The cost of an operation would then be calculated by multiplying the number of minutes the operation takes by this absorption rate.

The problem with this approach is that it is not realistic to assume that the cost per minute of all operations is the same. Some operations may require several surgeons and medical staff; others may require just one or two. Different equipment and different quantities of consumable materials will be used.

Examples of activities that could be used for an ABC approach to calculating the cost of an operation include:

Activity	Driver
■ Preparing the operating theatre	■ Number of operations—the cost of preparing the theatre does not vary significantly between different types of operations.
■ Activity of anaesthetist	■ Number of operations—calculated separately for those requiring a general anaesthetic and those requiring only local anaesthetics.
■ Anaesthetic drugs	■ Time taken from entering the anaesthetic room until entering the recovery room.
■ Activity of the physician	■ Time taken from "knife to skin" until closure.
■ Consumable items during surgery	■ Itemised list of consumables used during surgery, captured by a bar-coding device.
■ Overhead activity	■ A charge for management administration and staff training.

Summary

- Management accounting is concerned with the preparation and presentation of accounting information to assist management to plan, control and make decisions.

- Costing involves calculating the unit cost of a product or service. Traditional methods are absorption costing and marginal costing.

- Under absorption costing, a share of fixed production overheads is included in the unit cost. Steps used in absorption costing are:

  - As fixed overheads are incurred, they are allocated to, or apportioned between, the cost centres in the factory.

  - Overheads of the service cost centres are apportioned between the production cost centres.

  - Total costs in each production cost centre are absorbed into the unit cost using an appropriate basis (e.g. labour or machine hours).

- Activity-based costing aims to provide a more reliable calculation of the cost of a product, by relating the cost to the activities used in producing it.

- Steps in ABC:

  - Identify the activities which cause costs to be incurred.

  - Costs are allocated and apportioned between "activity pools"—where each pool represents an activity.

  - Identify the drivers related to each activity (a driver is a factor which causes the cost of the activity to rise).

  - The absorption rate per unit of driver is calculated.

  - The product cost is calculated using absorption rates based on the drivers.

- The main advantage of ABC is that it focuses on "more accurate" costs.

- The main disadvantage is its complexity, which makes it inappropriate for many organisations.

Session 1 Quiz
Estimated time: 15 minutes

1. List the main differences between management accounting and financial accounting. (1.2)
2. List the TWO traditional approaches to costing. (2)
3. List FOUR advantages of using ABC. (3.5.1)
4. List TWO disadvantages of using ABC. (3.5.2)

Study Question Bank
Estimated time: 40 minutes

Priority		Estimated Time	Completed
Q1	Gadget Co	40 minutes	

EXAMPLE SOLUTIONS

Solution 1—Overhead Absorption

(a) Overhead absorption rates

(i) Direct labour hour rate = $\dfrac{\$30,000}{100,000 \text{ hrs}}$ = $0.30

(ii) Direct material cost rate = $\dfrac{\$30,000}{\$40,000}$ = 75%

(iii) Direct labour cost rate = $\dfrac{\$30,000}{\$60,000}$ = 50%

(iv) Prime cost percentage rate = $\dfrac{\$30,000}{\$100,000}$ = 30%

(v) Machine hour rate = $\dfrac{\$30,000}{50,000 \text{ hrs}}$ = $0.60

(vi) Unit of output rate = $\dfrac{\$30,000}{200,000 \text{ units}}$ = $0.15

(b) Full absorption cost

	$
Materials	5
Direct labour	10
Prime cost	15
Overhead absorbed (0.5 machine hours x $10)	5
Absorption cost	20

Solution 2—Activity-Based Costing v Absorption Costing

(a) Traditional

Total overhead	=	$712,000
Total machine hours	=	178,000

Rate per hour = $\dfrac{\$712,000}{178,000}$ = $4/hour

	A $	B $
Direct material	20	60
Direct labour	50	40
Fixed overhead		
3 hrs @ $4	12	
4 hrs @ $4		16
Total	82	116

(b) ABC

Activities	Machine related	Set-up related	Purchasing related
Overheads	$178,000	$230,000	$304,000
Consumption of activities (cost drivers)	178,000 hrs	46 set-ups	152 orders
Cost per unit of driver	$1 per hour	$5,000 per set-up	$2,000 per order
Cost traced to products			
A	$18,000	$80,000	$104,000
B	$160,000	$150,000	$200,000

Overhead cost per unit

$$\text{A} \quad \frac{18,000 + 80,000 + 104,000}{6,000} = \$33.67$$

$$\text{B} \quad \frac{160,000 + 150,000 + 200,000}{40,000} = \$12.75$$

	A $	B $
Direct material	20.00	60.00
Direct labour	50.00	40.00
Fixed overhead	33.67	12.75
Total	103.67	112.75

(c) Comparison of costs under ABC and absorption costing

There is a significant difference in the cost per unit of Product A when using ABC compared to traditional absorption costing. Under absorption costing, the cost per unit was calculated as $82; under ABC, the cost per unit rose to $103.67, an increase of 26%. The difference in the cost per unit of Product B is less significant. It falls to $112.75 under ABC, compared to $116 under absorption costing, a drop of 3%.

The calculation of the cost of Product A is significantly understated when absorption costing is used. A significant factor in this would appear to be set costs. The total set-up costs apportioned to Product A were $80,000, equivalent to $13.33 per unit. Product B, by contrast, has total set-up costs of $150,000, equivalent to $3.75 per unit. Product A used 16 set-ups to produce 6,000 units, which is 375 units per set-up, and Product B used 30 set-ups to produce 40,000 units, achieving output of 1,333.33 per set-up.

Similarly in product-related costs, the cost per unit of Product A was $17.33 ($104,000/6,000 units) and the cost per unit of Product B was $5 per unit ($200,000/40,000). This is because, on average, one purchase order was used for 115 units of product A, (6,000/52) and one purchase order was used for 400 units of Product B (40,000/100).

These differences in the use of the activities are disguised when absorption costing is used, and all costs are absorbed based on a machine hour basis.

Developments in Management Accounting

FOCUS

This session covers the following content from the ACCA Study Guide.

A. Specialist Cost and Management Accounting Techniques

2. Target costing

a) Derive a target cost in manufacturing and service industries.

b) Explain the difficulties of using target costing in service industries.

c) Suggest how a target cost gap might be closed.

3. Life-cycle costing

a) Identify the costs involved at different stages of the life cycle.

b) Derive a life cycle cost in manufacturing and service industries.

c) Identify the benefits of life cycle costing.

4. Throughput accounting

a) Discuss and apply the theory of constraints.

b) Calculate and interpret a throughput accounting ratio (TPAR).

c) Suggest how a TPAR could be improved.

d) Apply throughput accounting to a multi-product decision-making problem.

5. Environmental accounting

a) Discuss the issues businesses face in the management of environmental costs.

b) Describe the different methods a business may use to account for its environmental costs.

Session 2 Guidance

■ **Know** the four new management accounting techniques this session introduces; understand the reasons for these techniques and be able to do the calculations. All of the areas are **highly examinable**.

■ **Read** the following articles to strengthen your understanding of this content—it is **highly examinable**. These and other technical articles relating to this exam are available on the ACCA website at www.accaglobal.com.

- "Environmental Management Accounting"
- "Throughput Accounting and the Theory of Constraints" parts 1 and 2
- "Target Costing and Lifecycle Costing"

■ **Understand** the rational behind target costing and be able to discuss ways that businesses can reduce the cost of making products and services (s.2).

(continued on next page)

VISUAL OVERVIEW

Objective: To explain the use of specialist management accounting techniques.

```
┌─────────────────────────────────────┐
│  DEVELOPMENTS IN MANAGEMENT          │
│            ACCOUNTING                │
│                                      │
│  • Traditional Management            │
│    Accounting                        │
│  • Business Environment              │
│    Changes                           │
│  • Growth of Services Industries     │
│  • Response of Companies             │
│  • Response of Management            │
│    Accountants                       │
└─────────────────────────────────────┘
```

TARGET COSTING	LIFE-CYCLE COSTING	THROUGHPUT ACCOUNTING	ENVIRONMENTAL MANAGEMENT ACCOUNTING
• Aim and Use	• Product Life Cycle	• Theory of Constraints	• Introduction
• Steps	• Costs Involved	• Throughput Contribution	• Importance
• Service Industries	• Benefits	• Throughput Accounting Ratio	• EMA
• Narrowing the Cost Gap	• Service Industries		• Environmental Costs
			• EMA Techniques

Session 2 Guidance

■ **Understand** the meaning of life-cycle costing and be able to calculate a life-cycle cost (s.3 and *Illustration 3*).

■ **Appreciate** the problem of bottlenecks, and the importance of maximising throughput per bottleneck hour (s.4).

■ **Know** how to calculate the throughput accounting ratio (s.4).

■ **Appreciate** the importance of environmental issues and how environmental management accounting can provide information to management.

1 Developments in Management Accounting

1.1 Traditional Management Accounting

Traditional management accounting was inward looking, focusing on controlling costs. The most important of these are:*

- costing systems (marginal and absorption costing);
- budgeting systems;
- standard costing and variance analysis; and
- working capital management.

*Commentary

*You should already be familiar with many of the techniques used in traditional management accounting from earlier exams.

1.2 Business Environment Changes

During the 1950s and 1960s, the Western industrialised nations enjoyed strong positions in international markets. There was little competition either on price or quality. Businesses could continue to be successful by just continuing to do what they had always done. During the 1970s, however, this stable business world began to disappear:

- Less protection in home markets and increased globalisation led to increased competition from newly emerging industrialised nations (particularly Japan).
- Introduction of computerised manufacturing systems led to the opportunity to reduce manufacturing costs while increasing the quality of products.
- Products' life cycles began to fall so there was increased demand for new products from consumers.
- The growth of service industries.
- Business combinations resulted in larger multinational organisations with diverse operations.
- Change in the structure of business with more decentralised decision-making.

1.3 Growth of Services Industries

Many of the traditional management accounting practices were aimed at manufacturing businesses. However, many "post-industrial" economies have developed that include a significant proportion of service industries. Service industries can be distinguished from manufacturing by the following characteristics:

- **Intangibility:** Tangible products have a physical presence, and customers can point to the specific features of a product and indicate the physical characteristics of it that they value. A service, on the other hand, does not have physical characteristics, and this makes it more difficult to identify what aspects of the service customers value.
- **Heterogeneity:** The standard of services will vary from service to service. For example, hairdressers in a salon will usually have different talents, and each haircut and styling that is performed will be different.*
- **Simultaneity:** The service is consumed at the same time as it is performed, so there is usually more emphasis on getting it right the first time, as there may be no second chances.

*Commentary

Several performance measures can be established for monitoring.

*Commentary

*This characteristic makes it more difficult to ensure that all services are of a consistently high standard.

■ **Perishability:** Services cannot be stored. Businesses therefore need to strike a careful balance between the need for sufficient resources to meet demand at peak times and the need for efficiency.

■ **Non-transferability of ownership:** Often there is no transfer of ownership when a service is provided. For example, a hotel guest has only a right of access to his hotel room and guest facilities during the period of his stay.

1.4 Response of Companies

Two developments in the commercial world are worth specific mention:

1. Total Quality Management*

2. Just-in-Time manufacturing

1.4.1 Total Quality Management (TQM)

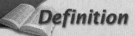

Total Quality Management—consists of continuous improvement in activities involving everyone in the organisation, managers and workers, in a totally integrated effort towards improving performance at every level.

*TQM is a philosophy of getting it right the first time. It is recognised that the costs of bad quality may exceed the costs of good quality.

The traditional Western approach to manufacturing was to produce to maximum capacity. Production was driven by internal plans rather than external demand. This led to a variety of weaknesses:

✗ Excessive holding of inventory with the associated costs of storage and obsolescence.

✗ Delays between the customer ordering products and the delivery of the products.

✗ Bottlenecks in the production process were not highlighted.

✗ A lack of flexibility in meeting changes in customer requirements.

1.4.2 JIT Manufacturing

A just-in-time (JIT) production system is driven by the demand for finished products so each component on a production line is only produced when needed for the next stage.

■ A "pull through philosophy"—customer demand drives production.

■ Requires careful planning of demand and production requirements.

JIT purchasing means the receipt of materials close to when they are used so that raw material stock is reduced to near-zero levels.

■ Achieved by having a series of small production units to which stock is delivered.

■ A few dedicated suppliers deliver defect-free components on time two or three times a day.

1.5 Response of Management Accountants

In response to the changing business environment, several new management accounting techniques evolved. The techniques included in the syllabus for F5 are:

- Activity-Based Costing (see *Session 1*)
- Target Costing
- Life-Cycle Costing
- Throughput Accounting
- Environmental Accounting.

2 Target Costing

2.1 Aim and Use

- In **traditional cost plus** pricing models, the cost of a product is the starting point for calculating price. Having determined the unit cost of a product, a profit margin is then added to calculate the price. In a competitive world, such an approach may not be realistic. The price calculated in this way may be too high for the market to accept.

- In a **competitive market,** the price of a product may be determined by the market. Companies therefore have to accept the market price.

- Target costing is an attempt to achieve an **acceptable margin** in a situation where the price of a product is determined externally by the market. This acceptable margin is achieved by identifying ways to reduce the costs of producing the product.*

*Commentary

*Traditionally, the cost of producing a product or service was something companies assumed was a variable over which they had little control. However, Japanese companies in particular showed that no matter how efficient operations are, there are always ways to identify further cost savings. This philosophy underlies target costing.

- Target costing may be used:
  - during the design phase of a product (where cost savings can be identified by changing the design of the product);
  - for existing products (where cost savings can be achieved without changing the design of the product).

2.2   Steps in Target Costing

1. Determine the price the market will accept for the product, based on market research. This may take into account the market share required.

2. Deduct a required profit margin from this price—this gives the target cost.

3. Estimate the actual cost of the product. If it is a new product, this will be an estimate.

4. Identify ways to narrow the gap between the actual cost of the product and the target cost.

Target costing can be illustrated by the following flow diagram:

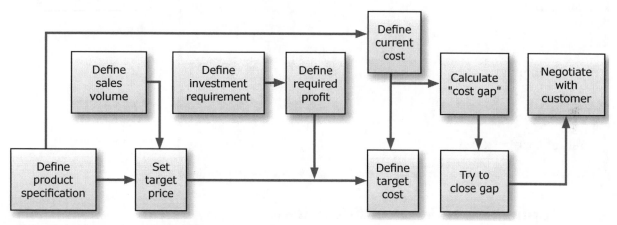

Source: Sakurai, M., Journal of Cost Management for the Manufacturing Industries, *Target Costing and How to Use It*, iii No. 2 (1989).

The flow diagram above summarises how the target price and profit may be determined:

■ The starting point is to define the product specification. This involves designing the product and determining, in detail, which features will be included.

■ The sales volume is defined and related target price set. This price will be based on the organisation's pricing strategy and market research, which will help to determine at what price the required volume of output can be sold.

■ The required profit may be based on the amount of investment required to produce the product and the return on investment required.

■ The target profit is then divided by the number of units to obtain a required profit per unit, which is deducted from the target price to give the target cost.

Example 1 Target Costing

Exclusive Motors is designing a new version of its luxury car, the Z123 series. The car will be launched next year. It is expected to have a life cycle of 10 years.

The production of the car will require an investment of $3 billion. The company requires a profit of 20% a year on this investment.

The marketing department believes that the car could be sold for a price of $40,000 each. 100,000 cars would be manufactured and sold each year.

Required:

Calculate the target cost of one Z123.

Solution

	$m
Expected revenue	
Required profit	
Total target cost	
Target cost per car	

2.3 Application to Service Industries

Target costing is likely to be most appropriate in manufacturing industries, where a volume of standard products is to be made. Although it can also be used in service industries, there may be additional challenges:

✗ In many service industries, the "products" are non-standard and customised. It is difficult to define a target cost when there is no standard product.

✗ A higher portion of costs in service industries are indirect (overheads). It is therefore harder to reduce these on a product-by-product basis.

✗ Reducing costs in a service industry may be at the expense of customer service or quality. In manufacturing industries, it may be possible to identify cost savings that remove parts of a product that are not valued by a customer anyway.

Illustration 1 Target Costing for Services

Gates & Jobs Co is a tax advisory business. There is a lot of competition for tax services in the market where Gates & Jobs is located, and one competitor has recently started to advertise that it will do tax returns for a flat rate of $100 a return.

Gates & Jobs Co has decided to match this price for a basic tax return, provided that the client does not have any capital gains tax to pay. Gates & Jobs currently aims to make a profit of 20% of all fees charged to clients.

The target cost of the tax return is therefore:

	$
Standard fee	100
Less: Required margin	20
Target cost	80

Based on observation and discussions with the management accountant, the actual cost of a "typical" tax return is as follows:

Direct costs	
Time of senior adviser (1 hour at $15 per hour)	15
Time of partner review (15 minutes at $100 per hour)	25
Total direct costs	40
Overheads apportioned at 150% of labour time	60
Actual cost	100

There is, therefore, a cost gap of $20. Although it can be argued that the price of the tax return of $100 does cover all direct costs, and therefore increases contribution, the partners are keen that all services should contribute to the overheads of the business at the rate of 150%.

Illustration 2 Cost Gap Reduction

Following on from *Illustration 1,* methods which might be used to reduce the cost gap include:

■ Reduce the time taken by the senior (e.g. using a software package).

■ Reduce partner time (e.g. the partner might not review really basic returns at all).

■ Reduce the overheads of the business (e.g. by using ABC methods to identify more accurately the drivers of overheads) and finding ways to economise.

2.4   Narrowing the Target Cost Gap

Target costing relies on multi-disciplinary teams, which discuss ways to reduce the gap between the actual (expected) cost and the target cost.

Some methods which have been used successfully in practice are:

✔ Reconsider the design to eliminate non-value added elements.

✔ Reduce the number of components or standardise components.

✔ Use less expensive materials.

✔ Employ a lower grade of staff on production.

✔ Invest in new technology.

✔ Outsource elements of the production or support activities.

✔ Reduce manning levels or redesigning the work flow.

Such methods may be assisted by the following techniques:

■ **"Tear down analysis"** (also called **"reverse engineering"**)—this involves examining a competitor's product to identify possible improvements or cost reductions.

■ **Value engineering**—involves investigating the factors which affect the cost of a product or service. The aim is to improve the design of a product so the same functions can be provided for a lower cost, or to eliminate functions which the customer does not value but which increase costs.

Some writers distinguish between four elements of value:

1. Utility or use value—how useful the product is to the owner.

2. Esteem value—how the product increases the owner's sense of well-being.

3. Scarcity value—the high value of diamonds is a result of their scarcity.

4. Exchange value—how much could the owner sell the product for.

■ **Functional analysis**—involves identifying the attributes/ functions of a product which customers value. The determination of a price the customer is prepared to pay for each of these functions is then performed. If the cost of providing the function exceeds the value, then the function is dropped.

Businesses should be careful to ensure that any steps taken to reduce product costs do not lead to a lower perceived (or actual) quality, as this may reduce the price the product could sell for. This would then reduce rather than increase the margin obtained from selling the product.

Increasing the sales price is **not** a viable method of reducing the gap.

■ The whole purpose of target costing is to achieve a reasonable margin when the price is determined competitively by the market.

■ Charging a higher price would lead to a big fall in demand for the product.

3 Life-Cycle Costing

3.1 Product Life Cycle

The product life cycle describes how demand conditions for a product, a brand and whole markets change with time.

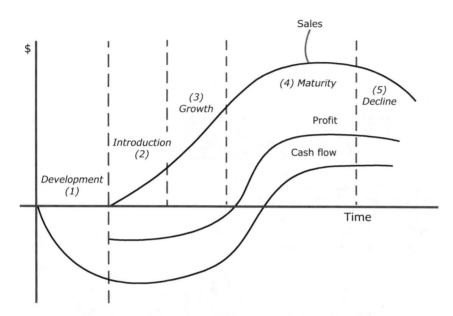

1. **Development stage (planning and design stage)**—During this stage the product is designed and developed. Prototypes may be produced. Manufacturing processes will also be designed, including any special machinery required to make the product. At this stage, cash flow will be negative, as there is no revenue.

2. **Introduction phase/launch**—Special pricing strategies may be used during the launch of a new product such as market skimming or market penetration. Companies also need to consider that the pricing strategy used at the introductory stage may affect demand in later years. For example, setting a low price initially may discourage competitors from entering the market. This will allow the company to enjoy higher demand later in the product life cycle.

3. **Growth**—Competition may rise due to new suppliers entering the market. This may force lower prices.

4. **Maturity**—Most profits are made during this phase. Prices may be stable. The company's price strategy during this phase is more likely to focus on maximising short-term profits, unlike in the *introduction* phase.

5. **Decline**—Prices may fall with demand, unless a niche market can be found.

   - In the modern manufacturing environment a high proportion of a product's costs will be incurred at the early stages in its life cycle (e.g. development, design and set-up costs). Revenues only arise, however, when the product is actually being manufactured and sold.

■ Traditional financial and management accounting systems focus only on costs and revenues incurred during the manufacturing stage of the product's life. They therefore ignore:

- costs incurred in developing and designing the product; and
- any abandonment and disposal costs at the end of the product's life.

■ Life-cycle costing estimates and accumulates costs over a product's entire life cycle to determine whether the profits earned during the manufacturing stage will cover the costs incurred pre- and post-manufacturing.

■ It traces development, design and set-up costs to individual products over their entire life cycles.

Illustration 3　Life-Cycle Costing

Zany developed a new computer game during the year 20X2 at a cost of $200,000. The game will be launched in the year 20X3. Budgeted revenues and costs of the game over its life cycle (life-cycle costing) are presented below:

	20X2 $000	20X3 $000	20X4 $000	20X5 $000
Sales (units)	0	16,000	34,000	12,000
Revenue	0	160	340	120
Variable costs	0	30	65	20
Contribution	0	130	275	100
Marketing costs	40	30	0	0
Development costs	200	0	0	0
Annual profit	(240)	100	275	100
Cumulative profit	(240)	(140)	135	235

Life-cycle cost per unit:	$000
Total variable costs	115 (30 + 65 + 20)
Marketing costs	70 (40 + 30)
Development costs	200
Total life-cycle costs	385
Total output (000 units)	62
Life-cycle cost per unit	$6.21

Managers can now see the expected profit of the product over its entire life, rather than simply on a year-by-year basis. Actual revenues and costs would be presented on a similar basis. The life-cycle cost per unit includes all costs, not just those relating to manufacturing.

3.2　Costs Involved

■ For the purposes of life-cycle costing, three stages can be identified in the product's life cycle:

- Planning and design stage
- Manufacturing stage
- Service and abandonment stage.

3.2.1 Committed Costs

■ During the planning and design phase, many of the decisions made about the product's design will determine the costs which will be incurred in the future. These are **committed costs.** Although they are not actually incurred during the design phase, the company is committed to incurring the expenditure in the future (mainly during the manufacturing stage).

■ Tools such as target costing (see previous) may be used to reduce such committed costs, if they exceed what is acceptable.

■ Clearly the pattern of expenditure will vary from industry to industry. It is not uncommon, however, for committed costs during the planning and design phase to reach 80% of the total costs over the product's life.

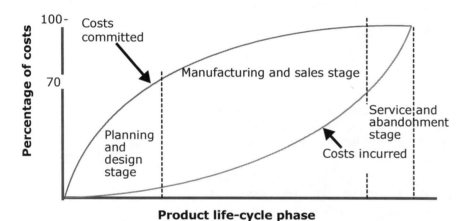

Product life-cycle phase

3.2.2 Cost Behaviour in the Product Life Cycle

The actual costs incurred during the product life cycle typically include the following:

Stage	Fixed Costs	Variable Costs
Planning and design	■ Product design ■ Building prototypes ■ Market research	
Manufacturing and sales	■ Marketing and advertising ■ Fixed production and sales overheads ■ Design updating	■ Materials and/or components ■ Direct labour ■ Variable production and non-production overheads ■ Sales commissions
Service and abandonment	■ Decommissioning factories ■ Disposal of products	■ Servicing (may be outsourced)

During the *manufacturing and design* phase, costs are likely to change as follows:

■ Marketing and advertising costs will initially be high when the product is first launched and for a period of time after this in which the manufacturer will want to raise market awareness. Later, costs of marketing and advertising will fall.

- Fixed production costs may also be higher in initial stages of manufacturing. Later, experience of the manufacturing process may enable cost savings to be made. However, some fixed costs may be stepped costs and so increase if production increases through the expansion of production facilities.

- Total variable costs will, by definition, increase as output increases. Output will be expected to increase at least during the start of the sales and manufacturing phase as demand for the product increases.

- Unit manufacturing costs calculated using traditional absorption costing will decrease as output increases, due to two factors:

  1. The fixed costs will be spread over a larger number of units leading to a lower fixed cost per unit; and

  2. The variable cost per unit may fall as output increases are a result of economies of scale and the learning effect.

3.2.3 Strategies to Extend Product Maturity

The life-cycle cost per unit can be reduced by extending the maturity of the product. The following strategies can be used for this:

- Issuing updated versions of the product which include new features. The costs of developing updates for an existing product are likely to be considerably less than the cost of developing an entirely new product.

- Repackaging the product to give it a new image. In this way, established products can be relaunched as if they were new.

- Selling the product in new markets. This could be new geographical markets or aiming the product at new market segments (e.g. by discounting the price).

3.3 Benefits

✔ Life-cycle costing encourages management to plan the pricing strategy for the whole product life, rather than on a short-term basis. (Pricing, and in particular the effect of the product life cycle on pricing decisions, is discussed later in *Session 6*).

✔ Identifying the costs which will be incurred throughout the product's life means that management understands the costs better and therefore enables management to control them better.

✔ By monitoring a product's revenues and costs on a cumulative basis over the life of the product, management is provided with more meaningful information for control than it would have by monitoring costs and revenues period by period.

✔ It is much easier to "design out costs" during the design phase of a product than to "control out costs" later in a product's life cycle. By considering the whole life cycle of the product at the design phase, management is more likely to achieve a reasonable cost base and therefore reasonable profits.

✔ Decisions about whether to continue to develop and manufacture products will be based on more complete information when the product life cycle is considered. Where costs and revenues are monitored on a period-by-period basis, there is a risk that products in the development phase will be scrapped because they do not bring in revenues.

3.4　Relevance to Services Industries

Life-cycle costing is relevant to services industries that provide services that require significant upfront research and development. An example is the software industry, in which considerable research and development is invested in a new application or operating system. The cost of this development must be recovered before the software becomes obsolete.

Life-cycle costing can also be performed in relation to customers. The costs of providing goods or services to customers may vary over their "life" as customers.

Some businesses incur high costs in setting up a new customer. However, having attracted new business, the cost of maintaining a customer relationship is likely to be much lower. Effort is therefore directed to ensuring customer loyalty.

For example, the following one-off costs might be incurred by a retail bank at the start of a new customer's life:

- Financial incentives (e.g. below-market-rate interest on borrowings for 12 months).
- Initial registration, including validation of personal details and identification documents.
- Creditworthiness checks if loans are to be provided.
- Setting up bank account access.
- Issuing user IDs and passwords for Internet banking.

Once the customer's accounts have been set up, many of the costs above will not need to be incurred again. The bank needs to ensure that the costs incurred at the start are recovered over the customer's life.

4　Throughput Accounting

4.1　The Theory of Constraints

During the 1980s, many factories in Western Europe and the US became heavily automated. At that time there was a general belief that automation would lead to reduced costs (by reducing labour) and higher profits. Management accountants, therefore, focused on performance measures of efficiency.

However, in spite of improved efficiency, many businesses did not see increased profits. Instead, they discovered the following problems:

- They were failing to meet customer orders on time, leading to customer frustration.
- The volume of work in progress and finished goods was growing significantly, leading to high costs of inventory obsolescence and lack of storage space in factories.

Goldratt and Cox, in their novel, "The Goal", pointed out that the cause of the apparent paradox between increased efficiency and reduced profits was production bottlenecks.

Bottlenecks are processes that are slower than the processes that precede and succeed them. They therefore slow down the whole production process.

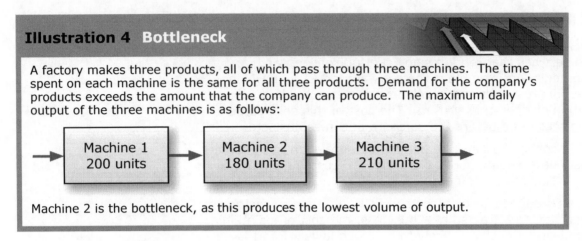

Illustration 4 Bottleneck

A factory makes three products, all of which pass through three machines. The time spent on each machine is the same for all three products. Demand for the company's products exceeds the amount that the company can produce. The maximum daily output of the three machines is as follows:

| Machine 1 | Machine 2 | Machine 3 |
| 200 units | 180 units | 210 units |

Machine 2 is the bottleneck, as this produces the lowest volume of output.

Goldratt and Cox pointed out the following:

- If the non-bottleneck processes operate at maximum efficiency, work in progress will build up in front of the bottleneck process.

   In *Illustration 4*, if Machine 1 continues to produce 200 units a day, 20 units a day work in progress will accumulate in front of Machine 2, which can only deal with 180 units a day.

- The bottlenecks themselves restrict the amount of inputs to the "downstream" processes.

   In *Illustration 4*, Machine 3 can only process 180 units a day, as this is all it receives as input from Machine 2. Thus, bottlenecks reduce the rate at which finished goods are produced.

What made the problem worse was that factories would set up machines for large production runs. After producing a large batch of one product, the machines would have to be set up for a different product. It was thought that large batches would reduce costs further by reducing set-up costs. However, it actually compounded the problems of a build-up of work in progress and the delays in meeting customer order deadlines.

Goldratt and Cox concluded that instead of focusing on efficiency, organisations should focus on "throughput" (i.e. focus on producing for sale, not producing for work in progress).

Goldratt and Cox proposed the following process to maximise profit when faced with bottlenecks:

1. Identify the systems bottlenecks. In the real world this will be more complex than the simplified *Illustration 4* here.

2. Decide which products to make, given the bottlenecks. This requires limiting factor analysis using the time spent on the bottleneck as the limiting factor (see *Example 3*).

3. Ensure that other resources do not produce at a higher rate than the bottleneck. In *Illustration 4*, if Machine 1 were to operate at its maximum capacity of 200 units per day, Machine 2 would only be able to take 180 units, so 20 units of work in progress would build up.

4. Eliminate the systems bottlenecks. This can be done, for example, by buying additional machines, training the machine operators or reducing the time spent on the bottleneck resource.

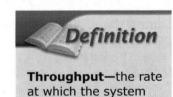

Definition

Throughput—the rate at which the system generates money through sales.

5. Once the bottleneck has been broken, another resource becomes the bottleneck. For example, if the capacity of Machine 2 were increased to 240 units per day, Machine 1 would become the bottleneck. Steps 1–4 are repeated. Therefore this is a process of continuous improvement.

The ideas above conflict with traditional management accounting:

■ The idea that Machine A should not operate at full capacity would lead to idle time of the operators of Machine A. Goldratt and Cox argue that this is fine as the cost of idle time is less than the cost of the work in progress which would build up if Machine A were to operate at full capacity.

■ Under traditional management accounting, the build-up of work in progress would not affect the profits of the business (since closing work in progress is part of closing inventory and deducted in determining cost of sales). Goldratt and Cox argue that this is wrong because the build-up of work in progress in front of a bottleneck is a cost to the company if the volume of work in progress is continually increasing.

4.2   Throughput Contribution

Goldratt and Cox introduced the idea of **"throughput contribution"** as the measure of performance.

They argue that all other costs which are traditionally treated as variable are fixed in the short run (e.g. labour). When using limiting factor analysis (see *Session 5*) to determine which products to produce, given a bottleneck they would advocate producing those products which produce maximum throughput contribution per hour of bottleneck.

Definition

Throughput contribution—sales revenue less direct material costs.

Example 2 Theory of Constraints

A factory produces two products, A and B. Both products pass through three processes; Process 1, Process 2 and Process 3. Process 2 has been identified as the bottleneck. There are 10 hours of Process 2 time available per day. Information relating to the two products is as follows:

	A	B
	$	$
Selling price per unit	100	80
Direct materials per unit	70	60
Direct labour per unit	5	10
Traditional contribution per unit	25	10
Maximum demand per day	8	14
Time on Process 2 per unit (hours)	1	0.5

Required:

Determine the daily production plan that would maximise throughput contribution.

Solution

	A	B
	$	$
Selling price per unit		
Direct materials per unit		
Throughput contribution per unit		
Time on Process 2 per unit (hours)		
Throughput return per hour of Process 2		
Ranking		

	Units produced	Hours used
B:		
A:		
Total throughput contribution		

4.3 Throughput Accounting Ratio ("TPAR")

4.3.1 Calculation

Based on the ideas of the theory of constraints, Galloway and Waldron developed the throughput accounting ratio ("TPAR") as a performance measure to be used for evaluation of factory managers. This aims to motivate factory managers to focus on maximising throughput. The ratio is calculated as follows:

$$\text{TPAR*} = \frac{\text{Return per factory hour}}{\text{Cost per factory hour}}$$

$$\text{Return per factory hour} = \frac{\text{Throughput per unit}}{\text{Hours of bottleneck resource used per unit}}$$

$$\text{Cost per factory hour} = \frac{\text{Other factory costs}}{\text{Bottleneck resource hours available}}$$

*Return per factory hour means throughput contribution per unit divided by time spent on the bottleneck where materials are the only variable cost.

Other factory costs means all costs incurred in the factory other than materials; since materials are considered to be the only truly variable costs, all other costs are fixed. The TPAR therefore shows:

$$\frac{\text{Contribution per hour}}{\text{Fixed cost per hour}}$$

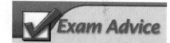

Other factory costs would **not** include administration or marketing costs—if these are mentioned in a question, they should be ignored.

4.3.2 Interpreting TPAR

- If TPAR > 1 the product is profitable; as the throughput contribution exceeds the fixed costs.
- If TPAR = 1 the product breaks even.
- If TPAR < 1 the product is loss making. The throughput contribution generated does not cover the fixed costs required to make it.

4.3.3 Ways to Improve the TPAR

TPAR is a performance measurement tool which may be used in evaluating the performance of managers. It is hoped that managers would take the following actions to increase their measured performance:

- Eliminate bottlenecks or reduce the time spent on bottleneck resources.
- Reduce other factory costs.

Mathematically the ratio could also be improved by increasing selling prices or reducing material costs. In a competitive environment, however, increasing selling prices may not be feasible. Reducing material costs may have implications on quality, so this may not be desirable.

Example 3 TPAR

Continuing on from *Example 2*. The factory costs per day are as follows:

	$
Labour costs	120
Variable overheads	180
Fixed overheads	50
Total costs per day	350

Required:

Calculate the TPAR for products A and B.

Solution

Throughput return per factory hour

	A	B
	$	$
Throughput return per hour of Process 2		

Fixed cost per factory hour

	A	B
TPAR		

5 Environmental Management Accounting

5.1 Introduction

Over the past 30 years, environmental issues have become an area of increasing interest. Environmental activists assert that current human activity is causing global warming, and warn of dire consequences for the planet unless we reduce our poor environmental behaviour. The most pressing issues are:

- Global warming, caused by the emission of greenhouse gasses.

- Many natural resources are scarce, and global reserves of these resources are being depleted. In particular, energy and water are resources that are forecast to become scarce over the next 50 years.

- Pollution is causing the loss of habitats for nature and for humans.

5.2 Importance of the Environment for Business

5.2.1 Environmental Behaviour and Performance

One of the pioneering articles on environmental management accounting was "The Green Bottom Line: Management Accounting for Environmental Improvement and Business Benefit", published by Martin Bennett and Peter James in 1998. This identified several ways in which a company can improve its performance by becoming more aware of the impact on the environment:

- Poor environmental behaviour can have an adverse effect on an organisation's image, which may lead to a loss of sales as customers boycott the organisation's products.

- Many governments may impose heavy fines on companies which harm the environment. Companies also may have to pay large amounts to clean up any pollution for which they are responsible.

- Increasing government regulations on environmental issues such as pollution has increased the costs of compliance for businesses.

- Improving environmental behaviour can reduce costs. For example, a programme of increasing energy efficiency will reduce the depletion of natural resources while also reducing energy costs for the companies concerned.

- Businesses as corporate citizens have a moral duty to play their part in helping to reduce the harm they do to the environment.

Exhibit 1   BP

The Deepwater Horizon oil spill in April 2010 was one of the worst environmental disasters on record. An exploratory oil rig in the Gulf of Mexico exploded, leading to a partially capped oil well a mile below the surface of the water. Experts estimate that from 35,000 to 60,000 barrels of oil a day leaked from this well, depending on weather conditions. It took approximately three months to re-seal the oil well and stop the leak.

BP was the majority owner of the oilfield. Although the rig was operated by a sub-contractor on behalf of BP, the US government stated that it held BP primarily responsible for the leak.

BP recognised a pre-tax cost of $40.9 billion in its 2010 financial statements relating to the oil spill (compared with a profit for the year 2009 of $16.6. billion). This included a fund of $20 billion which was set up to compensate the local community for damages caused as well as costs incurred on cleaning up the spill.

5.2.2   Achieving Environmental Benefits

Bennett and James suggested six ways in which business and environmental benefits could be obtained through environmental management accounting:

1. Taking account of environmental effects in making capital expenditure decisions.

2. Better understanding of environmental costs that are otherwise hidden in other overheads so management is not aware of them.

3. Reducing waste and saving energy.

4. Understanding environmental effects on life-cycle costs, many of which are incurred at the end of a product's life (e.g. to dispose of electronic goods in accordance with local laws on recycling).

5. Measuring environmental performance as stakeholders are becoming more interested in the impact that organisations have on the environment.

6. Involving management accountants in longer-term strategic planning for environmental-related issues.

5.3 Environmental Management Accounting

Traditional management accounting systems do not provide any analysis of environmental costs. Management are often unaware of them. The implication of this is that:

■ Management cannot do enough to manage environmental activities.

■ Management accounts underestimate the costs of poor environmental behaviour and underestimate the benefits of good environmental behaviour.

Environmental Management Accounting (EMA) aims to overcome this.

Definition

EMA—the identification, collection, analysis and use of two types of information for internal decision-making: physical information on the use, flows and rates of energy, water and materials (including wastes); and monetary information on environment related costs, earnings and savings.

—Environmental Management Accounting Research and Information Centre (EMARIC)

It is important to remember that there are two aspects to environmental management accounting:

■ Physical information, which focuses on the physical use of scarce resources and how much waste occurs.

■ Monetary information on environment-related costs, earnings and savings.

5.4 Defining Environmental Costs

The first step in dealing with environmental costs is to define what is meant by environmental costs. Various definitions or categories of environmental costs have been suggested. One of these is the definitions provided by the US Environmental Protection Agency (EPA), which identified the following categories of environmental costs:

■ **Conventional** costs: costs having environmental relevance (e.g. costs of buying energy and other scarce resources).

■ **Potentially hidden** costs: those environmental costs which are recorded, but simply included in general overheads, so management is not aware of them.

■ **Contingent** costs: potential future costs (e.g. costs of cleaning up damage caused by pollution).*

■ **Image and relationship** costs: the costs of producing environmental reports and promoting the company's environmental activities.

*Commentary

*In financial statements, contingent costs might be disclosed as contingent liabilities or provided for if they meet the definition and recognition criteria of IAS 37 *Provisions, Contingent Liabilities and Contingent Assets*.

An alternative categorisation of environmental costs was proposed by Hansen and Mendova, who came up with a definition based on total quality management:

■ Environmental **prevention** costs are the costs of activities undertaken to prevent the production of waste (e.g. spending on redesigning processes to reduce the amount of pollution released into the atmosphere).

■ Environmental **detection** costs are those incurred to ensure that the organisation complies with regulations and voluntary standards (e.g. costs of auditing the organisation's environmental activities).

■ Environmental **internal failure** costs are costs incurred to clean up environmental waste and pollution before it has been released into the environment (e.g. costs of disposing of toxic waste).

■ Environmental **external failure** costs are costs incurred on activities performed after discharging waste into the environment (e.g. costs of cleaning up an ocean after spilling oil).

5.5 EMA Techniques

Having identified the various types of environmental costs, it is necessary to provide useful information to management to help manage and control environmental activities—with the purpose of saving money and reducing the harm caused by operations to the environment. Various tools have been proposed for this:

■ An environmental cost report, based on the costs defined by Hansen and Mendova, with each category of costs shown as a percentage of revenues.

■ Environmental activity-based costing.

■ Input output analysis.

■ Flow cost accounting.

■ Life-cycle costing.

5.5.1 Environmental Activity-Based Costing

This applies ABC principles to environmental costs so that the environmental costs are apportioned "correctly" to the products which use the drivers which cause the costs to be incurred.

Normally many environmental costs are hidden in general overheads and therefore apportioned to products using inappropriate drivers. This can mean that product costs do not truly reflect the environmental costs associated with making them.

Environmental-related costs are removed from general overheads and allocated to environmental activities. Investigation of these activities occurs to identify the key drivers of the cost. For example, one activity may be monitoring emissions. The driver of this may be production time of products using a particular process which produces emissions. The costs of monitoring emissions can then be apportioned to the products based on the amount of production time used by each product.

The main methods of allocating the environmental cost (the allocation keys) to the various activities might be the following:

■ Volume of emissions or waste.

■ Toxicity of emission and waste treated.

■ Volume of emission treated.

■ The relative costs of treating different types of emissions.

5.5.2 Input Output Analysis

Input output analysis of "mass balance" aims to make it clear to management how much waste is being generated by their activities. The aim is simply to compare the output of a production process (in physical units) with the input on the basis that "what comes in must go out". What is not included in output must therefore be waste. Process flows are often used to show these more specifically. For example:

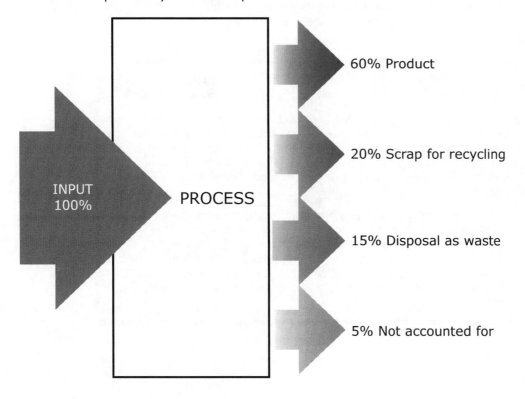

5.5.3 Flow Cost Accounting

Flow cost accounting is a more detailed version of input output analysis. Input output analysis considers only the physical inputs and ensures that these are accounted for as physical outputs at the *end* of the production process. Flow cost accounting considers the inputs and outputs for *each* process, to identify the waste at each process.

Flow cost accounting examines not only the physical quantities of material, but also the costs and values of output and waste for each process. So the costs of input into each process are calculated and apportioned between output of the process and waste using process costing principles.

The costs used in flow cost accounting are sometimes categorised as:

■ material costs;

■ system costs, which are the costs incurred within the various processes which add value to the product (e.g. wages and overheads); and

■ delivery and disposal costs, which are incurred in delivering goods to customers or disposing of waste.

5.5.4 Relevance of Life-Cycle Costing

Life-cycle costing is particularly relevant for environmental costs, because many environmental costs are not incurred during the production phase. Clean-up costs may be significant, but are not incurred until after the production process is finished. The European Union "End of Life Vehicles Directive" makes it compulsory for car manufacturers in the EU to collect and dispose of old cars which have reached the end of their useful life. Such costs should therefore be considered by manufacturers during life-cycle costing exercises.

Exhibit 2   XEROX

Xerox Corporation leases photocopying machines to clients. The machines are returned to the company at the end of their lives. One cost which had previously been ignored was the cost of packaging. Xerox would provide packaging for the new machines which were delivered to the customer. The customer would then dispose of this packaging, and have to pay to re-pack the old machine which was being returned to Xerox.

As a result of including the costs of packaging in the life-cycle costs of the photocopying, the company was able to see how large these costs were. The company now uses a standard re-usable pack. When a machine is delivered to a customer, the package in which it is delivered is used to pack the old machine which is being returned to Xerox. Two standard types of packing have been developed which cover all of Xerox's machines. This led to a reduction in packaging costs and increased customer satisfaction.

Summary

- The business environment within which companies operate has become more competitive. Products have shorter life cycles and there is emphasis on quality.

- New management accounting techniques have evolved to meet this new environment.

- Target costing is used to identify what unit costs would ensure that companies make sufficient profit to justify investment. Companies then try to narrow the gap between the actual cost and the target cost by redesigning the product, to "design out" costs.

- Life-cycle costing involves tracking the cumulative costs and revenues over the life of a product rather than using the traditional approach to accounting, where costs and revenues are reviewed on a period-by-period basis. Life-cycle costing enables managers to see more clearly how successful a product has been over its whole life.

- Throughput accounting is a system which aims to focus management attention onto bottlenecks. Throughput means sales revenue less material cost. Throughput accounting aims to maximise throughput generated per hour by eliminating bottlenecks.

- Environmental management accounting aims to provide management with monetary and non-monetary information to enable them to understand and manage the environmental impact of the organisation's activities.

Session 2 Quiz

Estimated time: 20 minutes

1. List FOUR factors which have occurred in the last 50 years which have led to a fundamental change in the environments within which businesses operate. (1.2)

2. List TWO goals of just-in-time manufacturing. (1.4.2)

3. State the FOUR steps which target costing involves. (2.2)

4. Suggest FOUR ways of reducing the target cost gap. (2.4)

5. Identify the main categories of costs which will be incurred during the following stages of the product life cycle (3.2):

   i. Planning and design stage.

   ii. Manufacturing and sales stage.

   iii. Service and abandonment stage.

6. Explain the difference between throughput contribution and traditional contribution. (4.2)

7. State the steps management should take to improve the measured throughput accounting ratio. (4.3.3)

8. Identify the FOUR categories of environmental costs according to the US Environmental Protection Agency's categorisation. (5.4)

Study Question Bank

Estimated time: 1 hour, 10 minutes

Priority		Estimated Time	Completed
Q2	Flopro	50 minutes	
Q3	Little Chemical Co	20 minutes	
Additional			
Q4	Scovet		

EXAMPLE SOLUTIONS

Solution 1—Target Costing

	$m
Expected revenue (100,000 × $40,000)	4,000
Required profit (20% × $3 billion)	600
Total target cost	3,400
Target cost per car ($3,400 million / 100,000)	34,000

Solution 2—Theory of Constraints

	A	B
	$	$
Selling price per unit	100	80
Direct materials per unit	70	60
Throughput contribution per unit	30	20
Time on Process 2 per unit (hours)	1	0.5
Throughput return per hour of Process 2	30	40
Ranking	2	1

	Units produced	Hours used
B:	14	7
A:	3	3
		10
Total throughput contribution: (14 x 20) + (3 x 30)		370

Solution 3—TPAR

Throughput return per factory hour

As calculated in 2 above:

	A	B
	$	$
Throughput return per hour of Process 2	30	40

Fixed costs per factory hour = $\dfrac{350\,^{*}}{10}$ = $35

	A	B
TPAR	$\dfrac{30}{35}$ = 0.86	$\dfrac{40}{35}$ = 1.14

*Commentary

*In thoughput accounting ALL costs except material costs are considered to be fixed in the short term.

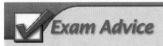

Exam Advice

Where, as in this Example, all products are produced in the same processes, they can be ranked based on return per hour as well as TPAR.

Relevant Cost Analysis

FOCUS

This session covers the following content from the *ACCA Study Guide.*

B. Decision-Making Techniques

1. Relevant cost analysis

a) Explain the concept of relevant costing.

b) Identify and calculate relevant costs for a specific decision situation from given data.

c) Explain and apply the concept of opportunity costs.

5. Make-or-buy and other short-term decisions

a) Explain the issues surrounding make v buy and outsourcing decisions.

b) Calculate and compare "make" costs with "buy-in" costs.

c) Compare in-house costs and outsource costs of completing tasks and consider other issues surrounding this decision.

d) Apply relevant costing principles in situations involving shut down, one-off contracts and the further processing of joint products.

Session 3 Guidance

■ **Note** that this is an important session; read all the material in this session. Relevant costing and decision-making are **highly examinable**.

■ **Work** through all the *Illustrations*.

■ **Appreciate** that for decision-making, only relevant costs and revenues should be considered. A cost or revenue is relevant if it is affected by the decision.

(continued on next page)

VISUAL OVERVIEW

Objective: Apply relevant costing principles in short-term decision-making.

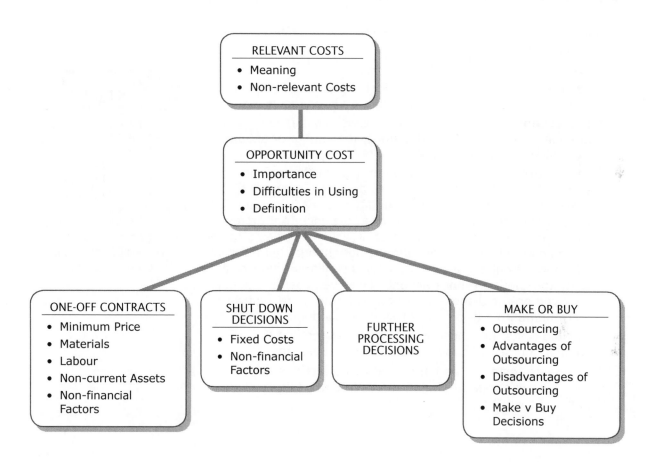

Session 3 Guidance

■ **Be** able to identify the relevant costs relating to one-off contracts (s.3 and *Examples 1–4*).

■ **Know** how to deal with shut down decisions (s.4) and further processing decisions (s.5).

1   Relevant Costs

1.1   Meaning

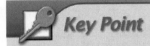

> **Key Point**
>
> Relevant costs are those costs that are appropriate to aiding the making of specific management decisions.

■ Only those costs (and revenues) which will be affected by a decision are "relevant".

■ Relevant costs are:

- **future** costs and revenues; historical costs and revenues are not relevant, as they have already been incurred;

- **incremental** (i.e. the amount by which costs/revenues will change as a result of the decision); if a course of action is **not** taken, incremental costs will be saved; and

- **cash flows** ignore depreciation and gains/(losses) on disposal, etc. Non-cash expenses and income are not relevant as they represent expenditure already made. For example, depreciation is a non-cash expense that arises from the accounting treatment of an asset that has already been acquired. That acquisition is not changed by a future decision. Profit or loss on disposal is similarly a non-cash item and therefore not relevant. However, cash proceeds received on the disposal of an asset would be relevant if incremental to a decision. (This is detailed in s.3.4.)

> **Key Point**
>
> Variable production materials costs are incremental; if production increases, costs of materials, labour, etc increase. Fixed production costs that do not increase are **not** incremental and therefore not relevant.

■ Avoidable costs (i.e. those which would be avoided if a particular course of action were taken) are relevant.

■ Controllable costs can be influenced by the actions of the person who controls the budget or cost centre (also called "managed costs").

Example 1 Incremental Costs

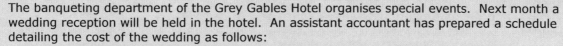

The banqueting department of the Grey Gables Hotel organises special events. Next month a wedding reception will be held in the hotel. An assistant accountant has prepared a schedule detailing the cost of the wedding as follows:

	Note	$	Solution Yes/No
Food and drinks		1,500	
Waiters' wages	1	200	
Supervisor's salary	2	100	
Flowers		500	
Administration	3	300	
Cleaning of function room	4	200	
Room rental	5	200	
Central management costs	6	300	
Total costs		3,300	

Notes

1. The waiters are not regular employees and work only when required for functions. They are paid $20 per day and 10 waiters would be required for the wedding.

2. The supervisor is a full-time employee of the hotel and is paid a fixed salary. The charge here is a portion of his basic salary for the time he will spend supervising the event.

3. Administration costs relate to the time spent by the banqueting department organising the event. All staff members in this department are full-time employees and are paid a fixed salary.

4. An external cleaning company is used to clean the function rooms before and after an event. It charges $200 per event.

5. The wedding reception will be held in one of Grey Gable's banqueting rooms. A notional rental charge for the room has been added. The hotel building is actually rented from a property company for a fixed annual rental.

6. When costing an event, the accounting department adds 10% to the cost of each event to cover central hotel management costs.

Required:

Indicate whether or not each of the costs in the accountant's schedule is incremental.

1.2 Non-relevant Costs

- Sunk costs concept—the historical cost of an asset is said to be "sunk" and is irrelevant to any decision.*
- Research and development costs already incurred are similarly "sunk".
- Committed costs (e.g. contract rental and lease payments) are not relevant—although future and cash flows, they are not incremental.*
- Fixed costs which are incurred regardless of the decision being taken are irrelevant (but an increment in a fixed cost will be relevant).
- Common costs (i.e. allocations and apportionments of shared costs) are subjective (even arbitrary) and not relevant to decisions (e.g. the apportionment of joint costs to joint products).
- Uncontrollable ("non-controllable") costs can be influenced only indirectly by the person in charge of the budget or cost centre. Typically these include "management charges" (i.e. reallocated non-production overheads).
- Notional costs (e.g. recharges of head office costs or management charges) which do not increase as a result of the decision are not relevant.

> ***Commentary***
>
> *Any realisable value, however, (an incremental, future cash flow) would be relevant (see s.3.4).

> ***Commentary***
>
> *If a contract is cancellable, such payments are not committed and any penalty costs incurred in cancelling the contract would be relevant.

2 Opportunity Cost

2.1 Importance

Key Point

Key Point
- *All* opportunity costs are "relevant".
- However, *only some* relevant costs are opportunity costs.*

2.2 Definition

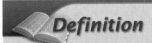

Definition

Opportunity cost—"The value of the benefit sacrificed when one course of action is chosen, in preference to an alternative. The opportunity cost is represented by the foregone potential benefit from the best rejected course of action."

—CIMA Official Terminology
(Chartered Institute of Management Accountants)

- Opportunity costs only apply to the use of **scarce resources**; where resources are not scarce, no sacrifice results from using them.
- For example, the contribution lost if a key worker is moved to a new project is an opportunity cost relevant to assessing that new project.

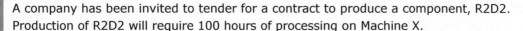

Illustration 1 Opportunity Cost

A company has been invited to tender for a contract to produce a component, R2D2.

Production of R2D2 will require 100 hours of processing on Machine X.

Machine X is working at full capacity producing 50 units of Product Z an hour. Each unit of Product Z makes a contribution of $2.

The lost contribution of $10,000 is an opportunity cost of producing R2D2 and should be taken into account when deciding how much to tender for the contract.

2.3 Difficulties in Using Opportunity Costs

✗ Estimating future costs/revenues and hence the benefit sacrificed.

✗ Identifying alternative uses and hence the best alternative forgone.

✗ Ignores effect on accounting profit. Accounting profits do not include opportunity costs and revenues. A course of action that reduces the reported accounting profit may be considered unacceptable even though it is the best decision under opportunity cost principles.

✗ Ignores non-financial factors (see s.3.5).

3 One-Off Contracts

One decision-making scenario is to decide how much to tender for a one-off contract. To make the decision, it is necessary to consider all the relevant costs of the contract to ensure that the revenue from the contract covers them.*

3.1 Minimum Price

The minimum price that may be quoted on a contract is equal to the relevant cost. At this price no profit or loss would be made on the contract. There are several reasons why a business might wish to know the minimum price of a contract:

■ It is useful for price negotiations to know the lowest price that can be charged for a contract; if a price is agreed to that is below the relevant cost the business would make a real loss.

■ A business may be prepared to undertake a contract at relevant cost in the hope that this may bring additional business in the future.

■ If a business has under-utilised resources during low season, it may be willing to take on additional contracts at this time (provided that no loss is made) as this may build up goodwill with potential customers.

3.2 Materials

Where materials are required for a one-off contract, the following guidance, as summarised in Figure 1, can be used to determine the relevant cost:

■ If the materials required have not already been acquired then clearly it will be necessary to buy them for the contract. The **current market price** is the relevant cost.

*Commentary

*All of the points discussed in s.1 and s.2 are relevant for decisions related to one-off contracts. This section provides further guidance in relation to materials, labour and non-current assets which may be required for such contracts.

Key Point

Historical costs or book values are *never* relevant costs of materials.

■ If the materials have already been acquired it is necessary to consider whether they are used regularly in the business:

  ● If used regularly, any materials consumed by the one-off contract will need to be replaced, so the **replacement cost** (which is also current market price) would be the relevant cost.

  ● If not used regularly (e.g. they were acquired some time ago and there is no current use for them), the relevant cost is their **opportunity cost.** This is often their scrap value (i.e. disposal proceeds if the materials can be sold if not used in the contract). If there is **no** scrap value, then the opportunity cost is **$0.**

Read exam questions carefully as they may contain irrelevant information.

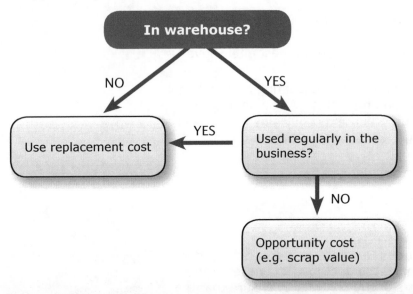

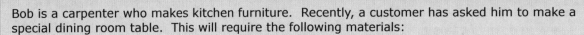

Example 2 Relevant Materials Costs

Bob is a carpenter who makes kitchen furniture. Recently, a customer has asked him to make a special dining room table. This will require the following materials:

1. 10m^2 of oak wood. Bob already has 20m^2 of oak in his storeroom that he bought last month for $2.50 per m^2. The current price of oak is now $2.75 per m^2. Bob frequently uses oak in his work.

2. Two tins of a particular varnish. Bob does not use this type of varnish regularly, so would have to buy it in. Each tin costs $20.

3. Four hinges, so that the ends of the table can be folded. Bob has four hinges in his storeroom that he acquired some years ago but never used. Bob remembers that the hinges cost $3.00 each. The price of such hinges in a shop today would be $3.50 each. Bob said, "I'm pleased that I can finally use these. They've been in the storeroom for years and if I don't use them on this table, they will stay in the storeroom for many more years. Nobody would want to buy second-hand hinges, would they?"

Required:

Explain what the relevant cost is for each of the three items above.

3.3 Labour

One-off contracts usually require some labour. The relevant cost of labour can be determined from the following situations:

■ If the organisation has spare (idle) labour time which can be used on the contract, then the relevant cost is **zero.** This might arise, for example, where workers are being paid a fixed weekly wage and are currently underemployed.

- If additional labour time is required and can be obtained *without* taking workers away from other activities, then the direct cost of the labour is relevant. This may be paid at a higher rate if overtime is involved.

- If there is a limit on the amount of labour available a contract may require workers to be taken away from other profitable activities. In this case, the relevant cost of labour is the direct cost plus the **lost contribution** from the other activities.*

*Learn this as a rule but see *Example 2* in *Session 6* for further explanation.

Example 3 Relevant Labour Costs

Omega Consulting specialises in helping clients implement new accounting software packages. The company has just received a request from a new client to implement a new accounting system, urgently, next week. You have been requested to calculate the relevant cost of the labour that would be required on the project.

1. A project manager would be needed. One project manager, Bill Bates, is available next week. Bill earns a fixed salary equivalent to $1,500 a week.

2. A business consultant would be required to work 30 hours on the contract. All consultants are busy next week. One consultant, Colin Carrington, is scheduled to deliver a training course to a client. This course will generate contribution of $10,000. If the course is cancelled Colin could work on the new client. Alternatively, the training course could be postponed to the following week, when Colin is available. The client would be charged $5,000 less if the course were delayed a week. Colin is on a fixed weekly salary of $1,000.

3. A technical consultant would be required for 10 hours to install the software and convert the data from the old system. All technical consultants are busy next week, but David Dawson, an experienced technical consultant, said he would be prepared to work overtime. He will work on the new project on Monday and Tuesday, and catch up with the 10 hours missed on his existing project the following weekend. David is paid a standard hourly rate of $50 and double time (i.e. $100 an hour) for weekend work. Alternatively, a freelance technical consultant is available. Freelance consultants charge $75 an hour.

4. An analyst would be required for 10 hours to document the new client's system. All analysts are busy next week, but a small project on which Edward Eaves was due to work can be cancelled, which would enable Edward to work on the documentation for the new client. If the other contract is cancelled, contribution of $1,000 would be lost. Edward is paid an hourly rate of $50.

Required:
Explain what the relevant cost is for each of the four items above.

3.4 Non-current Assets

Non-current assets, such as machinery, may be required for a contract. The relevant cost of such assets depends on how the organisation plans to obtain the use of it:

- If the asset is to be rented (or hired) the rental costs over the period of use are relevant.

- If the asset is to be acquired (purchased) for the contract, the cost of acquiring the asset would be relevant. It may be that when the contract is completed, the asset can be sold. In this case, the expected proceeds from the sale will be relevant income that should be deducted from the total cost of acquiring the asset when calculating the relevant cost.*

*Cost of acquiring may include not only the purchase cost but related costs, such as delivery and installation.

■ An asset such as the one that is required may already be owned. The relevant cost then depends on whether that asset is already being fully utilised on other activities.

  ● If the asset is not actually being used for any other purposes at the moment (or has space capacity), the relevant cost is the *fall in realisable value* that will arise if the asset is used for the contract.

  ● If the asset is already fully utilised its relevant cost is its *deprival value* (see s.3.4.2).

3.4.1 Fall in Realisable Value

> **Illustration 2 Fall in Realisable Value**
>
> Bob, a builder, owns a crane. He believes that he could sell it today for $150,000 in the used-crane market.
>
> He is tendering for a contract to renovate the town hall, which is expected to take a year to complete. If he wins this contract he will need to keep the crane. Once the town hall contract is complete he would sell the crane. He estimates that he would be able to sell it for $120,000 in one year's time.
>
> If he does not win the town hall contract, he will sell the crane straight away for $150,000.
>
> For the town hall contract, the relevant cost of the crane is $30,000. This is the fall in the realisable value of the crane if it is used on this contract.

3.4.2 Deprival Value

If an asset that is required for a contract is already owned but currently fully utilised in other activities, the relevant cost is its deprival value (i.e. the cost of depriving the business of the asset). Deprival value is determined by consideration of the "value in use" and the "replacement cost" of the asset:

Key Point

The lowest cost option will be chosen. This is the deprival value.

■ **Value in use** is the value to the business of the asset that is already owned. This is the higher of its *net realisable value* (i.e. the net amount that would be realised if it was disposed of) and its *economic value*. Economic value is the present value of the future earnings that the asset would generate for the business.*

  ● If economic value is less than net realisable value the asset should be sold.

  ● If economic value is more than net realisable value the asset should be kept.

■ **Replacement cost** is the cost of acquiring an equivalent asset (i.e. with the same operating capability).

***Commentary**

*The determination of future earnings is beyond the scope of F5.

The business needs to decide whether to:

■ buy an equivalent asset for the contract (i.e. incur the replacement cost); or

■ transfer the asset from existing activities (i.e. forego its value in use).

The determination of deprival value is summarised as follows:*

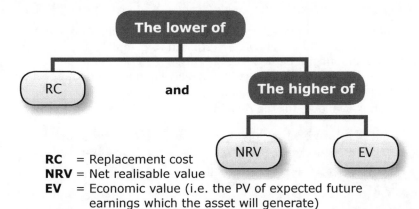

RC = Replacement cost
NRV = Net realisable value
EV = Economic value (i.e. the PV of expected future earnings which the asset will generate)

*This can be thought of as a two-stage decision:

Decision 1—should the asset be kept in use in the business or sold? (For assets in use, EV should be higher than NRV.)

Decision 2—if deprived of the asset (e.g. through sale or use elsewhere) will it be replaced?

Illustration 3 Non-current Asset Opportunity Cost

An asset which will be transferred to a new contract, if it is undertaken, has:

Replacement cost	$200,000
Net realisable value	$50,000
Economic value	$100,000

The opportunity cost of the asset is $100,000.

Example 4 Deprival Value

Identify the deprival value in each for the following cases:

Case	RC	NRV	EV	Deprival Value
1	500	600	550	
2	700	600	550	
3	700	600	650	

Example 5 Contract Quote

Stella is about to tender for a contract which requires two raw materials, steel and tungsten. Five hundred tons of steel and 1,000 tons of tungsten will be required to complete the contract. In addition, 2,000 hours of labour will be needed. Of this, 1,200 hours are in the assembly process and the remainder in the finishing process. Stella will quote a price that allows a 50% mark-up on relevant cost.

The following additional information is available for the resources required:

	In inventory now	Original price per ton	Current price per ton	Net realisable value
Steel	200 tons	$10	$12	$8
Tungsten	400 tons	$20	$23	$15

Steel cannot be used by Stella for any other purpose, but tungsten is used in all the company's manufacturing processes.

All labour is paid at $4 per hour, but to complete the contract in time, labour for the finishing process will have to be transferred from other work which generates contribution at a rate of $3 per hour (after labour costs). There is currently surplus capacity for assembly labour amounting to 1,000 hours for the duration of the contract. Owing to other urgent work, any additional assembly labour will have to be hired on a temporary basis at the rate of $5 per hour.

Required:

Determine the price Stella will quote on the contract.

Solution

	Working	$
Steel:		
Held		
Purchased		
Tungsten:		
Finishing labour:		
Cost		
Lost contribution		
Assembly labour:		
Relevant cost		
Mark-up		
Quote		

3.5 Non-financial Factors

From a financial point of view, a contract should proceed if the revenue from the contract exceeds its relevant cost. However, management should also take into account non-financial factors before making a final decision. Just some of the non-financial factors that may be considered are as follows:

- A contract may be undertaken even if the revenue is not sufficient to cover the relevant costs if there are other reasons why the contract is desirable. For example:

  - Undertaking a new type of contract may develop the business's knowledge and experience, which may be useful in obtaining subsequent business.

  - The contract may enhance the business's reputation (e.g. a contract for a high-profile customer).

- A profitable contract may be declined if there is a high risk of reputational damage.*

*Commentary

*For example, if the contract will harm the environment or involves activities that may be considered unethical.

4 Shut Down Decisions

4.1 Fixed Costs

Where managers are given an analysis of profits by division, it may be tempting to assume that loss-making divisions should be shut down. However, before such decisions are taken, managers must be aware of whether all the costs assigned to a division would actually be saved if the division were to be closed down. In particular, fixed costs may have been allocated to the division from the head office. These may not be saved if the division is closed down.

Example 6 Shut Down Decisions

Rolling Co is composed of four divisions: North, South, East and West. The directors are concerned about the performance of East and West divisions, which have consistently shown losses for the last three years.

The divisional income statements for the last year show the following:

	North $	South $	East $	West $
Sales	5,000	10,000	7,500	6,000
Variable costs	2,500	4,000	4,000	3,000
Contribution	2,500	6,000	3,500	3,000
Fixed costs	1,500	3,500	4,000	3,200
Profits/(losses)	1,000	2,500	(500)	(200)

Further analysis of the fixed costs reveals the following. It can be assumed that directly attributable fixed costs would be saved if the division were closed down. Allocated overheads would not:

	$	$	$	$
Directly attributable	500	1,500	2,500	2,000
Allocated (20% of revenue)	1,000	2,000	1,500	1,200
Total fixed costs	1,500	3,500	4,000	3,200

Required:

Calculate the financial impact on Rolling Co of closing divisions East and West. Based on your calculations, advise the management whether the divisions should be closed.

4.2 Non-financial Factors

When making shut down decisions, managers do not only consider whether closing a division would reduce losses. Managers should also take into account non-financial factors. For example:

- If closing a division would result in redundancies, this could lead to poor morale among remaining employees.

- The permanent loss of resources and specific skills may mean that it will not be possible to take advantage of future opportunities.

- Shutting down one division may affect demand for products produced by other divisions (e.g. if customers like to buy a range of products from one supplier, closing a particular division will limit the range that is available).

■ It may be possible to bring a loss-making division back to profitability by developing new products or services.

■ Shutting down a division may make it possible to sell assets such as buildings to raise finance for other divisions or to reduce debt.

5 Further Processing Decisions

Joint products and by-products arise where the manufacture of one product makes inevitable the manufacture of other products.

Joint products have significant relative sales value.

A **by-product** is produced in conjunction with one or more main products but has a small relative sales value. (So it is unlikely to influence the decision to produce main products.)

Products produced are not separately identifiable until a certain stage in the production process—the **split-off point (SOP)**.

Costs incurred before the SOP are **joint or pre-separation costs** and must be apportioned between the products produced.

Once the products have reached the split-off point:

■ It may be possible to sell the product immediately in its current state.

■ The product may require further processing before it can be sold.

■ The manufacturer may have a choice of selling the product immediately or processing further.

In making the further processing decision, the manufacturer needs to compare the additional revenue that can be gained by further processing the product against the additional costs of further processing.

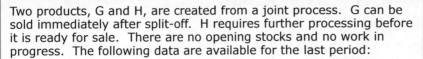

Illustration 4	Further Processing Decision*

Two products, G and H, are created from a joint process. G can be sold immediately after split-off. H requires further processing before it is ready for sale. There are no opening stocks and no work in progress. The following data are available for the last period:

	$	Product	Selling price per unit
Total joint production costs	384,000	G	$0.84 (400,000 units)
Further processing costs (product H)	159,600	H	$1.82 (200,000 units)

The relevant costs and revenues in determining whether H should be processed further are the additional revenue of $364,000 less the costs of further processing of $159,600. Further processing of H increases profits by $204,400, so H should be further processed.

Commentary

*The joint production costs incurred before the split-off point are a common cost and therefore not relevant to the further-processing decision. They will be relevant, however, to determining whether the overall process is viable.

Having determined whether or not to further process products after the split-off point, a decision needs to be made about the financial viability of the *overall* process. This should consider all revenues, less all relevant costs of further processing (if appropriate) and the main process.

Illustration 5   Overall Process

Continuing from *Illustration 4*, the following revenues and costs are relevant in deciding whether or not to go ahead with the whole process:

	$
Revenue from selling G (0.84 × 400,000)	336,000
Revenue from selling H (1.82 × 200,000)	364,000
Total joint production costs	(384,000)
Further processing costs (product H)	(159,600)
Total profit	156,400

6   Make or Buy

6.1   Outsourcing

Outsourcing is the practice of buying goods or services externally, rather than making or providing them internally. For many years now there has been a trend towards outsourcing of non-core services in particular. Examples of services that are often outsourced include:

- office cleaning
- canteen and catering services
- payroll services
- IT services
- security services.

Outsourcing is not limited to the provision of services; certain parts of manufacturing also may be outsourced. It is quite common for manufacturing companies to outsource some, or all, component parts. This trend has been strengthened by the reduced costs of international trade; many components may be made in lower-cost economies and the assembly of the final products may take place closer to the markets in which the products are sold. The decision companies may have to make, therefore, is whether to make components or to buy them in.

6.2   Advantages of Outsourcing

✔ **Lower cost.** Many companies have discovered that some goods or services may be purchased for less than it would cost to provide them internally. This may be assisted by the economies of scale enjoyed by the third-party provider.

✔ Services may become a **variable cost** rather than a fixed cost if outsourced. For example, the cost of outsourcing payroll services may be based on the number of personnel. If payroll services were sourced in-house, staff would have to be employed to provide this service (i.e. effectively a fixed, or stepped, cost).

✔ Outsourcing allows management to focus on the **core competencies** of the business without being distracted by managing peripheral areas.

✔ **Better quality** of the goods or service provided by a specialist third party.

✔ Access to a wider range of **expertise** as the provider deals with several clients. For example, a provider of IT services may have employees with a wider range of skills and knowledge than an internal IT function.

6.3   Disadvantages of Outsourcing

✗ The company relies on a third party to provide a reliable supply. It therefore loses **control** over a part of its business processes.

✗ Outsourcing may mean trusting a third party with **confidential** information about goods or services.

✗ Some costs may not be apparent (i.e. **hidden**) as anything not specifically covered by the contract is likely to incur additional charges.

✗ **Quality** may suffer especially if the contract price per unit is fixed (i.e. the third party can only increase its profit by reducing costs).

✗ Operational dependence on the outsourcing company is linked to its **financial stability.** If the third-party company fails, switching to another provider may be very costly.

✗ Outsourcing may **demotivate** the workforce if the decision to outsource is associated with job losses. (There may also be bad publicity where outsourcing is to another country.)

6.4   Make v Buy Decisions

When deciding whether to outsource the manufacture of a particular component, organisations will obviously want to calculate the financial effect. Although financial impact will not be the only factor to be considered, it is likely to be significant.

If a company outsources all production of an item there will be no in-house production for that item. This may lead to some fixed cost savings, since less production capacity will be required.

The approach here is to determine the costs that would be saved if in-house production were to cease, including any incremental fixed costs, and compare this with the costs of buying-in the component from an external supplier.

Example 7 Outsourcing All Production

Big Phones makes smart phones. The company sells 1 million phones each year. Each phone includes a standard rechargeable battery. Currently, the batteries are manufactured in-house, but the company has recently received an offer from Super Batteries to supply all the batteries required for a price of $2 each.

The management accountant has prepared a schedule showing the total costs of producing 1 million batteries last year as follows:

	$000
Materials	1,400
Direct labour	320
Machine running costs	240
Depreciation	250
Other overheads	400
Total	2,610

Depreciation includes depreciation of the factory building which is apportioned to each product. $75,000 has been apportioned to the battery manufacturing department. If the manufacture of batteries were to be outsourced, this part of the factory would remain empty, at least in the short term.

Other overheads include a $300,000 apportionment of general factory overheads that are not specific to making batteries.

Required:

Determine the costs that would be saved if the offer is accepted and hence advise Big Phones whether it should continue to manufacture the batteries in-house or outsource their manufacture to Super Batteries.

Solution

Cost savings

	$000
Materials	
Direct labour	
Machine running costs	
Depreciation	
Other overheads	
Total	2,610

Advice:

Summary

- In decision-making, the relevant costs and revenues are those which change as a result of the decision. All other revenues and costs should be ignored.

- Opportunity costs should be taken into consideration, as these are relevant to the decision.

- Decision-making scenarios include "one-off contracts" where the relevant cost of performing a contract is calculated.

- Shut down decisions involve the decision to close a loss-making division. In making such decisions, it should be recognised that some of the costs of the loss-making division may not be saved if the division is closed, and therefore are not relevant to the decision.

- Further processing decisions involve whether it is worthwhile processing joint products or by-products further.

Session 3 Quiz
Estimated time: 15 minutes

1. Distinguish between relevant and non-relevant costs. (1.1, 1.2)

2. Define opportunity cost. (2.2)

3. Summarise the principles relating to calculating the relevant cost of materials. (3.2)

4. Define the deprival value of a non-current asset. (3.4.2)

5. State under what circumstances it would be inappropriate to close down a loss-making division. Your answer should be based only on financial factors. (4)

6. State FOUR advantages and TWO disadvantages of outsourcing. (6.2, 6.3)

Study Question Bank
Estimated time: 1 hour, 10 minutes

Priority		Estimated Time	Completed
Q5	Parser	30 minutes	
Q6	Sniff Co	40 minutes	

EXAMPLE SOLUTIONS

Solution 1—Incremental Costs

	Relevant?	Explanation
■ Food and drinks	Yes	These costs are incurred specifically for the wedding party. If there were no wedding party, these costs would not be incurred.
■ Waiters' wages	Yes	Waiters are only paid when they work, so are being paid specially for the wedding.
■ Supervisor's salary	No	The supervisor is on a fixed salary, which does not change as a result of the wedding party.
■ Flowers	Yes	They are being purchased specifically for the wedding.
■ Administration	No	This cost relates to the salaries of the staff in the banqueting department. These are fixed and not increased by the wedding.
■ Cleaning of function room	Yes	The cleaning company is paid a fee per event. If the wedding did not take place, there would be no fee.
■ Room rental	No	The rent of the hotel building is fixed regardless of whether the rooms are occupied or vacant.
■ Central management costs	No	10% has just been added to the cost of the wedding to cover central overhead costs. These would probably have been incurred regardless of the wedding.*

Commentary

*Some overhead costs may increase as a result of the wedding (e.g. for light and heat) but as these amounts have not been identified, it is not possible to specify a relevant amount.

Solution 2—Relevant Materials Costs

1. Bob has sufficient oak in his storeroom to make the table. Since he uses oak regularly, any oak used to make the table would have to be replaced. The relevant cost is therefore the replacement cost (i.e. the current price of $2.75 per m^2).

2. Bob would have to buy the tins of varnish specifically for this order, so the relevant cost is the replacement cost (i.e. the current price of $20 a tin).

3. Bob already has the hinges needed for the table in the storeroom. The question is whether he would replace them if he used them for the table. The information clearly suggests not, as Bob has not used the hinges before. Any scrap value would therefore be the opportunity cost, but this would appear to be zero, as Bob has said that nobody would want to buy second-hand hinges.

Solution 3—Relevant Labour Costs

1. The relevant cost of the project manager is zero. Bill Bates, who would manage the new project next week, is paid a fixed salary and has spare time next week. There is, therefore, no additional cost to the company for Bill to manage this project.

2. The relevant cost of the business consultant would be the $5,000 discount given to the other client for agreeing to delay the training course by a week. Colin would have to be taken off a training course, but since he can deliver it a week later, the contribution on that course is not lost, so is not relevant. (Another way of looking at this is that the contribution is not entirely lost, but reduced by $5,000, in respect of the discount). Colin is also on a fixed salary, so no extra salary will be paid to him for working on the project.

3. There is a choice here between using the internal technical consultant, David Dawson, or an external consultant. The cost of the external consultant would be $750 (i.e. $75 an hour for 10 hours). If David were to be used, he would have to work overtime. Although the overtime rate of $100 would be incurred while working on his existing project, that overtime rate would not be paid if he were not used on the new project, so the cost of using David is $100 an hour. The external consultant is therefore the cheaper option, so the relevant cost would be $750.

4. The relevant cost is $1,500, which is the direct cost of Edward's time ($50 × 10) plus the opportunity cost of $1,000. The direct cost of Edward's time is relevant because he is paid an hourly wage of $50, which is a variable cost. The opportunity cost is the lost contribution on the other project that Edward would have worked on.

Solution 4—Deprival Value

Case	RC	NRV	EV
1	(500)	600	550
2	700	(600)	550
3	700	600	(650)

Solution 5—Contract Quote

	Working	$
Steel:		
Held (NRV)	200 tons @ $8	1,600
Purchased	300 tons @ $12	3,600
Tungsten:	1,000 tons @ $23	23,000
Finishing labour:		
—Cost	800 hours @ $4	3,200
—Lost contribution	800 hours @ $3	2,400
Assembly labour:	200 hours @ $5	1,000
Relevant cost		34,800
Mark-up 50% of relevant cost		17,400
Quote		52,200

Solution 6—Shut Down Decisions

	East	West
	$	$
Lost contribution	(3,500)	(3,000)
Saved fixed costs (attributable only)	2,500	2,000
Net savings/(losses)	(1,000)	(1,000)

Conclusion

Closing each division would lead to a reduction in profits of $1,000 per year. They should not be closed. The two departments make a positive contribution to the company's overall profits and only show a loss because of allocation of central fixed costs.

Solution 7—Outsourcing All Production

If manufacturing were to stop, the following costs would be saved each year:

	$000
Materials	1,400
Direct labour	320
Machine running costs	240
Depreciation (only attributable to batteries)	175*
Other overheads (excludes general overheads apportioned)	100*
Total	2,235

Costs of buying 1 million batteries from Super Batteries would be $2 million.

Advice: The cost of buying from Super Batteries is less than the savings made from stopping the manufacture of the batteries in-house (i.e. it is more expensive to make than to buy). The batteries should therefore be bought from Super Batteries.

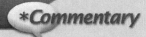

*Commentary

*It is assumed that attributable depreciation and overheads of $100 million would be saved if the production of batteries ceased. Factory depreciation and apportioned overheads would not be saved, so are not relevant savings.

Cost Volume Profit Analysis

FOCUS

This session covers the following content from the *ACCA Study Guide.*

B. Decision-Making Techniques

2. Cost volume profit analysis

a) Explain the nature of CVP analysis.

b) Calculate and interpret the breakeven point and margin of safety.

c) Calculate the contribution to sales ratio, in single and multi-product situations, and demonstrate an understanding of its use.

d) Calculate target profit or revenue in single and multi-product situations, and demonstrate an understanding of its use.

e) Prepare breakeven charts and profit volume charts and interpret the information contained within each, including multi-product situations.

f) Discuss the limitations of CVP analysis for planning and decision-making.

Session 4 Guidance

■ **Note** that if you studied F2 *Management Accounting*, then most of this session will be revision.

■ **Pay attention**, however; multi-product situations are new (s.4).

(continued on next page)

VISUAL OVERVIEW

Objective: To understand the concepts of breakeven and margin of safety, and to carry out CVP analysis.

BREAKEVEN ANALYSIS

- Breakeven Point
- Simplifying Assumptions

CHARTS

- Breakeven Chart
- Profit-Volume Chart

MATHEMATICAL APPROACH

- Contribution
- Breakeven Formulae
- C/S Ratio
- Margin of Safety

MULTI-PRODUCT ANALYSIS

- Assumption
- Calculation
- Multi-Product P/V Graphs

LIMITATIONS IN PLANNING AND DECISION-MAKING

- Simplifying Assumptions
- Multi-Product Situations

Session 4 Guidance

■ **Read** the article "Cost Volume Profit Analysis".

1 Breakeven Analysis

1.1 Breakeven Point

> ### Definition
>
> **Breakeven point**—the level of activity at which neither a profit nor a loss is made.

- It indicates the *lowest* activity level at which the activity is viable. (It may be regarded as a "life and death" measure.)*
- It is ascertained by a breakeven chart or calculation.

> ### *Commentary
>
> *Breakeven point—where total contribution = total fixed costs.

1.2 Simplifying Assumptions

- Within the range of activity under consideration, *total* cost behaves as a strictly linear semi-variable cost:
  - fixed costs remain fixed with the range;
  - total variable costs change proportionally with volume.
- Unit selling prices do not change with volume.
- Costs and income are matched (i.e. there is no significant change in inventory levels).
- Levels of efficiency and productivity do not change (as this would affect cost behaviour).
- There is only a single product or a constant sales mix of more than one product.

> ### Key Point
>
> Total costs and total revenue are linear functions of output.

2 Charts

2.1 Breakeven Chart

- The breakeven chart indicates approximate profit/loss at different levels of sales volume within a limited range.

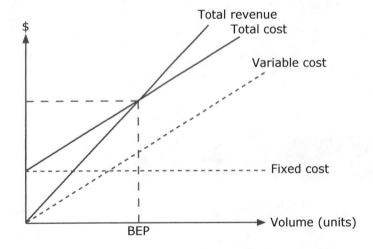

■ The variable cost and fixed cost lines add little to the above diagram, which is normally shown more clearly as:

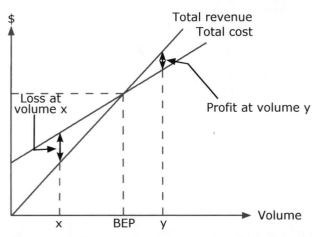

Diagram for the accountant's CVP model

Example 1 Breakeven Chart

A company makes one product, the gamma. The selling price per unit is $100. The variable cost per unit is $20. Fixed costs per year are $1,000,000.

Required:

Draw a breakeven chart for the gamma, and determine from the chart how many units of the gamma must be sold per year to break even.

2.2   Profit-Volume Chart

■ A "PV" chart is another way of presenting the same information as a breakeven chart but it emphasises profits and losses at different activity levels (i.e. sales volume or value).

■ To draw it requires only the following information:
 ● profit/(loss) at *any* (i.e. just one) level of sales; and
 ● total fixed costs.*

*At zero sales volume, total loss is the amount of the fixed costs.

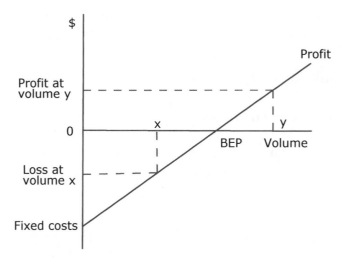

Example 2 PV Chart

A company makes one product, the beta. Annual fixed costs are $1 million. If sales of 60,000 units are made, profit will be $200,000.

Required:
Draw the PV chart and, using this, determine the breakeven point.

3 Mathematical Approach

3.1 Contribution

■ In the short term, the fixed costs of a business do not change with output.

■ Producing/selling one extra unit ⊃

- Extra revenue (the unit selling price).
- Extra costs (the *variable* cost per unit).

■ The *additional* profit made from selling one extra unit is known as the *unit contribution*.

Unit contribution = Selling price – Variable cost per unit

equally

Total contribution = Total revenue – Total variable cost

■ In any decision connected with varying the levels of production, fixed costs are not relevant as they do not change regardless of which course of action is taken.

■ It is the change in *contribution* which will affect the decision.

3.2 Breakeven Formulae

3.2.1 BEP

Profit
= Sales – Variable cost – Fixed cost
= Total contribution – Fixed cost

At BEP, profit = 0 Therefore, Total contribution = Fixed cost

But, Total contribution = Number of units x Unit contribution

Therefore,
Number of units to be sold to breakeven $= \dfrac{\text{Total fixed cost}}{\text{Unit contribution}}$

3.2.2 Target Profits

$$\text{Sales volume to achieve a target profit} = \frac{\text{Fixed cost} + \text{required profit}}{\text{Unit contribution}}$$

$$\text{Sales revenue to achieve a target profit} = \text{Sales volume to achieve a target profit} \times \text{unit selling price}$$

3.2.3 Breakeven Revenue

▦ BEP is expressed in terms of the number of units which must be sold to break even.

▦ Breakeven revenue is the revenue achieved at the BEP. One way of calculating this is simply to multiply the number of units at BEP by the unit selling price.

Example 3 Using the Formulae

Using the information in *Example 1* calculate:

(a) the breakeven point for the gamma using the numerical approach;

(b) the sales volume required to make a profit of $100,000;

(c) the revenue at the breakeven point.

3.3 C/S Ratio

3.3.1 C/S Ratio

▦ Contribution/sales ratio (also called *contribution margin*) is the proportion of selling price which **contributes to fixed overheads and profits.***

$$= \frac{\text{Contribution per unit}}{\text{Selling price per unit}} \left(\text{or } \frac{\text{Total contribution}}{\text{Total sales revenue}} \right)$$

Commentary

*Although this is also called the profit/ volume (or P/V) ratio, this is a misnomer. Profit is not the same as contribution and volume is not the same as sales.

3.3.2 Breakeven Revenue

▦ The C/S ratio can be used as an alternative way of calculating breakeven revenue, without calculating breakeven point.

$$\text{Breakeven revenue} = \frac{\text{Fixed cost}}{\text{C/S ratio}}$$

$$\text{Revenue required to achieve a target profit} = \frac{\text{Fixed cost} + \text{required profit}}{\text{C/S ratio}}$$

Example 4 C/S Ratio

Using the information in *Example 1* calculate:
(a) the C/S ratio for the gamma; and
(b) the breakeven revenue using the C/S ratio.

3.4 Margin of Safety

Definition

Margin of safety—the amount by which anticipated or existing activity exceeds (or falls short of) breakeven.

In units or $s: Margin of safety = Budgeted sales − Breakeven sales

As a percentage: $\dfrac{\text{Budgeted sales} - \text{Breakeven sales}}{\text{Budgeted sales}} \times 100\%$

Exhibit 1   TOYOTA

Toyota Motor Corporation had the capacity and flexibility of being able to meet expected demand plus or minus 20%. In 2008, in the wake of the financial crisis, demand for Toyota's cars fell by 35%. In the financial year ended 31 March 2009, the company made a loss of $4.2 billion. Fortunately the company returned to profit in the following financial year.

As a result of the loss in 2008/09, the company has endeavoured to reduce fixed costs in an attempt to achieve a margin of safety of 30%.

Example 5 Margin of Safety

Continuing on from *Examples 3* and *4*, the company expects to sell 20,000 units of the gamma per year.

Required:
Calculate the margin of safety in terms of number of units, and as a percentage.

Example 6 Target Revenue

A company manufactures a single product which has the following cost structure based on a production budget of 10,000 units.

	$
Materials—4 kg at $3/kg	12
Direct labour—5 hours at $7/hr	35

Variable production overheads are recovered at the rate of $8 per direct labour hour. Other costs incurred by the company are:

	$
Factory fixed overheads	120,000
Selling and distribution overheads	160,000
Fixed administration overheads	80,000

The selling and distribution overheads include a variable element due to a distribution cost of $2 per unit. The fixed selling price of the unit is $129.

Required:
(a)   Calculate how many units have to be sold for the company to break even.
(b)   Calculate the sales revenue which would give a net profit of $40,000.

Example 6 Target Revenue (continued)

Solution

(a) Breakeven number of units

	$
Materials	
Labour	
Variable overheads	
Distribution	
Total variable cost	
Selling price	
Unit contribution	

Fixed costs

	$
Factory	
Selling and distributing (after excluding variable element)	
Administration	
Total fixed cost	

BEP =

(b) Sales revenue ➲ Target profit $40,000

	$
Total fixed costs	
Profit required	
Total contribution required	

$$\frac{\text{Total contribution}}{\text{Unit contribution}} =$$

Total revenue required:

4 Multi-Product Analysis

4.1 Assumption

■ CVP analysis can be extended to multi-product situations if a predetermined sales mix is held to be constant.

■ If the assumption of standard mix is relaxed, there will be no unique BEP.

4.2 Calculation of Breakeven Point

4.2.1 Weighted Average C/S Ratio

■ The easiest way to calculate breakeven revenue in multi-product situations is to apply a C/S ratio (as in s.3.3).

■ The only difference is that the C/S ratio will be weighted:

$$\text{Weighted average C/S ratio} = \frac{\text{Total contribution (from all products)}}{\text{Total revenue (from all products)}} *$$

The C/S ratio specifies how much contribution will be generated by a \$1 increase in sales revenue. In multi-product situations, sales mix is assumed to remain constant.

The C/S ratio can be used to find:

■ breakeven revenue; and

■ sales revenue required to generate a target profit.

Simply apply the same formulae used above in single-product situations to a multi-product situation:

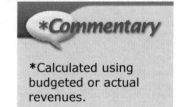

*Commentary

*Calculated using budgeted or actual revenues.

$$\text{Breakeven revenue} = \frac{\text{Fixed cost}}{\text{Weighted average C/S ratio}}$$

$$\text{Revenue required to achieve a target profit} = \frac{\text{Fixed cost} + \text{required profit}}{\text{Weighted average C/S ratio}}$$

Example 7 Multi-Product Analysis

Pear manufactures laptop computers and smart phones. The company has prepared the following forecast for the following financial period:

	Laptops	Smart phones
Budget sales	1,200	600
	$	$
Unit selling price	1,000	500
Unit variable cost	700	400
Unit contribution	300	100

Budget fixed costs are \$245,000 for the period.

Required:

(a)   The breakeven revenue, using the weighted average C/S ratio.

(b)   The sales revenue required to make a target profit of \$245,000.

4.2.2 Sales Units at Breakeven Revenue

▦ In multi-product situations, breakeven revenue shows the total revenue required to breakeven, assuming that the sales mix remains as per the budget. Decision makers may wish to analyse this revenue by product.

▦ This can be done by multiplying the total breakeven revenue by the revenue ratio for each product. The revenue ratio is simply the portion of total revenue that a particular product accounts for:

$$\text{Revenue ratio for product X} = \frac{\text{Budgeted revenue for product X}}{\text{Total budgeted revenue}}$$

At breakeven, Revenue from product X = Total breakeven revenue × Revenue ratio for product X.

Illustration 1 Sales Units at Breakeven Pointe

In *Example 7*, breakeven revenue was $875,000. Pear's management now wants to know how much of this revenue comes from laptop sales and how many laptops must be sold to achieve this.

$$\text{Revenue ratio for product laptops} = \frac{\text{Budgeted revenue for laptops}}{\text{Total budgeted revenue}}$$

$$= \frac{\$1.2 \text{ million}}{\$1.5 \text{ million}} = 0.8 \text{ or } 80\%.$$

Therefore, at breakeven point, revenue from laptops is $700,000 ($875,000 × 80%).

Because the unit selling price of a laptop is $1,000, this corresponds to the sale of 700 laptops.

4.3 Multi-Product P/V Charts

In a multi-product environment, sales revenue is drawn on the horizontal axis (x axis) and profit is drawn on the vertical axis (y axis). Two approaches are taken to drawing the line denoting profit/loss:

▦ constant (fixed) sales mix; or

▦ ranking of products by profitability.

4.3.1 Assuming a Constant Sales Mix

▦ Assuming a **constant** mix of products based on the budgeted sales it is only necessary to know profit for two values of sales (to plot on the graph and draw a straight line between them):

  ● The easiest point is where revenue = 0 (i.e. where the company makes a loss equal to fixed costs).

  ● For the second point it makes most sense to calculate profit for budgeted sales.

Illustration 2   Multi-Product P/V Chart

Company A makes two products, Exe and Wye. Details of these two products are as follows:

	Exe	Wye
Selling price	$40	$60
Contribution per unit	$24	$18
C/S ratio	0.6	0.3
Budgeted sales	10,000	10,000
Ranking (based on C/S) for *Illustration 2*	①	②
Total fixed costs	$100,000	

Maximum demand for both products is assumed to be the same as budgeted sales.

When sales revenue = 0, loss = $100,000 (fixed costs)

At budgeted sales revenue:

Revenue = (10,000 × 40) + (10,000 × 60) = $1,000,000.

Profit = Contribution − Fixed cost = (10,000 × 24) + (10,000 × 18) − 100,000 = 320,000.

The profit volume chart can then be plotted as follows:

Profit

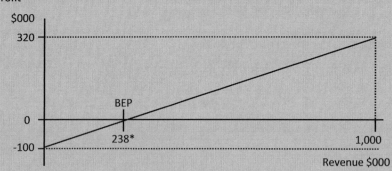

Where revenue is zero, the cumulative profit will be a loss that equates to total fixed costs. The breakeven point occurs where the line crosses the x axis, at the point where revenue = $238,000.

*Commentary

*It is unlikely that the BEP would be determined so accurately from the graph alone but the breakeven revenue could be checked using the formula.

4.3.2   Assuming Sales by "Profitability"

An alternative assumption is that sales are not made in a standard sales mix but by profitability of product (i.e. the company produces and sells the product with the highest contribution first). Products are therefore ranked according to the C/S ratios.

In this case, the PV chart will no longer be a straight line; it will be "kinked". To draw the graph, it is advisable to do a table first, calculating profit at the following points:

1. Sales revenue = 0

2. Maximum sales of the most profitable product, with no sales of the second product.

3. Maximum sales of the first and second products.

4. Maximum sales of the first, second and third products (if there are three products).

And so on.

Illustration 3   Sales by "Profitability"

Continuing from *Illustration 1*, assume now that company A decides to produce and sell product Exe first, as this has the highest C/S ratio, followed by product Wye. The calculation of profits at the key points is as follows:

	Contribution	Cumulative Profit/(loss)	Revenue	Cumulative Revenue
Sales revenue = 0	0	(100,000)	0	0
Max sales of Exe	240,000	140,000	400,000	400,000
Max sales of Wye	180,000	320,000	600,000	1,000,000

Drawing the line joining these key points gives the PV Chart:

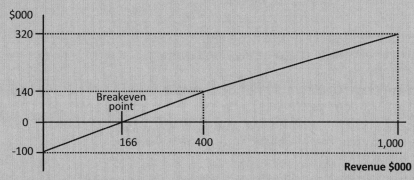

Up to revenue of $400,000, the company is selling only Exe. After this it starts to sell Wye. Since Wye generates contribution at a lower rate per $ of revenue than Exe, the line is more flat after this point.

The breakeven point is where the line crosses the x axis, at the point where sales = $166,000. This is lower than the breakeven point assuming a constant sales mix (*Illustration 1*). This is because the C/S ratio of product Exe is higher than the weighted average C/S ratio of the two products together.

Example 8 Multi-Product Breakeven Charts

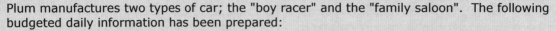

Plum manufactures two types of car; the "boy racer" and the "family saloon". The following budgeted daily information has been prepared:

	Boy racer	Family saloon
Budget sales	300	600
	$	$
Unit selling price	10,000	15,000
Unit variable cost	5,000	12,000
Unit contribution	5,000	3,000

Budgeted fixed costs are $1 million per day

Required:

Assuming that the budgeted sales represents maximum sales of each of the two products, draw the PV chart for the two products based on the assumption that:

(a) sales occur in the standard (budgeted) mix; and

(b) sales of the most profitable product occur first, followed by sales of the second product.

Draw both lines on one graph.

5 Limitations in Planning and Decision-Making

5.1 Simplifying Assumptions

The main limitations of CVP analysis for planning and decision-making relate to the assumptions which have to be made. In summary, these are:

- Fixed costs remain constant regardless of the production decision. In practice, fixed costs may not be truly fixed and may vary as output changes.

- Variable cost per unit is constant (which may not be the case due to discounts and other economies of scale).

- Selling price remains constant. This may not be true in practice, where an increase in volume of sales can only be achieved by lowering the price.

5.2 Multi-Product Situations

5.2.1 Product Mix

It is necessary to assume a fixed product mix to work with multi-product situations. If the product mix is allowed to vary, there could potentially be many breakeven points. In practice, a company would want to know how varying its product mix would affect profits.

5.2.2   PV Charts

✔ Multi-product PV charts enable the user to see easily the relationship between revenue and profit. Breakeven revenue can also be seen.

✔ Identifying the most and least profitable products should lead to improved decision-making.

✗ The PV chart assumes either a constant sales mix or assumes that products are sold in order of increasing C/S ratio. Actual sales mix is likely to deviate from these assumptions, making the conclusions about breakeven revenue incorrect.

✗ The chart shows only profits plotted against revenue. It does not show variable costs or output in units.

✗ The chart assumes that products can be sold in order of profitability, which ignores the fact that sales of one product may depend on sales of another.

Summary

- The breakeven point is the point at which a company makes a profit of zero. To break even a company needs to sell enough units to cover its fixed and variable costs.

- It is common in exams to see a breakeven chart which shows how total costs and total revenues vary with output. Another type of chart is the PV (Profit-Volume) chart, which shows how profit varies with output.

- The following formulae are all easily derived and are **not** provided in the examination:

  - $\text{Breakeven point} = \dfrac{\text{Total fixed cost}}{\text{Unit contribution}}$

  - $\text{C/S ratio} = \dfrac{\text{Contribution per unit}}{\text{Selling price per unit}}$

  - $\text{Breakeven revenue} = \dfrac{\text{Fixed cost}}{\text{C/S ratio}}$

- In multi-product situations, a standard product mix is assumed. Breakeven revenue can then be calculated by dividing fixed costs by a weighted average C/S ratio.

- The usefulness of CVP analysis is limited by the assumptions that have to be made to make it workable.

Session 4 Quiz
Estimated time: 30 minutes

1. State FIVE simplifying assumptions made in breakeven analysis. (1.2)
2. Give the total cost on a breakeven chart, when output is zero. (2.1)
3. State the formula for contribution per unit. (3.1)
4. What is the formula for calculating the breakeven point (in units)? (3.2.1)
5. Give the formula for the C/S ratio. (3.3.1)

Study Question Bank
Estimated time: 20 minutes

Priority		Estimated Time	Completed
Q7	A to C Co	20 minutes	

EXAMPLE SOLUTIONS

Solution 1—Breakeven Chart

From the diagram below, it can be seen that the breakeven level of sales is 12,500 units.

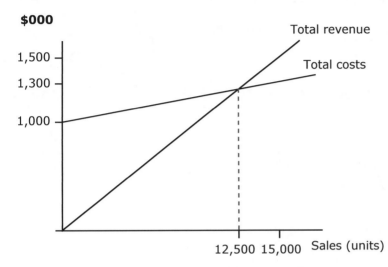

In order to draw each line, it is necessary to calculate total cost or total revenue at two levels of output, and draw a straight line between them:

Total Revenue

When output is 0, total revenue is zero. An output level of 15,000 units was chosen at random. At an output level of 15,000 units, total revenue would be $1.5 million ($100 per unit × 15,000 units).

Total Costs

When output = 0, total costs = fixed costs, = $1 million.

At output level of 15,000 units (chosen at random) total variable costs are $300,000 ($20 per unit × 15,000). Fixed costs are $1 million. Therefore total costs are $1,300,000.

Solution 2—PV Chart

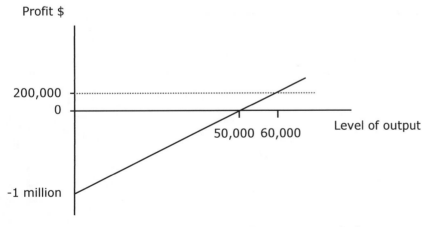

By plotting profit known at two points and drawing a straight line between them, BEP can be seen to be $50,000, because this is the point at which the line crosses the axis (where profit = 0).

Solution 3—Using the Formulae

(a) $\qquad \text{BEP} = \dfrac{\text{Total fixed cost}}{\text{Unit contribution}} = \dfrac{1,000,000}{\$100 - \$20} = 12,500 \text{ units}$

(b) $\qquad$ Sales volume required to make a profit of $100,000

$$= \dfrac{\text{Fixed cost} + \text{Required profit}}{\text{Unit contribution}} = \dfrac{1,000,000 + \$100,000}{\$80} = 13,750 \text{ units}$$

(c) $\qquad$ Revenue at BEP = $100 × 12,500 units = $1,250,000.

Solution 4—C/S Ratio

(a) $\qquad$ The C/S ratio $= \dfrac{\text{Contribution per unit}}{\text{Selling price per unit}} = \dfrac{\$80}{\$100} = 0.8 \text{ (or 80\%)}.$

(b) $\qquad$ Breakeven revenue $= \dfrac{\text{Fixed cost}}{\text{C/S ratio}} = \dfrac{\$1,000,000}{0.8} = \$1,250,000.$

This is the same as was calculated in *Example 3* part (c).

Solution 5—Margin of Safety

In units $\qquad$ Margin of safety = Budgeted sales – Breakeven sales
$\qquad\qquad$ = 20,000 – 12,500 = 7,500 units.

As a percentage $\qquad \dfrac{\text{Budgeted sales} - \text{Breakeven sales}}{\text{Budgeted sales}}$ x 100%

$$\dfrac{20,000 - 12,500}{20,000} \text{ x } 100\% = 37.5\%.$$

This means that sales can fall by 37.5% before the company will no longer make a profit.

Solution 6—Target Revenue

(a) Breakeven number of units

	$
Materials	12
Labour	35
Variable overheads	40
Distribution	2
Total variable cost	89
Selling price	129
Unit contribution	40

Fixed costs	$
Factory	120,000
Selling and distributing (after excluding variable element)	140,000
Administration	80,000
Total fixed cost	340,000

$$\text{BEP} = \frac{\text{Total fixed costs}}{\text{Unit contribution}} = \frac{340,000}{40} = 8,500 \text{ units}$$

(b) Sales revenue ⊃ Target profit $40,000

	$
Total fixed costs	340,000
Profit required	40,000
Total contribution required	380,000

$$\frac{\text{Total contribution}}{\text{Unit contribution}} = \frac{\$380,000}{40} = 9,500 \text{ units}$$

Total revenue required: 9,500 × $129 = $1,225,500

Solution 7—Multi-Product Analysis

The weighted average C/S ratio is: $\dfrac{\text{Total (budgeted) contribution}}{\text{Total (budgeted) sales}}$

Total budgeted contribution is $(1,200 \times 300) + (600 \times 100) = \$420,000$
Total budgeted revenue is $(1,200 \times 1,000) + (600 \times 500) = \$1,500,000$

Weighted average C/S ratio is therefore $\dfrac{420,000}{1,500,000} = 0.28$

(a) Breakeven revenue

$= \dfrac{\text{Fixed cost}}{\text{Weighted average C/S ratio}} = \dfrac{245,000}{0.28} = \$875,000.$

(b) Sales revenue to make a profit of $245,000

$= \dfrac{\text{Fixed cost + Required profit}}{\text{Weighted average C/S ratio}} = \dfrac{245,000 + 245,000}{0.28} = \$1,750,000$

Solution 8—Multi-Product Breakeven Charts

(a) Assuming that sales occur in the budgeted sales mix

When sales = 0, loss = $1,000,000 (fixed costs).
When sales are as per budget:
Revenue = (300 × 10,000) + (600 × 15,000) = $12,000,000.
Profit = Contribution − Fixed costs = (300 × 5,000) + (600 × 3,000) − 1,000,000 = $2,300,000.

(b) Assuming that most profitable products are sold first

The C/S ratio of the boy racer is higher, 50%, compared to 20% for family saloons. Therefore, boy racer would be produced first.
Revenue and profits at the key points are as follows:
The amounts are as follows:

	Contribution	Cumulative Profit/(loss)	Revenue	Cumulative Revenue
	$000	$000	$000	$000
Sales revenue = 0	0	(1,000)	0	0
Max sales of boy racers	1,500	500	3,000	3,000
Max sales of family saloons	1,800	2,300	9,000	12,000

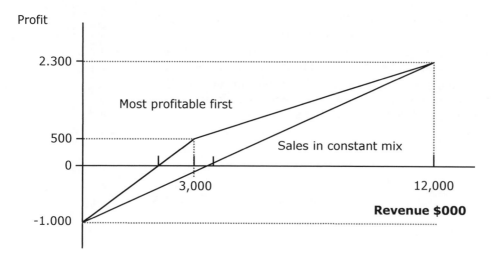

Limiting Factor Decisions

FOCUS

This session covers the following content from the *ACCA Study Guide.*

B. Decision-Making Techniques

3. Limiting factors

a) Identify limiting factors in a scarce resource situation and select an appropriate technique.

b) Determine the optimal production plan where an organisation is restricted by a simple limiting factor, including within the context of "make" or "buy" decisions.

c) Formulate and solve multiple scarce resource problems both graphically and using simultaneous equations as appropriate..

d) Explain and calculate shadow prices (dual prices) and discuss their implications on decision-making and performance management.

e) Calculate slack and explain the implications of the existence of slack for decision-making and performance management. (Excluding simplex and sensitivity to changes in objective functions.)

Session 5 Guidance

■ **Work** through this session on limiting factor decisions. Most of this will be revision from F2.

(continued on next page)

VISUAL OVERVIEW

Objective: To understand how to make production decisions in situations in which there are one or more constraints.

```
                    ┌─────────────────────┐
                    │   LIMITING FACTOR   │
                    │     DECISIONS       │
                    └─────────────────────┘
```

LIMITING FACTORS	MAKE OR BUY	MULTI-LIMITING FACTORS	FURTHER CONSIDERATIONS
• Key Factor Analysis • One Limiting Factor • Shadow Price • Throughput Accounting	• Decisions • Shadow Prices	• Linear Programming • Drawing the Graph • Objective Function Method • Simultaneous Equations • Assumptions	• Shadow Price • Slack • More Than Two Variables

Session 5 Guidance

■ **Pay particular attention to** shadow price and slack; these are new concepts (s.4). You should be able to discuss these concepts and explain their relevance to management.

1 Limiting Factors

1.1 Limiting Factor Analysis (Key Factor Analysis)

■ In the short term, sales demand may be greater than productive capacity. For example, output may be restricted by a shortage of:
   * labour;
   * materials;
   * machinery; or
   * factory space.
■ Where such *limiting factors* apply, contribution (and therefore profit) is maximised by using scarce resources on the product(s) which make the "best use" of them.

1.2 One Limiting Factor

Rule: Where resources are unlimited—make all those products which give "positive contribution".

Rule: Where a factor of production is limited—contribution and profit (because the difference is **fixed** costs) will be maximised by concentrating production on the product(s) which make(s) "best use" of the scarce resource.

1.2.1 Approach

The following approach is used to decide which product(s) to make to maximise profit (which means maximising contribution), where one of the factors of production is limited:

1. Identify the **limiting factor**. To find this calculate how many units of each resource is required to produce sufficient quantities of each product to meet *maximum* demand. If a resource is insufficient to meet maximum demand, it is a limiting factor.

2. Calculate **contribution per unit** of each product.

3. Calculate **contribution per unit of limiting factor** for each product:

$$\frac{\text{Contribution per unit}}{\text{Units of scarce resource used}}$$

4. **Rank** the products according to the contribution per unit of limiting factor; and

5. Concentrate production on those products with the highest contribution per unit of limiting factor—until all of the scarce resource is used up.

Example 1 Limiting Factor Analysis

Material I is restricted to 12,000 kilos.

Product	A	B	C
Contribution per unit ($)	16	10	24
Kilos of I per unit	4	2	8

Required:

Calculate the maximum contribution which can be achieved.

Solution

Product	A	B	C
Contribution per unit			
No. of kilos per unit			
Contribution per kilo			
Rank			

Therefore produce _____ units of _____

Maximum contribution _____

Example 2 Sales Restrictions

Suppose in *Example 2* that sales of B are restricted to 4,000 units.

Required:

Calculate the maximum contribution which can now be achieved.

Solution

	kg
4,000 units of B uses up	
_____	

Therefore maximum contribution $

From B

_____

1.2.2 Limitations of This Approach

✗ Assumes constant variable cost per unit and constant total fixed costs.

✗ Takes no account of loss of customer goodwill.

✗ Can deal with only one scarce resource.

✗ Applies only to situations where capacity constraints cannot be removed in the short term.

1.3 Shadow Price

■ The shadow price (or dual price) is a term which is applied to limited resources. It is the additional contribution the company would generate if one more unit of the resource becomes available.

■ The significance of the shadow price is that companies may be able to obtain additional quantities of a scarce resource if they are prepared to pay a higher price. The shadow price represents the maximum **premium** over the normal price the company would be prepared to pay for each additional unit.

■ It is not worth paying more than the normal price plus the shadow price for additional units, as the additional contribution from producing extra units is more than offset by the extra price paid.

Illustration 1 Shadow Price

Referring back to *Example 2*, if any additional supplies of Material I were to be made available, they would be used for product A, because all demand for product B has been satisfied and product A has the second highest contribution per unit of I.

The shadow price of I is therefore $4. This is equal to the contribution that is generated by every kilogram of I used in making product A.

If additional supplies of Material I were to become available at a higher price than normal, it would be worth paying any price up to $4 above the normal price, as contribution would still be achieved. However, if the price were more than $4 above the normal price, product A would cease to be profitable.

1.4 Throughput Accounting

Throughput accounting was detailed in *Session 2*. It is worth noting that limiting factor analysis may also be used with throughput contribution if the objective is to maximise throughput. Usually the limiting factor is the amount of time available on the bottleneck resource.

The following approach is used:

1. Calculate the **throughput per unit** generated by each product. Throughput per unit is sales price less direct materials cost.

2. Calculate the **throughput return per hour of bottleneck resource** for each product.*

   This is calculated as:

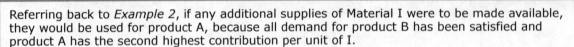

$$\frac{\text{Throughput per unit}}{\text{Bottleneck hour required to produce one unit}}$$

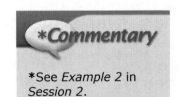

*Commentary

*See *Example 2* in *Session 2*.

3. **Rank** the products based on the return per hour of bottleneck resource (from highest to lowest).

2   Make or Buy

2.1   Decisions

Session 3 introduced outsourcing and "make v buy" decisions in situations that consider producing **all** output of a particular product or component.

This section deals with situations in which only some production will be outsourced due to a limiting factor that prevents the business from producing all that is needed. The limiting factor could be a scarce material, a particular type of skilled labour or any other resource that is in limited supply. The following assumptions apply:

- The business makes several products that use the limiting factor.
- The cost of making items in-house is less than the cost of outsourcing.
- Due to the limiting factor, it is not possible to produce the required quantities of all products. Some production needs to be outsourced.

Assuming that the company can decide which components to make in-house and which to outsource, it should:

- make those components or products where the biggest savings can be made; and
- outsource the remainder.*

Method: To decide which products should be made and which should be bought, calculate the **saving per unit of scarce resource** from making the product rather than from buying it:

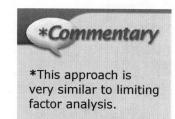

*This approach is very similar to limiting factor analysis.

$$\text{Saving per unit of scarce resource} = \frac{\text{Buy-in price} - \text{Variable cost to make}}{\text{Number of units of scarce resource used per unit}}$$

The products with the greatest saving per unit of scarce resource should be given the highest priority for manufacture.

Example 3 Make or Buy

A company requires three components, X, Y and Z, for use in the manufacture of its main product, the Galaxia. The company can make these components or it can buy them externally. All three components require Material B in their manufacture. Monthly supplies of Material B are restricted to 8,000 kilos.

Product/Component	X	Y	Z
Units required each month	2,000	2,500	4,000
Variable cost to make ($ per unit)	10	12	14
Buy-in price ($ per unit)	13	17	16
Number of kgs of B used per unit	3	2	1

Required:

Determine which products/components the company should make and which it should buy.

Solution

	X	Y	Z
Savings per unit of scarce resource			
Ranking			

Conclusion:

Utilisation of B

	kg of B
Total B overall	8,000

2.2 Shadow Prices in Make v Buy

Shadow prices may also be relevant in a make v buy situation where:

- internal production is limited due to the shortage of a particular factor; and
- production of some items is being outsourced.

If additional units of a factor become available, then more production can be brought in-house, leading to greater savings.

> **Key Point**
>
> The shadow price in this case would be the **savings per unit of scarce resource**.

Illustration 2 Shadow Price in Make v Buy

In *Example 3*, the company has a shortage of Material B that is used in the manufacture of three components. Due to this shortage, 1,000 units of product Z and 2,000 units of product Y should be outsourced.

If additional units of Material B were to become available, they would initially be used to produce product Z, since the saving per kilogram of material B is higher for product Z than for product Y.

The shadow price of material B is the saving per kilogram on making product Z in-house, which is $2 per kilogram.

3 Multi-Limiting Factors

3.1 Linear Programming

In situations in which more than one factor is limited, an alternative approach is used to determine the optimal production so as to maximise contribution (and therefore profit). This technique is linear programming:

- A mathematical technique for problems of rationing scarce resources between products to achieve optimum benefit.
- Objective function—quantifies the objective. For example:
  - profit maximisation (which is always by maximising contribution);
  - cost minimisation.
- Based on the assumption that the objective and the constraints may be expressed as linear equations.
- The syllabus only includes situations involving *two* variables this allows the equations to be plotted as straight lines on a graph.
- The graph can be used to *identify* the optimal solution.*

*Commentary

*Do **not** merely read from the graph—the graph is relatively crude and, although it should be sufficiently reliable to **identify** the optimal solution, it should not be relied on to specify the solution.

- The optimal solution **must** be *solved* algebraically (e.g. using simultaneous equations).

3.2 Drawing the Graph

Step 1 *Define* unknowns. For example, x = Number of units of output of one of the products and y = Number of units of output of the other product.

Step 2 Formulate the *objective* function (use contribution **not** profit).

Step 3 Express *constraints* in terms of inequalities (including non-negativity). Constraints may include resource constraints, production constraints and/or levels of demand.

Step 4 Plot **all** constraints on a graph and identify the *feasible region.*

Having drawn the graph, the optimal solution can be solved using one of two methods:

1. The objective function method—also referred to as the iso-contribution method (see s.3.4).

2. The simultaneous equation method (see s.3.5).

3.3 Problem Formulation

Illustration 3 Linear Programming

A company makes two products, cabinets and chests. Each product passes through two departments, carpentry and polishing. The time spent in each department is as follows.

	Departmental time (hours)	
	Carpentry	Polishing
Cabinets	3	2
Chests	4	6

There are 4,800 hours available in each department.

Annual production of cabinets must not exceed 1,200 units. Apart from this, all items produced can be sold.

The contribution to profit and fixed overheads is $100 for a cabinet and $150 for a chest.

Required:

Calculate the optimal product mix which will maximise the total contribution to profit.

Solution

Step 1—Define unknowns

Let: x = Number of **cabinets** to be produced per annum

y = Number of **chests** to be produced per annum

C = Total contribution to profit

Step 2—Formulate the objective function

The function to be maximised is the total contribution to profit (i.e. C). Since **cabinets** and **chests** contribute $100 and $150 respectively, for each item produced:

C = $100x + 150y$

Step 3—Formulate constraints

■ 4,800 carpentry hours are available to provide 3 hours per cabinet and 4 hours per chest:

$3x + 4y \leq 4,800$

■ 4,800 polishing hours are available to provide 2 hours per cabinet and 6 hours per chest:

$2x + 6y \leq 4,800$

■ Production of cabinets must not exceed 1,200 units:

$x \leq 1,200$

■ Because production cannot be negative:

$x \geq 0, y \geq 0$

Summary

The model is therefore: Maximise $C = 100x + 150y$

Subject to: $3x + 4y \leq 4,800$

$2x + 6y \leq 4,800$

$x \leq 1,200$

$x, y \geq 0$

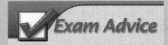

Exam Advice

Although obvious, the programme and the examiner require any "non-negativity" to be explicitly stated.

Illustration 3 Linear Programming (continued)

Solution

Step 4—Present graphically

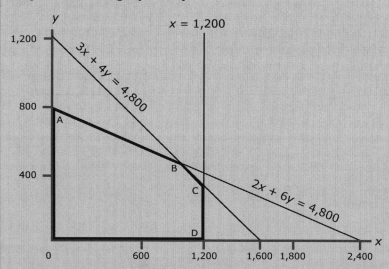

Plotting lines on a graph

1. Find the point where each line crosses the y axis, by setting the value of x to 0.

2. Fine the point where each line crosses the x axis by setting the value of y to 0.

3. Draw a straight line between each of the points.

For carpentry hours:

　If $x = 0$ then $4y = 4,800 \Rightarrow y = 1,200$

　If $y = 0$, then $3x = 4,800 \Rightarrow x = 1,600$

For polishing hours:

　If $x = 0$ then $6y = 4,800 \Rightarrow y = 800$

　If $y = 0$ then $2x = 4,800 \Rightarrow x = 2,400$

Feasible region

■ With the given constraints, all possible values for x and y lie in the boxed area of the graph 0ABCD, called the *relevant* or *feasible region*. The point on the boundary of this area must now be found where the contribution to profit (C) has a maximum value.

3.4 Objective Function Method

3.4.1 Iso-Contribution Lines

The objective function shows how contribution varies with output of the products. In *Illustration 1* the contribution function was:

$C = 100x + 150y$

Contribution lines can be draw showing all combinations of x and y that would produce a particular value of contribution. For example, some of the values on the line $C = 15,000$ would be as follows:*

x	y	C
150	0	15,000
90	40	15,000
60	60	15,000
0	100	15,000

All the combinations of x and y that produce contribution of $15,000 can be plotted on the graph as follows:

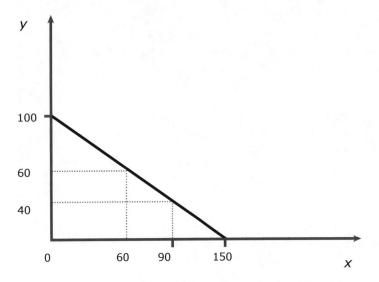

*You must understand where the values in the table came from. For example, if $y = 60$, contribution from y is $9,000 (60 × 150). Contribution from x must therefore be $6,000 to achieve total contribution of $15,000. Since each unit of x generates contribution of $100, 60 units of x must be sold.

Key Point

Only the two points on the axes need to be plotted to draw any straight line.

Another contribution line could be shown for another value of contribution, for example C = 18,000.

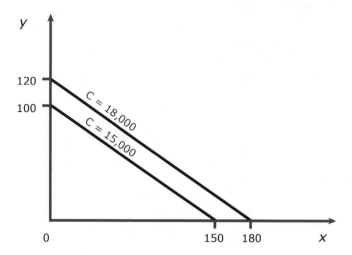

Such lines are called **iso-contribution lines** (i.e. every point on each line gives the same value of contribution).

Two important principles can be deduced from above:

- Contribution lines with a higher value of contribution are further away from the origin (the point $x = 0$, $y = 0$) than contribution lines with a lower value.

- All iso-contribution lines are parallel to each other. Just as the iso-contribution line C = 18,000 is parallel to the iso-contribution line C = 15,000, all other possible contribution lines would be parallel to this.*

*The gradient, or slope, of each line is fixed by the relative amounts of contribution for the two products.

3.4.2 Contribution and the Feasible Region

Illustration 1 showed how the feasible region represents all possible combinations of x and y that can be produced and sold, given the constraints.

The diagram below shows a feasible region represented by the area 0ABCD with three iso-contribution lines:

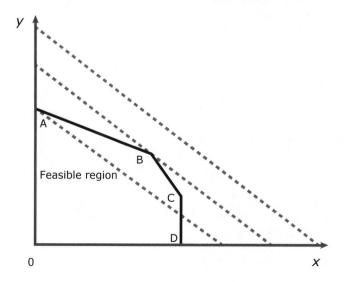

The line representing the lowest value of contribution is the line closest to the origin. The line furthest from the origin is outside of the feasible region. This means that this level of contribution could not be achieved.

The middle contribution line lies mostly outside of the feasible region, but there is one point, B, that is on the boundary of the feasible region. Point B represents the combination of production that is feasible at which contribution is maximised.

3.4.3 Slope of the Contribution Line

In the previous diagram, the point of maximum contribution was represented by point B. However, had the contribution line been "flatter", point A could be the point of maximum contribution.

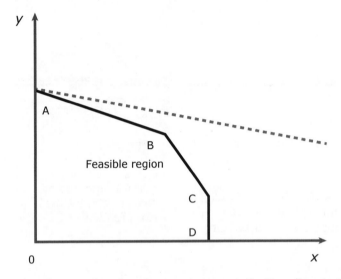

The reason for drawing an iso-contribution line is therefore to identify which of the points A, B, C or D represents maximum contribution.

3.4.4 Approach in Exam Questions

In exam questions, you should always use the iso-contribution method unless the examiner asks specifically for the equation method (see next section). These are the steps to identify the point of maximum contribution:

1. Having drawn a graph showing all the constraints and the feasible region (as in *Illustration 3*), "randomly" choose a value of contribution and draw a sample contribution line on the graph.

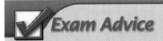

Random choice needs to be sensible for ease of plotting. Choose a point on the x axis that lies below all the constraint lines, preferably a round number. Calculate C at this point. Then calculate which point on the y axis gives the same value of contribution. Draw a straight line through these two points for a sample contribution line.

2. Place your ruler against the contribution line. Move it away from the origin ensuring that it remains parallel to the sample contribution line. Stop at the furthest point from the origin that is on the boundary of the feasible region. This will be the point of maximum contribution.*

*Commentary

*You should appreciate that if the sample contribution line happens to be parallel to a constraint line the optimal solution may not be a single point (of intersection) but an infinite number of combinations of *x* and *y*. In this case, the maximum contribution can still be calculated at one point, as in *Illustration 3*.

3. Identify the constraints that intersect at this optimal point. Find the value of *x* and *y* at this point by solving, simultaneously, the equations that correspond to these constraints.

4. If the question asks for maximum contribution (or profit), calculate maximum contribution by putting the values of *x* and *y* (as determined in *Illustration 3*) into the contribution function.*

5. Answer the question. State in words how many units of product *x* and how many units of product *y* must be sold to maximise contribution (and therefore profit).

*Commentary

*If asked for profit, remember to deduct **total** fixed overheads from total contribution (i.e. do not fall into the trap of using unit profits).

Continuing with *Illustration 3*

Illustration 3 Linear Programming (continued)

Solution

Step 5—Plot the objective function

To plot $C = 100x + 150y$ a value is assumed for C which will allow the line to be easily plotted on the axes.

For example, below, the line $100x + 150y = 150,000$ has been plotted.

The value chosen is irrelevant. It is the gradient of the line which is important, because other values for C would plot as lines parallel to that drawn. Rule of thumb: choose a value which is a multiple of the coefficients of x and y.

The highest possible value of C lies on that particular line furthest from the origin on the edge of the feasible region.

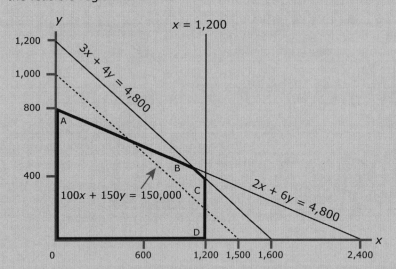

*Commentary

*Note that if the gradient of the objective function were less steep than the line B-C, the optimal solution would be at A. If the gradient were steeper, the optimal solution would be at C. Therefore, it must not be assumed that the optimal solution will lie at the intersection of two resource constraints.

Place the edge of a ruler parallel to the objective line, and push it outwards until it leaves the feasible region. In this case, it can be seen that B is the optimal solution.*

Step 6—Solve

B is at the intersection of the two lines:

$$3x + 4y = 4,800 \ ❶$$

and $\quad 2x + 6y = 4,800 \ ❷$

Solving simultaneously:

1½ x ❷	$3x + 9y = 7,200$	(new equation ❸)
	$3x + 4y = 4,800$	(original equation ❶)
❸-❶	$5y = 2,400$	
Therefore	$y = 480$	

Substitute for y in (1):

$$3x + 1,920 = 4,800$$
$$3x = 2,880$$

Therefore $\quad\quad\quad x = 960$

Step 7—Optimal solution

The optimal solution is to produce 960 cabinets and 480 chests.

This will give a contribution of $C = 100x + 150y = (\$100 \times 960) + (\$150 \times 480) = \$168,000$

3.5 Simultaneous Equations Method

After plotting the feasible region, it is possible to identify the point of maximum contribution without using the objective function method. In the diagram below, the point of maximum contribution must be represented by one of the corner points A, B, C or D. However, which point is the optimal solution cannot be determined from the diagram.*

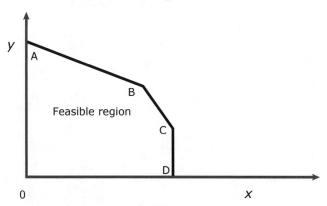

*It is therefore necessary to calculate contribution at each point.

The procedure is as follows:

1. Determine the value of x and y at each point of intersection. Use simultaneous equations for points where two constraints intersect.*

2. Calculate the contribution at each point of intersection by substituting the values of x and y into the contribution function.

3. Compare the values of C at each point. Select the point that corresponds to the highest value of C.

*Do not forget the points on the x and y axes (where $y = 0$ and $x = 0$ respectively) that represent non-negativity constraints.

As the simultaneous equations method is more time consuming than the objective function method, you should not use it unless the examiner specifically requires it.

Continuing with *Illustration 3*

Illustration 3 Linear Programming (continued)

The graph showing the feasible region was drawn in Step 4 as follows:

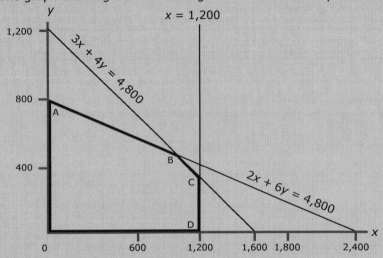

The point of maximum contribution will be either point A, B, C or D.

D can be eliminated as a possible candidate for the optimal solution because the value of x is the same at both C and D, while the value of y is zero at point D and greater than zero at point C. So contribution at point C must be higher than contribution at point D.

Point A lies on the intersection of:

$x = 0$ ❶
$2x + 6y = 4,800$ ❷
Substitute ❶ into ❷: $6y = 4,800$
⮑ $y = 800$.

Total contribution = $100x + 150y$ ⮑ $100 \times 0 + 800 \times 150 = \$120,000$.

Point B lies on the intersection of:

$3x + 4y = 4,800$ ❶
$2x + 6y = 4,800$ ❷
Multiply ❷ by 1.5:
$3x + 9y = 7,200$ ❸
$5y = 2,400$ ❸ − ❶
⮑ $y = 480$

Substitute y into ❶:
$3x + 1,920 = 4,800$ ⮑ $3x = 2,880$ ⮑ $x = 960$
⮑ at B, $x = 960$ and $y = 480$
Contribution = $100 \times 960 + 150 \times 480 = \$168,000$

Point C lies at the intersection of:

$x = 1,200$ ❶
$3x + 4y = 4,800$ ❷
Substitute ❶ into ❷ gives:
$3,600 + 4y = 4,800$ ⮑ $4y = 1,200$, $y = 300$
⮑ at C, $x = 1,200$ and $y = 300$
Contribution = $100 \times 1,200 + 150 \times 300 = \$165,000$.

Comparing the calculations of contribution, it is highest at point B where $x = 960$ and $y = 480$.

Conclusion: To maximise profits, the company should produce 960 cabinets and 480 chests each year.

Example 4 Objective Function Method

A manufacturer produces two types of garden furniture—tables and benches. Both use the same material and are produced by the same workforce, which consists of skilled and unskilled workers. The managing director is trying to decide on the optimal production plan to maximise contribution each week.

The following standard cost cards apply:

	Table	Bench
	$	$
Material ($5/kg)	15	10
Skilled labour ($10/hour)	50	20
Unskilled labour ($4/hour)	16	4
Variable overhead ($2/hour)	18	6
Total variable cost	99	40
Selling price	134	50
Contribution per unit	35	10

There is a shortage of the required material and only 120 kilos are available each week. There are four skilled workmen, each working a 35-hour week. Unskilled labour is employed on a part-time basis and there are 100 hours available per week.

Required:

Determine graphically how many units of each type of furniture should be produced each week to maximise contribution. Calculate the maximum weekly contribution.

3.6   Assumptions

The following assumptions give rise to limitations using the graphical method:

■ **Linearity**—contribution per unit and resource utilisation per unit are the same for any quantity produced and are sold in the range under consideration.

■ Infinite **divisibility**—of products and resources. Solution may **not** have integer values (e.g. 12 $1/4$ units of x and 9 $3/4$ units of y) and should **not** be rounded. For example, for an optimisation problem:

• rounding up will be to a point **outside** the feasible region;

• if rounding down, it will depend on the gradient of the objective function which integer value lies furthest from the origin.

■ Solution is dependent on the quality of the input data. It must be complete, accurate and valid.

■ Only one *quantifiable* objective can be satisfied. Non-quantifiable objectives are not considered at all.

■ Single value estimates (e.g. expected values) can be used for uncertain variables.

■ Only two "products" for graphical solution (but see s.4.3).

4 Further Considerations

4.1 Shadow Price

Shadow prices (see s.1.2) can also be calculated in linear programming situations. To calculate the shadow price of a particular factor:

1. Restate the constraint for that factor with the number of units available increased by 1.

2. Recalculate the solution to the linear programme. For such a small change it is reasonable to assume that the same point on the graph would be the point of maximum contribution. However, since the equation for the line has changed (increase of 1), it is necessary to recalculate the value of x and y at that point using simultaneous equations.

3. Calculate the revised value of contribution.

4. Deduct the original value of contribution from the revised value. The increase in contribution is the shadow price of the limiting factor.

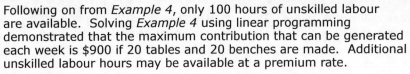

Illustration 4 Shadow Price

Following on from *Example 4*, only 100 hours of unskilled labour are available. Solving *Example 4* using linear programming demonstrated that the maximum contribution that can be generated each week is $900 if 20 tables and 20 benches are made. Additional unskilled labour hours may be available at a premium rate.

Required:
Calculate the shadow price of unskilled labour.

Illustration 4 Shadow Price (continued)

Solution

The constraint for unskilled labour now becomes: $4x + y \leq 101$.

The other constraints remain the same. In summary, therefore, it is necessary to solve the linear program:

Objective function to maximise contribution (C) given by: $C = 35x + 10y$

Subject to constraints:

Materials: $3x + 2y \leq 120$

Skilled labour: $5x + 2y \leq 140$

Unskilled labour: $4x + y \leq 101$

Non-negativity: $x \geq 0, y \geq 0$

Plotting the equations graphically:

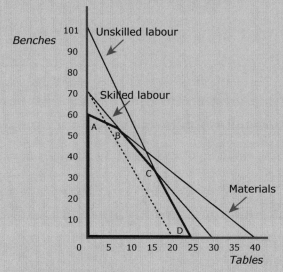

The feasible region is 0ABCD.

A sample contribution line, C = 700, is represented by the broken line.

Because the unskilled labour equation has changed, the line showing the skilled labour constraint becomes very slightly steeper. The optimal point C is the intersection of the skilled and unskilled constraints:

Solving simultaneously

$$5x + 2y = 140 \qquad (1)$$
$$4x + y = 101 \qquad (2)$$

$$2 \times (2) \qquad 8x + 2y = 202 \qquad (3)$$
$$(3) - (1) \qquad 3x = 62$$
$$x = 20.67$$

By substitution in (2)
$$82.68 + y = 101$$
$$y = 18.32$$

Contribution becomes (20.67 x $35) + (18.32 x $10) = $906.65.

This compares to contribution of $900 when only 100 hours of unskilled labour were available (*see Example 4* solution).

This means that the availability of one additional hour of unskilled labour increases contribution by $6.65. This is the shadow price of unskilled labour.

Of course, in practice, it is not possible to manufacture 20.67 tables or 18.32 benches. However, the method itself is valid, as it shows the extra contribution available per extra hour.

4.2   Slack

4.2.1   Non-binding and Binding Constraints

In linear programming problems involving several constraints, it is possible that not all constraints are binding at the optimal point (i.e. at the level of production which maximises contribution, not all of the available supply of one or more of the inputs is used).

Referring once again to *Example 4*, the graph showing the constraints was drawn as:

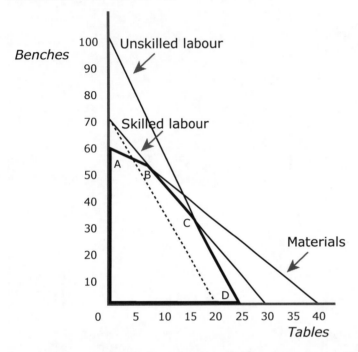

At the optimal point, C, all available skilled and unskilled labour are being utilised (because this point lies on the lines representing these resources). Thus both skilled and unskilled labour are binding constraints.

Materials, however, is not a binding constraint. Point C lies below the materials line, which means that not all available materials will be used in achieving maximum contribution.

The term *slack* means the difference between maximum resources available and resources used at the optimal point. For binding constraints, the value of slack is **zero.**

Slack can be calculated for each resource as maximum available, less the amount used at the optimal point. It can be calculated by rearranging the equations for each constraint and then substituting in the values of *x* and *y* at the maximum point.

Demand can also be a slack variable if there is unfulfilled demand for a particular product at the point of optimal contribution.

Illustration 5 Slack

Calculate the slack for materials, unskilled labour and skilled labour in *Example 4*.

Solution

Let x = number of tables made per week. At optimal point, $x = 20$.

Let y = number of benches made per week. At optimal point, $y = 20$.

For each of the inputs, the slack is calculated as the maximum available less the use of the resource in making 20 tables and 20 benches:

Materials = 120 kilos − $(3x + 2y)$ = 120 − (60 + 40) = 20 kilos

Skilled labour = 140 hours − $(5x + 2y)$ = 0

Unskilled labour = 100 hours − $(4x + 1y)$ = 0

The slack for the skilled labour and unskilled labour is zero. This is as expected as they are binding constraints. The slack for materials is 20 kilos meaning that each week the company would use 20 kilos less than the maximum available supply.

Slack may also relate to demand. If there is a limit to demand for a particular product (say Product X) this would be included as a constraint in the formulation of the linear programme. Having solved the linear programme and determined the optimal production of products, it may be that production of Product X is below the maximum demand. In this case there will also be slack.

This slack can be expressed in units as:

Maximum demand for product X − Output of Product X

4.2.2   Implications of Slack

It is useful to know the amount of slack for the following reasons:

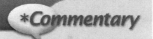

Commentary

■ If the amount of slack for a particular resource is low, there is a danger that the resource could become a binding constraint if the availability of other scarce resources increases. Management may therefore start to plan for additional supplies of the resource before they are needed.*

■ If slack is high, it means that the availability of the resource exceeds the amount used by a significant amount. It may be possible to use this resource elsewhere in the business or sub-contract it to another business.

4.3   More Than Two Variables

■ A linear program can be *formulated* for any number of variables and any number of constraints.

■ However, the methods used in this session based on drawing graphs are limited to *solving* problems where there are only two variables—represented by the *x and y* axes—although there can be any number of constraints.

■ There are several methods of solving for more than two variables including:

  ● the dual problem; and

  ● simplex.*

*In *Illustration 5,* both skilled and unskilled labour are binding constraints. If additional labour hours became available, output would increase. However, because the slack for materials is fairly low, output would not be able to increase much before production would also be constrained by the availability of materials.

Commentary

*These methods are not examinable at F5, only awareness that problems with more than two variables can be solved.

Summary

- Where factors of production are scarce, production decisions have to be made to maximise **contribution** (and hence profit) given limited resources.

- Where **one** resource is scarce, the approach is to **rank** products by **contribution** generated per unit of scarce resource.

- For make or buy decisions, the method is to **rank** products by **saving** per unit of scarce resource.

- Where there is more than one constraint, use linear programming:

  1. Define variables.

  2. Define the objective function (usually to maximise contribution).

  3. Formulate constraints.

  4. Plot constraints on a graph and determine the feasible area.

  5. Draw a sample contribution line and use this to find the point on the feasible region which generates the highest contribution.

  6. Solve the equation(s) for the optimal point in (5.) to specify the corresponding values of the variables.

  7. Answer the question. Maximum profit **MUST** be calculated as maximum contribution less total fixed overheads **never** using unit profit.

- The **shadow price of** a resource is the amount by which contribution would be increased if one more unit of the scarce resource were available.

- **Slack** arises where the company does not use all of the resource available. Slack can be calculated as resource available less resource used.

Session 5 Quiz
Estimated time: 15 minutes

1. State the assumptions behind the approach taken to maximising contribution when there is one limiting factor. (1.2)
2. State the meaning of the shadow price of a resource. (1.3)
3. State the meaning of "objective function" in a linear program. (3.1)
4. Give the non-negativity constraint for X in a linear program, where X is the output of product A. (3.3)
5. Give the assumptions behind linear programming. (3.6)
6. State the meaning of slack in a linear program. (4.2.1)

Study Question Bank
Estimated time: 40 minutes

Priority		Estimated Time	Completed
Q8	BVX	20 minutes	
Q9	Optimal Production Plan	20 minutes	

EXAMPLE SOLUTIONS

Solution 1—Limiting Factor Analysis

Product	A	B	C
Contribution per unit	$16	$10	$24
No. of kilos per unit	4	2	8
Contribution per kilo	$4	$5	$3
Rank	2	1	3

Therefore produce $\dfrac{12,000}{2}$ = 6,000 units of B

Maximum contribution = 6,000 × 10 = $60,000

Solution 2—Sales Restrictions

	kg
4,000 units of B uses up (4,000 × 2)	8,000
1,000 units of A uses up (1,000 × 4)	4,000
	12,000

	$
Therefore maximum contribution	
From B (4,000 × $10)	40,000
From A (1,000 × $16)	16,000
	56,000

Solution 3—Make or Buy

	X	Y	Z
Savings per unit of scarce resource	$\dfrac{13-10}{3}=1$	$\dfrac{17-12}{2}=2.5$	$\dfrac{16-14}{1}=2$
Ranking	3	1	2

Comment: Therefore, the firm should initially make Ys and then make as many Zs as possible.

Utilisation of B

	kg of B
2,500 Ys x 2 kg each uses	5,000
3,000 Zs x 1 kg each uses	3,000
Total B overall	8,000

Comment: The additional 1,000 Zs and 2,000 Xs required should be bought in.

Solution 4—Objective Function Method

Let x be the number of tables made per week.
Let y be the number of benches made per week.
Objective function to maximise contribution (C), given by $35x + 10y$

Subject to constraints:

Materials	$3x + 2y \le 120$
Skilled labour	$5x + 2y \le 140$
Unskilled labour	$4x + y \le 100$
Non-negative	$x, y \ge 0$

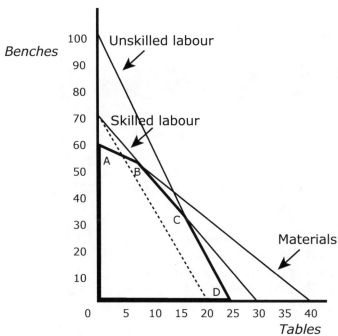

Feasible region is 0ABCD.

A sample contribution line, C = 700, is represented by the broken line.

The optimum point is at C, the intersection of the skilled and unskilled constraints.

Solving simultaneously:

$$5x + 2y = 140 \qquad (1)$$
$$4x + y = 100 \qquad (2)$$

$2 \times (2)$
$$8x + 2y = 200 \qquad (3)$$

$(3) - (1)$
$$3x = 60$$
$$x = 20$$

By substitution in (2)
$$80 + y = 100$$
$$y = 20$$

So to maximise contribution, the company should make and sell 20 of each type of unit.

The contribution will be $(20 \times \$35) + (20 \times \$10) = \$900$

Session 6

Pricing

FOCUS
This session covers the following content from the *ACCA Study Guide.*

B. Decision-Making Techniques

4. Pricing decisions

a) Explain the factors that influence the pricing of a product or service.

b) Explain the price elasticity of demand.

c) Derive and manipulate a straight line demand equation. Derive an equation for the total cost function (including volume-based discounts).

d) Calculate the optimum selling price and quantity for an organisation, equating marginal cost and marginal revenue.

e) Evaluate a decision to increase production and sales levels, considering incremental costs, incremental revenues and other factors.

f) Determine prices and output levels for profit maximisation using the demand based approach to pricing (both tabular and algebraic methods).

g) Explain different price strategies, including:
    i)   All forms of cost-plus
    ii)   Skimming
    iii) Penetration
    iv) Complementary product
    v)   Product-line
    vi) Volume discounting
    vii) Discrimination
    viii) Relevant cost

h) Calculate a price from a given strategy using cost-plus and relevant cost.

Session 6 Guidance

- **Understand** all the different methods of pricing.
- **Know** and **discuss** the advantages and disadvantages of each method of pricing.

(continued on next page)

VISUAL OVERVIEW

Objective: To identify, discuss and implement a range of product-pricing methods applicable in particular market situations.

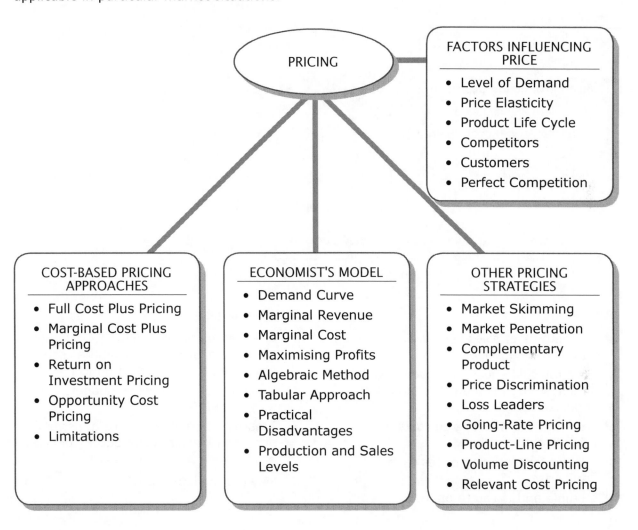

PRICING

FACTORS INFLUENCING PRICE
- Level of Demand
- Price Elasticity
- Product Life Cycle
- Competitors
- Customers
- Perfect Competition

COST-BASED PRICING APPROACHES
- Full Cost Plus Pricing
- Marginal Cost Plus Pricing
- Return on Investment Pricing
- Opportunity Cost Pricing
- Limitations

ECONOMIST'S MODEL
- Demand Curve
- Marginal Revenue
- Marginal Cost
- Maximising Profits
- Algebraic Method
- Tabular Approach
- Practical Disadvantages
- Production and Sales Levels

OTHER PRICING STRATEGIES
- Market Skimming
- Market Penetration
- Complementary Product
- Price Discrimination
- Loss Leaders
- Going-Rate Pricing
- Product-Line Pricing
- Volume Discounting
- Relevant Cost Pricing

Session 6 Guidance

■ **Know** how to calculate the profit maximising output and price using the marginal revenue = marginal cost (Economist's) model.

■ **Be aware** of practical pricing methods and when they would be appropriate.

1 Cost-Based Pricing Approaches

1.1 Full Cost Plus Pricing

The price of a product using full cost plus pricing is found as follows:

	$/unit
Direct production costs	x
Absorption of overheads	
Variable production overhead	x
Fixed production overhead	x
Variable non-production overhead	x
Fixed non-production overhead	x
Full cost	x
Mark-up percentage	x
Selling price	x

$$\text{Selling price per unit} = \frac{\text{Total budgeted production cost} + \text{Total budgeted non-production cost}}{\text{Budgeted sales units}} + \text{Mark-up}$$

Advantages

✔ If the budget sales level is achieved, profit will be made.

✔ The full cost should be readily available if a system of standard costing is in operation.

✔ Appropriate where fixed costs are significant.

✔ Useful for justifying prices (and price rises).

✔ Simple and cheap to operate.

Disadvantages

✗ The method of accounting for overheads will have a large impact on the costs calculated for different products.

✗ If actual sales are below budget, losses may occur.

✗ Ignores external factors (e.g. demand/price relationship, competitors' prices).

✗ Size of mark-up is arbitrary.

✗ May not maximise profits.

Full cost plus pricing is a *long-term* pricing method. It ensures that prices cover all variable and fixed costs.

The problems regarding overheads can be reduced by using *activity-based costing* (see *Session 1*). A margin is added to this cost.

1.2   Marginal Cost Plus Pricing

$$\text{Selling price per unit} = \frac{\text{Budgeted variable production cost} + \text{Budgeted variable non-production cost}}{\text{Budgeted sales units}} + \text{Mark-up}$$

Advantages

✔ Mark-up represents contribution, which is useful in short-run pricing decisions (e.g. market penetration policy).

✔ Appropriate where fixed costs are relatively small.

Disadvantages

✘ May lead to failure to recover fixed costs.

✘ Not appropriate for *long-term* pricing, particularly where fixed costs are significant.

1.3   Return on Investment (ROI) Pricing

Prices are set to achieve a target percentage return on the capital invested in production.

$$\text{Selling price per unit} = \frac{\text{Budgeted full cost} + (\text{target ROI percentage} \times \text{capital employed})}{\text{Budgeted sales units}}$$

ROI pricing is a *long-term* pricing method.

Advantages

✔ Links price to both short-term costs and long-term capital employed.

✔ Consistent with ROI as a performance measure.

✔ Target ROI can be set to take account of risk.

Disadvantages

✘ Ignores external factors.

✘ Problems in calculating capital employed (e.g. whether to use book values or replacement cost).

✘ Subjective split of shared investment between products.

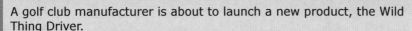

Example 1 Cost Plus and Target ROI

A golf club manufacturer is about to launch a new product, the Wild Thing Driver.

Buildings and equipment needed for production will cost $2,000,000, and working capital requirements are estimated at $10 per unit per annum.

Expected sales levels are 40,000 units per annum.

Variable production costs are $30 per unit.

Fixed production costs will be $300,000 per annum and fixed non-production costs will be $100,000 per annum.

Required:

(a) Calculate selling price using:

    (i)   Full cost plus 20%.

    (ii) Marginal cost plus 40%.

    (iii) Target ROI of 10%.

(b) If *actual* sales are only 20,000 units and selling price was set using full cost plus 20%, calculate profit for the year.

Example 1 Cost Plus and Target ROI
(continued)

Solution

(a) Setting prices

(i) **Full cost plus 20%**	**$/unit**
Variable costs	
Fixed costs	
Full cost	
20% mark-up	
Selling price	

(ii) **Marginal cost plus 40%**	**$/unit**
Variable costs	
40% mark-up	
Selling price	

(iii) **Target ROI**	**$**
Buildings and equipment	
Working capital	
Capital employed	
Profit required	

	$/unit
Variable cost	
Fixed cost	
Profit	
Selling price	

(b) Profit for the year	**$000**
Sales	
Variable costs	
Fixed costs	
Net profit/(loss)	

1.4   Opportunity Cost Pricing

Opportunity cost pricing, also called "relevant cost pricing", is a short-run method used to price:

- one-off projects;
- special orders; and
- tenders for contracts.

Production will use existing resources and hence a *relevant costing* approach is used:

Price = Relevant costs + mark-up

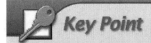 **Key Point**

A relevant cost basis provides a **minimum** price that can be used as the basis for a quotation. (The concept of relevant costs for decision-making have already been covered in *Session 3*.)

Example 2 Opportunity Cost Price

After spending $500 on market research, Bobco Engineering wants to bid on an important one-off contract and needs to ensure its costing is both competitive and commercially rational. To complete the project it will need to devote the following resources to its construction:

- **1,500 kg of standard steel regularly used in its production process.** It currently has inventory of 6,000 kg purchased at an average price of $8/kg. With recent market conditions, the purchase cost is now $9.35/kg.
- **500 kg of speciality steel.** It has 500 kg of such steel in inventory. This was purchased 16 months ago at $12/kg. As it has not been used since purchasing, the auditors insisted on a write-down to estimated net realizable value of $4/kg. The purchasing manager figures that he can sell it for scrap at $2/kg. If sold, the costs to remove it from the warehouse and deliver it would be $1,000.
- **380 hours of unskilled labour.** Although the existing union contract pays $6/hour for such labour, extra workers would have to be hired in the "temporary" labour market at $7/hour.
- **196 hours of semi-skilled labour being paid $9/hour under the existing union contract.** Currently, there is a surplus of such labour in the plant.
- **51 hours of skilled labour being paid $18/hour under the current union contract.** The workers are currently busy in another department, where they are producing output which is sold for $96 and which uses $15 of direct material, $9 of skilled labour, $27 of semi-skilled labour, $15 of variable overheads and $8 fixed-cost overheads allocated. It takes a half hour of skilled labour to work on this existing product. The department head has agreed to release his skilled workers but he must be compensated so he is no worse off.
- **Use of equipment which was scheduled to be disposed of this period for $12,000.** If used in the project, it will have to be disposed of later at an estimated selling price of $4,000.
- **Exclusive use of a piece of manufacturing equipment (a fibrillator) which will not survive its use in the project.** The machine originally cost $51,000 and currently has a carrying (i.e. book) value of $6,000. It could be currently sold in the used fibrillator market for $8,000 (because new ones cost $45,000). If it was left in its existing use, it could generate cash flows with an estimated present value of $5,000.
- **38 kg of Ecotox which was originally purchased for $600/kg.** Under current government environmental rules, Bobco will have to pay $3,000 for the recycling company to take it away if it is not used in the contract.

Required:

Calculate the price which Bobco should bid for the contract on the assumption that it wishes to charge a price equal to relevant cost plus 25%.

1.5 Limitations of Cost-Based Approaches

The four cost-based approaches discussed share the following limitations:

✗ They ignore external factors (e.g. demand).

✗ They may not lead to profit, revenue or market share maximisation (common objectives).

✗ They may result in prices completely different from those charged by competitors.

Therefore, the following practical considerations should be taken into account before the final price is decided.

2 Economist's Model

2.1 Demand Curve

2.1.1 The Concept

■ Demand means the *total quantity* of a product or service the buyers in a market would wish to buy in a given period.

■ Demand depends on the price charged by suppliers. For most goods, as the price falls, demand for the goods rises.

This can be shown graphically as follows:

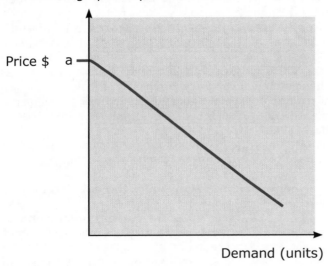

2.1.2 Equation

The demand curve can be expressed as an equation of the form:

$$P = a - bQ$$

where:

P is the price which would achieve a given demand, Q;

a = price when Q = 0;

b is the slope of the line—it shows by how much the price must change to achieve a given increase in demand:

$$b = \frac{\text{change in price}}{\text{change in quantity}}$$

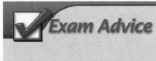

Exam Advice

The formula for the demand curve is given in the exam formula sheet.

Illustration 1 Demand

Alex owns the only bakery in a small town in England, and is the only supplier of doughnuts in the area. Based on an analysis of his sales over the past 12 months, he has calculated that the daily demand for doughnuts follows the following demand curve:

P = 500 − 0.1 Q

Where P is the price in cents and Q is daily demand in units.

If Alex wishes to sell 1,000 doughnuts per day, he should charge a price of 400 cents (500 − 0.1 × 1,000).

The value of b is −0.1. This means that to increase the quantity sold by one unit, Alex should reduce the price by 0.1 cents.

2.2 Marginal Revenue

2.2.1 The Concept

Marginal revenue is the increase in total revenues resulting from selling one more unit of a product or service.* There are two effects on total revenue of selling one more unit:

1. An additional unit has been sold; this increases revenue.

2. To sell an extra unit, the price will have had to be reduced *for all units* sold; this reduces total revenue.

The marginal revenue function can be derived from the demand function as follows:

Price: $P = a - bQ$

Revenue = Price × quantity ➲ Revenue = $aQ - bQ^2$

It can be shown using the mathematical technique of calculus that:

Marginal revenue = $a - 2bQ$

Exam Advice

The formula for marginal revenue is given in the exam formula sheet.

2.2.2 Graphically

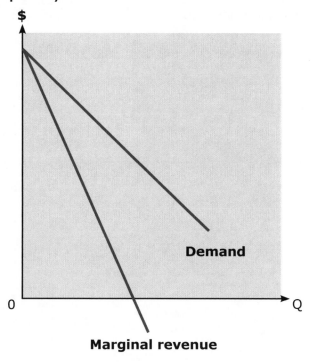

Demand

Marginal revenue

Example 3 Marginal Revenue

A firm has estimated that it faces the following price/quantity relationship:

Selling Price $	Quantity Demanded Units
40	10
25	20
10	30

Required:

(a) Plot the demand function on a graph and find its equation.

(b) Find the total revenue function.

(c) Find the marginal revenue function.

2.3 Marginal Cost

Marginal cost is the increase in total cost from producing and selling one additional unit of a product or service.

Economists assume that marginal cost changes as output increases. Initially, marginal cost falls as output rises, due to economies of scale. However, once the firm reaches its lowest marginal cost, marginal cost begins to rise as output increases further.

Accountants (and examiners) take a simpler approach and assume that marginal cost is equal to variable cost per unit (at least until full capacity is reached).

Marginal cost is normally constant since it is generally assumed that the variable cost of each unit does not change, regardless of how many units are produced. However, where there are **volume-based discounts** on raw materials or components (i.e. discounts are available when agreed quantities are purchased), marginal cost will fall to a lower amount for all subsequent units produced.

Key Point

Marginal cost is incremental and therefore *relevant* in evaluating a decision to increase production and sales.

Illustration 2 Volume-Based Discount

The variable cost of product Y is as follows:

	$
Materials—1 kg at 100 per kg	100
Labour—2 hours at $20 per hour	40
Variable overhead—2 hours at 15 per hour	30
Marginal cost	170

If more than 1,000 kilograms are purchased in a month, the supplier will give a 5% discount on all materials.

The marginal cost would then be as follows:

More than 1,000 units

When the discount is achieved the marginal cost becomes:

	$
Materials—1 kg at 95 per kg	95
Labour	40
Variable overhead	30
Marginal cost	165

Between 950 units and 1,000 units

The material cost of producing 1,000 units is $95,000 as the discounted price applies. This is the same as the material cost of producing 950 units without the discount. Therefore, to produce 951 units or more, 1,000 kilos should be purchased to take advantage of the discount. So the marginal cost for between 950 units and 1,000 units is as follows:

Output		Total variable cost	Marginal cost
		$	$
950 units (950 × 170)		161,500	170
951 units—Materials (1,000 × 95)	95,000		
Labour and overhead (951 ×70)	66,570		
		161,570	70
952 units—Materials	95,000		
Labour and overhead (952 ×70)	66,640		
		161,640	70

No additional materials would be acquired until production exceeds 1,000 units, so the marginal cost is $70 up to 1,000 units.

Fewer than 950 units

For fewer than 950 units, the marginal cost is the variable cost without discounts—that is $170 per unit.

Summary of marginal costs

	$
Up to 950 units	170
951 units to 1,000 units	70
Above 1,000 units	165

2.4 Maximising Profits

The objective of most businesses is to maximise profits. The economist's model is used to find the price that will meet this objective. This is determined as follows:

■ Identify the quantity of sales (Q) that would lead to maximum profits. This is the quantity at which:

> Marginal cost = Marginal revenue

■ Calculate the price that must be set in order to achieve this level of sales by putting the value of Q into the demand function:

> $P = a - bQ$

Graphically*

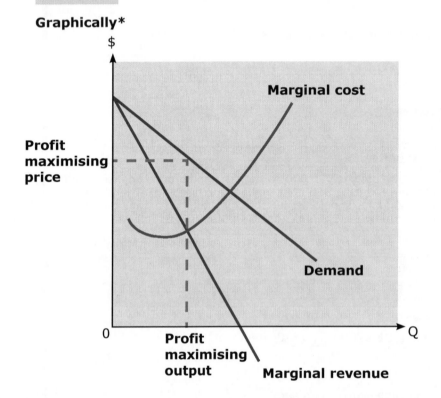

*Marginal revenue always has twice the gradient of the demand function.

If the firm's output is below the output at which marginal cost equals marginal revenue, then marginal cost is greater than marginal revenue. This means that if output is increased by one unit, the extra revenue is greater than the extra cost.

After the point at which marginal cost equals marginal revenue, marginal cost becomes more than marginal revenue. This means that if output is increased further, the additional cost exceeds the additional revenue, so it is not worthwhile producing more.

Therefore, the profit maximising point is Marginal Cost = Marginal Revenue.

Example 4 Profit Maximisation

The firm in *Example 3* now estimates its total costs at various activity levels:

Total Cost $	Quantity Units
350	10
400	20
450	30

Required:

(a) Find the total cost and marginal cost functions and plot these on the same graphs as the total revenue and marginal revenue functions, respectively.

(b) Find profit maximising output and selling price.

2.5   Summary of Algebraic Method

The method used above to calculate the profit maximising output is referred to as the algebraic method. A summary of the steps that would be taken to identify the profit maximising output and price is as follows:

1. Establish the demand function, which has the form $P = a - bQ$.

2. Establish the equation for marginal revenue, which has the form $MR = a - 2bQ$.

3. Identify the marginal cost function. Normally marginal cost = variable cost, so the marginal cost function will be in the form $MC = x$ (where x is a number).

4. Solve the equation $MC = MR$. This gives the value of Q at the point of maximum profit.

5. Put the value of Q into the demand function (from Step 1) to determine the price that should be charged so that demand equals Q.

2.6   Tabular Approach

An alternative approach to identifying the profit maximising point of output is to use the tabular approach. This approach may be used where information has been given about the level of demand for a small number of different prices and:

- due to the small number of items there is insufficient data to calculate a price equation accurately; or
- the relationship between the price and demand does not appear to be linear.

In these cases, marginal revenue and marginal cost can be calculated for each set of data. There may not be any point where marginal cost = marginal revenue exactly. In this case, produce up to the last point where marginal revenue exceeds marginal cost.

Illustration 3 Tabular Approach

The information in *Example 3* can be used to calculate total revenue in a table. The total cost information in *Example 4* can then be added, and a final column, total profit, can be calculated:

Quantity demanded (units)	Selling price $	Total revenue $	Total costs $	Profit $
10	40	400	350	50
20	25	500	400	100
30	10	300	450	(150)

The table shows that profit is maximised when output of 20 is chosen, which implies a price of $25.

This is not as accurate as the algebraic method, as the only possible solutions considered are those included in the table. The algebraic method suggested a profit maximising output of 16.67 with a price of $30.

Example 5 Tabular Method

A baker has just introduced a new type of cake. He has been experimenting with the price to determine daily demand. On each of the last 10 business days, for which he charged a different price, he recorded actual demand and production costs as follows:

Price (cents)	Quantity demanded	Total cost (costs)
460	1	385
420	2	570
380	3	749
360	4	932
325	5	1,100
302	6	1,280
269	7	1,467
244	8	1,656
212	9	1,847
180	10	2,030

Required:

(a) Using a tabular approach, calculate the marginal revenue and marginal cost at each price and output level. Based on this, determine the price to maximise profit and associated quantity to be produced.

(b) Calculate total profit at each price and confirm that the price and quantity calculated in (a) maximise profit.

Example 5 Tabular Method (continued)

Solution

(a) Marginal cost and marginal revenue

Price	Quantity	Total revenue	Marginal revenue	Total cost	Marginal cost
460	1			385	
420	2			570	
380	3			749	
360	4			932	
325	5			1,100	
302	6			1,280	
269	7			1,467	
244	8			1,656	
212	9			1,847	
180	10			2,030	

Profit is maximised by setting the price at ⬚ and producing and selling ⬚ cakes each day.

(b) Total profit

Price	Quantity	Total revenue	Total cost	Total profit
460	1		385	
420	2		570	
380	3		749	
360	4		932	
325	5		1,100	
302	6		1,280	
269	7		1,467	
244	8		1,656	
212	9		1,847	
180	10		2,030	

2.7 Practical Disadvantages of the Economist's Model

Although the economist's model appears to be logical, it is difficult to apply in practice for the following reasons:

✗ Firms are unlikely to be able to estimate demand curves for their products with any degree of accuracy.

✗ The demand curve ignores exogenous variables (i.e. variables outside of the control of management which may affect price), such as market conditions.

✗ In practice, demand for products may be interrelated. However, demand curves treat demand for each product as independent of demand for other products.

✗ Companies may have strategies other than profit maximisation (e.g. maximisation of market share or achieving a particular target profit).

2.8 Production and Sales Levels

A decision to increase production and sales levels should, like any decision, consider relevant costs (see *Session 3*). These clearly include consideration of marginal revenue and marginal cost. However, there are many other factors, some of which are inter-related, that can make evaluation of this decision quite difficult. For example:

■ One of the implications of increasing production may be the need for increased storage space for raw materials and/or finished goods. The cost of additional storage space is not a variable cost but a fixed cost.*

■ Selling price usually has a significant effect on demand. When following a particular pricing strategy (see next section), a business will need to have production capacity to meet the demand generated.

■ Increasing production may have consequences on the quality of the product (e.g. more defective items). This would not only result in additional costs (e.g. in monitoring quality control and repairs) but might lead to:

  ● customers turning to other suppliers of more reliable products;

  ● the selling price being driven down; and/or

  ● reputational damage (of a brand name).

Commentary

*Inventory holding costs and the economic order quantity (EOQ) model are assumed knowledge from F2 *Management Accounting*.

3 Other Pricing Strategies

3.1 Market Skimming

Market skimming is often used when a product is launched. A high price is set initially, which generally means that demand will be low. However, a large profit margin can be made during this stage.

Later, when the elite segment of the market is satisfied, the price may be lowered so that sales can be made to a larger market segment.

Market skimming is most likely to be used in the following situations:

▓ A new product is being launched into a market where there is no existing competition. This is typically a "breakthrough" product.*

▓ The product confers some status on the customer. For example, when mobile phones were first launched commercially in the 1980s, the cost of a handset was about $2,500. Having a mobile telephone was a symbol of importance.

▓ The product has a short life cycle, and it is desirable to recover the development costs as quickly as possible.

*Commentary

*Examples of breakthrough products include the car, penicillin, laptop computer, Windows operating system, ATM, and iPad. Breakthrough services include orthodontistry, the Internet and online shopping.

3.2 Market Penetration

Market penetration may also be used when launching a product into a new market. However, it is the opposite of market skimming, as a low price is charged initially in order to attract new customers. The initial price may even lead the manufacturer to make a loss in the short term. Once a customer base has been established, the price is increased.

Market penetration is most likely to be used in the following situations:

▓ For commodity-type products where there are many existing products available. The only way to break into the market is to sell for a lower price than the existing products.

▓ For price-sensitive products (i.e. a small reduction in price is expected to result in a large increase in demand).*

▓ For products where economies of scale exist (i.e. if large quantities are produced the cost per unit falls significantly).

*Commentary

*This high *price elasticity* of demand is discussed in more detail later in this session.

3.3   Complementary Product Pricing

The use of one product often requires the purchase of a second product (e.g. cars cannot run without fuel; printers require ink cartridges). Demand for such complementary products is therefore linked.

Complementary product pricing requires understanding of the impact that the price of one product may have on demand for the other. When setting prices the impact on demand for the complementary product may be considered to be more important than the demand or profit relating to the first product.

For example, printers are often sold at a relatively low price; once a particular model of printer has been acquired, the user has to buy a particular print cartridge. The price of the print cartridges is then relatively high because a large margin can be made on them.*

*Consumers have no choice but to buy those cartridges unless they invest in a new printer.

3.4   Price Discrimination

Price discrimination involves setting different prices for a product or service in different markets. Customers in some markets may be willing to pay higher prices than customers in other markets, so price discrimination aims to achieve the maximum price in each available market.

For price discrimination to be feasible there must be barriers between markets (otherwise arbitrageurs would buy in the lower price market and resell in the higher price market).*

*This would undermine the objective of discriminating.

Examples of price discrimination include:

- Where switching can be prevented by selling a product to consumers for:
  - unique moments in time (e.g. airline tickets for a specific flight that cannot be resold under any circumstances, or cheaper rail tickets that are valid for a specific rail service);
  - unique locations (e.g. a return airline or train ticket from location A to location B may be priced differently from a return ticket from location B to location A).
- Software businesses (e.g. Microsoft) often offer heavy price discounts for educational users. For example, Office 2007 was made available at a 90% discount for students in the summer of 2009. Educational purchasers must provide evidence of their status.
- Different tariffs of service charges (e.g. for telephone and Internet communications) for commercial and residential customers.

3.5   Loss Leaders

A loss leader is a product that is sold at a loss to attract customers who will then buy other products. Loss leaders may be used in complementary pricing, where one product (e.g. the printer) is sold at a loss to lock customers into buying another (e.g. ink cartridges).

Loss leaders are common in supermarket promotions, where products are advertised at very low, loss-making prices. The supermarkets know that once customers have entered the supermarket to buy the promotional product, they are likely to buy other goods that they had not planned to purchase.

3.6 Going-Rate Pricing

This simply means charging the prevailing market price. This approach might be used in competitive markets (i.e. where charging above market price would lead to a loss of the majority of customers and selling below market price would not bring additional customers).

Going-rate pricing is common for homogeneous products that have very little variation (e.g. commodities such as aluminium or beef).

3.7 Product-Line Pricing

Some products are related because they are sold to the same customer or through the same outlets. Product-line pricing involves setting the price of the products in the product line together. There are two particularly common approaches:

1. Product bundling (i.e. a group of products are sold together for a price that is less than the total of the individual products). This is common in fast-food restaurants (e.g. "meal deals" containing a burger, soft drink and french fries for less than the total price of the individual items).*

2. Set differentials between different products in a range. For example, a price is set for a basic car with a 1.4 litre engine and all other versions (e.g. a 1.6 litre engine) are sold for the basic price plus a pre-determined differential.

Commentary

*The rationale is that the extra revenue from the third item, compared with just two, exceeds the cost of the third item.

3.8 Volume Discounting

Many organisations offer discounts to customers who buy a certain number of products. In retail stores, for example, it is quite common to see "buy one, get one for 50%".

The reason for using such a strategy is twofold:

1. To offer a more competitive price overall (as the average price paid for two items will obviously be lower than the price for one).

2. To acknowledge the law of diminishing marginal utility (i.e. the idea that the consumer gets most satisfaction from the first unit of a product or service). As subsequent units of a product or service are consumed, the satisfaction derived from them declines. Offering the second item for a lower price encourages consumers to buy it even though it offers less satisfaction.

3.9 Relevant Cost Pricing

Relevant cost pricing, also referred to as opportunity cost pricing, is often used for one-off contracts or orders. The relevant cost of the contract is calculated, and then a mark-up added to get the price (see *Example 2* earlier in this session).

4   Factors Influencing the Price of a Product

4.1   Level of Demand

Demand is the quantity of a good which consumers want, and are willing and able to pay for. In practice, firms may not know what the demand curve is for their product. The level of demand, however, will still influence pricing. If demand is high, firms are able to charge a higher price for a product or service.

Demand is influenced by the following:

- **Income.** Demand for most goods rises when consumers' incomes rise. However, demand for inferior goods (e.g. cheap meat) might fall as incomes rise.

- **Price of substitute goods.** If substitutes are available for a much lower price, consumers may buy the substitutes instead.

- **Price of complementary goods.** Complementary goods are goods which are bought together, for example, petrol and cars. US car manufacturers expect to see a fall in demand for large-sized cars when the price of petrol increases.

- **Consumer tastes and fashion.** For example, in Western Europe, there is a trend towards buying organically grown vegetables, so demand for these products is high.

- **Advertising.** Spending on advertising can increase a product's demand.

4.2   Price Elasticity of Demand

The price elasticity of demand (PED) is the degree of sensitivity of demand for a good to changes in the price of that good.

The following graph can be used to illustrate the calculation of the PED:

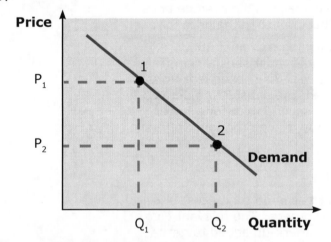

$$\text{PED at point 1* } = \frac{\dfrac{(Q_2 - Q_1)}{Q_1}}{\dfrac{(P_2 - P_1)}{P_1}}$$

Commentary

*PED will normally be negative, since a rise in price leads to a fall in demand. By convention, the minus sign is ignored when describing PED (e.g. if calculated as "– 1.5" it is described as "1.5").

Demand for a product can be described as:

- Elastic—meaning that demand is very responsive to changes in price. The change in the quantity of goods demanded will be relatively greater (i.e. in percentage terms) than the change in price. The PED will be greater than one.

- Inelastic—meaning that a change in price will have little impact on demand. Demand will change by a relatively small amount (i.e. in percentage terms) than the change in price. The PED will be less than one.

If demand is elastic (i.e. PED > 1.0), then increasing the price may lead to reduced revenue.

If demand is inelastic (i.e. PED < 1.0), then price rises can increase revenue (e.g. necessity goods).

Example 6 Price Elasticity of Demand

Alex, a baker, has ascertained that the daily demand for doughnuts has the following demand function:

$P = 500 - 0.1Q$

Where P is the price in cents, and Q is the daily demand in units.

Required:

Calculate the price elasticity of demand based on Alex increasing the price by 5 cents, assuming that his current price per doughnut is:

(a) $4

(b) $2

4.3   Product Life Cycle

One influence on a product's price is its life cycle (see *Session 2*). Different pricing policies might be adopted at different stages as follows:

- **Introduction stage:** Price skimming or penetration pricing may be used (see above).

- **Growth phase:** If price skimming has been used, the price will be reduced during this phase. If penetration pricing has been used, the price will start to rise during this phase once the business is confident about having sufficient customer loyalty.

- **Maturity phase:** At this stage, it is likely that profit maximisation pricing policies will be used (see the economist's model described previously).

- **Decline phase:** Lower prices may be charged to sell off excess inventories. However, in some industries, products that have reached the end of their life cycles may become specialty items, where there is still demand from a small section of the market. For example, vinyl records of music up until the 1980s are collector items for those who prefer vinyl to CDs, etc.*

*Commentary

*Record companies still produce a small number of vinyl records.

4.4   Competitors

If there are many competing suppliers in the market, then an individual firm may have little power to influence prices. On the other hand, a monopolist can dominate the market and set the price.

If a firm has competitors, it must consider their possible reaction to its pricing policy. For example, cutting prices could lead to retaliation—a price war (this is common in supermarkets).

4.5   Customers

If the firm has one dominant customer, the firm may find it difficult to increase prices and might be forced to offer bulk buying discounts.

Firms in the service sector sometimes try to attract "prestige" clients by offering low prices. The hope is to improve reputation and attract other clients, who will be paying normal prices.

4.6   Perfect Competition

Perfect competition is a theoretical concept in which there are:

- many sellers;
- many buyers;
- identical/homogeneous products;
- no barriers to entry; and
- perfect information.

The selling price is set by the market; it is the market clearing price.

Individual firms are not big enough to influence the total output of the market significantly. They are "price takers"—they must accept the market price.*

Commentary

*With perfect competition, firms have no decision to make regarding price.

Market   **Individual Firm**

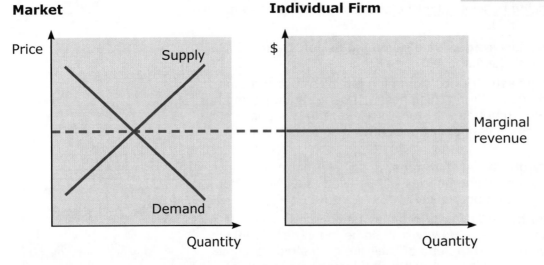

If an individual firm charges a price higher than the market price, that firm will not make any sales, because buyers have perfect information and will know that they can buy at a lower price from the other suppliers in the market.

There is no incentive for firms to sell for a price below the market price because the firm could sell all of its output for the market price.

In a competitive market, firms will charge the market price.

Summary

- Cost plus pricing methods involve adding a given margin to the cost of a product. The cost may be the marginal cost, the full cost or even the relevant cost.

- Full cost plus pricing is a *long-term* pricing method. It ensures that prices cover all variable and fixed costs.

- With return on investment pricing, prices are set to achieve a target percentage return on the capital invested in production.

- Opportunity cost pricing (relevant cost pricing) is a *short-run* pricing method.

- Cost plus methods of pricing:

  - do not consider external factors (e.g. what the market will pay for a product);

  - may not lead to the maximisation of profit, revenue or market share; and

  - may lead to a price which is completely different from what competitors are charging.

- In the economist's model, price is a function of the quantity supplied. As the quantity supplied rises, the price falls. The quantity provided is determined as the point at which the marginal cost = marginal revenue.

- Marginal revenue is the increase in total revenues resulting from selling one more unit of a product or service.

- For the exam, marginal cost is equal to variable cost per unit (at least until full capacity is reached).

- The price elasticity of demand is the degree of sensitivity of demand for a good to changes in the price of that good.

- Pricing is a strategic decision, and in practice there are several pricing strategies which may be adopted.

Session 6 Quiz
Estimated time: 15 minutes

1. List FOUR advantages of using full cost plus method of pricing. (1.1)

2. List TWO situations where opportunity cost pricing may be used. (1.4)

3. State THREE practical disadvantages of using the economist's model for pricing. (2.7)

4. List and describe FOUR price strategies that are not cost plus methods of pricing. (3)

5. List and briefly describe FOUR practical points which a company may consider when choosing a price. (4)

Study Question Bank
Estimated time: 40 minutes

Priority		Estimated Time	Completed
Q10	Tabular Approach	20 minutes	
Q11	Albany	20 minutes	

EXAMPLE SOLUTIONS

Solution 1—Cost Plus and Target ROI

(a) Setting prices

(i) Full cost plus 20%

		$/unit
Variable costs (given)		30
Fixed costs	$\dfrac{300,000 + 100,000}{400,000}$	10
Full cost		40
20% mark-up (20% x $40)		8
Selling price		48

(ii) Marginal cost plus 40%

	$/unit
Variable costs (given)	30
40% mark-up (40% x $30)	12
Selling price	42

(iii) Target ROI

	$
Buildings and equipment (given)	2,000,000
Working capital ($10 x 40,000)	400,000
Capital employed	2,400,000
Profit required ($2,400,000 x 10%)	240,000

	$/unit
Variable cost (given)	30
Fixed cost (given)	10
Profit ($240,000 / 40,000 units)	6
Selling price	46

(b) Profit for the year

	$
Sales (20,000 x $48)	960,000
Variable costs (20,000 x $30)	(600,000)
Fixed costs ($300,000 + 100,000; do not vary with sales)	(400,000)
Net profit/(loss)	(40,000)

Solution 2—Opportunity Cost Price

	$
Market research (sunk cost, therefore, not relevant)	0
Standard steel (regular use, so replacement cost = 1,500 kg x $9.35)	14,025
Speciality steel (not used regularly, therefore, scrap value of 500 x $2)	1,000
Less delivery costs (cost not incurred by using it)	(1,000)
Unskilled labour (380 hours × $7)	2,660
Semi-skilled labour (surplus, work can be done in spare time)	0
Skilled labour: Direct cost (51 hours × $18)	918
Opportunity cost (W) (51 × 60)	3,060
Use of equipment (reduced scrap value)	8,000
Fibrillator (deprival value)	8,000
Ecotox (saved disposal costs)	(3,000)
Total relevant cost	33,663
Mark-up of (25%) ($33,663 x 25%)	8,416
Bid Price	42,079

Working: Opportunity Cost of Skilled Labour

Each half hour of skilled labour used on the contract results in one lost unit of production for the department where the labour is normally employed. The opportunity cost is the lost contribution. The lost contribution per hour is as follows:

	$
Lost revenue (per unit, given)	96
Less: Direct materials (per unit, given)	(15)
Skilled labour (per unit, given)	(9)
Semi-skilled labour (per unit, given)	(27)
Variable overheads (per unit, given)	(15)
Fixed costs (not relevant)	0
Lost contribution per unit	30
Units per hour	2
Lost contribution per hour of skilled labour	60

Solution 3—Marginal Revenue

(a) Demand function

Graph

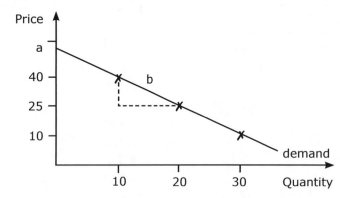

Equation: P	=	a − bQ
		$55 + \left(\dfrac{25-40}{20-10}\right)Q$
		$55 - 1.5Q$

(b) Total revenue, TR   = $55Q - 1.5Q^2$

(c) Marginal revenue, MR

Marginal revenue   =   a − 2bQ

From part (a) a = 55, b = 1.5 therefore marginal revenue = 55 − 3Q.

Solution 4—Profit Maximisation

The total cost function takes the form TC = a +bQ

Where a is the total fixed costs, b is the variable cost (marginal cost) per unit, and Q is output.

To find a and b, use the "high low method":

b = variable cost per unit = (Total costs at highest output-total costs at lowest output)/(Units at highest output-units at lowest output)

= (450–350)/(30–10) = $5 per unit.

The equation Total costs = Fixed costs + Variable costs

can be rearranged to Fixed costs = Total costs – Variable costs

At the 30 units level of output: Fixed costs = 450 – (30 × $5) = $300

So the total cost function is: Total cost = 300 + 5Q

(a) Total cost function   =   300 + 5Q

    Marginal cost function   = $\dfrac{\Delta \text{TC}}{\Delta \text{Q}} = \dfrac{400-350}{20-10} = \dfrac{450-400}{30-20}$

Combined graphs:

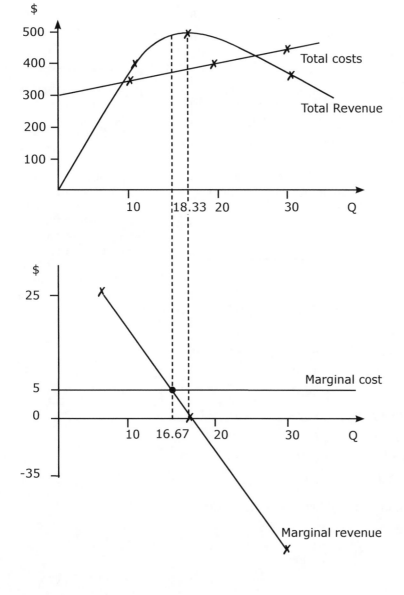

Solution 4—Profit Maximisation (continued)

(b) Profit maximising output   =

Profit maximisation, where MR = MC

$$55 - 3Q = 5$$
$$3Q = 50$$
$$Q = 16.67$$

Profit maximising price   = $55 - (1.5 \times 16.67) = \$30$

Note: When profit maximisation is the goal, the quantity is lower and the price is higher than they are when trying to maximise revenues.

Solution 5—Tabular Method

(a) Marginal cost and marginal revenue

Price	Quantity	Total revenue	Marginal revenue	Total cost	Marginal cost
460	1	460	460	385	385
420	2	840	380	570	185
380	3	1,140	300	749	179
360	4	1,440	300	932	183
325	5	1,625	185	1,100	168
302	6	1,812	187	1,280	180
269	7*	1,883	71	1,467	187
244	8	1,952	69	1,656	189
212	9	1,908	(44)	1,847	191
180	10	1,800	(108)	2,030	183

Profit is maximised by setting a price of 302 cents and producing and selling 6 cakes each day (since this is the point at which marginal revenue is almost the same as marginal cost).

(b) Total profit

Price	Quantity	Total revenue	Total cost	Total profit
460	1	460	385	75
420	2	840	570	270
380	3	1,140	749	391
360	4	1,440	932	508
325	5	1,625	1,100	525
302	6	1,812	1,280	532
269	7	1,883	1,467	416
244	8	1,952	1,656	296
212	9	1,908	1,847	61
180	10	1,900	2,030	(130)

This table confirms the conclusion in part (a) that the profit maximising price is 302 cents for 6 cakes.

*Commentary

*The marginal revenue and cost for 7 cakes show that if production is increased to 7, revenue would increase by 71 cents, and costs would increase by 187 cents. Therefore it would not be worth producing that seventh unit.

Solution 6—Price Elasticity of Demand

(a) Current Price $4

At a price of $P_1 = 400$ cents, daily demand (Q_1) is 1,000 doughnuts (W). If the price rises by 5 cents to $P_2 = 405$ cents, daily demand (Q_2) will fall to 950 doughnuts.

$$PED = \frac{(Q_2 - Q_1) \div Q_1}{(P_2 - P_1) \div P_1} = \frac{(950 - 1,000) \div 1,000}{(405 - 400) \div 400} = \frac{-0.05}{0.0125} = -4.$$

Ignoring the minus sign, elasticity is 4 when the current price is $4. As this is greater than 1, demand is *elastic* at this point.

(b) Current Price $2

At a price of $P_1 = 200$ cents, daily demand (Q_1) is 3,000 doughnuts (W). If the price rises by 5 cents to $P_2 = 205$ cents, daily demand (Q_2) will fall to 2,950 doughnuts.

$$PED = \frac{(2,950 - 3,000)}{3000} \div \frac{(205 - 200)}{200} = \frac{-0.167}{0.025} = -0.67$$

Ignoring the minus sign elasticity is 0.67 when the current price is $2. This shows that elasticity of demand *varies* along the demand curve.

Working

Demand function: $P = 500 - 0.1Q$
At the current price of 400 cents:
$400 = 500 - 0.1Q$
➲ $0.1Q = 100$
➲ $Q = 1,000$ (i.e. daily demand 1,000 doughnuts)

Similarly:

If $P = 405$: $405 = 500 - 0.1Q$ ➲ $0.1Q = 95$, $Q = 950$.
If $P = 200$: $200 = 500 - 0.1Q$, ➲ $0.1Q = 300$, $Q = 3,000$.
If $P = 205$: $205 = 500 - 0.1Q$ ➲ $0.1Q = 295$, $Q = 2,950$

Risk and Uncertainty

FOCUS

This session covers the following content from the *ACCA Study Guide.*

B. Decision-Making Techniques

6. Dealing with risk and uncertainty in decision-making

a) Suggest research techniques to reduce uncertainty (e.g. focus groups, market research).

b) Explain the use of simulation, expected values and sensitivity.

c) Apply expected values and sensitivity to decision-making problems.

d) Apply the techniques of maximax, maximin and minimax regret to decision-making problems, including the production of profit tables.

e) Draw a decision tree and use it to solve a multi-stage decision problem.

f) Calculate the value of perfect and imperfect information.

C. Budgeting and Control

2. Quantitative analysis in budgeting

e) Apply expected values and explain the problems and benefits.

Session 7 Guidance

■ **Understand** approaches to decision-making in situations where the outcome of making a decision is not known with certainty at the time the decision is made.

■ **Know** the numerical ways of dealing with risk.

(continued on next page)

VISUAL OVERVIEW

Objective: To explain techniques which allow for uncertainty and risk in decision-making.

```
                    ┌─────────────────────────────┐
                    │  DECISION-MAKING IN A WORLD  │
                    │           OF RISK            │
                    │─────────────────────────────│
                    │   • Context                  │
                    │   • Methods                  │
                    └─────────────────────────────┘
```

EXPECTED VALUE	RISK ATTITUDE AND DECISION RULES	SENSITIVITY ANALYSIS AND SIMULATION	REDUCING UNCERTAINTY
• The Concept • Profit Tables • Value of Perfect Information • Value of Imperfect Information • Decision Trees	• Three Types of Decision-Makers • Decision Rules	• Sensitivity Analysis • Simulation	• Focus Groups • Market Research

Session 7 Guidance

■ **Know** the practical ways of dealing with, or reducing, uncertainty.

■ **Remember** to not only **focus** on the numerical aspects but also on equally important discursive aspects.

■ **Read** the article "Decision Trees".

1   Decision-Making in a World of Risk

1.1   Context

So far, decision-making questions have assumed that the results of various courses of action are known with certainty. In the real world, this is seldom the case. Decisions often have to be made where various uncertain outcomes could result from the decision being made.

1.2   Methods

There are several methods of dealing with risk in decision-making. The methods which are dealt with in the syllabus for F5 are:

- Expected value
- Value of perfect information
- Decision trees
- Maximax
- Maximin
- Minimax regret.

Definition

Risk—the existence of several possible outcomes, which are known in advance along with the related probability.

Uncertainty—the potential outcomes of a decision that are not known in advance. Clearly, then, associated probability cannot be known, either.

Exam Advice

You must also be aware of practical ways to deal with **uncertainty** (see *s.5*).

2   Expected Value (EV)

2.1   The Concept

The expected value represents the average outcome that would be achieved if a decision were to be repeated many times.

> Expected value (EV) = Weighted arithmetic mean of possible outcomes
>
> $= \Sigma \, (x_i \, p(x_i))$

This formula represents the sum (Σ) of each possible outcome (X_i) multiplied by its probability of occurring ($p(x_i)$).

Illustration 1   Expected Value

When an unbiased six-sided die is thrown, each side has an equal chance ($\frac{1}{6}$) of being obtained. The expected value of throwing a die many times is calculated as:

Value x_i	Probability $p(x_i)$	Product $x_i \, p(x_i)$
1	$\frac{1}{6}$	$\frac{1}{6}$
2	$\frac{1}{6}$	$\frac{2}{6}$
3	$\frac{1}{6}$	$\frac{3}{6}$
4	$\frac{1}{6}$	$\frac{4}{6}$
5	$\frac{1}{6}$	$\frac{5}{6}$
6	$\frac{1}{6}$	$\frac{6}{6}$
Total $\Sigma \, (x_i \, p(x_i))$		$\frac{21}{6}$

The EV is therefore $\frac{21}{6}$ or $3\frac{1}{2}$.

Example 1   Expected Value

A decision-maker must select one of three mutually exclusive projects. The outcome from each project depends on the state of the market, which can be diminishing, static or expanding. The profit for each project under each of the three outcomes is shown in the following payoff (profit) table:

State of the market	Probability	Project 1	Project 2	Project 3
Diminishing	0.4	100	0	180
Static	0.3	200	500	190
Expanding	0.3	1,000	600	200

Required:

Determine the expected value (EV) for each project and select which project to pursue.

Solution

$000

Project 1	EV =		
Project 2	EV =		
Project 3	EV =		

Based on the EVs, Project ☐ should be undertaken.

2.1.1   Advantages of EV

✔ It reduces the information to one number for each choice.

✔ The idea of an average is easily understood.

2.1.2   Limitations of EV

✗ The probabilities of the different possible outcomes may be difficult to estimate.

✗ The average may not correspond to any of the possible outcomes.

✗ Unless the same decision has to be made many times, the average will not be achieved; it is therefore unsuitable for decision-making in "one-off" situations.

✗ The average gives no indication of the spread of possible results (i.e. it ignores risk).

2.2   Profit Tables

A profit table (also referred to as a payoff matrix) shows all possible "payoffs" (NPVs, contribution, profits, etc) which may result from a decision-maker's chosen strategy. The data given in *Example 1* is in the form of a payoff matrix.

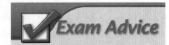

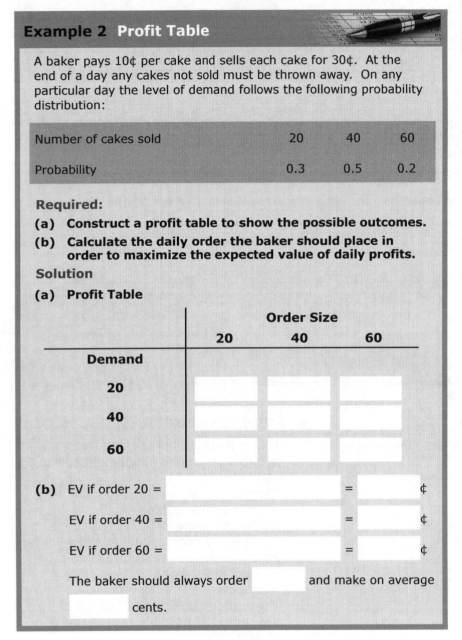

Example 2   Profit Table

A baker pays 10¢ per cake and sells each cake for 30¢. At the end of a day any cakes not sold must be thrown away. On any particular day the level of demand follows the following probability distribution:

Number of cakes sold	20	40	60
Probability	0.3	0.5	0.2

Required:

(a)   Construct a profit table to show the possible outcomes.

(b)   Calculate the daily order the baker should place in order to maximize the expected value of daily profits.

Solution

(a)   Profit Table

	Order Size		
Demand	20	40	60
20			
40			
60			

(b) EV if order 20 = _____ = _____ ¢

EV if order 40 = _____ = _____ ¢

EV if order 60 = _____ = _____ ¢

The baker should always order _____ and make on average

_____ cents.

2.3 Value of Perfect Information

2.3.1 The Concept

Imagine that, in a situation of uncertainty, it is possible to buy an accurate forecast which predicts with certainty what the uncertain variable is going to be each time a decision has to be made.

The value of perfect information is the maximum amount a decision-maker would be willing to pay for advance information to know which outcome *will occur.*

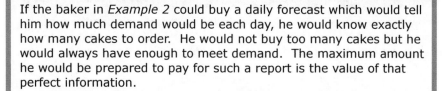

Illustration 2   Perfect Information

If the baker in *Example 2* could buy a daily forecast which would tell him how much demand would be each day, he would know exactly how many cakes to order. He would not buy too many cakes but he would always have enough to meet demand. The maximum amount he would be prepared to pay for such a report is the value of that perfect information.

2.3.2 Calculation

Even if the baker in Example 2 were to order a daily forecast which would provide him with accurate data about daily sales, he would still face risk. The risk arises because although the daily forecasts would be accurate, the baker would not know what the forecasts would say for each day.

Expected value with perfect information is the expected daily profit the baker would earn if he ordered the forecast and acted on it. Some days the forecast will say that demand will be 20 cakes, other days 40 cakes and so on. It is assumed that the probability distribution of the forecast is the same as the probability distribution of the underlying variable (i.e. demand for cakes).

Value of perfect information = EV with perfect information − EV *without* perfect information

Example 3 Value of Perfect Information

The baker in *Example 2* opts to buy a daily forecast which tells him in advance of placing the day's order what demand for that day will be with certainty.

Required:

Calculate the value of this perfect information.

Solution

Daily forecast	Cakes ordered	Daily contribution (¢)	Probability	Expected value (¢)

EV with perfect information
Less: EV without perfect information (*Example 2*)   620

Value of perfect information

2.4 Value of Imperfect Information

In the real world, it is unlikely that any forecast would be perfect. In the case of the baker, the daily forecast would not always be accurate. Even with an inaccurate forecast, however, the baker may make a higher expected return than with no forecast at all.*

Commentary

*EVs of perfect and imperfect information can be calculated more easily using decision trees, which follow.

Value of imperfect information = $\dfrac{\text{EV with imperfect}}{\text{information}}$ _ $\dfrac{\text{EV } \textit{without}}{\text{information}}$

Illustration 3 Imperfect Information

A news agent has to decide how many newspapers to buy each day. Demand is uncertain and can either be high, with a probability of 60%, or low, with a probability of 40%. A profit table shows the profits for the possible combinations of order size and demand:

		Order Size	
		High	**Low**
Demand	**High**	1,000	400
	Low	(200)	400

EV without information

Without any additional information, the news agent would order the quantity which gives the highest expected profit:

Expected outcome of placing a high order: $520 ((1,000 × 0.6) + ((200) × 0.4)).

Expected outcome of placing a low order: $400 ((400 × 0.6) + ((400) × 0.4)).

EV with imperfect information

The news agent can commission a survey which will tell him what demand will be on a particular day. If the survey says demand will be high on a particular day, then he will place a high order; if it says demand will be low on a particular day, he will place a low order. There is a 60% chance that the survey will say high and a 40% chance that the survey will say low. The survey is not always correct, and there is a 90% chance that it will be correct.

If the news agent commissions the survey, then the following profits, along with their associated probabilities, would be possible:

	Profit ($)	Probability
Survey says high and is correct	1,000	0.54 (0.6 × 0.9)
Survey says high and is incorrect	(200)	0.06 (0.6 × 0.1)
Survey says low and is correct	400	0.36 (0.4 × 0.9)
Survey says low and is incorrect	400	0.04 (0.4 × 0.1)

EV with imperfect information = (1,000 × 0.54) + ((200) × 0.06) + (400 × 0.36) + (400 × 0.04) = $688.

The value of imperfect information in this case is:

	$
EV with the survey	688
EV without the survey	520
	———
Value of imperfect information	168

2.5 Decision Trees

2.5.1 Concept

Decision-making often involves multi-stage decisions. At each stage in the decision-making process, the decision-maker has to choose between two or more decisions. The possible outcomes of each decision will be specified, along with the associated probability. Having made the first decision, a second decision or possibly even more decisions may be required.

A "decision" tree helps visualise and evaluate outcomes in the decision-making process. It is a pictorial representation of the decisions which need to be made at each stage, along with their potential outcomes and associated probabilities.

2.5.2 Conventions and Process

The following conventions are used in drawing decision trees:

■ **Decision fork (point)**—this is a point at which a decision-maker has to decide between two or more decisions.

■ **Chance fork (outcome point)**—this occurs where there are several possible outcomes. Normally, for each decision taken, there will be two or more possible outcomes.

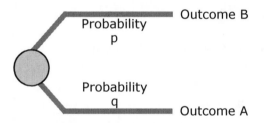

Key Point

The sum of the probabilities of all outcomes at each chance fork must equal 1 or 100%.

Having drawn the decision tree, it is necessary to calculate the expected outcome at each decision fork. To do this process, start at the right-hand side of the decision tree and work back to each decision fork to identify which is the best decision at each fork.

Ultimately, the decision tree enables the decision-maker to determine the best decision to make at the first stage.

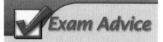

Exam Advice

Mark with a cross each branch that is a decision not taken as you work "backwards" through the tree.

Illustration 4 Decision Tree Process

A firm is considering investing in a new machine. This would involve an initial expenditure of $50,000 on patent rights, and profit in the coming year could be:

$300,000   with probability 0.6

or $200,000   with probability 0.4

If the firm does not invest in the machine, next years' profits will be:

$250,000   with probability 0.7

or $150,000   with probability 0.3

This can be illustrated as follows:

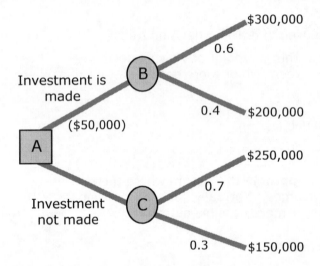

At chance fork B: Expected profits are $260,000 ((0.6 × 300,000) + (0.4 × $200,000)).

At chance fork C: Expected profits are $220,000 ((0.7 × 250,000) + (0.3 × $150,000)).

At decision point A:

   Either invest: Expected outcome is $210,000 (260,000 − 50,000).
   Or do not invest: Expected profit is $220,000.

Conclusion: The investment should not be made.

Example 4 Decision Trees

Slim Foods is considering launching a non-sugar snack bar into a new market. Although the company has not yet undertaken any market research, the marketing director estimates that the product has a 60% chance of success and a 40% chance of failure in the market.

A market research company has offered to do research in the new market prior to any decision being made whether to launch the product. Management believes that there is a 60% chance the market research will recommend the launch and a 40% chance it will advise Slim Foods not to launch the product. The cost of the market research will be $30,000.

The market research company has admitted that its research findings do not always turn out to be as expected once the product has been launched. The company advises that if it recommends the launch, there would be an 80% chance the product would succeed and a 20% chance it would fail. If it does not recommend the launch, there would be a 30% chance that the product would succeed if management were to launch it, and a 70% chance that it would fail.

In all cases, if the product succeeded, the present value of future profits from the product would be $10 million (excluding the market research costs) and, if the product failed, the net present value of the loss would be $4.5 million (excluding the market research costs).

The directors of the company are trying to decide whether to accept the offer of the market research company or to make a decision based only on the gut feel of the marketing director.

Required:

(a) **Draw a decision tree to illustrate the possible decisions and their associated potential outcomes.**

(b) **Advise management how they should proceed.**

(c) **Calculate the value of the imperfect information provided by the market research company.**

3 Risk Attitude and Decision Rules

3.1 Three Types of Decision-Makers

1. **Risk seekers** are those who seek the maximum possible return regardless of the probability of it occurring. As optimists, they consider the best-case scenario.

2. **Risk neutral** are those who consider the most likely outcome.

3. **Risk averse** are those who make decisions based on the worst possible outcome.

3.2   Decision Rules

MAXIMAX	Select the alternative with the maximum possible payoff (i.e. highest return under the best-case scenario). The risk seeker's (i.e. optimist's) rule.
MAXIMIN	Select the alternative with the highest return under the worst-case scenario. The pessimist's rule (i.e. risk averse).
MINIMAX REGRET	Select the alternative with the lowest maximum *regret*. Regret is defined as the opportunity loss from having made the wrong decision. Minimax regret is suitable for risk averse investors.
EXPECTED VALUE (EV)	Select the option that gives the highest EV. Those who use EVs may be described as risk neutral (i.e. they are not concerned with the amount of risk associated with each option only the amount of the expected return).

Example 5   Decision Rules

The payoff table from *Example 1* is reproduced below:

State of the market	Probability	Project 1	Project 2	Project 3
Diminishing	0.4	100	0	180
Static	0.3	200	500	190
Expanding	0.3	1,000	600	200

Required:

Determine which project would be chosen, using each of the following decision rules:

(a) Maximax; (b) Maximin; (c) Minimax regret.

Solution

(a) Maximax

Project selected — [   ]

(b) Maximin

Project selected — [   ]

(c) Minimax Regret: Table of Regrets

State of the market	Outcome at best	Project 1 regret	Project 2 regret	Project 3 regret
Diminishing				
Static				
Expanding				
Maximum regret				

Project selected — [   ]

4 Sensitivity Analysis and Simulation

Sensitivity analysis and simulation provide alternatives to the methods used above to deal with risk and uncertainty in decision-making.

4.1 Sensitivity Analysis

■ Sensitivity analysis calculates how responsive a decision is to changes in any of the variables used to calculate it.

■ It looks at one variable at a time and measures how much the variable can change by (in percentage terms) before the decision changes.

Example 6 Sensitivity Analysis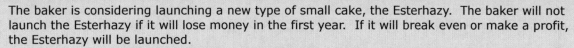

The baker is considering launching a new type of small cake, the Esterhazy. The baker will not launch the Esterhazy if it will lose money in the first year. If it will break even or make a profit, the Esterhazy will be launched.

An accountant has prepared a forecast profitability analysis for the Esterhazy, which shows that it will be profitable. The accountant's analysis is as follows:

	$
Selling price	3
Variable costs	1.5
Contribution per unit	1.5
Budgeted sales per day	50
Daily contribution	75
Additional daily fixed costs	50
Additional daily profits	25

Because the cake is forecast to make a profit, the baker has decided to launch it. The baker is worried, however, about how reliable the accountant's estimates are and wishes to know how sensitive his decision is to changes in the underlying estimates.

Required:

(a) Calculate how sensitive the decision to launch the Esterhazy is to changes in:

    (i) Selling price

    (ii) Volume of daily sales

    (iii) Additional fixed costs.

(b) State to which of these variables the decision is most sensitive.

Example 6 Sensitivity Analysis (continued)

Solution

(a) Sensitivity to:

(i) Selling price

Price must fall [   ] % to change the decision.

(ii) Volume of daily sales

Volume must fall [   ] % to change the decision.

(iii) Additional fixed costs

Fixed costs must rise [   ] % to over the forecast to change the decision.

(b) State to which of these variables the decision is most sensitive.

The forecast is most sensitive to the change in [   ]

Advantages

✔ It gives an idea of how sensitive the decision taken is to changes in any of the original estimates.

✔ It can be readily adapted for use in spreadsheet packages.

Limitations

✗ Although it can be adapted to deal with multi-variable changes, sensitivity is usually only used to examine what happens when one variable changes and others remain constant.

✗ Without a computer, it can be time consuming.

4.2 Simulation

 **Definition**

Simulation—a mathematical model constructed to represent the operation of a real-life process or situation.

▣ **Simulation** is a technique which allows more than one variable to change at the same time.

▣ Most real-life problems are complex as there is more than one uncertain variable. Models can be generated which "simulate" the real-world environment within which the decision must be made.

Illustration 5 Simulation

A computer model could simulate the conditions which exist for the baker in *Example 6*. Each time the simulation is run (each trial), the model would randomly generate a selling price per unit, daily demand and daily fixed cost. The profit for the trial would then be calculated. The simulation would be run many times. Based on the results of the simulation, a probability distribution of daily profit of the baker could be constructed.

Although a simulation is not likely to be used in such a simple situation (as alternative models are available), it may be the only suitable method of analysing more complex situations where there are many variables which could change.

One example of a mathematical model used in simulation is the "Monte Carlo" method.*

> ***Commentary**
>
> *"Monte Carlo" was the code name given to this method by the physicists who developed simulations to estimate the probability of success in nuclear weapon projects.

4.2.1 Stages

1. Specify the major variables (excessive detail will over-complicate).

2. Specify the relationship between the variables.

3. Attach probability distributions to each variable and assign random numbers to reflect the distribution.

4. Simulate the environment by generating random numbers.

5. Record the outcome of each simulation.

6. Repeat each simulation many times to obtain a probability distribution of the likely outcomes.

4.2.2 Advantages and Limitations

Advantages

✔ It overcomes the limitations of sensitivity analysis by examining the effects of all possible combinations of variables and their realisations.

✔ It therefore provides more information about the possible outcomes and their relative probabilities.*

✔ It is useful for problems which cannot be solved analytically by other means.

Limitations

✗ It is not a technique for making a decision, only for getting more information about the possible outcomes.

✗ It can be very time consuming without a computer.

✗ It could prove expensive in designing and running the simulation on a computer.

✗ It relies on reliable estimates of the probability distributions of the underlying variables.

> ***Commentary**
>
> *This helps in highlighting implausible assumptions and detecting bias (e.g. in optimistic assumptions).

5 Reducing Uncertainty

5.1 Focus Groups

Much of the uncertainty which companies face in the real world relates to new products and whether they will be successful. To reduce this uncertainty, focus groups may be used prior to the launch of a product.

■ A group of people are asked to give their opinion about a new product or service. The discussion takes place in an interactive environment in which participants are free to give their opinions and discuss them with other members of the group.

■ Members of the group are chosen at random. Often they are approached by employees of the marketing organisation in the street and asked to participate.

■ Prior to the meeting, the members of the group may be screened to ensure they belong to the target market to which the product is aimed.

■ A moderator may be present to ease the discussion.

■ During the meeting, the participants may be observed, usually without their knowledge, by marketing professionals who examine their body language, facial expressions and group behaviour.

5.2 Market Research

Market research is the systematic gathering of information about customers, competitors and the market. The type of information gathered in market research seeks to answer the following types of question:

■ Who are the customers?

■ Where are they located?

■ What quantity and quality do they want?

■ What is the best time to sell?

■ What is the long-term price?

■ Who are the competitors?

Market research can be used to help companies make decisions about the development and marketing of new products. The earlier the market research is conducted in the development of a product, the better, from a risk point of view.

Market research can be based on primary or secondary data.

■ Primary data means the company collects its own original data, for example, by conducting interviews.

■ Secondary data means that already published data is used, such as published statistics.

Summary

- Various techniques can be used to make decisions in situations of uncertainty.

- EV analysis involves choosing the highest expected outcome. This is based on probabilities, and is an average value. It may not be appropriate for one-off decisions.

- A profit table (payoff matrix) shows all possible payoffs which may result from the strategy chosen by the decision-maker.

- Value of perfect information shows the maximum amount a company would be prepared to pay for an accurate forecast of the uncertain variables it faces. It is defined as:

  > EV with perfect information (the forecast) less EV without perfect information

- Imperfect information has value if it results in a higher expected return than the expected value without it.

- Decision trees may be used to document multi-stage decisions with various potential outcomes at each stage.

- Maximax decision-making involves choosing the option with the highest potential outcome. Maximax decision-makers are risk seekers.

- Maximin decision-makers are pessimists, who assume that only the worst outcome will occur. They therefore select the option where the worst outcome is higher.

- Sensitivity analysis calculates how responsive a decision is to changes in any of the variables used to calculate it.

- Simulation allows for more than one variable to change at a time.

- In the real world, much of the risk that commercial organisations face comes from new products. Such risk can be reduced by focus groups or other forms of market research.

Session 7 Quiz

Estimated time: 15 minutes

1. List THREE disadvantages of using expected values as a criterion for choosing which decision to take. (2.1.2)

2. State the formula for calculating the value of perfect information. (2.3.2)

3. True or False? In a decision tree, a decision fork is denoted by a square. (2.5.2)

4. Describe the attitude towards risk of a person who makes decisions using the maximax decision-making rule. (3.2)

5. Describe the purpose of a focus group. (5.1)

Study Question Bank

Estimated time: 1 hour, 20 minutes

Priority		Estimated Time	Completed
Q12	Shifters Haulage	40 minutes	
Q13	Decision Trees	40 minutes	

EXAMPLE SOLUTIONS

Solution 1—Expected Value

		$000
Project 1	EV = (100 × 0.4) + (200 × 0.3) + (1,000 × 0.3)	400
Project 2	EV = (0 × 0.4) + (500 × 0.3) + (600 × 0.3)	330
Project 3	EV = (180 × 0.4) + (190 × 0.3) + (200 × 0.3)	189

Based on the EVs, Project 1 should be undertaken.

Solution 2—Profit Table

(a) Profit Table (in cents)

	Order Size		
Demand	**20**	**40**	**60**
20 (Pr 0.3)	400	200	0
40 (Pr 0.5)	400	800	600
60 (Pr 0.2)	400	800	1,200

Sample working:

If order q = 20 and demand = 20, profit = (20 × 30) – (20 × 10) = 400

If order q = 20 and demand = 40, sales are limited to 20,

therefore profit = (20 × 30) – (20 × 10) = 400.

(b) EV if order 20 = (400 × 0.3) + (400 × 0.5) + (400 × 0.2) = 400 cents

EV if order 40 = (200 × 0.3) + (800 × 0.5) + (800 × 0.2) = 620 cents

EV if order 60 = ((0 × 0.3) + (600 × 0.5) + (1,200 × 0.2)) = 540 cents

The baker should always order 40 and make on average 620 cents.

Solution 3—Value of Perfect Information

Daily forecast	Cakes ordered	Daily contribution (¢)	Probability	Expected value (¢)
20	20	400	0.3	120
40	40	800	0.5	400
60	60	1,200	0.2	240
EV with perfect information				760
Less: EV without perfect information (*Example 2*)				620
Value of perfect information				140

Conclusion: The value of perfect information is 140 cents per day. This is the maximum amount the baker would be prepared to pay for a daily forecast which would provide him with the exact demand for each day.

Solution 4—Decision Trees

(a) Decision Tree

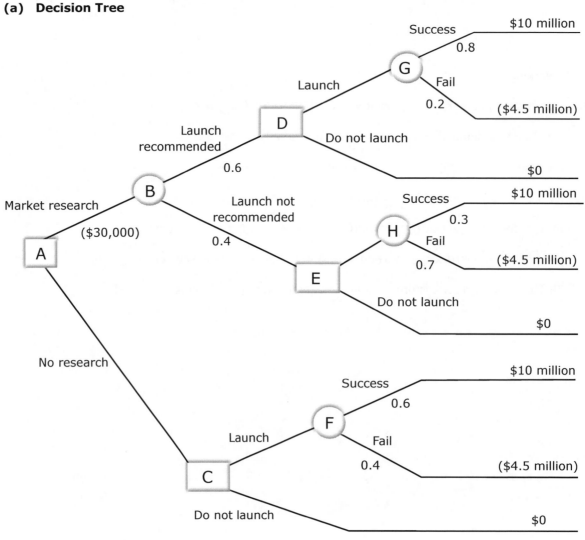

(b) Advice to Management

Expected Present Value of Profits With Market Research

At outcome point G (launching), the EV is $7,100,000 ((10 million × 0.8) + (-4.5 million × 0.2)).
This is higher than zero (not launching), so the decision at point D would be to *launch*, and EV here is $7,100,000.

At outcome point H, EV is − $150,000 ((10 million × 0.3) + (−4.5 million × 0.7)).
This is less than not launching the product, so the decision at point E is *not to launch* the product.

Therefore, at outcome point B (market research recommendation), if the product launch is recommended, it *will be* launched. If it is not recommended, then it *will not be* launched.

At outcome point B, the expected outcome is $4,260,000 ((0.6 × 7,100,000) + (0.4 × 0)).
To get from point A to point B, the company has to pay $30,000 for market research.
The expected value of proceeding with the market research is therefore $4,230,000.

Expected Present Value of Profits Without Market Research

At outcome point F, the expected net present value of profits is $4,200,000 ((10 million × 0.6) + (-4.5 million × 0.4)). The decision at point C is therefore to *launch*, as the net present value of not launching is zero. Therefore, the expected present value of profits at C is also $4,200,000.
No cost is involved in getting from A to C, so the expected net present value of profits is $4,200,000 if market research is *not* carried out.

Conclusion: The market research should be undertaken. This is because the net present value of profits is higher by $30,000 ($4,230,000 − $4,200,000) with market research.

(c) Value of Imperfect Information

The value of imperfect information is simply the difference between the expected value if the market research is commissioned and the expected value if it is not:

	$000
EV with the market research	4,260 (point B)
EV without market research	4,200 (point C)
Value of imperfect information	60

Solution 5—Decision Rules

(a) Maximax

Project selected — 1 (it has the highest return in an expanding market).

(b) Maximin

Project selected — 3 (it has the highest return in a diminishing market).

(c) Minimax Regret: Table of Regrets

State of the market	Outcome at best	Project 1 regret	Project 2 regret	Project 3 regret
Diminishing	180	80	180	0
Static	500	300	0	310
Expanding	1,000	0	400	800
Maximum regret		300	400	800

Project selected — 1. A minimax regret decision-maker would choose Project 1 as it has the lowest minimum regret. If Project 1 is chosen, no matter what the outcome is, the decision-maker will never be more than $300 below the best outcome

Solution 6—Sensitivity Analysis

(a) (i) Sensitivity to price

Let p = price per unit.
Contribution per unit = p – 1.5.
At breakeven point, total contribution = total fixed costs

Breakeven price (based on budgeted sales of 50 units per day):
(p – 1.5) × 50 = 50
50p – 75 = 50
50p = 125
p = 2.50

If the price is below 2.5 then a loss will be made.
Price must fall 16.67% (0.5/3) to change the decision.

(a) (ii) Sensitivity to volume of daily sales

Let v = daily sales in units
Total contribution = 1.5
At breakeven, $1.5v = 50
v = 33.33
Forecast volume = 50 units per day
Volume must fall 33.34% (16.67/50) to change the decision.

(a) (iii) Sensitivity to additional fixed costs

Budgeted contribution per day is 75.
If budgeted fixed costs exceed 75 per day, then a loss will
be made.
Forecast fixed cost is 50.
Fixed costs must rise 50% (25/50) over the forecast in order to
change the decision.

(b) State to which of these variables the decision is most sensitive.

The forecast is most sensitive to the change in price. This
is the variable where the lowest change would result in the
decision changing.

Budgeting

FOCUS

This session covers the following content from the *ACCA Study Guide.*

C. Budgeting and Control

1. Budgetary systems and types of budget

a) Explain how budgetary systems fit within the performance hierarchy.

b) Select and explain appropriate budgetary systems for an organisation, including top-down, bottom-up, rolling, zero-based, activity-based, incremental and feed-forward control.

c) Describe the information used in budget systems and the sources of the information needed.

d) Indicate the usefulness and problems with different budget types (including fixed, flexible, zero-based, activity-based, incremental, rolling, top-down, bottom-up, master, functional).

e) Prepare flexed budgets, rolling budgets and activity-based budgets.

f) Explain the beyond budgeting model, including the benefits and problems that may be faced if it is adopted in an organisation.

g) Discuss the issues surrounding setting the difficulty level for a budget.

h) Explain the benefits and difficulties of the participation of employees in the negotiation of targets.

j) Explain how budget systems can deal with uncertainty in the environment.

i) Explain the difficulties of changing a budgetary system or type of budget used.

7. Performance analysis

c) Identify the factors which influence behaviour.

Session 8 Guidance

- **Understand** similar topics covered in F2.
- **Know** the purpose of budgets.
- **Understand** how budgets affect the performance of an organisation.
- **Read** the article "Comparing Budgeting Techniques".
- **Understand** the Beyond Budgeting model and the rationale behind it.

VISUAL OVERVIEW

Objective: To describe, illustrate and comment on the planning and control uses of budgeting.

BUDGETARY CONTROL SYSTEMS

OBJECTIVES

- Introduction
- Objectives

PERFORMANCE HIERARCHY

- Long-Term Planning
- Mission
- Corporate Objectives
- Unit Objectives
- Setting Strategies
- Role of Budgeting

TYPES

- Introduction
- Top Down v Bottom Up
- Rolling
- Incremental
- Zero Based (ZBB)
- Activity Based (ABB)
- Feedback and Feed Forward

INFORMATION USED

- Quality Aspects
- Sources of Data

DIFFICULTIES OF CHANGING

- Traditional Approaches
- Difficulties

UNCERTAINTY IN THE ENVIRONMENT

- Forecasting
- Flexible Budgets
- Flexed Budgets

BEHAVIOURAL ASPECTS

- Factors Which Influence Behaviour
- Hopwood
- Level of Difficulty
- Standards
- Participation

BEYOND BUDGETING

- Criticisms of Traditional Budgeting
- Beyond Budgeting Model
- Evaluation of Beyond Budgeting

1 Objectives of a Budgetary Control System

1.1 Introduction

A budgetary control system is a way of achieving financial control of an entity. The typical budgetary control system consists of the following stages:

1. A budget is prepared for a calendar year. This shows budgeted revenues, costs and possibly cash flows and statements of financial position. Normally, the budgets are divided into monthly periods.

2. Shortly after the end of each month, when the accounts for that month have been prepared, the actual results are compared with the budgeted results. Any differences (variances) between the actual results and budgeted amounts are investigated.

3. Action is taken to ensure such variances do not occur in future months.

1.2 Objectives*

1.2.1 Coordination

- Of the different activities of an organisation.
- Should help achieve *goal congruence.*
- Particularly important in decentralised organisations.

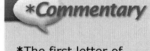

Illustration 1 Coordination

> Without a budget, the production department may not plan sufficient resources to meet the sales planned by the selling department.

Commentary

*The first letter of each of the objectives of budgeting spells the word "CRUMPET". This may help you to remember the objectives of budgeting.

1.2.2 Responsibility

A budget is a way of delegating responsibility by showing managers which revenues and costs they are responsible for.

1.2.3 Utilisation

Having a budget should lead to better resource utilisation. Decisions such as ordering inventory and hiring staff will be guided by the budget, meaning that organisations do not acquire resources in excess of their needs.

1.2.4 Motivation

Research shows that giving managers a target in the form of a budget may improve their performance compared with giving them no target. If the target becomes too difficult, however, it can demotivate managers.

1.2.5   Planning

Budgets are a financial plan. Requiring managers to prepare budgets forces them to think about the budget period. It makes them consider what conditions may exist and how they will respond to them. This should lead to better decision-making than simply taking each day as it comes.

Budgets cover a short-term time frame, typically one year. Most organisations have a long-term plan as well. The budget should be consistent with the long-term plan as it shows, in detail, how the budgeted period will contribute to the longer-term objectives.

1.2.6   Evaluation

Managers' performance is likely to be evaluated, at least in part, by how they perform against the budget they are given. In some organisations, managers may receive bonuses based on how they perform relative to the budget. Promotions may also depend on this. In such situations, managers will be extremely keen to ensure that they achieve the budget.

1.2.7   Telling

Budgets are a means by which superiors communicate their expectations of the managers below them.

2   The Performance Hierarchy

2.1   Long-Term Planning

A budget typically covers 12 months. Many organisations prepare longer-term plans. This section looks at how the budgeting process fits in with the performance hierarchy.

The first stage of long-term planning involves setting out the long-term, strategic objectives of the organisation. These objectives are often set out using a hierarchical structure, the performance hierarchy.

A typical hierarchy of objectives is as follows:

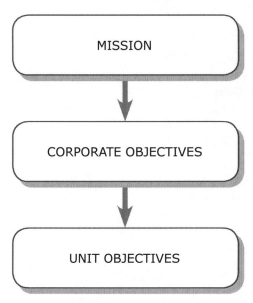

MISSION

CORPORATE OBJECTIVES

UNIT OBJECTIVES

2.2 Mission

The **mission** of an organisation can be described as the reason for the organisation's existence. In the case of commercial organisations, the mission is normally to maximise the wealth of shareholders.

Not-for-profit organisations' missions will not normally be to maximise the wealth of shareholders, but will be based on achieving some other aim.

Exhibit 1   GREENPEACE

The mission of the environmental group Greenpeace, for example, is set out in a mission statement. It includes the following statement:

"Greenpeace is an independent global campaigning organisation that acts to change attitudes and behaviour, to protect and conserve the environment and to promote peace."

Source: greenpeace.org/international

2.3 Corporate Objectives

Whether an organisation is achieving its mission is often a matter of opinion, as it is not normally set out in quantifiable terms. Corporate objectives are more concrete and set out what the organisation must do to achieve its mission. Corporate objectives are specific and quantifiable.

Examples of corporate objectives are as follows:

- To increase revenues by 10% per year.
- To increase dividends by 5% per year.
- To reduce global emissions of carbon gasses by 10% by 2021.

2.4 Unit Objectives

Once objectives are set for the organisation as a whole (corporate objectives), objectives may then be set for each business unit. These should be consistent with the corporate objectives.

2.5 Setting Strategies

Having established the objectives of the organisation, possibly using the performance hierarchy approach, organisations need to determine what actions to take to achieve those objectives. These strategies may be set out in a long-term plan.

2.6 Role of Budgeting in Long-Term Planning

A budget is concerned with implementing the long-term plan for the budget period. The budget will be more detailed than the long-term plan, and shows essentially how the budget period will contribute to the long-term plan.

Figure 1 summarises the discussion about how budgetary systems
fit within the performance hierarchy.

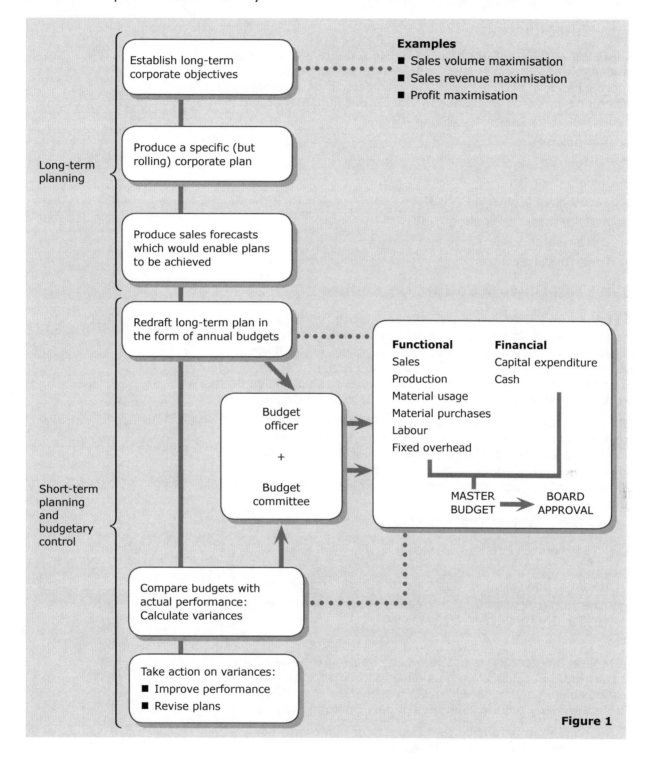

Figure 1

3 Different Types of Budgetary Systems

3.1 Introduction

A number of different approaches to the preparation of budgets have evolved. It is important to understand what these approaches are, and to appreciate which would be appropriate for different types of organisations. The approaches mentioned in the ACCA Study Guide are as follows:

- Top-down
- Bottom-up
- Rolling budgets
- Zero-based budgeting (ZBB)
- Activity-based budgeting (ABB)
- Incremental
- Feed-forward control.

3.2 Top-Down v Bottom-Up Budgeting

An important factor in budgeting is how much participation managers enjoy in preparing their own budgets. In some organisations, budgets are prepared centrally, by the finance department, with the input of senior management. These budgets are then imposed on junior managers, who are then expected to work towards operating their departments within budget.

Other organisations allow a more participative approach. The managers of each department prepare the first draft of their budget, which is then discussed with senior managers. After some negotiation, changes may be made to the draft to ensure that the final budget meets the objectives of the whole organisation, before it is approved.

Definition

Top-down budgeting—budgets are prepared by senior management.

Bottom-up (participative) budgeting—managers participate in the preparation of their department's budget.

In reality, the decision is not between choosing top-down or bottom-up, but in deciding how much participation managers of responsibility centres should have in preparing their budgets. There are many different degrees of participation, for example:

- Managers prepare their own budgets or plans with no intervention by senior management.
- Managers prepare the first draft, which is then amended by senior managers.
- Senior managers prepare the budgets after discussion with the managers responsible.
- Senior managers prepare the budget entirely and the departmental managers have no input at all.

3.2.1   Factors to Consider

The following factors may be considered in deciding how much participation should be allowed:

Commentary

*In this case, a top-down approach may be more appropriate.

■ The attitudes of junior managers to their work. Some may be very proactive and want to participate in all aspects of managing their department. If they are not allowed to participate they will become disappointed and demotivated. Others may be less proactive and require detailed guidance from above.*

■ The skills of junior mangers relating to budgeting. If their financial skills are weak, then participation may be limited.

■ The amount of interdependence between departments. If departments rely on each other (e.g. services of one department are consumed by another) then more coordination of the budgeting process will be necessary. This will require some intervention by senior management.

■ In periods of financial difficulty, when control of the resources and cash flows of the organisation is essential for survival, senior management should be intervening.

■ The amount of "local" knowledge of senior managers. In very large organisations, senior head-office management may have little knowledge of local conditions at ground level (i.e. in the divisions or branches). In this case, the participation of local managers in the preparation of their own budgets is advisable.

Commentary

*Such organisations are more likely to adopt a participative approach.

■ Culture of the organisation. In a "command and control" approach to management, everything is centrally planned and all junior staff are told what they must do. Top-down budgeting is often a feature of such organisations. Other organisations may adopt a more delegated approach, in which managers are given autonomy. They will be given broad guidelines about what is expected of them, but allowed to do the detailed planning without central intervention.*

3.2.2   Participation and the Objectives of Budgeting

Participation in the budget preparation process may help or hinder the objectives of budgeting:

■ **Planning:** Budgets force managers to take time away from managing day-to-day operations to plan the future of their departments. Clearly, the more involvement junior managers and staff have in the budgeting process the more they will be forced to plan.

■ **Coordination:** Coordination of the various departments in budgeting is easier if budgeting is performed centrally and there is less participation.

Commentary

*That is, understating budgeted revenues and/or overstating budgeted costs to make budgets easier to achieve.

■ **Motivation:** Managers are more likely to be motivated if they are involved in setting their own budgets. Managers given responsibility for a department but not allowed to participate in their budgets may become demotivated.

■ **Evaluation of performance:** If managers are evaluated on their performance against budget, the budget must be set at an appropriate level of difficulty. It should be challenging, but realistic. If managers participate in preparing their own budgets, there is a risk of "budgetary slack".*

3.2.3   Advantages and Disadvantages

Example 1   Advantages

Suggest FOUR advantages of top-down budgeting and FOUR advantages of bottom-up budgeting.

3.3   Rolling Budgets (Rolling Forecasts)

In a **rolling budget**, the budget horizon (typically one year) is kept constant by adding another month (or quarter) to the end of the budgeted period as each month (or quarter) expires.

Definition

Rolling budget—a system of budgeting in which the budget is continuously updated.

Illustration 2   Rolling Budgets

A budget is prepared for the year 20X2.

At the end of January 20X2, the actual performance for the month of January is compared against the budget. Based on this comparison, it may be decided that the budgets for 1 February to 31 December 20X2 should be changed to reflect changes in external factors. Once this has been done, a budget is also prepared for January 20X3. The new budget, therefore, covers 1 February 20X2 to 31 January 20X3.

3.3.1   Usefulness of Rolling Budgets*

✔ The budget is always updated to reflect external changes. It is therefore more relevant and more valid for comparison against actual performance.

✔ There will always be a budget for the next 12 months. This can be useful for planning things such as cash flows.

✔ Managers will be more motivated as the budget is more realistic, because it will be updated to take account of changes which occur outside of their control.

Commentary

*The mechanics of Rolling budgets are described in *Session 9*.

3.3.2   Problems With Rolling Budgets

✗ Time consuming.

✗ Budgets may be changed to hide operational inefficiencies.

✗ Not necessary in a stable environment.

3.3.3   Appropriateness of Rolling Budgets

Rolling budgets are likely to be more appropriate in industries which are dynamic, where external changes can lead to the original budget quickly becoming out of date. In stable industries, little benefit may be obtained by continuously updating the budget, so a rolling budget may be less useful.

Example 2 Rolling Budgets

For organisations in each of the following industries, discuss whether rolling budgets would be appropriate:

Solution

- A food retailer

- A developer of handheld computer devices and mobile phones

- An airline

- An advertising agency

- A retail bank

Example 3 Rolling Budgets

Homeland Airways uses rolling forecasts. At the start of the year, the following quarterly budget was prepared:

	Quarter 1 $m	Quarter 2 $m	Quarter 3 $m	Quarter 4 $m
Revenue	200	230	400	170
Costs:				
Fuel	70	81	120	60
Labour	60	65	70	60
Other	20	23	40	17
Profit	50	61	170	33

It is now the end of Quarter 1, and the company wishes to update the budget as follows:

1. Due to a rise in the world price of oil, budgeted fuel costs for Quarters 2, 3 and 4 should increase to 120% of the amount shown in the original budget.

2. The original budget was based on the assumption that an increase in staff costs of 10% would be negotiated with the unions. In the event of that, a pay rise of only 5% was agreed.

3. There is no change in budgeted revenues or other costs.

4. Quarter 1 of the following year should be based on the assumption that all items are 10% higher than budgeted for Quarter 1 of the current year, with the exception of fuel, which should be 44% higher.

Required:

Prepare the rolling budget for the four quarters starting with Quarter 2 of the current year.

3.4 Incremental Budgeting

3.4.1 Use of Historical Data

An incremental budget is a budget prepared using a previous period's budget or actual performance as a basis with incremental amounts added for the new budget period. The allocation of resources is based on allocations in the previous period. It is not generally recommended as it fails to take into account changing circumstances. Also, it encourages a "spend it or lose" mentality, as spending the budget is likely to ensure a reasonable allocation in the next period.

3.4.2 Usefulness of Incremental Budgeting

✔ The budget is stable, and change is gradual.

✔ Managers can operate their departments on a consistent basis.

✔ The system is relatively simple to operate and easy to understand.

✔ Conflicts should be avoided if departments can be seen to be treated similarly.

✔ Coordination between budgets is easier to achieve.

✔ The effect of change can be seen quickly.

3.4.3 Problems With Incremental Budgeting

✗ Assumes activities and methods of working will continue in the same way.

✗ No incentive for developing new ideas.

✗ No incentives to reduce costs.

✗ Encourages "spend it or lose" mentality so that the budget is maintained next year.

✗ The budget may become out of date and no longer relate to the level of activity or type of work being carried out.

✗ The priority for resources may have changed since the budgets were set originally.

✗ There may be budgetary "slack" built into the budget, which is never reviewed.*

*Commentary

*Managers may have overestimated their requirements in the past to obtain a budget which is easier to work to, and which will allow them to achieve favourable results.

3.5 Zero-Based Budgeting (ZBB)

3.5.1 Weakness of Incremental Budgeting

✗ When a budgeting system has been in operation for some time, there is a tendency for the next year's budget to be justified by reference to the levels currently being achieved. However, the analysis process should take into account all changes which should affect the future activities of the organisation.

✗ Even using such an analytical base, some organisations find that historical comparisons, and particularly the current level of constraints on resources, can inhibit innovative changes in budgets. This can severely handicap an organisation because the budget should be the first year of the long-term strategic plan. If changes are not started in the budget period, it will be more difficult for the organisation to make the progress necessary to achieve long-term objectives.

One way of breaking out of this "cyclical" budgeting problem is to go back to basics and develop the budget from an assumption of no existing resources (i.e. a "zero base"). Using this basis, all resources have to be justified, and the chosen way of achieving any specified objectives has to be compared with the alternatives. For example, in considering budgeted sales, the current existing sales force would be ignored, and the optimum means of achieving the sales objectives in a particular market for a particular product or service would be developed. This might not include any of the sales force, or a different-sized team, and the company then has to plan how to implement this new strategy.

3.5.2 Features of ZBB

Traditional budgets are normally produced using a "line item" approach, which lists each type of expense (e.g. staff costs, depreciation, etc) and the amount budgeted by each department. ZBB is based around activities or programmes that focus on what each department would actually like to undertake.

A three-stage approach to ZBB may be as follows:

1. Each manager identifies activities or programmes to undertake in the budgeted period. A "decision package" is then prepared for each activity. This is a mini–budget that shows how much will need to be spent on the activity. There also may be some narrative explaining the benefits of the package and quantifying any revenues (or cost savings) if appropriate.

2. A budget committee reviews all the decision packages and ranks them (in decreasing order of benefits). Management accepts each package up to the point at which the total budgeted expenditure is reached.

3. Resources are allocated to the activities selected in Step 2. The budget is then a consolidation of all the accepted packages.

3.5.3 Decision Package

A decision package is produced for each activity that the managers wish to undertake in the following year. For example, in a large accountancy firm a decision package might relate to "ACCA training".

A package may be broken down into:

- a "base level" package, specifying the minimum level of service that would be required; and
- incremental packages with additional expenditure.

A base package for ACCA training might include exam registration and study materials. An incremental package could include training courses.*

Decision packages also may be mutually exclusive (i.e. two or more packages are alternative approaches to the same problem). For example, one package may be to make a component in-house; another might be to outsource it. It would clearly not make sense for the budget committee to select both packages.

Definition

Discretionary cost—a capital or revenue expense that can be curtailed, eliminated or postponed without affecting short-term profitability.

*Commentary

*When ranking packages, the budget committee can decide whether to accept just the base package or provide funds for the incremental package also.

3.5.4 Usefulness of ZBB

▦ Forces budget setters to examine every item.

▦ Allocation of resources is linked to results and needs.

▦ Develops a questioning attitude.

▦ Wastage and budget slack should be eliminated.

▦ Prevents budgets "creeping" based on previous year's figures with a percentage add-on.

▦ Encourages managers to look for alternatives.

3.5.5 Problems With ZBB

✗ It is a complex and time-consuming process.*

✗ Short-term benefits may be emphasised to the detriment of long-term planning.

✗ Internal politics can result in annual conflicts over budget allocation.

Commentary

*Hence, the full process may be carried out only every five years (for instance). An alternative approach is to look in-depth at one area of the business each year on a rolling basis so that each area prepares a ZBB every five years.

3.5.6 When ZBB Is Appropriate

ZBB is most appropriate in organisations that have a high portion of discretionary costs (e.g. research and development, training and advertising). Expenditure on such items may be reduced without the organisation ceasing to function; however, such expenditure does bring benefits. ZBB enables organisations to reassess how much they spend on such discretionary items.

Organisations which enjoy few such discretionary items of expenditure would not gain as much from introducing ZBB.

3.5.7 Use of ZBB in the Public Sector

ZBB is increasingly being used by public sector bodies due to the following factors:

▦ Showing a budget based on activities rather than on line items is more transparent. A budget that shows the total amount that will be spent on employee costs does not provide useful information to taxpayers. However, if the budget shows the amount to be spent building a new motorway, taxpayers can appreciate where their taxes are being spent.

▦ The ranking of decision packages can be very useful in allocating limited public sector resources, where governments face demands for funds from numerous programmes. Ranking helps ensure that taxpayers' money is spent where it will best meet the objectives of the government.

▦ A large proportion of expenditure, but not all, will be discretionary. This means that a mixed approach might be taken to budgeting, where some expenditure will be budgeted using an incremental approach and some using a ZBB approach.

Illustration 3 ZBB in a Hospital

In preparing its annual budgets, a hospital might take the following approaches to certain costs:

■ Salaries of medical staff: An incremental approach may be relevant since staff costs will be similar to those of the previous year, requiring changes only for the number of staff and any pay rises.

■ Setting up a new research centre: A ZBB approach may be taken here. A decision package should be prepared for the research centre and a budget prepared for the likely costs and benefits. It may be appropriate to prepare a base-level package with incremental packages specifying higher levels of excellence.

Example 4 ZBB in Central Government
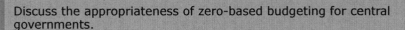

Discuss the appropriateness of zero-based budgeting for central governments.

3.6 Activity-Based Budgeting (ABB)

3.6.1 Principles of ABB

Most budgeting techniques assume that costs vary with the level of output. However, costs of support activities do not necessarily depend on the number of units produced or sold (see *Session 1*). For these types of costs, a more sophisticated type of budgeting is appropriate.

Activity-based budgeting (ABB) follows principles of activity-based costing (ABC) "in reverse". Having decided how many units to produce and sell, the organisation then needs to define the cost of the activities required to produce them. These depend on the drivers identified for each activity.

3.6.2 Preparation of AB Budgets

Preparing activity-based budgets is rather like performing ABC in reverse. The following steps are used:

1. Estimate the budgeted volume of sales and production, in units.

2. For each activity (e.g. machine set-up), estimate the number of units of driver which would be required to support the budgeted volume of sales and production (e.g. the number of production runs).

3. Determine the cost of each unit of driver. This may require an analysis of factors such as labour time required, labour cost per unit, etc.

4. Calculate the budgeted cost of each activity (number of drivers × cost per unit of driver).

Example 5 Activity-Based Budgeting

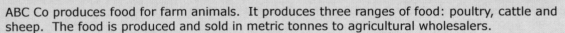

ABC Co produces food for farm animals. It produces three ranges of food: poultry, cattle and sheep. The food is produced and sold in metric tonnes to agricultural wholesalers.

The company is preparing its budgets for the next financial year, and wishes to use an activity-based approach to budgeting for its overheads.

Directs costs per tonne are as follows:

	Poultry	Cattle	Sheep
Materials	$500	$700	$850
Labour cost	$120	$140	$800
Weekly production	1,000	750	900

The company uses ABC, and has identified the following support activities for which overhead costs are incurred:

Activity	Driver
Machine set-ups	Number of production runs
Ordering materials	Number of orders
Storage	Tonne days of storage

The expected number of drivers that will be used each week by each of the three products is shown as follows:

	Poultry	Cattle	Sheep
Production runs	8	15	9
Purchase orders	20	25	30
Tonne days of storage	45	18	36

The management accountant has already calculated the cost per unit of driver for the machine set-ups and storage as follows:

Activity	Cost per unit of driver
Machine set-ups	$500 per production run
Storage	$10 per tonne day

Unfortunately, the management accountant quit at the end of the last month, and you have been asked to complete the budget.

You have discovered the following information about the purchase order process:

1. Each order takes 30 minutes to process (on average). The cost of employing clerical staff is $10 per hour. Clerical staff would work a minimum of 40 hours per week.

2. Office supplies are estimated to be $180 per clerk per week.

3. Each clerk would require a desktop computer. The cost of providing the computer is estimated at $20 per week.

Required:

(a) **Calculate the cost per purchase order, based on the information provided.**

(b) **Prepare the weekly budgeted costs, showing the total budgeted cost of each activity separately.**

3.6.3   Advantages of ABB

✔ Management attention is focused on the activities of the organisation. These are something which management can control more easily than focusing on total costs.

✔ Better understanding of what causes costs to be incurred may provide opportunities for cost reductions.

✔ May identify *non-value added activities* which can be estimated.

3.6.4   Disadvantages of ABB

✗ Complicated and expensive to implement. More suited to large organisations with multiple products and many drivers.

✗ Many fixed costs do not vary with changes in the volume of drivers in the short run—so ABB may provide misleading information.

3.6.5   Appropriateness of ABB

ABB is a complex method. It is likely to be used only in large companies which have the resources to implement such an approach. It is most appropriate in these situations:

◾ The organisation has a large volume of overheads.

◾ There are several different activities to which the overheads relate.

◾ The organisation has many products with differing production times and methods.*

*See *Session 9* for an example of preparing an activity-based budget.

3.7   Feedback and Feed-Forward Control

3.7.1   Feedback Control

A feedback control system is a system in which outputs are monitored against a predetermined standard, and if there are any deviations from the standard, action is taken to remedy these. The feedback is the information concerning the difference between the actual output and the desired output.

A budgetary control system is an example of a feedback control system. For each period, the actual results are compared against the budget. If the budget was not achieved, then action can be taken to correct the factor which caused the budget to be missed.

3.7.2 Closed-Loop System

A closed-loop system is any system with feedback. Reliance on feedback makes such systems reactive rather than proactive.

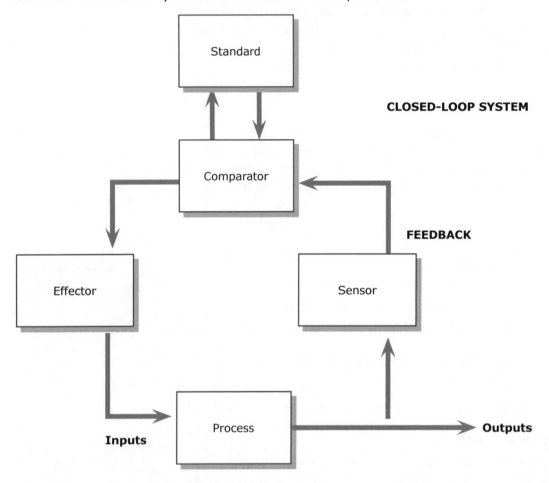

- **Standard:** What the system is aiming for (e.g. the budget).
- **Sensor:** Measures the output of the system (i.e. accumulation of actual data).
- **Comparator:** Compares the information from the sensor to the standard (e.g. variance analysis).
- **Effector:** Control action (e.g. management action to minimise future adverse variances and repeat favourable variances).

3.7.3 Open-Loop System

An open-loop system is a system without feedback. There are two reasons for the absence of feedback:

1. Feedback is not produced (e.g. variance analysis not undertaken).

2. Feedback is produced but not used appropriately (e.g. variances are not communicated to the appropriate manager).

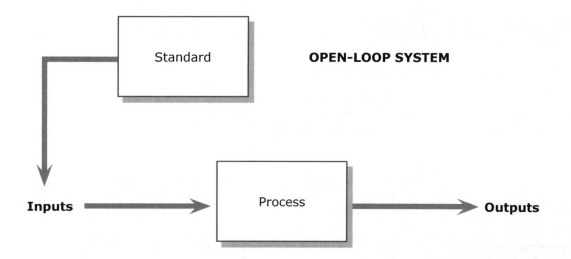

3.7.4 Positive and Negative Feedback

Positive feedback means that the output has achieved or even exceeded the plan.

Negative feedback means that the output is below the plan (e.g. actual profits are below budget for a particular period). The cause of negative feedback should be investigated so that corrective action can be taken to reduce the likelihood of repetition in the future.

Positive results (e.g. favourable variances) should also be investigated, to determine whether they can be repeated.*

3.7.5 Feed-Forward Control

The major problem with feedback control systems is that by the time the feedback is received, it is too late to take action to correct the deviation for the period under review. If actual costs are higher than budget, for example, action can be taken which will stop the same deviation from occurring in future periods. The current period, however, is already history, and no action can be taken to change that.

In feed-forward control systems, predicted future results are compared against the desired outcome. If it appears that the desired outcome will not be achieved based on the current prediction, action can be taken now so that the desired outcome is achieved.*

*Commentary

*However, care must be taken here (e.g. a favourable sales price variance might actually *reduce* profits if demand is sensitive to price changes).

*Commentary

*Target costing (see *Session 3*) is an example of feed-forward control. The expected cost per unit is compared with the desired cost per unit and action is taken to eliminate the gap.

Illustration 4 Feed-Forward Control

Alpha operates in a business which is not subject to seasonal variations in demand or costs. The company has budgeted to make a profit of $10 million for the current financial year, which ends on 31 December. On 30 June, profits for the first half of the year are $4 million. Based on this, the directors forecast that profits for the year will be only $8 million, not $10 million, unless some action is taken.

Because this information is available halfway through the year, the directors can take action to remedy the situation to try to achieve the budgeted profit figure of $10 million for the year. The forecast profit of $8 million is therefore feed-forward.

---

4   Information Used in Budgetary Systems

4.1   Aspects of Information Quality

In considering the sources of information for use in budgetary systems, attention should be paid to aspects of the quality of information. These may be summarised as "PROMPT".

Aspect	Meaning	Considerations
Presentation	Information is clearly communicated.	Language, layout, structure, etc.
Relevance	Information matches the needs of the user.	Level of detail, summary information, exception reporting.
Objectivity	The information is not biased (e.g. by the person providing it).	What vested interests might lie in the information, whether the language is emotive or "value-laden".
Method (e.g. research reports)	The means by which underlying data has been collected.	Population size, sample size, selection method.
Provenance	It is clear where and from whom the information has been obtained.	Identification of source, format of report, protection of information contained (e.g. from unauthorised changes).
Timeliness	It is clear when the information was produced.	Date, time, possible obsolescence, alternative sources available.

4.2   Sources of Data and Information

Data and information come from multiple sources—both internal (inside the business) and external. Businesses need to capture and use information which is relevant and reliable.

4.2.1   Internal

Accounting records are a primary source. They detail past transactions which may be used as the basis for planning (e.g. preparing a financial budget or forecast). They are primarily used to record what has happened to the financial resources of a business. For example, how cash has been obtained and spent; what assets have been acquired; and what profits or losses have been made on business activities.

Accounting records also provide non-financial information. For example, documented reasons for raising debit notes to suppliers or credit notes to customers can provide useful information about the quality of materials purchased/finished goods sold. Data analysed from sales invoices provide a profile of which products, to whom and in which markets sales are being made.

A lot of internal information is related to the accounting system—but not a direct part of it. For example:

- Employee records (personal details, wage rates or salary, skills and experience, training records);
- Costings for tenders for contracts;
- Production department data (e.g. number of machines, operating capacity, repairs and maintenance records);
- Records of direct contact with customers (e.g. complaint letters, calls received by a customer service centre).

Not all internal information is provided formally. For example, relevant and reliable information may be communicated through regular meetings without formal documentation.

4.2.2 Categories of External Information

- Information about ways in which business activities need to be undertaken. For example:
  - Businesses must keep records to collect taxes on behalf of the government, and so need regular and up-to-date information about the taxation system (e.g. VAT, corporate profits tax) and what actions needs to be taken (e.g. returns submitted, payments made).
  - Businesses need to be aware of laws which affect their activities (e.g. environmental legislation, health and safety regulations, labour law).
- "Market" or "competitive intelligence" (i.e. information about the markets in which a business operates). This may be obtained through market research.

5 Difficulties of Changing a Budgetary System

5.1 Traditional Approaches to Budgeting

The traditional approach to budgeting uses an incremental approach. Changes to budgetary systems are likely to occur when organisations move away from traditional approaches to budgeting to more sophisticated methods (e.g. ZBB or ABB).

5.2 Difficulties

In changing the approach to budgeting, organisations are likely to encounter the following obstacles:

- ✗ Resistance to change—employees who do not appreciate the value of change may be reluctant to help, particularly if it requires additional work.
- ✗ Scepticism—particularly at senior management levels. Managers who do not understand the benefit of the change may not give their full support.
- ✗ Training everyone involved in the process of change. New methods will require an investment in training so that all those involved will be competent to perform the new types of budgets.
- ✗ Additional time and costs involved in moving to a new system. This may include costs of consultants and overtime for staff.

6 Uncertainty in the Environment

6.1 Forecasting

A budget is effectively a forecast of what can be achieved. The forecast has to make assumptions about the external environment.

The following are some of the factors that may cause uncertainty in the budget-setting process:

- The overall economic performance of the markets in which the business sells. Economic growth may lead to increased demand for products or services.

- Actions of competitors. A competitor's launch of a great new product may reduce demand considerably.

- Performance of employees. It may be difficult to estimate how productive employees will be and how many employees will actually be required.

- Market prices of inputs. The prices of many commodities (e.g. metals and oil) are determined by highly developed international markets and can be very volatile.

- Demand for new products will be uncertain. Popularity will not be known until the products have been launched.*

The following methods can be used to deal with uncertainty:

- Flexed or flexible budgets
- Rolling budgets
- Revision of the budgets at the end of the period before comparing with actual results.

*This can be mitigated by market research.

6.2 Flexible Budgets

Flexible budgeting involves preparing two or more budgets, using different assumptions for each about the level of sales or production. At the end of the financial period, the budget with the activity level closest to the actual activity level is used for comparing the actual performance.

6.3 Flexed Budgets

At the end of the year, prior to comparing the actual figures against the budget, the budgets are re-calculated (flexed) using the original budget assumptions, but the actual activity levels. This means that the comparison is more valid.*

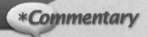

*When flexing the budget, a decision has to be made about how to deal with fixed costs. One view is that fixed costs are fixed and, therefore, they should *not* be flexed. Sometimes, however, fixed costs are flexed, particularly if absorption costing is used. Because budgeting is an internal process, there are no "rules". You may come across some examples where the fixed cost has been flexed, and other examples, such as the flexed budget in *Illustration 5*, where the fixed cost has not been flexed.

Illustration 5 Flexed Budgets

Original Budget

		$000
Sales	(50,000 items @ $100)	5,000
Production	(55,000 units)	
Materials	(55,000 × 40)	2,200
Labour	(55,000 × 3)	165
Variable overheads	(55,000 × 9)	495
Fixed overheads	(55,000 × 15)	825
Budgeted cost of production		3,685
Less: Closing inventory	(5,000 @ $67)	(335)
Standard cost of goods sold		3,350
Budgeted profit (50,000 @ $33)		$1,650

Actual sales were 53,000 units and production was 56,000 units. The flexed budget would be calculated as follows:

Flexed Budget

		$000
Sales	53,000 × $100	5,300
Production costs		
Materials	56,000 × $40	2,240
Labour	56,000 × $3	168
Variable overheads	56,000 × $9	504
Fixed overheads		825
Less: Closing inventory		(201)
Cost of goods sold		3,536
Profit		1,764

 Exam Advice

This is assumed knowledge. See *Session 10* for an example.

7 Behavioural Aspects of Budgeting

7.1 Factors Which Influence Behaviour

In many organisations, managers are at least partly evaluated on how they perform in relation to the budget. The budget is, therefore, likely to influence the behaviour of those managers. It is hoped that the budget will motivate managers to achieve higher profits for the organisation. Several factors will influence this.

7.2 Hopwood's Management Styles

One of the first management writers to consider the effect of budgets on behaviour was Hopwood, who carried out a survey of budgeting practices during the 1970s to identify how budgets influenced the behaviour of managers. He identified three different management styles in the companies he visited: budget constrained, profit conscious and non-accounting.

7.2.1 Budget-Constrained Style

Managers are evaluated on their ability to meet budgets in the short term. Failure to meet budgets means that managers will have poor evaluations, even if there was a good reason for exceeding the budget.

7.2.2 Profit-Conscious Style

In the profit-conscious company, managers are judged more on their ability to contribute to long-term success rather than simply meeting the budget. Budgets are used, but are applied more flexibly. For example, if the budget was not reached, but there was a good reason for this, the manager would not be penalised.

7.2.3 Non-accounting Style

Accounting data is not important for performance evaluation. Qualitative factors are seen as more important (e.g. customer satisfaction).

The following table summarises the effect of these styles on the behaviour of managers:

Style Features	Budget-constrained	Profit-conscious	Non-accounting
Involvement with costs	High	High	Low
Job-related tension	High	Medium	Medium
Manipulation of data	Extensive	Little	Little
Relationships with superiors and colleagues	Poor	Good	Good

7.3   Setting the Level of Difficulty of the Budget

▓ Research has shown that:

  ● Targets can be used to motivate employees;
  ● If individuals have higher levels of *intended* achievement, then *actual* achievement rises.

▓ But if targets are too easy to achieve (e.g. basic standards), individuals will *not* be motivated to improve performance.

▓ On the other hand, targets which are too difficult (e.g. ideal standards) can be *demotivating*.

▓ Research suggests that targets which are *just out of reach* are optimal for motivation (e.g. just above the current standard).

▓ This is only a general rule. The optimal target may be different from individual to individual.

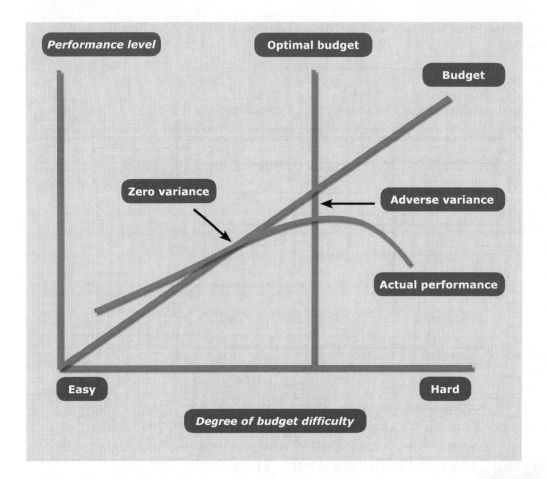

■ Note that an adverse variance will be produced even though performance has been maximised. Care must be taken to ensure that the budget holder does not react adversely to this.*

7.4 Standards

When setting the level of budget difficulty, four approaches can be used to setting standards:

7.4.1 Ideal Standard

■ Calculated assuming 100% efficiency from all factors of production (e.g. no losses, no idle time, etc).

■ Too difficult as a target, therefore, may lead to demotivation.

7.4.2 Basic Standard

■ Long-run (underlying) average standard.

■ Based on historical data (i.e. past performance).

■ Out of date.

■ Likely to be too easy to achieve in the future.

7.4.3 Expected Standard

■ Based on normal efficiency (e.g. after normal loss, expected idle time, normal machine downtime).

■ May be a useful standard to use in variance analysis.

■ But it may not be an appropriate target for motivation as it can be met without any improvement over normal efficiency.

*Commentary

*A solution to the adverse variance might be to use a lower standard for performance evaluation.

7.4.4 Current Standard

- A standard established for use over a short period, reflecting current conditions.
- Obtained by adjusting the expected standard.
- Use is time consuming (e.g. new current standards must be recalculated each month).

7.5 Benefits and Difficulties of Employee Participation

The benefits of bottom-up budgeting, whereby managers or employees participate in the setting of their budgets, have already been discussed in this session. The same benefits apply to setting other performance targets

7.5.1 Benefits of Employee Participation

✔ Employees are more likely to accept and work towards targets they have been involved in setting.

✔ Employees will be more motivated if they are given more autonomy

✔ The targets should be realistic, as employees would not agree to targets which are not.

7.5.2 Potential Problems of Employee Participation

✗ Employees may try to set targets which are too easy. In budgets, they may add "slack" to the budgets. Budgetary slack means adding expenses to the budget in excess of what is really needed.

✗ Setting the targets is likely to be more time consuming if employees are involved.

✗ Setting of targets may not be fair, given that some employees will be better negotiators than others and will, therefore, be able to negotiate lower targets.

8 Beyond Budgeting

8.1 Criticisms of Traditional Budgeting

For many years there has been much criticism of the traditional budgetary processes. Hope and Fraser detail these criticisms in their book *Beyond Budgeting*. This looks at the problems inherent in the traditional budgeting process, and suggests an alternative approach to performance management, the "Beyond Budgeting" model.

In discussing budgets, Hope and Fraser use a broader definition of budgeting than simply producing a financial plan. They mean the whole performance measurement process of agreeing on the targets, setting reward schemes based on achieving those targets, using budgets to allocate resources, and controlling performance based on this process. They refer to this as the "fixed performance contract".

The main criticisms of this budgeting model as described by Hope and Fraser are as follows:

8.1.1   Budgets Take Up Too Much Time

■ The budgeting process takes up too much of the time of senior management, and does not add sufficient value to the organisation to justify this.

8.1.2   Budgeting Is Out of Kilter With the Modern Business Environment

■ In the more competitive environments that have existed since the 1980s, businesses must react quickly to customer needs. This requires transferring power from the centre to managers who are closer to the customers. The old "command and control" structure of organisations represented by traditional budgeting process has become outdated.

■ The primary drivers of shareholder value in the modern business world are intellectual capital such as brands, loyal customers and proven management teams. These are outside of the orbit of the budgetary control system.

8.1.3   The Extent of Gaming

Budgets were initially introduced as a planning tool for managing costs and cash flows. However, over time budgets also came to be used as performance management tools for managing the business. The **"fixed performance contract"** was introduced, as follows:

■ A fixed target—usually expressed in terms of budgeted sales, costs, profits and ratios such as return on capital employed.

■ Incentives were introduced based on achieving these targets, such as bonuses and promotions for achieving the budgets.

■ Resources are allocated to departments based on the budget.

This system sounds good in theory, but in practice it can lead to an annual **"performance trap"** whereby the actions of all managers are focused on meeting the performance targets of the current year.

This may lead to dysfunctional behaviour, or gaming. Gaming means manipulating a system to achieve some advantage. During their research, Hope and Fraser encountered the following examples of gaming:

■ Managers negotiate the lowest targets and the highest rewards.

■ Always make the bonus whatever it takes (e.g. by "window dressing").*

■ Never put the customer above the sales targets.

■ Never share knowledge or resources with other teams.

■ Ask for more resources than you need. You will be cut back to what you actually need.

■ Always spend what's in the budget or you will lose it.

■ Always be able to explain adverse variances on causes beyond your control.

■ Never provide accurate forecasts—hide bad news or you will be expected to compensate.

■ Always meet the numbers, never beat them.

■ Never take risks.

Commentary

*A "window dressing" example could be ensuring that sales targets are met by making sales on a "sale or return" basis at the end of the financial year to a friend. The following year the goods are returned.

8.2 Beyond Budgeting Model

Hope and Fraser suggest that the traditional budgetary control process should be replaced by the following system:

- Replace **financial** targets with targets based on **key performance indicators** (KPIs) and use "stretch goals" for planning that are not linked to reward schemes.

- Appraise managers using comparisons with peers and benchmarks and **reward** them accordingly.

- Devolve responsibility for **planning** away from the centre.

- Manage **resources** to be available for worthwhile opportunities.

- Use rolling forecasts, performance league tables and other KPIs to measure and **control performance** rather than just relying on comparison of actual performance against the budget.

Definition

Beyond Budgeting— a set of guiding principles to enable an organisation to manage its performance and decentralise its decision-making process without the need for traditional budgets.

8.2.1 Setting Targets

Where managers rewards are linked to achieving fixed financial targets, managers negotiate the lowest targets. This means that the organisation does not achieve its potential. Beyond budgeting encourages managers to set challenging targets or "stretch goals" that cannot be achieved by making small improvements to existing performance.

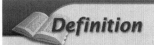

- Managers are asked what their department could achieve if it aimed to maximise performance over the short to medium term.

- Since their rewards will not depend on achieving these targets managers will not have an incentive to simply negotiate easy targets.*

- Setting targets based on KPIs is quicker than setting detailed financial budgets, therefore reducing the time spent on budgeting.

- Targets set are more aligned with the strategy of the organisation than financial targets.

Definition

Stretch goal—a goal that requires an organisation or person to push themselves to their limits.

*Commentary

*Raising targets encourages maximum profit potential.

8.2.2 Rewarding People

In traditional budgeting, fixed targets are set at the start of the year and managers are rewarded if they achieve those targets, regardless of any external changes in the environment. This leads to manipulation of data and gaming—an attitude of "make the target whatever it takes".

- Beyond budgeting uses relative targets (e.g. how managers perform compared to peers) or benchmarks (e.g. profits compared to competitors or market share).*

- Targets are therefore more relevant and realistic, unlike internally set targets.

- Targets are also fairer, as they take into account changes in the external environment automatically; if the economy is not doing well in a particular year, the competitor's profits will also be lower. This helps to eliminate gaming as managers now see that the targets are fair.

*Commentary

*The best performers are rewarded, rather than the skilled budget negotiators.

8.2.3 Action Planning

In traditional budgeting, budgets are often prepared at the start of the year using top-down methods. These fix the behaviour that is expected of the managers. The problem is that in a dynamic business environment, organisations need to be able to react quickly to changes (e.g. to customer demand). The traditional budget limits such reaction.

■ In the beyond budgeting model, business unit managers and front-line staff develop their own plans for maximising customer satisfaction and shareholder wealth.

■ The role of senior management is to provide higher-level targets and to challenge the plans produced by business unit managers.

■ Unit managers will typically prepare medium-term goals on an annual basis and short-term goals on a quarterly basis. They can therefore respond to changing demand and anticipate business threats and opportunities.*

*Commentary

*This continuous and open process allows teams to create value.

8.2.4 Managing Resources

In traditional budgeting, budgets are used as the basis for deciding how resources should be allocated to each department. If new projects become available that were not envisaged when the budget was prepared, funds may not be made available for them. This may lead to good business opportunities being missed.

■ In the beyond budgeting model, resource decisions are devolved to front-line teams, making them more responsive.*

■ Funds are allocated to projects based on a "fast track" review process (i.e. if front-line teams need additional resources, they will be approved if they meet agreed criteria).

*Commentary

*Managers are more accountable; there is greater ownership and less waste.

8.2.5 Coordinating Actions

In traditional budgeting, the budgets of all departments are coordinated. According to Hope and Fraser, although the departments may be coordinated with each other, they are not aligned with the strategy of the organisation. An additional problem is that it is not enough to perform this coordination once every year.

■ In beyond budgeting, coordination occurs through cross-company interaction.

■ Service level agreements between the different departments are used to coordinate their activities. Under such agreements one department commits to providing goods or services to another, based on expected demand, covering an appropriate time frame.

■ Operating capacity rises and falls according to demand, rather than to meet a predetermined budget.*

*Commentary

*Production is more flexible and there is less waste as fewer items are made for inventory.

8.2.6 Controlling Performance

In traditional budgeting systems, control is exercised by comparing actual performance against budget and asking managers to explain any variances. Corrective action is then taken to bring actual performance back into line with the budget. This leads to too much focus on the short term, according to Hope and Fraser. Few organisations focus beyond the end of the current financial year.

- Beyond budgeting model uses a more diverse range of forward-looking indicators to manage performance.*

- Extensive use of rolling forecasts and leading indicators provide managers with a view of what will happen in the future.

- There is also greater use of comparison of KPIs achieved against benchmarks and the use of league tables. This provides managers with a more sophisticated view of performance and should eliminate manipulation of data.

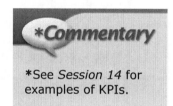

*Commentary

*There is a greater focus on trends and forecasts.

8.3 Evaluation of Beyond Budgeting

8.3.1 Advantages

✔ Divisional managers will be more motivated as they will be given autonomy to plan for their own business units.

✔ Creates a climate based on competitive success. Using relative performance measures and comparing performance with external benchmarks encourages managers to focus on beating competitors rather than other managers.

✔ Quicker response to changes in customer needs as managers will not be committed to a budget that is out of date. Resources will also be made available for new projects if they are worthwhile even if not originally in the budget.

✔ Performance is not only focused on financial numbers but on KPIs, which reflect more faithfully the overall objectives of the organisation.*

✔ More customer-focused attitude of departments that supply other internal departments.

*Commentary

*See *Session 14* for examples of KPIs.

8.3.2 Disadvantages

✗ The organisational culture may not support this approach (e.g. where senior managers are accustomed to a command-and-control style of management).

✗ May not be appropriate in organisations in which financial control is crucial to success (e.g. in public sector organisations where funds are limited).

Summary

- A budgetary control system is a means of management exercising control over the organisation by setting budgets, and comparing the performance of the organisation against the budget. Action is taken to remedy deviations from the budget.

- The main objectives of budgetary control system are planning, coordination of the activities of the organisation and ensuring better resource utilisation.

- Budgets may also be used to delegate responsibility to managers, who are then evaluated on how they perform relative to the budget.

- Budgets should contribute towards the long-term plans of the organisation.

- Top-down budgeting means that budgets are prepared by senior management and imposed on the departments responsible for achieving them.

- Bottom-up budgeting means that departments participate in preparing their own budgets.

- Incremental budgeting is where the starting point for the preparation of a budget is the previous year's budget or actual figures.

- ZBB is where the preparation of the budget starts from zero and the costs and benefits of all activities have to be quantified and justified.

- Activity-based budgets use ABC principles to calculate the budgeted overhead costs.

- Budgets influence the behaviour of managers, because their evaluation depends on whether they achieve the budget.

- The Beyond Budgeting model aims to replace traditional budgetary control systems with a more modern approach:

  - Targets and stretch goals are linked to objectives. Rewards do not depend on achieving them;

  - Appraisals are based on comparing the performance of managers against peers and benchmarks rather than a pre-set, fixed target;

  - Responsibility for planning is devolved from head office to divisional managers;

  - Resources are made available to worthwhile projects even if they were not included in the budget;

  - Continuously updated rolling budgets and forecasts are used rather than a fixed budget, which can become outdated.

Session 8 Quiz
Estimated time: 25 minutes

1. Explain FOUR objectives of budgeting. (1.2)

2. Describe what is meant by an organisation's mission. (2.2)

3. Describe top-down budgeting. (3.2)

4. State the type of budgeting system which might be appropriate for companies which operate in a changing environment. (3.3)

5. State the type of situation in which activity-based budgeting may be appropriate. (3.6.5)

6. Define feed-forward control. (3.7.5)

7. List the aspects of the quality of information summarised in the acronym PROMPT. (4.1)

8. True or False? With flexible budgeting, two or more budgets are prepared which use different assumptions about the level of sales or production. (6.2)

9. List the THREE types of management styles identified by Hopwood concerning approaches to budgeting. (7.2)

10. List THREE weaknesses of the traditional budgetary process. (8.1)

11. List the FIVE parts of the Beyond Budgeting model. (8.2)

Study Question Bank
Estimated time: 40 minutes

Priority		Estimated Time	Completed
Q14	BRT Co	40 minutes	
Additional			
Q15	Zero-Based Budgeting		
Q16	PC Co		

EXAMPLE SOLUTIONS

Solution 1—Advantages

Top-Down Budgeting

✔ Senior management have greater control of the budgetary process. The budgets will, therefore, reflect more accurately the corporate objectives and the long-term plan.

✔ Where managers prepare their own budgets, and are assessed on how they perform relative to these, there is a temptation for the managers to add "budgetary slack" (i.e. they overstate budgeted expenses or understate budgeted revenues to make their budgets easier to achieve). Using top-down budgeting avoids this risk.

✔ Since budgets are prepared centrally, the activities of the various departments should be better coordinated.

✔ It may be difficult for managers with little financial or accounting knowledge to prepare budgets for their own departments. Top-down budgeting means that these managers would not have to prepare their own budgets.

✔ The various budgets are more likely to be set at the same level of difficulty and would, therefore, be fairer than if bottom-up budgeting is used.

Bottom-Up Budgeting

✔ Managers are more likely to accept the budgeted targets for their departments and work towards achieving them if they have been involved in setting the budgets.

✔ Managers have a more detailed knowledge of the work which their departments do than senior management and, therefore, can produce more realistic budgets.

✔ Managers may feel more motivated if they are given greater autonomy and more responsibility for their departments. Giving managers greater autonomy would normally include giving them the right to participate in preparing their own budgets.

✔ At the end of the budget period, when managers' performance is being assessed, the managers cannot claim that the budget was unrealistic if they prepare the budget.

✔ Managers will better understand the financial objectives of the organisation if they are involved in budgeting. Thus, the budget process can be seen as a type of education given to non-financial managers.

Solution 2—Rolling Budgets

Food Retailer

Food retailing is a stable business. Few unexpected external changes are likely to occur. Therefore, little benefit would be gained by continuously updating budgets, so rolling budgets are unlikely to be used.

Manufacturer of Mobile Computer Devices and Mobile Phones

This industry is very dynamic as new products are constantly being developed. As competitors introduce new products, this may well change demand for the companies' own products. It also may affect whether existing development projects are accelerated, scrapped or changed. Accordingly, rolling budgets may be useful in this type of business.

Airlines

Airlines are also subject to many external factors. Fuel typically accounts for 50% of the total costs of many airlines, so changes in the market price of oil will affect profits. Economic factors heavily affect demand, because travel is a "discretionary" activity for many people. Accordingly, rolling budgets may be useful, as otherwise budgets quickly could become out of date.

Advertising Agencies

Budgeting is likely to be very difficult in advertising agencies. Revenues may vary significantly from month to month depending on whether clients decide to spend on campaigns. Accordingly, rolling forecasts could be useful.

Retail Banking

Retail banking is a fairly stable business. As such, little benefit may be gained from using rolling budgets.

Solution 3—Rolling Budgets

	Quarter 2 $m	Quarter 3 $m	Quarter 4 $m	Quarter 1 $m
Revenue	230	400	170	220
Costs:				
Fuel	97	144	72	101
Labour	62	67	57	66
Other	23	40	17	22
Profit	48	149	24	31

Notes:

1. Fuel for Q2 to Q4 is the original budget amount multiplied by 1.2.
2. Staff costs are calculated by multiplying the original budget amounts by $\frac{105}{110}$.

Solution 4—Zero-Based Budgeting

In practice, many governments use incremental budgeting. Due to the sheer size of central government budgets, introducing ZBB would be very time consuming.

There are, however, very good arguments in favour of using ZBB in central governments. Much government spending is discretionary in nature. ZBB would enable governments to re-examine the benefits associated with this discretionary expenditure and decide whether to continue to allocate so much of the state's funds to these types of activities.

Since the financial crisis of 2008 many countries have been forced to implement austerity measures to reduce government deficits. As a form of budgeting that is associated with cutbacks, the use of elements of ZBB has undoubtedly increased.

Certain areas of government expenditure may not be discretionary (e.g. spending in areas of welfare benefits and health services may be determined by demand for those services). As such, ZBB would not be appropriate. In other areas (e.g. funding for arts and culture and defence), ZBB could be useful as these are areas in which governments have discretion as to how much to spend.

Due to the huge amount of work involved in ZBB, it is unlikely that it would be carried out annually. However, it could be performed over a longer period (e.g. every five years) with incremental budgeting used during the interim periods.

Solution 5—Activity-Based Budgeting

(a) Cost per purchase order

	$
Clerical staff costs (one member of staff)*	400
Office supplies	180
Computer (one clerk)	20
Total weekly cost	600
Number of purchase orders	75
Cost per order	8

*Based on the number of purchase orders, 37.5 hours of clerical time per week would be required. Since clerks work for a minimum of 40 hours per week, it would be necessary to employ one full-time clerk.

(b) Weekly budgeted costs

	$	$
Materials (500 × 1,000) + (700 × 750) + (850 ×900)		1,790,000
Direct labour (120 × 1,000) + (140 × 750) + (800 × 900)		945,000
Total direct costs		2,735,000
Indirect costs:		
Machine set-ups (500 × (8 + 15 + 9))	16,000	
Purchase orders (8 × (20 + 25 + 30))	600	
Storage costs (10 × (14 + 18 + 36))	680	
Total indirect costs		17,280
Total costs		2,752,280

Quantitative Analysis in Budgeting

FOCUS

This session covers the following content from the *ACCA Study Guide.*

C. Budgeting and Control

2. Quantitative analysis in budgeting

a) Analyse fixed and variable cost elements from total cost data using the high-low method.

b) Estimate the learning rate and learning effect.

c) Apply the learning curve to a budgetary problem, including calculations on steady states.

d) Discuss the reservations with the learning curve.

f) Explain the benefits and dangers inherent in using spreadsheets in budgeting.

Session 9 Guidance

■ **Know** the learning curve theory because it is an important area which is relevant in both budgeting and variance analysis (s.2).

■ **Note** that the learning curve formula is provided in the exam so you do not need to memorise it.

■ **Read** the article "The Learning Rate and Learning Effect".

VISUAL OVERVIEW

Objective: To master the quantitative aids which might be required in budgeting.

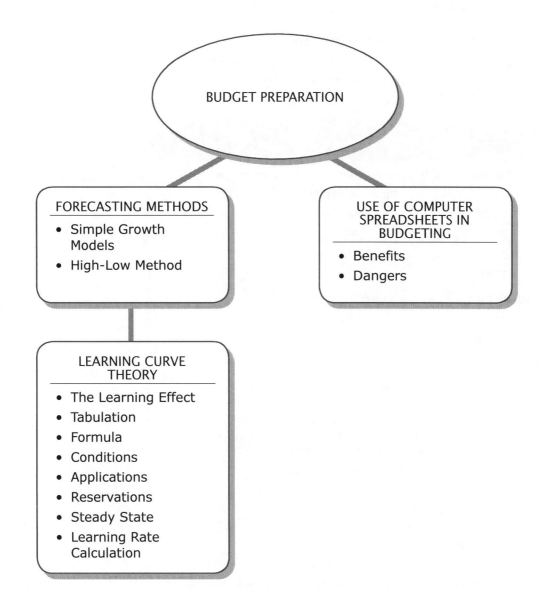

1 Forecasting Methods

1.1 Need for Forecasting

Management accountants need to use forecasts for many areas of their work. In budgeting, for example, it is useful to be able to forecast sales. This session looks at some mathematical forecasting techniques.

1.2 Simple Average Growth Models

Such models take average growth from the past, using the geometric mean, and assume that this level of growth will continue in the future.

Illustration 1 Geometric Mean

The sales of Beta during the last three years were as follows:

Year	Sales in $000
20X2	100
20X3	180
20X4	210
20X5	300

The growth rate of sales each year is as follows:

20X3	80% (180 − 100)/100
20X4	16.67% (210 − 180)/180
20X5	42.9% (300 − 210)/210

The simple average growth rate is 46.5% calculated as (80% + 16.67% + 42.9%)/3.

This overstates the rate of growth, however: If the 20X2 sales of $100,000 were to increase by 46.5% each year for three years, the sales in 20X5 would be $314,000, not $300,000.

The more accurate growth rate is obtained using the **geometric mean**.

Growing by 80% is the same as multiplying by 1.8 , so the geometric mean for the three years is $\sqrt[3]{1.8 \times 1.1667 \times 1.429}$ = 1.442, so the average growth rate is 44.2%.

This can then be used to calculate expected sales in future period.

1.3   High-Low Method

■ A crude method of estimating a value of *y* (cost) for a value of *x* (volume).

■ It selects costs associated with the highest and lowest levels of *activity* (i.e. *x*) and assumes all other costs lie on a straight line.

■ This method is limited by its crudeness. Furthermore, using extreme values to determine the relationship between two variables is probably dangerous, as extreme values are likely to be atypical.

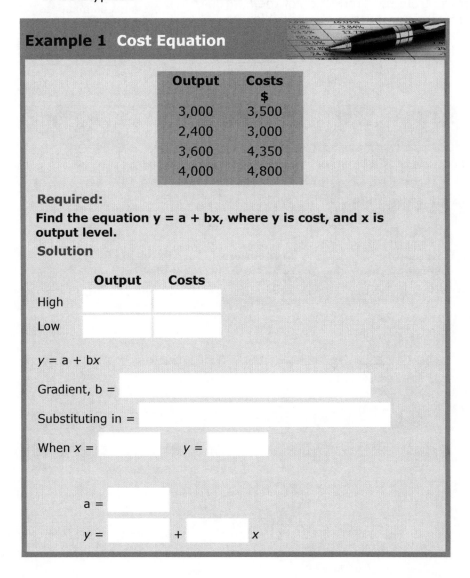

Example 1   Cost Equation

Output	Costs $
3,000	3,500
2,400	3,000
3,600	4,350
4,000	4,800

Required:

Find the equation y = a + bx, where y is cost, and x is output level.

Solution

	Output	Costs
High		
Low		

y = a + b*x*

Gradient, b =

Substituting in =

When *x* =   *y* =

a =

y =   +   *x*

2 Learning Curve Theory

*Commentary

2.1 The Learning Effect

■ If workers specialise, there is a tendency for labour hours per unit to fall as they become more familiar with the task.

■ During World War II, empirical evidence from aircraft production found the rate of improvement to be so regular that it could be reduced to a formula.

■ The learning effect starts from the production of the *first* unit/batch. Each time cumulative production then doubles, the cumulative average time per unit falls to a fixed percentage of the previous average time.*

*The theory states that as cumulative output doubles (e.g. from two to four units), the cumulative average time taken per unit will fall to a given percentage of the previous cumulative production. This percentage is the **learning rate**.

2.2 Tabulation

Example 2 Tabulation

A product will take 100 hours for the first unit, and an 80% learning curve applies.

Required:

Complete the table and graph which follow.

Solution

Table

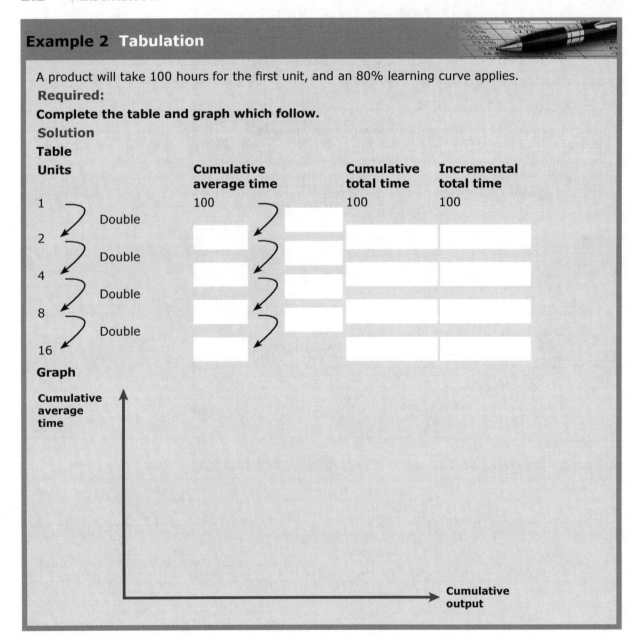

Units		Cumulative average time		Cumulative total time	Incremental total time
1	Double	100		100	100
2	Double				
4	Double				
8	Double				
16					

Graph

Cumulative average time

Cumulative output

What is the cumulative average time to produce 10 units?
The table does not cover this.

2.3   Learning Curve Formula

Although the graph could be used to provide an estimate, it is more accurate to use the following exam formula:

$$y = ax^b$$

The formula is provided in the exam

Where y = cumulative average time per unit to produce x units

        a = time taken for the first unit of output

        x = the cumulative number of units produced

        b = the index of learning (log LR/log 2)

        LR = the learning rate as a decimal.

Example 3   Using the Learning Curve Formula

Based on the information in *Example 2*, use the formula to check the cumulative average time for 8 units.

Note: The index of learning b is given as −0.3219.

Solution

    Y = [   ] hour

Example 4   Learning Curve Formula

It is estimated that it will take 500 hours to produce the first unit of a new product. Workers have a 95% learning effect.

Required:

Calculate how long it will take to produce the seventh unit.

Note: The index of learning b is given as −0.074.

Solution

	Average	Total
Cumulative average time for first seven units		
Total time for first seven units		
Cumulative average time for first six units		
Total time for first six units		
Total time for the seventh unit		

Example 5 Labour Cost

McSporran is a new business. It is budgeting costs for the production of kilts.

Work studies show that the first batch will have a labour cost of $2,000 and an 85% learning effect applies.

In period 1, budget production is 5 batches.

In period 2, budgeted production is 7 batches.

The wage rate per hour will be constant.*

Required:

Calculate the budgeted labour cost for period 2.

Note: The index of learning b is given as −0.2345.

Solution

Total cost for 12 batches =	$
Total cost for 5 batches =	$
Labour cost for period 2 =	$

*Commentary

*As the wage rate is constant, it is possible to use $s rather than hours in the formula.

In practice (and in many questions), the learning curve effect does not continue forever. At some point, a "steady state" is reached—beyond this point, hours per unit is constant.

2.4 Conditions for a Learning Curve to Apply

■ The activity is labour intensive.

■ The units are identical (i.e. a repetitive task).

■ Low labour turnover.

■ No prolonged breaks in production.*

*Commentary

*Thus the conditions for a learning curve to apply may lead to low morale and, hence, reduce the learning effect.

2.5 Applications of Learning Curve Theory

■ **Standard setting**—the labour standard should be set/revised based on the expected learning effect.

■ **Budgeting**—variable costs are expected to fall with an increase in production—particularly important to cash budgeting.

■ **Pricing decisions**—an accurate labour cost may be predicted into the future.

■ **Work scheduling**—manpower planning (e.g. as part of MRPII).*

*Commentary

*MRPII is a manufacturing resource planning system which integrates production scheduling, job costing, control of workforce, performance measurement, etc.

2.6 Reservations About the Learning Curve

✗ Knowing what the learning rate will be for new products. The usual assumption is that it will be similar to products made in the past. This may not always be a valid assumption.

✗ The learning curve is useful in situations where production of a product takes place on a continuous basis. If there is a break in production, however, workers may "forget" the skill and the learning curve will not be so predictable.

✗ In the modern business world, many products are tailor-made for customers. The idea of mass producing identical items, which is where learning curves are strongest, is not always appropriate.

✗ In some heavily unionised industries, there may be "go slow" agreements where workers agree not to work to their full capacity in order to save jobs.

2.7 Steady State

As cumulative output increases, the effect of the learning curve diminishes. When cumulative output reaches a certain point, there will be no further learning. The time taken per unit reaches a steady state and all units produced beyond this point will take the same amount of time per unit.

Example 6 Learning Curve and Steady State

Supercars produces cars on a production line. One of the production line processes, Process 10, is labour intensive.

A new model, the XY123, will be introduced to production next month. As this is a new model, the labourers in Process 10 will have to learn how to apply this process specifically to XY123.

The time taken for the first car is expected to be one hour. A learning rate of 85% is expected. The effect of the learning curve is expected to stop after 30 units have been produced and all subsequent units will take the same time to produce as the 30th unit.

Supercars has budgeted to manufacture 100 XY123s in the first month of production.

Required:

(a) Calculate the labour time per unit which will apply for the 30th and subsequent units.

(b) Calculate the total labour time to make the first 100 units of the XY123.

Note: The index of learning b is given as -0.2345.

2.8 Estimating the Learning Rate

2.8.1 Tabular Approach

A learning rate for a new product can be estimated using a tabular approach based on production to date and the time taken.

When the learning rate stops (i.e. when a "steady state" is reached, as described above) can also be calculated. This is the point at which the incremental time per unit becomes constant.

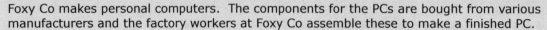

Example 7 Learning Rate

Foxy Co makes personal computers. The components for the PCs are bought from various manufacturers and the factory workers at Foxy Co assemble these to make a finished PC.

Production of a new type of PC has just begun. The management accountant has asked one of the workers to keep a record of how much time he took to make each new computer. The worker provided the following summary for the first month:

	Incremental time taken (minutes)
1st unit	340
2nd unit	204
3rd and 4th units	326
5th to 8th units	522
9th to 16th units	964
17th to 32nd units	1,929
Total	4,285

The time shown within each band is the total for that band, not the average per computer.

Required:

(a) Calculate the learning rate that applied to the new PC.

(b) Estimate the point at which the learning period finishes.

2.8.2 Algebraic Approach

An alternative approach to the tabular approach is an algebraic approach.

This has to be used when only information about the cumulative average time is for two levels of output.

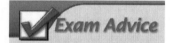

Exam Advice

This might be the case in a multiple-choice question.

Illustration 2 Algebraic Approach to Learning Rate

The first unit of a product took 300 minutes; the total time taken for the first 8 units was 2,056 minutes.

The cumulative average time per unit for the first 8 units is therefore 257 minutes (2,056 ÷ 8).

Cumulative output has doubled three times since the production of the first unit (from 1 to 2, to 4, then to 8) and the cumulative average time per unit has fallen to 257. If the learning rate is r:

$$\Rightarrow 300 \times r^3 = 257$$

$$\Rightarrow r^3 = \frac{257}{300} = 0.8567$$

$$\Rightarrow r = \sqrt[3]{0.8567} = 0.9497 \text{ i.e. approximately 95\%}$$

Example 8 Expected and Actual Learning Rates

Go Fast Cars has just started the manufacture of a new model of its "lightning" sports car. The time taken for one process was two hours for the first car produced. A budget was prepared using an expected 80% learning rate based on prior experience.

Recently, the company invested in sophisticated new manufacturing equipment. Workers are assisted by robots and computerised machine tools in the process in question. As this has enabled the company to reduce the workforce, a number of labourers have recently been made redundant.

The actual production time of the first 16 units was higher than expected, suggesting that the learning rate might be greater than 80%. The budgeted and actual cumulative total times for the first 16 units are given below in minutes:

Cumulative output	Cumulative total time budgeted	Cumulative total time actual	Cumulative average time actual
1	120	120	
2	192	216	
4	307	389	
8	492	700	
16	786	1,260	

Required:

(a) Calculate the actual learning rate experienced for this process.

(b) Suggest reasons why the actual learning rate was higher than expected.

3 Use of Computer Spreadsheets in Budgeting

The use of spreadsheet applications, such as Microsoft® Excel®, is widespread in most organisations and budgeting is one area in which spreadsheets are likely to be used.

3.1 Benefits of Using Spreadsheets in Budgeting

✔ Budgets may contain many lines of detail. Any line of the budget in a spreadsheet can easily be changed and totals, for example, will be automatically updated.

✔ Flexed budgets can easily be performed using a spreadsheet. When the quantity in the sales units' cell is changed, all the other cells are automatically recalculated.

✔ Master budgets, which are summarised budgets for the whole organisation, can be prepared in the same spreadsheet and linked into the subsidiary budgets so that any changes to the subsidiary budgets will automatically be reflected in the master budget.

3.2 Dangers of Using Spreadsheets in Budgeting

✗ It is easy for errors to appear in formulae in spreadsheet models. Thus budgeted figures may be incorrect if they are based on an incorrect formula.

✗ Because users may be familiar with spreadsheet models, they may change parts of the standard budgeting pro forma documents without authorisation.

✗ Spreadsheet models are often developed and designed by the users of the spreadsheets. This means the organisation does little to control the development of spreadsheets.

✗ Few users are given any meaningful training in how to use Excel® or similar products.

Summary

- The high-low method is a crude method used to find the relationship, which takes only the highest and lowest values from the sample.

- Learning curve theory is based on the concept that the time taken to make a unit of a product or service falls as workers become more experienced. As cumulative output doubles, the cumulative average time taken falls to a given factor.

Session 9 Quiz
Estimated time: 50 minutes

1. Distinguish between the simple average growth forecasting model and the high-low model. (1.2, 1.3)

2. List and explain the applications of the learning curve formula. (2.5)

3. Identify TWO benefits and TWO dangers of using spreadsheets in budgeting. (3.1, 3.2)

Study Question Bank
Estimated time: 1 hour

Priority		Estimated Time	Completed
Q17	Tompkins Co	10 minutes	
Q18	Mermus Co	50 minutes	

EXAMPLE SOLUTIONS

Solution 1—Cost Equation

	Output	Costs
High	4,000	4,800
Low	2,400	3,000

$y = a + bx$

Gradient, $b = \dfrac{4,800 - 3,000}{4,000 - 2,400} = \dfrac{1,800}{1,600} = \dfrac{18}{16} = 1.125$

Substituting in low level of activity (alternatively, use high level)

When $x = 2,400$ $y = 3,000$

$3,000 = a + 1.125 \times 2,400$

$3,000 = a + 2,700$

$a = 300$

$y = 300 + 1.125\,x$

Solution 2—Tabulation

Units		Cumulative average time		Cumulative total time	Incremental total time
1	⟍ Double	100	⟍ × 80%	100	100
2	⟍ Double	80	⟍ × 80%	160	60
4	⟍ Double	64	⟍ × 80%	256	96
8	⟍ Double	51.2	⟍ × 80%	409.6	153.6
16		40.96		655.36	245.76

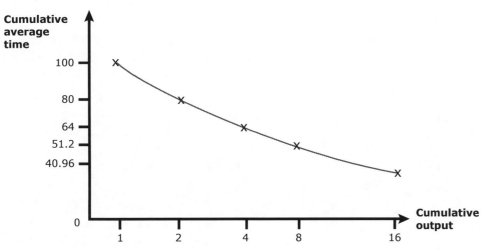

Solution 3—Using the Learning Curve Formula

$Y = 100 \times 8^{-0.3219} = 100 \times 0.512 = 51.2$ hour

Solution 4—Learning Curve Formula

	Average	Total
Cumulative average time for first seven units $(Y = 500 \times 7^{-0.074})$	432.95	
Total time for first seven units (7 x 432.95)		3,030.65
Cumulative average time for first six units $(Y = 500 \times 6^{-0.074})$	437.91	
Total time for first six units (6 x 437.91)		2,627.46
Total time for the seventh unit		403.19

Solution 5—Labour Cost

Labour cost for period 2 = Total cost for 12 batches – Total cost for 5 batches

                           (period 1 and 2)   (period 1)

Total cost for 12 batches = 12 $(2,000 \times 12^{-0.2345})$ = \$13,401

Total cost for 5 batches = 5 $(2,000 \times 5^{-0.2345})$ = \$6,856

Labour cost for period 2 = 13,401 − 6,856 = \$6,545

Solution 6—Learning Curve and Steady State

(a) Labour time for the 30th and subsequent units

	Hours
Total time taken to make the first 30 units (W)	13.513
Less: Total time taken to make the first 29 units (W)	13.166
Time taken to make the 30th and subsequent units	0.347

Working*

Using the formula $Y = ax^b$

$b = -0.2345$ (given)

$a = 1$

For first 30 units:

Cumulative average time per unit, $Y = 30^{-0.2345}$	0.45042	
Total time (30 × 0.45042)		13.513

For first 29 units:

Cumulative average time per unit, $Y = 29^{-0.2345}$	0.45401	
Total time (29 × 0.45401)		13.166

Commentary

*For the total hours to be accurate to 3 decimal places it is necessary to calculate the average times per unit to 5 decimal places (because they are to be multiplied by numbers between 10 and 100). If the numbers of units were less than 10, the average times would need to be only to 4 decimal places.

(b) Total labour time for the first 100 units*

	Hours
Total time taken to make the first 30 units (per (a))	13.51
Time taken to make the next 70 units (70 × 0.347)	24.29
Time taken to make the first 100 units (hours)	37.80

Commentary

*After the 30th unit, the time per unit remains constant at 0.347 hours per unit, the same as the time taken for the 30th unit since the learning effect ceases at this point.

Solution 7—Learning Rate

(a) Learning rate

Cumulative output (units)	Cumulative total time (minutes)	Cumulative average time per unit (minutes)
1	340	340
2	544	272
4	870	218
8	1,392	174
16	2,356	147
32	4,285	134

As cumulative output doubles:

From 1 to 2 units: 272/340 = 80%

From 2 to 4 units: 218/272 = 80%

Therefore the learning rate appears to be 80%.

(b) End of learning period

The learning rate ends when the incremental time per unit becomes constant. Because there is no information about the time taken for each individual item, it is necessary to calculate the average incremental time for each group or band of units produced. When this becomes constant, the learning process ends:

	Incremental time taken	Average incremental time
1st unit	340	340
2nd unit	204	204
3rd and 4th units	326	163
5th to 8th units	522	131
9th to 16th units	964	120.5
17th to 32nd units	1,929	120.5

The time taken per unit becomes constant at 120.5 from the start of the band that includes the 9th to the 16th unit.

Conclusion: The learning effect ends after the 8th unit.

Solution 8—Expected and Actual Learning Rates

(a) Actual learning rate

Cumulative output	Cumulative total time budgeted	Cumulative total time actual	Cumulative average time actual
1	120	120	120.00
2	192	216	108.00
4	307	389	97.25
8	492	700	87.50
16	786	1,260	78.75

As cumulative output doubles from 1 to 2, cumulative average time falls to 90% (108/120). This is repeated as cumulative output doubles from 2 to 4 (97.25/108), 4 to 8 (87.5/97.25) and 8 to 16 (78.75/87.5).

The actual learning rate is therefore 90%. This is higher than the expected learning rate of 80%, leading to the actual time taken being higher than budgeted.

(b) Possible reasons for higher learning rate*

In the past, Go Fast Cars experienced learning rates of 80% when introducing new models. The new model has a higher learning rate of 90%, to the surprise (and no doubt disappointment) of management. It is necessary to identify the factors that may have led to this.

The learning curve is most significant in more labour-intensive industries where the tasks are repetitive, there is low labour turnover and staff members are motivated. In such situations, staff will learn more quickly, leading to a lower learning rate.

Several developments at Go Fast Cars may have reduced the learning effect and led to a higher learning rate.

- The introduction of technology means that the processes are less labour intensive. There is therefore less scope for learning, as much of the process is likely to be automated anyway and automated processed are likely to work at a constant rate.

- The recent redundancies may have demotivated the remaining staff members, as they may believe that the company has little loyalty towards them. When morale is low, employees are less likely to work as productively as they can, leading to a higher learning rate.

*Commentary

*It is potentially confusing that a higher learning rate means that the effect of learning is lower. In this example, the actual learning rate was 90% compared with a budgeted learning rate of 80%. The higher rate meant that the actual time taken to produce the first 16 units exceeded the time budgeted.

Session 10

Standard Costing

FOCUS

This session covers the following content from the *ACCA Study Guide.*

C. Budgeting and Control

3. Standard costing

a) Explain the use of standard costs.

b) Outline the methods used to derive standard costs and discuss the different types of cost possible.

c) Explain and illustrate the importance of flexing budgets in performance management.

d) Explain and apply the principle of controllability in the performance management system.

Session 10 Guidance

- **Note** that this is a theoretical session which explains why standard costing and variance analysis is used. Pay attention; the topics here could form a small part of a longer variance analysis question.
- **Learn** the uses of standard costs, particularly in budgeting (s.1).
- **Understand** standard setting; distinguishing between the ideal and practical approaches (s.2).

(continued on next page)

VISUAL OVERVIEW

Objective: To examine the purpose of standard costing and the principles behind setting standards and budgets.

```
┌─────────────────────────────────┐
│      USE OF STANDARD COSTS      │
│                                 │
│  • By Management                │
│  • Variance Investigation       │
│  • Uses of Standard Costing     │
│    Systems                      │
│  • Examples                     │
│  • In Budgeting                 │
└─────────────────────────────────┘
                 │
┌─────────────────────────────────┐
│       DERIVING STANDARDS        │
│                                 │
│  • Setting Standards            │
│  • Ideal Standards              │
│  • Practical Standards          │
│  • Information Used for Setting  │
│    Standards                    │
└─────────────────────────────────┘
                 │
┌─────────────────────────────────┐
│                                 │
│        CONTROLLABILITY          │
│                                 │
└─────────────────────────────────┘
                 │
┌─────────────────────────────────┐
│        FLEXING BUDGETS          │
│                                 │
│  • Importance                   │
│  • Usefulness                   │
│  • Preparation                  │
└─────────────────────────────────┘
```

Session 10 Guidance

■ **Understand** that the controllability principle (s.3) is a particularly important concept in performance management. Attempt *Example 1*.

■ **Work** *Example 2* and practice preparing a flexed budget (s.4).

1 Use of Standard Costs

1.1 By Management

Production costs are affected by internal factors over which management has a large degree of control. An important role of executive management is to help departmental managers to understand their part in contributing to the success of the firm.

Standard costs and the variances which arise from them:

- Keep management informed about the economy, efficiency and effectiveness of production processes.
- Facilitate supervisory personnel being made directly responsible for the variances under their control.

Variances provide a measure of the fairness of standards and facilitate further analysis, investigation and action (e.g. to eliminate causes of undesirable variances).

- Adjustments should be made to an unreasonable standard if variance analysis is to be meaningful.
- Variance analysis should encourage and reward cost control commensurate with desired levels of performance.

Definition

Standard cost—the predetermined cost of producing a single unit (or batch) of a product (goods or service) during a specific period in the near future. It is the planned cost of a product under current and/or anticipated operating conditions.

Definition

Variances—differences between actual prices and standard prices and actual quantities and standard quantities.

Variance analysis—the process of calculating and interpreting variances.

An example of a calculation of a standard cost, often referred to as a "standard cost card", is shown in *Illustration 1*.

Illustration 1 Standard Cost Card

Product XYZ

		$ Per Unit
Sales price		100
Production		
Materials	(2 kg @ $20/kg)	40
Labour	(1.5 hrs @ $2/hr)	3
Variable overhead	(1.5 hrs @ $6/hr)	9
Fixed overhead	(1.5 hrs @ $10/hr)	15
Standard cost of production		67
Standard profit per unit		33

A standard provides a "benchmark" or "norm" for measuring performance. Standards are widely used (recommended daily allowances (RDA), drinking measures, materials standards for building constructions, quality standards, health and safety standards).

In management accounting, standards generally relate to two aspects of inputs used in producing goods/services:

1. **Quantity standards** specify how much resource (raw materials, labour) *should be input* to produce a unit of product/ service.

2. **Price (or cost) standards** stipulate how much *should be paid* for each unit of resource.

The main reason for categorising standards—into price and quantity—is because different managers are usually responsible for the activities of buying and using inputs which occur at different points in time. For example:

- The purchasing manager's responsibility is exercised when materials are purchased.

- The production or factory manager's responsibility is exercised only when the materials are used, which could be months later (even in a different budget period).

Management should investigate the significant variances revealed (by a comparison of actual quantities and prices against the standards) to establish their cause(s) and to take corrective action to prevent their reoccurrence. Management "by exception" is facilitated because investigation is unnecessary if deviations are insignificant.*

*Commentary

*An expectation that has not been met is an opportunity to uncover the root of the problem. If the underlying cause is not discovered and corrected, the problem is likely to recur and may worsen.

1.2   Variance Investigation

The main purpose of **variance investigation** is to improve operations.

- Actual cost and performance is compared with the standard cost of actual performance reports and the level of actual performance against what was expected (budgeted).

- The differences between actual results and what should have happened according to the standards are **variances**.

- Management should consider both the nature ("why did it arise?") and magnitude ("how much has it increased"?) of any variance.

- A corrective action could include re-calibrating/re-setting the specifications of an item of equipment or changing a supplier.

- An amended standard cost may be prepared for the next period.

VARIANCE INVESTIGATION

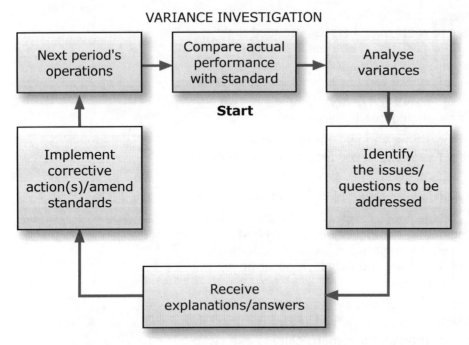

1.3 Uses of Standard Costing Systems

✔ To assist in planning by providing management with insights into the probable effect of decisions on cost levels (and profits).

✔ To help establish budgets (see later).

✔ To control costs, direct and motivate employees and measure efficiencies.

✔ To highlight opportunities for possible cost reductions.

✔ To simplify costing of products and facilitate reporting of costs on a timely basis.

✔ To assign cost (e.g. through processes of allocation, apportionment and absorption) to inventories of raw materials, work in process and finished goods.

✔ To provide a cost basis on which to tender for contracts/set sales prices (see sessions on relevant costing and pricing).

1.4 Examples of Use

■ **In production**, many manufacturing companies use "standard cost cards" to specify the standard amount of resources (components, materials, different grades of labour, machine time, overheads, etc) and the standard price for each product.

■ **Service centres** for national chains of car service centres (e.g. Kwik Fit) set standard labour times and parts to be used in routine car maintenance tasks (e.g. changing spark plugs, replacing exhaust/tyres, etc). Actual performance can be compared against standard for each service centre.

■ **Restaurant and drink retail outlets** (e.g. Pizza Express, Starbucks) have standards for ingredients (quality, quantity and price), speed of service, etc.

■ **Hotel chains** may use standards for many aspects of their operations—laundry, housekeeping, restaurants and bars.

1.5   Use of Standards in Budgeting

Budgeting is a method by which reliable information relating to the operation and control of an entity is obtained on a timely basis. Like budgets, standard costs:

✔ facilitate control and highlight possibilities for cost reductions;

✔ use predetermined costs for the budget period; and

✔ provide information for reports which compare actual costs with predetermined costs (see operating statements later).

	Budget	**Standards**
Scope	A statement of expected costs (to direct activities to an agreed action plan).	Specify what costs should be for a level of performance achieved.
Highlights	Volume of activity and level of costs to be maintained (as desired by management).	Level to which costs should be reduced (to increase profit).

2   Deriving Standards

2.1   Setting Standards

Standard setting calls for the combined expertise of those responsible for procuring resource inputs and overseeing their use. For a production company, this usually will include accountants, buyers, engineering and factory supervisors and managers.

Historical records provide information which might be used in setting standards. Standards should be set, however, to encourage efficient future operations (so not attainable all of the time) rather than repeat past inefficiencies.

When setting standards, two approaches can be taken regarding the level of difficulty; ideal or practical.

2.2   Ideal Standards

These are standards which can only be achieved under ideal operating circumstances. They do not make allowances for:

▉ Machine breakdowns

▉ Interruptions to schedule

▉ Idle time/capacity.

The usefulness of ideal standards may be viewed both positively and negatively:

✔ They are a constant reminder to strive to improve economy, efficiency and effectiveness.

✗ They are demotivating, as managers know that they will never be able to achieve them.

✗ When examining variances, it is difficult to assess how much of the adverse variance is because the standard is unrealistic and actual operating conditions are inefficient.

2.3 Practical Standards

Practical standards are challenging but should be attainable under existing operating conditions. They do make an allowance for a normal (i.e. expected) level of:

- machine breakdowns; and
- breaks (rests) by the workforce.

They do, however, require a high, though reasonable, level of efficiency. Practical standards are more likely than ideal standards to be used because:

✔ They are achievable so managers will be motivated.

✔ Any variances will highlight only abnormal conditions for the attention of management. This is useful for assisting in "management by exception".

2.4 Information Used for Setting Standards

In setting standards, for each input used two standards have to be determined:

1. Price per unit of input (kgs, hours).

2. Quantity used per unit of output.

There are multiple methods which might be used for setting these standards.

2.4.1 Price per Unit of Input

- The price is normally set to reflect current market prices for the budgeted period.

- The difficulty with prices is that they may change due to external factors. A solution to this is that the budget or standard may be revised prior to performing variance analysis to take this into account. Revisions of budgets are dealt with in a later session.

2.4.2 Quantity of Materials

- Quantity may be determined by a "bill of materials" prepared by product design, the engineering department or a works foreman.

- Allowance may be made for an expected level of waste.

2.4.3 Direct Labour Hours

- "Time and motion" studies of operations may be used to determine the most efficient production method.

- Time measurements determine standard hours for the typical worker to complete a job.

2.4.4 Wage Rates

- Wage rates are determined by company policy/negotiations between management and unions. Sometimes standards may have to be set before the annual wage negotiations have been concluded.

2.4.5   Variable Overheads

▪ A standard variable overhead rate per unit of activity is calculated. This may be labour hours.

▪ If there is no observable direct relationship between resources and output, past data is used to predict.

▪ The activity measure which exerts the greatest influence on costs is investigated—usually direct labour hours (although an alternative is to use machine hours).

2.4.6   Fixed Overheads

▪ Because fixed costs are largely independent of changes in activity, they are constant over wide ranges in the short term.

▪ Therefore, for control purposes, a fixed overhead rate per unit of activity is inappropriate.

▪ For inventory valuation purposes, IAS 2 requires standard fixed overhead rates.

3   Controllability

The controllability principle is that managers should be judged only on things within their control.

In a system of responsibility accounting, managers are given responsibility for particular areas of the organisation. At the end of the period, the performance of managers may be judged at least in part by:

▪ **variances** which are attributed to their department;

▪ **differences** between actual and budgeted revenues, costs and profits.

Managers' remuneration may also be linked to this (e.g. bonuses could be paid if managers achieve their budgeted profit figures). It is clearly important therefore that the performance management system is fair.

Example 1   Controllability

Ron is the production manager of a factory making ball bearings. His performance is judged using variance analysis. The variance analysis for the last month has just been performed and includes the following:

• An adverse materials price variance due to a change in the supplier. The supplier was changed because the production manager complained that the quality of the products sold by the old supplier was substandard.

• A labour idle time variance caused by two factors:

  1. A strike lasting two days over pay.

  2. A machine breakdown, meaning staff could not work until the machine was fixed.

• A fixed overhead variance caused by an increase in factory rent. All rental contracts are dealt with by the company's legal department.

Required:

Discuss which of the events above (if any) are outside of Ron's control and should, therefore, be ignored when assessing his performance.

---

4 Flexing Budgets

4.1 Importance of Flexed Budgets

At the start of the year when a budget is prepared, estimates are made about the volume of sales and production. It is unlikely that the actual volume of sales and production will be the same as per the budget. This makes it difficult to compare actual performance against the budget, as they are based on different levels of activity.

The budget can be **flexed** at the end of the period before this comparison takes place.

The flexed budget is then compared to the actual results. This results in a more valid comparison, as like is being compared with like.

Finally, three figures arise:

1. Original budget
(standard costs/revenues at expected activity level) } Volume variances

2. Flexed budget
(standard costs/revenues at actual activity level) }

3. Actual results } Other variances

> **Key Point**
>
> Flexing the budget simply means that the budget is recalculated based on the original budget assumptions (such as cost per unit, selling prices, etc) but uses the *actual* volume of sales and production.

Illustration 2 Budgeted v Actual Results

The following are extracts from a firm's budgeted and actual results:

Budgeted production	100 units
Budgeted materials cost per unit	$5
Actual production	200 units
Actual materials cost per unit	$4

The three relevant figures here are as follows:

Original budget	100 × $5 =	$500
Flexed budget	200 × $5 =	$1,000
Actual cost	200 × $4 =	$800

The $500 difference between the original budget and the flexed budget reflects the additional expected cost which resulted from higher-than-expected volume. The $200 difference between the flexed budget and the actual cost reflects the fact that $200 less was spent on materials than expected given the volume of activity. This variance is the more useful assessment of performance.

4.2 Usefulness

✔ The flexed budget is prepared at the same level of activity as actual output.

✔ Actual revenues and costs are compared to what budgeted costs and revenues should be for the actual level of activity achieved. This highlights variances caused by higher or lower prices and costs than budgeted, and different levels of activity.

✔ The difference between the original budgeted profit and the flexed budget profit shows the effect on profit of operating at a different activity level from plan.

4.3   Preparation of Flexed Budgets

Example 2 Flexed Budgets

A company has obtained the following information regarding costs and revenue for the past financial year:

Original budget:

Sales	10,000 units
Production	12,000 units

Standard cost per unit:

	$
Direct materials	5
Direct labour	9
Fixed production overheads	8
	22
Standard selling price	30

Actual results:

Sales	9,750 units
Revenue	$325,000
Production	11,000 units
Material cost	$65,000
Labour cost	$100,000
Fixed production overheads	$95,000

There were no opening stocks.

Required:

Produce a flexed budget statement showing the flexed budget and actual results. Calculate the total variances (differences) between the actual and flexed figures for the following:

- sales;
- materials;
- labour; and
- fixed production overhead.

Solution	Flexed budget	Actual results	Variances	
Sales—units				
Production—units				
	$000	$000	$000	Adverse/ favourable
Sales price				
Cost of sales				
Opening inventory				
Production costs:				
Materials				
Labour				
Fixed production overheads				
Total production costs				
Closing inventory				
Total cost of sales				
Profit				

Summary

- A standard cost is a planned cost for a product or service. Actual costs are compared against the standard, and the resulting variances are investigated to identify the cause. Thus, standard costing is an important element in financial control.

- Ideal standards, which assume perfect operating efficiency, may be set. This is unlikely to be achieved in practice, so the use of ideal standards is demotivating. An alternative method is to set practical standards which are challenging but achievable under existing operating conditions.

- Controllability principle is the principle that managers should be evaluated only on things which are within their control. Controllability is an important factor to take into account when using variance analysis to assess a manager.

- Budgets may be "flexed" prior to comparison with actual results. Flexing a budget means recalculating the budget based on the original budget assumptions, at the actual level of activity.

Session 10 Quiz
Estimated time: 15 minutes

1. List THREE uses of a standard cost. (1.3)

2. Briefly explain the meaning of "ideal standard". (2.2)

3. True or false? Standards should never include an allowance for a normal or expected level of waste. (2.4.2)

4. Summarise the meaning of the controllability principle. (3)

EXAMPLE SOLUTIONS

Solution 1—Controllability

Materials price variance. This variance was caused by Ron's decision to switch supplier. He should, therefore, be held responsible for the variance. His decision to switch supplier may have been sensible, and may reflect positively on some of his other variances, but the price variance was caused by Ron.

Idle time variance—the strike. There is no clear-cut answer to this. On the one hand, it could be argued that the strike was caused by the unions rather than by Ron so he was not to blame. On the other hand, it could be that as factory manager, Ron is ultimately responsible for decisions about hiring staff, and therefore the strike could have been averted. It partly depends on how much responsibility Ron has for agreeing and negotiating wages.

Idle time variance—machine breakdown. At first it may appear that the machine breakdown was outside of Ron's control. However, as factory manager, Ron is responsible for the maintenance of the machines in the factory and, therefore, any breakdowns.

Fixed overhead variance. It seems fairly clear-cut that this particular expense is outside of Ron's control. He has no responsibility for negotiating the rent. Therefore, he should not be "blamed" for this variance.

Solution 2—Flexed Budgets

	Flexed budget	Actual results	Variances	
Sales—units	9,750	9,750		
Production—units	11,000	11,000		
	$000	**$000**	**$000**	**Adverse/ favourable**
Sales price (30 × 9,750)	292.5	325	32.5	favourable
Cost of sales				
Opening inventory	0		0	
Production costs:				
Materials (5 × 11,000)	55	65	10	adverse
Labour (9 × 11,000)	99	100	1	adverse
Fixed production overheads (8 × 12,000)	96	95	1	favourable
Total production costs	250	260	10	adverse
Closing inventory (22 × (11,000–9,750))	(27.5)	(27.5)		
Total cost of sales	222.5	232.5		
Profit	70	92.5	22.5	favourable

Basic Variance Analysis

FOCUS

This session is a revision of F2 and covers the following content from the F2 *ACCA Study Guide.*

D. Standard Costing

1. Standard costing systems

a) Explain the purpose and principles of standard costing.

b) Explain and illustrate the difference between standard, marginal and absorption costing.

c) Establish the standard cost per unit under absorption and marginal costing.

2. Variance calculations and analysis

a) Calculate sales price and volume variance.

b) Calculate materials total, price and usage variance.

c) Calculate labour total, rate and efficiency variance.

d) Calculate variable overhead total, expenditure and efficiency variance.

e) Calculate fixed overhead total, expenditure and, where appropriate, volume, capacity and efficiency variance.

f) Interpret the variances.

g) Explain factors to consider before investigating variances, explain possible causes of the variances and recommend control action.

h) Explain the interrelationships between the variances.

i) Calculate actual or standard figures where the variances are given.

3. Reconciliation of budgeted and actual profit

a) Reconcile budgeted profit with actual profit under standard absorption costing.

b) Reconcile budgeted profit or contribution with actual profit or contribution under standard marginal costing.

Session 11 Guidance

■ **Note** that this session is revision of the F2 variances; however there is one new variance, the labour idle time variance, so be sure to study this carefully.

■ **Pay** attention that although these variances are F2 level, there have been many questions on them in past F5 exams for which marks have been awarded.

VISUAL OVERVIEW

Objective: To revise basic variances for sales, materials, labour and overheads. To produce an operating statement under either absorption costing or marginal costing principles.

VARIANCE ANALYSIS

- Introduction
- Sales Variances
- Materials Variances
- Labour Variances
- Variable Overhead Variances
- Fixed Overhead Variances

THE OPERATING STATEMENT

MARGINAL COSTING APPROACH

- Differences
- Pro Forma

INVENTORY AT ACTUAL COST

- Profit
- Variances
- Accounts

CAUSES OF VARIANCES

- General Causes
- Specific Causes
- Interdependence of Variances

1 Variance Analysis

1.1 Introduction

This session revises the "basic variances" examined in F2 Management Accounting and introduces the labour idle time variance.*

Commentary

*Although "basic" variances are examined in F2 *Management Accountant*, they are also examined in F5. However, at this level there is more emphasis on understanding the possible causes.

Example 1 Variance Analysis

The standard revenue and cost of a squidget is as follows:

		$ per unit
Standard		
Sales price		100
Costs:		
Material	(2 kg @ $20/kg)	40
Labour	(1½ hrs @ $2/hr)	3
Variable overheads	(1½ hrs @ $6/hr)	9
Fixed overheads	(1½ hrs @ $10/hr)	15
Cost of production		67
Profit per unit		33

Original budget		$ per unit	$000
Sales	(50,000 squidgets @ $100)	100	5,000
Production	(55,000 squidgets)		
Materials	(110,000 kg @ $20/kg)	40	2,200
Labour	(82,500 hrs @ $2/hr)	3	165
Variable overheads	(82,500 hrs @ $6/hr)	9	495
Fixed overheads	(82,500 hrs @ $10/hr)	15	825
Standard cost of production		67	3,685
Less: Closing inventory	(5,000 @ $67)		(335)
Standard cost of goods sold			3,350
Budgeted profit	(50,000 @ $33)	33	1,650

Example 1 Variance Analysis (continued)

		$000	$000
Actual results			
Sales	(53,000 squidgets @ $95)		5,035
Production	(56,000 squidgets)		
Materials			
Purchased	130,000 kg	2,700	
Closing inventory	20,000 kg @$20	(400)	
			2,300
Labour	(85,000 hrs paid)		180
	(83,000 hrs worked)		
Variable overhead			502
Fixed overhead			935
			3,917
Closing inventory	(3,000 @ $67)		(201)
			3,716
Actual profit			1,319

A calculation of the **flexed budget** shows the following variances:

		Flexed budget	Actual	Variance
		$000	$000	$000
Sales	(53,000 × $100)	5,300	5,035	265 Adverse
Production costs				
Materials	(56,000 × 2kg × $20)	2,240	2,300	60 Adverse
Labour	(56,000 × 1½ hrs × $2)	168	180	12 Adverse
Variable overheads	(56,000 × 1½ hrs × $6)	504	502	2 Favourable
Fixed overheads	(56,000 × 1½ hrs × $10)	840	935	95 Adverse
Less: Closing inventory		(201)	(201)	
Cost of goods sold		3,551	3,716	
Profit		1,749	1,319	

Required:

(a) **Calculate the variances for:**

   (i)   **Sales volume**

   (ii) **Materials usage**

   (iii) **Labour and variable overhead**

(b) **Draft an operating statement under:**

   (i)   **Absorption costing**

   (ii) **Marginal costing**

Note:
The information in *Example 1* will be used in the calculations in subsequent pages. You may wish to bookmark it for ease of reference.

1.2 Sales Variances

1.2.1 Sales Volume Variance

This variance shows the effect of selling more or less than the budgeted quantity on profits.

> **Example 1 Variance Analysis (continued)**
>
> **(a) Variances**
>
> | **(i) Sales Volume** | | **Units** |
> |---|---|---|
> | Actual sales | | |
> | Budgeted sales | | |
> | Difference | | |
> | × standard profit per unit | $ | |
> | Sales volume variance | $ | |
>
> *Note:*
> Here, the difference between actual and budgeted sales is multiplied by the standard profit per unit, as absorption costing is being used. If marginal costing is used, multiply the difference by the **standard contribution** per unit.

1.2.2 Sales Price Variance

Shows the effect on profit of selling at a higher or lower price than the standard:

> **Example 1 Variance Analysis (continued)**
>
> **(a) Variances**
>
> | **(ii) Sales Price** | **$000** |
> |---|---|
> | Actual sales × actual price (actual revenue) | |
> | Actual sales × standard price | |
> | Sales price variance | |
>
> *Note:*
> Variances are categorised as **favourable** if they would lead to an increase in profits or adverse if they would lead to a fall in profits.

1.3   Materials Variances

1.3.1   Causes

The total cost variance of $60,000 Adverse from the flexed budget in *Example 1* can be broken down into two further variances:

- **Price,** if the price paid per kilogram is not at standard.
- **Usage,** if more (or less) than should have been for the production achieved.

1.3.2   Materials Price Variance

> **Example 1   Variance Analysis** (continued)
>
> **(a)   Variances**
>
> **(iii) Materials Price**   **$000**
>
> Actual materials purchased at actual price
>
> Actual materials purchased at standard price
>
> Materials price variance
>
> *Note:*
> The **materials price variance** is based on the quantity of materials purchased during the period. If more materials are purchased than used, the unused materials go into inventory at standard cost.

1.3.3   Materials Usage Variance

> **Example 1   Variance Analysis** (continued)
>
> **(a)   Variances**
>
> **(iv) Materials Usage**   **Kilos**
>
> Materials used
>
> Standard materials for actual production
>
> Difference
>
> × standard price per kilo $
>
> Materials usage variance $
>
> *Note:*
> When calculating **usage and efficiency variances,** always compare actual usage to the standard for actual output, not to the original budgeted usage.

1.4 Labour Variances

1.4.1 Causes

The total labour cost variance of $12,000 Adverse from the flexed budget in *Example 1* can be broken down into three variances.

1. Rate, if a non-standard hourly rate is paid.

2. Idle time, if there were unproductive hours.

3. Efficiency, if more (or fewer) hours were worked than should have been.

1.4.2 Labour Rate Variance

Example 1 Variance Analysis (continued)

(a) Variances

(v) Labour Rate Variance $000

Hours paid at actual rate

Hours paid at standard rate

Labour rate variance

1.4.3 Idle Time Variance

Example 1 Variance Analysis (continued)

(a) Variances

(vi) Idle Time Variance Hours

Hours paid

Hours worked

Idle time

× standard hourly rate $

Idle time variance $

1.4.4 Labour Efficiency Variance

Example 1 Variance Analysis (continued)

(a) Variances

(vii) Labour Efficiency Variance   **Hours**

Labour hours worked

Standard labour hours for actual production

Difference

          × standard rate per hour $

Labour efficiency variance $

Note:
In principle, the **labour rate variance** is the same as the materials price variance, and the **labour efficiency variance** is the same as the materials usage variance.

1.5 Variable Overhead Variances

1.5.1 Causes

The total variable overhead cost variance of $2,000 Favourable from the flexed budget in *Example 1* can be broken down into two variances where variable overheads are accounted for on a labour hour basis:

1. Rate, if the actual rate incurred is non-standard.

2. Efficiency, which is identical in cause to the labour efficiency variance but is calculated using the standard variable overhead absorption rate.

1.5.2 Variable Overhead Rate Variance

Example 1 Variance Analysis (continued)

(a) Variances

(viii) Variable Overhead Rate Variance   **$000**

Labour hours worked × actual rate (actual variable overhead cost)

Labour hours worked × standard variable overhead rate per hour

Variable overhead rate variance

Note:
It is assumed that variable overheads are incurred during *productive* labour hours.

1.5.3 Variable Overhead Efficiency Variance

Example 1 Variance Analysis (continued)

(a) Variances

(ix) Variable Overhead Efficiency Variance	**Hours**
Labour hours worked	
Standard labour hours for actual production	
Difference	
× standard variable overhead rate per hour	$
Variable overhead efficiency variance	$

Note:
As for the labour efficiency variance, the **variable overhead efficiency variance** compares the actual hours worked with the standard labour hours. The logic is that if more/less hours are worked than the standard, not only will management have to pay more/less wages, but variable overheads will increase/decrease, because these are incurred when people are working. Machines will be working, for example, so additional power costs will be incurred.

1.6 Fixed Overhead Variances

1.6.1 Causes

Two possible variances arise:

1. The **expenditure variance** compares the actual fixed cost with the original budget. If the company uses marginal costing, this is the only variance which is calculated.

2. If the company uses absorption costing, a second variance is calculated, called the **volume variance.** A "favourable" fixed overhead volume variance corrects profits for over-absorption and an "adverse" variance corrects for under-absorption.

1.6.2 Fixed Overhead Expenditure Variance

Example 1 Variance Analysis (continued)

(a) Variances

(x) Fixed Overhead Expenditure Variance	**$000**
Actual fixed cost	
Budgeted fixed cost	
Fixed overhead expenditure variance	

1.6.3 Fixed Overhead Volume Variance

(a) Variances

(xi) Fixed Overhead Volume Variance | **Units**

	Units
Actual production	
Budgeted production	
Difference	
× standard fixed overhead rate per unit	$
Fixed overhead volume variance	$

1.6.4 Fixed Overhead Capacity and Efficiency Variances

If the fixed overhead is absorbed using labour hours, then the fixed **overhead volume variance** can be further analysed into two additional variances: the capacity variance and the efficiency variance.

The **capacity variance** compares actual labour hours worked with the original budget. If more hours were worked than budgeted, then more fixed overheads are absorbed, so there will be a favourable variance. If fewer hours were worked than budgeted, then there will be an adverse variance.

The **efficiency variance** is similar to the labour efficiency and variable overhead efficiency variances. It compares the actual labour hours worked with the standard labour hours for actual output.

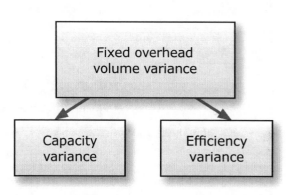

(a) Variances

(xii) Fixed Overhead Capacity and Efficiency Variance

	Hours			Hours
Actual labour hours		Actual labour hours		
Budgeted labour hours		Standard hours for actual output		
Difference				
× standard rate per hour	$	× standard rate per hour	$	
Capacity variance	$	Efficiency variance	$	

2   The Operating Statement

The operating statement is a formal reconciliation of budgeted profit (under absorption costing) to actual profit. The reconciling items are the individual variances.

Example 1   Variance Analysis (continued)

(b)   Operating Statement for Period
(i)   Absorption costing

		Favourable $000	Adverse $000	$000
Budgeted profit (BQ × standard profit per unit)				1,650
Sales margin variances				
Price (AP – SP) AQ				
Volume (AQ – BQ) standard profit per unit				
Standard profit on actual sales				
Cost variances				
Materials	• price (SP – AP) AQ_p			
	• usage (SQ – AQ_u) SP			
Labour	• rate (SR – AR) AH_p			
	• idle time (SH – AH_p)SR			
	• efficiency (SH – AH_w) SR			
Variable overhead	• rate (SR – AR) AH_w			
	• efficiency (SH – AH_w) SR			
Fixed overhead	• expenditure budget – actual			
	• capacity (AH_w – BH) SR			
	• efficiency (SH – AH_w) SR			
Actual profit				1,319

Note:
All inventories must be stated at **standard absorption cost** in determining actual profit.

---

3 Marginal Costing Approach

3.1 Differences

There are two differences between this and the total absorption approach just seen:

1. The only **fixed overheads variance** will be the expenditure variance. There can be no volume variances, as there is no attempt to absorb fixed overheads into production.

2. The **sales volume variance** needs to be re-calculated in terms of standard contribution, rather than standard profit.

In *Example 1* the figures will be:

▪ Budgeted contribution 50,000 × (100 − 52) = $2,400,000;

▪ Fixed overhead expenditure variance $110,000 A;

▪ Sales volume variance $48 per unit × (53,000 − 50,000 units) = $144,000 F;

▪ Profit is now:

	$
Revenue	5,035,000
Costs	(3,917,000)
Closing inventory 3,000 × $52	156,000
	1,274,000

3.2 Pro Forma

Example 1 Variance Analysis (continued)

(b) Operating statement for period
(ii) Marginal costing

	Favourable $000	Adverse $000	$000
Budgeted contribution			
(BQ × standard unit contribution)			
Sales margin variances			
Price **as before**			
Volume (AQ – BQ) standard unit contribution			
Standard contribution on actual sales			
Cost variances **as before**			
Materials Price			
Usage			
Labour Rate			
Idle time			
Efficiency			
Variable overhead Rate			
Efficiency			
Fixed overheads			
Budgeted			
Expenditure variance **as before**			
Actual profit (with inventory at standard marginal cost)			

It is not part of the operating statement, but absorption costing (AC) and marginal costing (MC) actual profits can be reconciled as follows:

	$000	$000
Actual profit (MC)		X
Finished goods inventory at MC	X	
Finished goods inventory at AC	X	
		X
Actual profit (AC)		X

4   Inventory at Actual Cost

4.1   Profit With Inventory at Actual Cost

▓ In *Example 1,* in determining the actual profit for the period, inventory was valued at $201,000 (3,000 × $67), its standard cost.

▓ If inventory were valued at its actual cost, the value would be:

$$\frac{3,000}{56,000} \times \$3,917,000 = \$209,839$$

actual   actual cost
production   of production

▓ Actual profit with inventory at actual cost is:

	$
Sales	5,035,000
Costs	(3,917,000)
Closing inventory	209,839
Actual profit	1,327,839

▓ This represents an increase of $8,839 over the actual profit with inventories at standard cost (the profit is higher because the inventory value is higher).

4.2   Variances*

▓ $8,839 represents:

$$\frac{3,000}{56,000} \times \$165,000$$

total production cost variances

4.3   Accounts

▓ For internal (management control) purposes, inventory is normally valued at its standard cost to highlight variances and to encourage any necessary remedial action to be taken.

▓ For external financial reporting (e.g. annual accounts), inventory is normally valued at its actual cost.

*Commentary

*When inventory is valued at actual cost, some of the current period's production cost variances are carried forward in the inventory value, rather than being expensed in profit or loss (which is what happens when inventory is valued at its standard cost).

5 Causes of Variances

5.1 General Causes

Variances may be caused by:

- Planning errors (e.g. inaccurate standards)
- Measurement errors (e.g. time recording errors)
- Random factors (e.g. natural disasters)
- Operational factors (e.g. management policies).

Operational factors may indicate that the process is out of control, and it is these which are considered below.

 Exam Advice

If asked to discuss or comment on the causes of variances, read the scenario carefully to identify the clues to the potential causes. Suggestions of rote-learnt causes that are irrelevant to the scenario or contradict the clues provided will not earn marks.

5.2 Specific Causes

	Favourable	Adverse
Materials price	Bulk discounts Good purchasing	Market price increase (shortage) Bad purchasing Delivery costs
	Different supplier Different material Change in quality	
Materials usage	Better quality More efficient	Defective material Theft Excessive waste or spoilage Stricter quality control
	Different batch sizes Change in mix	
Labour rate	Lower skilled labour	Wage rise Overtime working Bonus payments
	Different skill mix	
Idle time		Strikes Lack of material Breakdowns Injury/Illness Lack of orders
Labour efficiency	Motivation Higher pay Better equipment Learning effect Better material Higher grade	Lower pay Poor equipment Slow working Poor material Lower grade
Overhead expenditure	Cost savings/cutbacks	Cost increases Excessive service usage
	Incorrect split of semi-variable and fixed costs	
Overhead efficiency	(see Labour efficiency)	
Overhead capacity	Increase in productive hours	Excessive idle time Shortage of plant capacity
Sales price	Market shortage	To achieve increase in volume
	Change in quality Response to competitors Pass on cost changes	
Sales volume	Increase in market share Increase in market size	Fall in market share Fall in market size

5.3   Interdependence of Variances

Frequently, two or more opposing variances will be caused by the same operational factor.

It is necessary to consider the overall effect when considering any course of action.

5.3.1   Examples

- Purchase high-quality material:
  - Adverse materials price
  - Favourable materials usage.
- Raise the selling price:
  - Favourable sales price
  - Adverse sales volume.
- Use highly skilled labour:
  - Adverse labour rate
  - Favourable labour efficiency
  - Favourable variable overhead efficiency
  - Favourable fixed overhead efficiency.

5.3.2   A More Complex Example

Purchase high-quality material:

- Adverse materials price
- Favourable materials usage
- Favourable labour efficiency
- Favourable variable overhead efficiency
- Favourable fixed overhead efficiency
- Favourable sales price
- Adverse sales volume.

- ■ Variance analysis is a detailed investigation into why actual profits differ from budget, and it compares the actual costs against the standards.

- ■ Formulae for the variances are as follows:
  - ● Notation:
    - —AQ = Actual quantity (AH = Actual hours)
    - —BQ = Budgeted quantity (SH = Standard hours)
    - —AP = Actual price (AR = Actual rate)
    - —SP = Standard price (SR = Standard rate)
    - —SMn = Standard margin
  - ● Sale variances:
    - —Sales volume: $(AQ - BQ)\ SMn$
    - —Sales price: $(AP - SP)\ AQ$
  - ● Materials variances:
    - —Price: $(SP - AP)\ AQp$
    - —Usage: $(SQ - AQu)\ SP$
  - ● Labour variances:
    - —Rate: $(SR - AR)\ AHp$
    - —Idle time: $(AHw - AHp)\ SR$
    - —Efficiency: $(SH - AHw)\ SR$
  - ● Variable overheads:
    - —Rate: $(SR - AR)\ Ahw$
    - —Efficiency $(SH - AHw)\ SR$
  - ● Fixed overheads:
    - —Expenditure: Budget − Actual
    - —Volume: $(AQ - BQ) \times$ Standard rate per unit or $(SH - BH)\ SR$ (Absorption costing only)
    - —Capacity: $(AH - BH)\ SR$ (Absorption costing only)
    - —Efficiency: $(SH - AH)\ SR$ (Absorption costing only)
    - —Capacity + Efficiency = Volume

- ■ The budgeted quantity in usage variances and standard hours in efficiency variances is always "budgeted for actual production".

- ■ The only differences between variance analysis using absorption and marginal costing are:
  - ● Sales volume variance is valued at standard profit per unit for absorption, and standard contribution per unit for marginal.
  - ● There is only one fixed overhead variance for marginal costing; the expenditure overhead.

- ■ Variances could be caused by planning, measurement, random factors or operational factors. As far as investigating variances are concerned, operational factors are more important.

Session 11 Quiz

Estimated time: 15 minutes

1. The formula for the sales price variance can be shown as (AQ × AP) − (AQ × SP), where A means actual, Q means quantity and P means price. Using similar notation, write down the formulae for:

    a) Materials price variance. (1.3)

    b) Labour efficiency variance. (1.4)

    c) Variable overhead efficiency variance. (1.5)

    d) Fixed overhead capacity variance. (1.6)

2. State the TWO differences between variance analysis using absorption costing and variance analysis using marginal costing. (3.1)

3. List FOUR possible causes of adverse materials usage variance. (5.2)

4. List FOUR possible causes of favourable labour efficiency variance. (5.2)

5. Explain how an adverse material price variance may cause favourable labour variances. (5.3.2)

Study Question Bank

Estimated time: 20 minutes

Priority		Estimated Time	Completed
Q20	Portland	20 minutes	

EXAMPLE SOLUTIONS

Solution 1—Variance Analysis

(a) Variances

(i) Sales Volume

	Units	
Actual sales	53,000	
Budgeted sales	50,000	
Difference	3,000	
× standard profit per unit	$33	
Sales volume variance ($000)	99	Favourable

(ii) Sales Price

	$000	
Actual sales at actual price (actual revenue)	5,035	
Actual sales at standard price (53,000 × $100)	5,300	
Sales price variance	265	Adverse

(iii) Materials Price

	$000	
Actual materials purchased at actual price	2,700	
Actual materials purchased at standard price (130,000 x $20)	2,600	
Materials price variance	100	Adverse

(iv) Materials Usage

	Kilos	
Materials used (130,000 − 20,000)	110,000	
Standard materials for actual production (56,000 x 2)	112,000	
Difference	2,000	
× standard price per kilo	$20	
Materials usage variance ($000)	40	Favourable

(v) Labour Rate Variance

	$000	
Hours paid at actual price	180	
Hours paid at standard price (85,000 × 2)	170	
Labour rate variance	10	Adverse

(vi) Idle Time Variance

	Hours	
Hours paid	85,000	
Hours worked	83,000	
Idle time	2,000	
× standard hourly rate	$2	
Idle time variance ($000)	4	Adverse

(vii) Labour Efficiency Variance

	Hours	
Labour hours worked	83,000	
Standard labour hours for actual production (56,000 × 1.5)	84,000	
Difference	1,000	
× standard rate per hour	$2	
Labour efficiency variance ($000)	2	Favourable

(viii) Variable Overhead Rate Variance*

	$000	
Actual variable overhead cost	502	
Labour hours worked × standard variable overhead rate per hour (83,000 × $6)	498	
Variable overhead rate variance ($000)	4	Adverse

*Commentary

*It is assumed that variable overheads are incurred during productive labour hours.

(ix) Variable Overhead Efficiency Variance

	Hours	
Labour hours worked	83,000	
Standard labour hours for actual production	84,000	
Difference	1,000	
× standard variable overhead rate per hour	$6	
Labour efficiency variance ($000)	6	Favourable

(x) Fixed Overhead Expenditure Variance

	$000	
Actual fixed cost	935	
Budgeted fixed cost	825	
Fixed overhead expenditure variance	110	Adverse

(xi) Fixed Overhead Volume Variance

	Units	
Actual production	56,000	
Budgeted production	55,000	
Difference	1,000	
× standard fixed overhead rate per unit	$15	
Fixed overhead volume variance ($000)	15	Favourable

(xii) Fixed Overhead Capacity and Efficiency Variance

	Hours		Hours
Actual labour hours	83,000	Actual labour hours	83,000
Budgeted labour hours	82,500	Standard hours for actual output	84,000
Difference	500		1,000
× standard rate per hour	$10	× standard rate per hour	$10
Capacity variance ($000)	5	Efficiency variance ($000)	10

(b) Operating statement for period

(i) Absorption costing

		Favourable	Adverse	
		$000	$000	$000
Budgeted profit (BQ × standard profit per unit)				1,650
Sales margin variances				
Price (AP − SP) AQ			265	
Volume (AQ − BQ) standard profit per unit		99		(166)
Standard profit on actual sales				1,484
Cost variances				
Materials	• price (SP − AP) AQ_p		100	
	• usage (SQ − AQ_u) SP	40		
Labour	• rate (SR − AR) AH_p		10	
	• idle time (SH − AH_p)SR		4	
	• efficiency (SH − AH_w) SR	2		
Variable overhead	• rate (SR − AR) AH_w		4	
	• efficiency (SH − AH_w) SR	6		
Fixed overhead	• expenditure budget − actual		110	
	• capacity (AH_w − BH) SR	5		
	• efficiency (SH − AH_w) SR	10		
		63	228	(165)
Actual profit				1,319

(ii) Marginal costing

	Favourable $000	Adverse $000	$000
Budgeted contribution			2,400
(BQ × standard unit contribution)			
Sales margin variances			
Price **as before**		265	
Volume (AQ − BQ) standard unit contribution	144		(121)
			2,279
Standard contribution on actual sales			

Cost variances **as before**

		Favourable $000	Adverse $000	$000
Materials	Price		100	
	Usage	40		
Labour	Rate		10	
	Idle time		4	
	Efficiency	2		
Variable overhead	Rate		4	
	Efficiency	6		
		48	118	(70)
				2,209
Fixed overheads				
Budgeted			825	
Expenditure variance **as before**			110	
				(935)
Actual profit*				1,274

*Commentary

	$000	$000
Actual profit (MC)		1,274
Finished goods inventory at MC (3,000 × 52)	156	
Finished goods inventory at TAC (3,000 × 67)	201	
		45
Actual profit (AC)		1,319

Session 12

Advanced Variance Analysis

FOCUS

This session covers the following content from the *ACCA Study Guide.*

C. Budgeting and Control

4. Material mix and yield variances

a) Calculate, identify the cause of, and explain mix and yield variances.

b) Explain the wider issues involved in changing mix (e.g. cost, quality and performance measurement issues).

c) Identify and explain the relationship of the material usage variance with the material mix and yield variances.

d) Suggest and justify alternative methods of controlling production processes.

5. Sales mix and quantity variances

a) Calculate, identify the cause of, and explain sales mix and quantity variances.

b) Identify and explain the relationship of the sales volume variances with the sales mix and quantity variances.

Session 12 Guidance

■ **Recognise** that this session builds on the "basic" variances covered in *Session 11,* which is revision of the F2 variances. Materials mix and yield variances (s.1) and sales margin mix and quantity variances (s.2) are **examined fairly regularly**, so know these well.

■ **Understand** the relationship between the material in this session and the corresponding material in F2.

■ **Know** the calculations process for materials mix and yield variance, and **understand** the information provided by mix variances and yield variances when used together (s.1).

(continued on next page)

VISUAL OVERVIEW

Objective: To calculate materials mix and yield variances, and sales mix and quantity variances.

MATERIALS MIX AND YIELD VARIANCES

- The Concept
- Mix Variance
- Yield Variance
- Interpretation
- Inter-relationship
- Product Mix Issues
- Alternative Control Methods

SALES MIX AND QUANTITY VARIANCES

- The Concept
- Sales Mix Variance
- Sales Quantity Variance
- Interpretation

Session 12 Guidance

■ **Know** the calculations process for sales margin mix and quantity variances, and **understand** the information provided by sales mix and quantity variances when used together (s.2).

■ **Read** the article "Materials Mix and Yield Variances".

1 | Materials Mix and Yield Variances

1.1 The Concept

The basic variances examined in the previous session included variances for materials: the materials price and usage variances. The basic variances assumed that the production process used only one type of material. Clearly, real world products use more than one material. The standard cost of a product makes an assumption about the quantity of the materials used. Actual production costs may differ from the standard in the following ways:

- The prices paid for the materials may differ from the standard price. This will be reflected in the **price variance**. This is calculated in the same way as before, except that it is necessary to calculate price variances for *each* material used.

- The materials may be used in different portions to the standard. This may lead to a different average cost. This is reflected in a variance called the **mix variance**.

- The standard may assume that there is some level of standard loss. The actual loss may be more or less than the standard loss. This is reflected in a **yield variance**.

Illustration 1   Mix and Yield Variances

A perfume is made by mixing essential oils with alcohol. Essential oils cost $15,000 per litre. Alcohol costs $10 per litre. In the standard, 1% of the liquid input is essential oil, and 99% is alcohol. If the production manager uses more oil and less alcohol, this would lead to a more expensive mix, as essential oil costs more than alcohol. This would result in an adverse mix variance.

When making one litre of perfume a normal loss of 37.5% of input occurs. In order to make one litre, therefore, the standard specifies using 1.6 litres of liquid. If the production manager input 1.6 litres of inputs and managed to make more than 1 litre, this would result in a favourable yield variance.

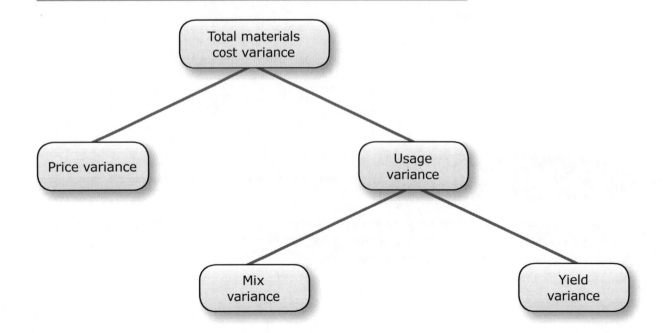

1.2   Calculating the Mix Variance

▓ A tabular approach best illustrates how to calculate the mix variance:

	Actual quantity used litres/kgs	Actual quantity in standard mix litres/kgs	Difference litres/kgs	Variance $
	A	B	(B − A)	(B − A) × standard cost
Material 1				
Material 2				
Material 3				
Total	x	x	0	$y

▓ *Actual quantity used* describes the actual amount of each material employed in production.

▓ *Actual quantity in the standard mix* equals the total actual quantity used (total column A) multiplied by the standard portions. The quantity totals for columns A and B will be the same.

▓ *Variance due to materials mix* equals the third column multiplied by the standard price for each unit of input.

▓ This method determines variance as actual quantity of each material less standard quantity for each material (represented as column A less column B). Using more of a particular material compared to its standard means additional cost (i.e. an adverse variance).

1.3   Calculating Yield Variance

▓ The yield variance compares actual output with the output expected based on the actual input.

▓ Yield variance equals the difference between expected and actual output multiplied by standard cost per unit.

Pro Forma Calculation	
	Units
Actual output	A
x litres/kgs should yield	B
Difference	(A − B)
	× standard cost per unit
Yield variance	x

The alternative tabular approach takes longer, but may be conceptually easier to understand:

	Actual quantity in standard mix litres/kgs A	Standard quantity for actual output litres/kgs B	litres/kgs (B − A)	Variance $ (B − A) × standard cost
Material 1				
Material 2	_____	_____		_____
Total				
	_____	_____		_____

Example 1   Materials Mix and Yield

The standard material cost of a unit of a product is:

				$
Material X	2 kg	@	$3	6
Material Y	1 kg	@	$2	2
	3 kg			8

The actual production was 5,000 units and the materials used were:

Material X   9,900 kg costing $27,000
Material Y   5,300 kg costing $11,000

Required:

Calculate the following variances:

(a)   Total materials cost

(b)   Materials price

(c)   Materials mix

(d)   Materials yield

(e)   Materials usage.

Example 2 Materials Mix and Yield

The Imperial Chemical Company (ICC) makes various chemicals. Chemical X is made by combining three substances in a furnace. The following is the standard cost of 100 kg of Chemical X:

	Input	Cost per	Total cost
	kg	kg	$
Material A	75	0.7	52.5
Material B	25	1.3	32.5
Material C	25	3.0	75.0
	125		160

The loss of 25 kg in production is expected due to evaporation.

Variances are calculated every day. Yesterday's output of 1,300 kg was obtained from the following inputs:

	kg
Material A	850
Material B	300
Material C	350
	1,500

Required:

(a) **Calculate the materials mix variance.**

(b) **Calculate the yield variance.**

1.4 Interpreting Material Mix and Yield Variances

■ A favourable overall materials mix variance means an actual mix cheaper than standard. Cheaper materials have been substituted for more expensive ones. The perfume manufacturer in *Illustration 1* would have a favourable mix variance if he used less than 1% of essential oils in the mix.

■ While a cheaper mix saves money, it may imply poorer quality of the final product. This may mean a loss of customers in the longer run.

■ Yield variance means that actual output exceeds output expected for the given input units. This could result from:

• less spillage due to production methods; or

• less waste due to quality of materials used as inputs.

1.5 Inter-relationship Between Price, Mix and Yield Variances

■ Price variance may be outside the control of the production manager. Prices may be seasonal, or based on a market rate, which the production manager cannot influence.

■ In some situations, managers may obtain cheaper inputs by buying from alternative suppliers. This will result in favourable price variances. However, the cheaper materials may be of lower quality, and this may increase materials waste resulting in an unfavourable yield variance.

■ A manager who observes a favourable mix variance due to using an increased proportion of less expensive material may inadvertently cause an unfavourable yield variance.

1.6 Wider Issues Relating to Product Mix

The materials mix may vary from standard for many products.

> **Illustration 2 Varying Materials Mix**
>
> Imagine cooking a meal at home. Perhaps you are following a recipe from a cookbook. Do you always weigh the ingredients precisely so that your mix is exactly the same as the cookbook (the standard)? Or perhaps you vary them slightly based on your own personal taste, or perhaps simply because you do not measure everything precisely; you just roughly estimate how much you have put in. You know that you will still have a meal in the end and hopefully one that tastes good.

The standard product mix was likely set after considering the following issues:

■ **Balancing mix and yield**—using a cheaper "mix" of materials often leads to a lower yield. The standard mix attempts to minimise costs at an acceptable yield.

■ **Quality**—a cheaper mix may lead to lower cost, but this may also lower the quality.

1.6.1 Reasons for Varying the Mix

In practice, managers may move away from the standard mix for the following reasons:

■ The price of materials may change away from the standard, so one becomes relatively more or less expensive.

■ Inaccurate measurement of inputs due to carelessness or mistake.

■ Intentionally using a cheaper mix to get a favourable mix variance.

1.6.2 Impact of Varying the Mix

A cheaper mix will lead to a favourable mix variance. However, adverse effects may also result.

✗ It may lead to a lower yield. When assessing the financial performance of the manager, the mix and yield variance need to be considered together. If the mix and yield variance added together yields an overall favourable variance, then from a financial perspective that may be considered to be good.

✗   It may reflect lower output quality. In the longer term, this
    will lead to a fall in sales reflected in an adverse sales volume
    variance. The sales volume variance will take some time to
    show and may occur in a later period, making it difficult to
    assess management performance in the current period.

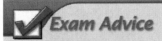

Exam Advice

Always look for the whole picture when answering exam questions.
Favourable mix and yield variance may result in an unfavourable
non-financial impact (e.g. quality, customer satisfaction).

1.7   Alternative Methods of Controlling Production Processes

■   Where production managers are evaluated on materials mix
    and yield variances, as we have seen in the previous material,
    they may take actions to improve the measured variances at
    the expense of other important factors—particularly quality.

■   To overcome this, manager performance evaluation should
    consider additional measures, such as quality. Measuring
    quality is not always easy, however, as this may be subjective.

2   Sales Mix and Quantity Variances

2.1   The Concept

Where the company sells more than one product, the budget will
include the budgeted quantity of each product sold. The actual
sales can be compared with the budget, and the sales volume
variance calculated. The overall sales volume variance can be
analysed into two further categories:

■   The sales mix variance shows the effect on contribution or
    profit of selling a different "mix" to the standard. This implies
    that sales of different products may be dependent such that
    consumers decide to substitute sales of one product for
    another. If the products have different margins, then this will
    affect profits.

■   The quantity variance compares the actual quantity of goods
    sold for each product in units with the *budgeted mix* of
    products at the actual total quantity.

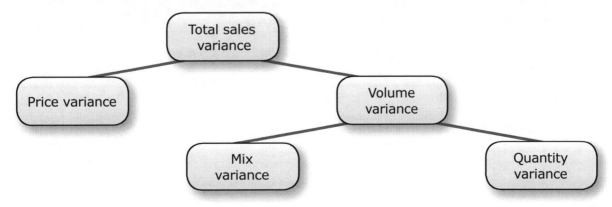

2.2　Calculating the Sales Mix Variance

The best way to calculate the sales mix variance is to use a table:

Product	Actual sales in units	Actual sales units in budgeted mix	Difference in units	Standard margin $	Sales mix variance $
	A	B	A − B	C	(A − B) x C
X					
Y					
Z					
	_____	_____	_____		_____
	_____	_____	_____		_____

In principle, the calculation of sales mix variance is similar to the materials mix variance. Sales mix variance calculates the difference between actual product sales and actual total sales allocated in the budgeted product sales mix, then multiplies that difference by the standard margin per unit. Standard margin would normally be contribution per unit, although if absorption costing is used, standard profit per unit may be used. If in doubt, use standard contribution per unit.

Exam Advice

Standard margin is either standard contribution per unit or standard profit per unit. If standard contribution, the variance is "sales mix contribution variance". If standard profit, the variance is the "sales mix profit variance".

2.3　Calculating the Sales Quantity Variance

The starting point for the quantity variance is actual sales, adjusted to standard mix. This is then compared with budgeted sales, and the differences multiplied by the standard margin.

Product	Actual sales in budgeted mix (units)	Budgeted sales (units)	Difference (units)	Standard margin $	Sales quantity variance $
	A	B	A − B	C	(A − B) x C
X					
Y					
Z					
	_____	_____	_____		_____
	_____	_____	0		_____

Example 3 Sales Price, Mix and Quantity Variances

A company sells three related products, Q, P and R. The budgeted sales mix is 50% for Q and 25% for each of products P and R. The current period budget and actual sales are:

	Products		
Budget	**Q**	**P**	**R**
Unit sales	200	100	100
Price	$20	$25	$30
Contribution	$3	$4	$6
Actual			
Unit sales	180	150	170
Price	$22	$22	$26

Required:
Calculate the sales price, sales mix contribution variance and sales quantity variances.

2.4   Interpreting the Sales Mix and Quantity Variance

2.4.1 Usefulness of Sales Mix and Quantity Variances

When product sales are unrelated the demand and price for each product will be considered separately to optimise profits. The budgeted sales mix has no significance. The sales price and volume variance calculated on a product-by-product basis should provide sufficient information for management to identify any particular products which are under performing. Sales mix and quantity variances will not provide additional useful information.

Analysing the sales volume variance into mix and quantity variances is only likely to be useful in situations in which sales of the various products are interrelated. The analysis may indicate that products are substitutes or complements. The products could be similar in nature, but differentiated by package size or by brand. In such situations, the mix of products may have been considered when the budget was prepared, and management will therefore be interested in the sales mix and quantity variances.

2.4.2 Meaning of Sales Mix Variances

An adverse mix variance means that customers are buying less of the higher-margin products and instead buying lower-margin ones. It implies substitution of one product for another, rather than reducing the overall quantity of goods acquired.

> **Illustration 3 Contribution Margin**
>
> A smoker decides to stop buying a premium brand of cigarettes and switches to a cheaper brand, but continues to buy the same quantity of cigarettes. This would reduce the contribution margin of the tobacco company.

2.4.3 Meaning of Sales Quantity Variance

The sales quantity variance shows the actual quantity of goods sold against the budget. An adverse variance may be due to poor economic conditions or a new competitor. This variance identifies factors which affect sales of all the products.

2.4.4 Inter-relationships Between Variances

The variances above are likely to be inter-related, so any analysis of variances should look at all the variances together rather than individually. For example:

- Sales price and sales volume variances: a fall in selling prices for products would lead to an adverse price variance. However, if it also leads to higher demand for the products, the volume variance would be favourable.

- Sales mix and quantity variances: an adverse sales mix variance may be due to customers switching to cheaper ranges or brands as these may be considered better value. If these "better value" products attract customers from other products too, this will lead to a favourable quantity variance.

Summary

- Materials mix variances measure the effect of using a different mix of inputs in the production process.

- Materials yield variances compare actual output with expected output, given the input material quantities and standard wastage.

- Sale mix variances consider how changing the mix of products affects contribution.

- Sales quantity variances consider the effect on budgeted sales of selling a higher or lower quantity.

- Expenditure variances in activity-based costing analyses the actual overhead cost against the standard cost for the driver units used.

- An efficiency variance compares the actual driver units with the standard driver units, given actual output.

- Organisations with unrelated product sales need not worry about how selling more of one product affects the bottom line.

- Organisations with products which complement or substitute for other products must consider the overall profit effect of a change in volume of one product; a sales decrease will result in lower sales for the complementary product and a sales increase for a substitute product.

- An unfavourable sales price variance can result in increasing product sales and a favourable volume variance. Sales mix variance results can signify a more complicated result regarding profits.

Session 12 Quiz

Estimated time: 15 minutes

1. State the "basic" variance which is obtained by adding the mix variance to the yield variance. (1.1)

2. True or false? If the production manager uses a higher portion of cheaper materials and a lower portion of the more expensive materials in the product mix, it will lead to an adverse mix variance. (1.4)

3. State whether the quality of the output is likely to be better than standard or worse than standard if the mix variance is favourable. (1.6)

4. Due to a machine overheating, more materials were wasted in the production process. Describe the effect this would have on the yield variance. (1.6)

5. During a budget period, actual revenue was as per budget, but the sales mix reflected more sales of product B than product A than per the budget. Product B has a lower contribution margin than product A. State whether the resulting mix variance would be favourable or adverse. (2)

Study Question Bank

Estimated time: 50 minutes

Priority		Estimated Time	Completed
Q21	Milbao Co	20 minutes	
Q22	Pan Ocean Chemicals	30 minutes	

EXAMPLE SOLUTIONS

Solution 1—Materials Mix and Yield

(a) Total materials cost variance

	$	
Standard cost of actual production (5,000 units × $8)	40,000	
Actual cost of actual production (27,000 + 11,000)	38,000	
	2,000	Favourable

(b) Materials price variance

Material	Actual quantity at actual price $		Actual quantity at standard price $	Variance $	
X	27,000	(9,900 × 3)	29,700	2,700	
Y	11,000	(5,300 × 2)	10,600	(400)	
	38,000		40,300	2,300	Favourable

(c) Materials mix variance

	Actual quantity used kgs		Actual quantity in standard mix kgs	Difference kgs	Variance $	
X	9,900	(2/3)	10,133	233 @ $3	699	
Y	5,300	(1/3)	5,067	(233) @ $2	(466)	
	15,200		15,200	0	233	Favourable

> ### *Commentary
>
> *The mix variance is favourable because using a higher proportion of material Y has led to a cheaper mix.

(d) Materials yield variance

	Units	
15,200 kgs should yield (3 kilograms per unit ⊃ 15,200 ÷ 3)	5,067*	
Actual output	5,000	
Difference (shortfall)	(67)	
× standard cost per unit	$8	
Yield variance ($)	(536)	Adverse

> ### *Commentary
>
> *Rounding up the units gives rise to a small rounding difference in the variance calculation.

Alternative approach to yield variance

	Actual quantity in standard mix kgs	Standard quantity for actual output kgs	Difference kgs	Variance $	
X	10,133	10,000	(133)	(399)	
Y	5,067	5,000	(67)	(134)	
	15,200	15,000*		(533)	Adverse

*Actual output was 5,000 units. Standard usage is 2 kg of X and 1 kg of Y per unit.

(e) Materials usage variance

	Actual quantity in standard mix kgs	Standard quantity for actual output kgs	Difference kgs	Variance $	
X	9,900	10,000	100	300	
Y	5,300	5,000	(300)	(600)	
	15,200	15,000		(300)	Adverse

Materials usage variance = mix variance + yield variance
= 233 − 533 = 300 adverse.

Solution 2—Materials Mix and Yield

(a) Mix variance

Material	Actual quantity used kg	Actual quantity in standard mix (W) kg	Difference kg	Variance $
A	850	900	50 @ 0.7	35
B	300	300	0	0
C	350	300	(50) @ 3	(150)
	1,500	1,500	0	(115)

The mix is adverse, because a higher proportion of the more expensive material (C) was used compared with the standard mix.

Working

Standard proportions are:

Material A: 75 ÷ 125 = 0.6 (i.e. 60%)
Material B: 25 ÷ 125 = 0.2
Material C: 25 ÷ 125 = 0.2

These proportions are applied to the actual quantity used (1,500) to calculate the actual quantity in standard mix.

(b) Yield variance

125 kg of input yields 100 kg of output so the standard yield is 80% (100 ÷ 125).

	kg
1,500 kg should yield (80%)	1,200
Actual output	1,300
Difference (excess)	100
× standard cost per unit ($160 ÷100)	$1.60
Yield variance ($)	160

The yield variance is favourable because more output was achieved than expected, given the input.

Alternative approach

Actual	Actual quantity in std mix kg	Standard quantity for actual output* kg	Difference kg	Variance $
A	900	975	75 @ 0.7	52.5
B	300	325	25 @ 1.3	32.5
C	300	325	25 @ 3	75.0
	1,500	1,625	0	160

Commentary

*Actual output was 1,300 kg. The simplest way to calculate the standard quantity for 1,300 kg is to multiply the standard quantity for 100 kg by 13, for each material.

Solution 3—Sales Price, Mix and Quantity Variances

Price variance

		$
Q	(180 × (22 − 20))	360
P	(150 × (22 − 25))	(450)
R	(170 × (26 − 30))	(680)
		(770)

Sales mix contribution variance*

Product	Actual sales (units)	Actual sales in budgeted mix (units)	Difference (units)	Standard contribution $	Sales mix contribution variance $	
Q	180	250	(70)	3	(210)	
P	150	125	25	4	100	
R	170	125	45	6	270	
	500	500	0		160	Favourable

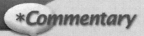

Commentary

*The sales mix variance is favourable because customers have switched from product Q, which has the lowest contribution margin, to products P and R, which have higher margins.

Quantity variance

Product	Actual sales in budgeted mix (units)	Budgeted sales (units)	Difference (units)	Standard contribution $	Sales quantity variance $	
Q	250	200	50	3	150	
P	125	100	25	4	100	
R	125	100	25	6	150	
		400			400	Favourable

Planning and Operational Variances

FOCUS

This session covers the following content from the *ACCA Study Guide.*

C. Budgeting and Control

6. Planning and operational variances

a) Calculate a revised budget.

b) Identify and explain those factors that could and could not be allowed to revise an original budget.

c) Calculate, identify the cause of and explain planning and operational variances for:

  i)   sales, including market size and market share;

  ii) materials;

  iii) labour, including the effect of the learning curve.

d) Explain and discuss the manipulation issues involved in revising budgets.

7. Performance analysis

a) Analyse and evaluate past performance using the results of variance analysis.

b) Use variance analysis to assess how future performance of an organisation or business can be improved.

d) Discuss the effect that variances have on staff motivation and action.

e) Describe the dysfunctional nature of some variances in the modern environment of JIT and TQM.

f) Discuss the behavioural problems resulting from using standard costs in rapidly changing environments.

Session 13 Guidance

■ **Understand** why a variance may be revised prior to variance analysis taking place and that managers may try to "bend" the system by having variances revised to disguise inefficiencies (s.1).

■ **Recognise** the difference between planning variances and operational variances (s.2.1). **Master** the calculations of planning and operational variances.

(continued on next page)

VISUAL OVERVIEW

Objective: To consider when standards and budgets should be revised, the calculations in such circumstances and the effect of using variance analysis on the behaviour of managers and employees.

REVISION OF BUDGETS AND STANDARDS

PLANNING AND OPERATIONAL VARIANCES

- Problems of Traditional Analysis
- Calculations
- Learning Curve and Labour
- Market Volume and Market Share
- Advantages and Disadvantages
- Manipulation

BEHAVIOURAL ASPECTS
OF STANDARD COSTING

- Staff Motivation and Action
- Variances and Performance Evaluation
- Relevance Under JIT and TQM
- Behavioural Patterns

Session 13 Guidance

■ **Know** the method of accounting for a learning curve when determining a standard (s.2.3).

■ **Recognise** how unrealistic standards affect morale and output (s.3).

1 Revision of Budgets and Standards

At the end of a budget period, prior to comparing the actual performance of an organisation against the budget, budgets may be revised to take account of changes within the environment which were not anticipated when the budget was prepared. The reason for such revision is that because managers are judged on how they performed relative to the budget, it is unfair to use a budget that turns out to be "wrong".

The principles that should be applied when revising budgets are as follows:

- If something occurred during the budget period that was outside the control of the manager and meant that the actual budget was not achieved, then the budget should be revised.

- If, in retrospect, it appears that the original budget was unrealistic, then the budget may also be revised.

- Management should not revise budgets to hide inefficiencies.

- Senior management should approve only appropriate revisions.

Example 1 Budget Revisions

The budget for an airline for the year ended 31 December 20X1 was prepared in October 20X0. Since the budget was prepared, the following events occurred:

- The price of oil increased 25% on world markets. This caused airline fuel prices to increase. Fuel accounts for 25% of the airline's costs.

- Due to a strike, the airline could not operate for four weeks of the year. There was no revenue during this period.

- The airline lost an additional two weeks of revenue due to the eruption of the Eyjafjallajokull volcano in Iceland and the associated ash cloud.

Required:

For each of the events above, discuss which should result in budget revisions and which should not.

---

2 Planning and Operational Variances

2.1 Problems of Traditional Variance Analysis

Traditional variance analysis compares:

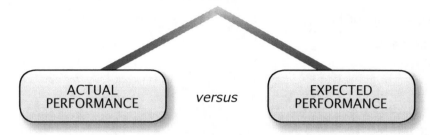

ACTUAL PERFORMANCE   *versus*   EXPECTED PERFORMANCE

▪ If the actual environment differs from what was anticipated when the original standard was set, then management should consider revising the standard (ex-post standard).

▪ Even if the environment has not changed, hindsight might show that an unrealistic standard was used (e.g. ideal standard). Again, management should consider revising the standard.

▪ The factors to consider in deciding whether to revise a standard are essentially the same as whether to revise a budget, discussed in section 1.

▪ The variances calculated by comparing actual performance are referred to as **operational** (or operating) **variances**. Their calculation is exactly the same as for calculating standard variances; the only difference is that a revised standard has been used.

▪ The difference between the *ex-ante* and *ex-post* targets is known as the **planning variance**.*

> *Commentary*
>
> *Planning variances can relate to any element of the standard product specification.

> ### Definition
>
> **Planning variance**—a classification of variances caused by *ex-ante* budget being changed to an *ex-post* basis.
>
> **Operational variance**—a classification of variances in which non-standard performance is defined as that which differs from an *ex-post* standard.

2.2 Calculations

There are various methods of calculating planning variances. The following approach starts with the traditional variance (e.g. a material price variance) that is then analysed into planning and operational variances.

> ✓ *Exam Advice*
>
> This is the current examiner's preferred approach.

2.2.1 Materials Price and Labour Rate

The approach to calculating the materials price and labour rate variances is the same, so these two variances are dealt with together here.

- For materials, the references to quantity are to quantities of materials;
- For labour, the quantities are labour hours.

Traditional Price/Rate Variance

	$
Actual quantity x *Actual* price	X
Actual quantity x *Revised standard* price	X
Price variance	X

If the standard price has subsequently been revised, the traditional variance can be analysed into planning and operational, as follows:

Planning Price Variance*

This shows the effect of revising the standard cost by comparing the standard cost of actual materials under the old and new standard cost:

	$
Actual quantity x *Original* standard price	X
Actual quantity x *Revised* standard price	X
Planning price variance	X

✗ This is adverse if the revised standard price is higher than the original standard price.

*Commentary

*Planning variances are sometimes referred to as "budget revision variances".

Operational Price Variance

The calculation of the operational price variance is very similar to the calculation of the traditional price variance. The only difference is that the actual price is compared with the *revised* standard instead of the original standard:

	$
Actual quantity x *Actual* price	X
Actual quantity x *Standard* price	X
Operational price variance	X

✔ This is favourable if the actual cost is less than the revised standard cost.

Example 2 Materials Price Variances

The standard cost of Material X is $4 per kilo. During the month, 10,000 kilos were purchased at a total cost of $42,500.

Required:

(a) Calculate the traditional material price variance for the month.

(b) After the variance report was produced, the purchasing manager argued that the original standard cost turned out to be unrealistic. Market prices of Material X rose considerably during the month, and it has been agreed that a more realistic standard cost would have been $4.50 per kilo.

Required:

Calculate the planning price and operational price variances for the month.

(c) Comment on how the operational price variance provides a fairer indication of the performance of the purchasing manager than the traditional price variance.

Solution

(a) Traditional price variance

	$
Actual materials at actual price	
Actual materials at standard price	
Materials price variance	

(b) Planning and operational variances

Planning variance

	$
Actual materials at original standard price	
Actual materials at revised standard price	
Planning price variance	

Operational variance

	$
Actual materials at actual price	
Actual materials at revised standard price	
Operational price variance	

(c) Comment

2.2.2 Usage and Efficiency*

Traditional Usage/Efficiency Variance

	Kilos/Hours, etc
Actual quantity used	x
Standard quantity for actual output	x
Difference	x
At standard price/rate per unit/hour	$x
Materials usage (labour efficiency) variance	$x

*The approach to calculating the materials usage and labour efficiency variances is the same, so they are dealt with together here.

Planning Usage/Efficiency Variance

	Kilos/Hours, etc
Original standard quantity for actual output	x
Revised standard quantity for actual output	x
Difference	x
At standard price/rate per unit/hour	$x
Materials usage/labour efficiency planning variance	$x

✗ This is adverse if the revised standard quantity exceeds the original standard quantity.

Operational Usage/Efficiency Variance

	Kilos/Hours, etc
Actual quantity used	x
Revised standard quantity for actual output	x
Difference	x
At standard price/rate per unit/hour	$x
Materials usage/labour efficiency operational variance	$x

Example 3 Labour Efficiency Variances

At the start of a month, a standard cost was set for a new product. The standard for the labour component was 0.25 hours at $10 per hour. In the last month, actual output of the product was 1,000 units and 320 labour hours were worked.

At the end of the month, it was agreed that the factory accountant had been a little unrealistic in setting a standard of 0.25 hours per unit. A more appropriate standard would have been 0.3 hours per unit. It has been agreed that the standard will therefore be revised to this amount. There was no idle time and no learning curve effect.

Required:

(a) Calculate the traditional labour efficiency variance.

(b) Calculate the labour efficiency planning and operational variances.

(c) Comment on how the operational efficiency variance gives a more appropriate indication of the performance of the factory manager than the traditional efficiency variance.

Example 4 Materials

Standard material cost/unit:	4 kg at $2.50 =$10
Budgeted output:	20,000 units
Actual output:	22,000 units
Materials actually used:	86,000 kg at $3

With hindsight, a better standard would have been 3.75 kg per unit at $2.80 per kg.

Required:

(a) Calculate the traditional variances:

    (i)   Price variance

    (ii) Usage variance

    (iii) Overall material variance (price + usage).

(b) Analyse the price variance into planning and operational.

(c) Analyse the usage variance into planning and operational.

2.3 Learning Curve and Labour Variances

- Where learning curves apply, standard costs based on the cost of producing the first unit of a product may quickly become out of date, meaning that the variances will become meaningless.

- In order to adjust for this, the "standard hours for actual production" in the labour efficiency variance should take into account the learning curve (see *Session 9*).

Example 5 Learning Curves and Variances

Martin Co developed a new product. It set a standard labour cost based on the expected time to make the first unit of the product, which was 100 minutes. A 90% learning rate is expected to apply, and the budgeted cost per hour of labour time is $12 per hour. This learning rate was not incorporated into the standard.

The actual time taken to make the first four units was 350 minutes and the cost was $80.

Required:

(a) Calculate traditional labour rate and efficiency variances.

(b) Re-calculate the labour efficiency variance to take account of the learning rate.

2.4 Market Volume and Market Share Variances

2.4.1 The Concept

Traditional sales volume variance may result from:

- market size variance where the size of the market was different from expected due to a change in the external environment (e.g. economic growth); or

- market share variance where the share of that market was different from budget (e.g. due to effective advertising).

The sales volume variance can therefore be split:

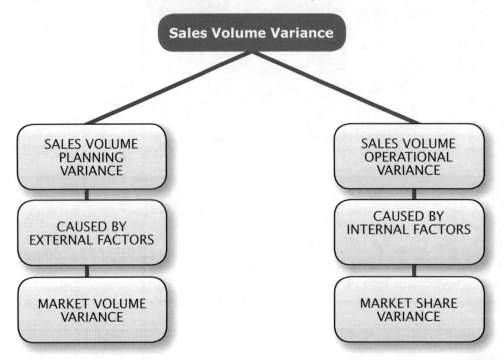

- Sales managers can control the market share variance, but cannot control the sales volume variance.*

2.4.2 Market Volume Variance

	Units
Budgeted sales quantity	x
Revised budgeted quantity (Actual market size × Budgeted market share)	x
Difference	x
× Standard contribution/profit* per unit	x
Market volume variance	$x

2.4.3 Market Share Variance

	Units
Actual sales quantity	x
Revised budgeted quantity	x
Difference	x
× Standard contribution/Profit* per unit	x
Market share variance	$x

*If marginal costing is used, multiply the differences by standard contribution per unit. If absorption costing is used, multiply the differences by the standard profit per unit.

*Commentary

*Perhaps any bonus for the sales manager should be linked to the market share variance, not the sales volume variance.

Example 6 Sales Planning and Operational Variances

Acme has a sales budget of 1,795 units at a unit contribution of $20.00. This is based on the company maintaining a 5% market share. Total sales volume for the industry was estimated to be 35,900 units.

Actual sales volumes were as follows:

Acme	1,850 units
Industry	37,500 units

Required:

Calculate for Acme:

(a) **the traditional sales volume variance; and**

(b) **the market volume and market share variance.**

2.5 Advantages and Disadvantages

Advantages

✔ Distinguishes between those variances caused by bad planning or unavoidable factors and those which are the result of operating factors.

✔ Adverse operating variances provide feedback control on processes which need correcting.

✔ Planning variances can be used to update standards to current conditions.

✔ Motivation may improve if managers know they will only be assessed on variances under their control (i.e. operational variances).

Disadvantages

✗ Extra data requirements (e.g. market volume).

✗ More time consuming.

✗ Managers may claim that all adverse variances have external causes and all favourable variances have internal causes (i.e. manipulation of revised standards).

2.6 Manipulation

From the previous discussion, it should be apparent that budgets and standards prepared at the start of the year may need revision at the end of the year if they are inappropriate because of factors which occurred outside of the control of the organisation.

Care clearly must be taken to ensure that budget revisions are only made when appropriate. Managers who have not achieved their budget targets, or who experience adverse variances, may try to hide these by revising the budgets and standards.

In practice, there may be some debate about whether an organisation should revise a standard or a budget.

3   Behavioural Aspects of Standard Costing

3.1   Effect on Staff Motivation and Action

■ Standard costing and variance analysis may be used as part of the performance evaluation of managers and staff. As such, variance analysis will have some effect on motivation.

✔ As for budgets, a challenging target can motivate managers and staff to work harder, compared with having no target.

■ However, there are many potential problems related to the use of variance analysis:

✗ If managers use variance information insensitively, morale may suffer. Employees (workforce and supervisors) should be congratulated on tasks well done but management by exception tends to focus on what has gone wrong. If employees are berated or disciplined for adverse variances they may attempt to conceal them or take actions to ensure that the variances within their control are favourable, which may not be in the best interests of the firm. For example, in rushing to increase productivity at the end of the budget period to avoid an unfavourable labour efficiency variance, the quality of output may suffer.

✗ Accurate preparation of standards can be difficult. For example, workers may operate below their ability during standard-setting runs to build "slack" into the standard.

✗ Labour quantity standards and efficiency variances make two assumptions that may not hold true:

   1.   Output increases if workers speed up (i.e. the pace of production is dictated by labour). However, the volume of output may be influenced more by the processing speed of equipment.

   2.   Labour is a variable cost. However, the cost of a workforce may be essentially fixed. Undue emphasis on efficiency can result in an excessive build-up of work in progress and finished goods inventories.

3.2 Variances and Performance Evaluation

This session and the three preceding sessions have mentioned the use of variances to evaluate performance. This section provides comprehensive guidance on this aspect of variance analysis.

3.2.1 Identify the Cause of the Variance

Possible causes of traditional variances were discussed in *Session 11,* and *Session 12* gave reasons for materials mix and yield variances. In the real world (and in examination questions) there may be other causes. The first stage in using variances to evaluate performance is to understand what caused them.

Having identified the cause of a particular variance, it is worth identifying whether other variances were also affected. For example:

■ A favourable materials price variance may have been caused by buying cheaper materials, but this may also have resulted in an adverse materials usage variance.

■ It would be meaningless therefore to say that the favourable price variance was "good" and that the adverse usage variance was "bad".

All variances that have been caused by a common factor should be considered together. It may be worthwhile to add the variances together (treating favourable variances as positive and adverse variances as negative) to appreciate the total financial impact.

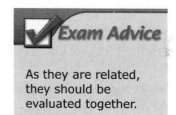

Exam Advice

As they are related, they should be evaluated together.

3.2.2 Identify Who Is Responsible

It may be that variances are being used to assess the performance of a particular manager (e.g. a factory manager). Managers should only be judged on variances that are within their control. Variances are normally the responsibility of the following departments and their managers:

■ Materials price variance—the purchase department. However, look for signs that the purchase department may have been put under pressure to buy from a particular supplier. Or, if the purchase was requisitioned at very short notice, the purchasing department may have been unable to obtain a favourable price that it might have had otherwise.

■ Labour rate variances—this depends on who makes the decisions about how much to pay particular workers. It could be the human resources department or the factory manager.

■ Labour efficiency variances are normally assumed to be the responsibility of the person who supervises the workers—this could again be the factory manager. However, these variances may also be related to the rate variance—a higher grade of labour will generally lead to an adverse rate variance, but the labourers might work more efficiently.

■ Material usage variances are also associated with a production manager. However, variances may also have been caused by the purchase manager buying a quality of material different from the standard.

- Mix and yield variances are normally considered to be under the control of the production manager who supervises the production process. However, these may also be affected by the quality of materials used, which could be the responsibility of the purchasing manager.

- Overhead variances will be the responsibility of the appropriate managers—equipment maintenance expenditure, for example, would depend on the maintenance manager.

3.2.3 Consider Whether the Standard Was Fair

As previously explained, if an original standard becomes out of date, or is otherwise unreasonable (e.g. it was a poor estimate), it should be revised. Operational variances are generally a more reliable indicator of performance than traditional variances.

3.2.4 Non-financial Factors

Variances reflect only the financial view. Non-financial factors such as quality may be equally important, but these are ignored by variances.*

If variances are favourable, this means costs are being kept under control. However, if this is at the expense of quality, it may be a bad thing.

*Be aware of this limitation.

Illustration 1 Non-financial Factors

A past exam question involved a company that manufactured soup. The production manager had been told that his performance would be judged on the reported variances. He had successfully kept costs down, reporting large favourable mix and yield variances. From a financial point of view this seemed positive.

The sales manager, on the other hand, was angry that customers were complaining about the quality of the soup. This was clearly related to the fact that, in order to reduce costs, the production manager was diluting the soup and the quality was suffering. In the long term this threatened to lead to a fall in demand, which would lead to a fall in profits.

3.2.5 Improving Future Performance

After identifying the causes of variances, appropriate action can be taken to ensure that future performance improves. For example:

- Including non-financial factors as well as variances in managers' appraisal systems.

- Regular review and updating of variances to reflect changes in the external environment.

- Using target costing to identify ways to reduce costs further.

3.3   Relevance of Variances in the Modern Environment of JIT and TQM

Many writers have argued that variance analysis is not relevant in the modern, rapidly changing business world and that it can lead to dysfunctional behaviour for these reasons:

■ Use of a standard costing system may lead to overemphasis on **quantitative** elements of performance. It is important that qualitative performance is not neglected (e.g. customer satisfaction, employee morale, innovation), particularly in a total quality management environment.

■ Just-in-time (JIT) systems and flexible manufacturing systems aim to provide more tailored production to meet customers' needs. There may, therefore, be less standardisation of production, which makes comparison with a standard less meaningful.

■ JIT purchasing systems emphasise forging close, long-term relations with suppliers. Under such a system, input costs will likely be known with certainty in advance, so there will be no price variances.

■ Traditional standard setting is based on a company's *own* costs and procedures. This may be too inward looking where the company operates in a rapidly changing, competitive market.

A more modern approach is *benchmarking*, which also takes into account the practices of other organisations in the industry (i.e. external information).

3.4   Behavioural Problems in Rapidly Changing Environments

The use of standard costing and variance analysis can have adverse effects on behaviour in a rapidly changing environment.

✗   Merely meeting standards may be insufficient to ensure the survival of a firm in a competitive environment. Thus, it may be necessary to focus on trends in variances which aim for continual improvement.

✗   Standards provide an internal focus to management. In a rapidly changing environment, an external focus would be more appropriate.

✗   New products come online more frequently. There may be learning curves associated with these. Standards which fail to reflect learning curves may not set an appropriate target. They could be too easy, which would not challenge staff, or too difficult, which would be demotivating.

Summary

■ Actual performance is compared with budgets at the end of each budget period. Prior to performing this comparison, it may be appropriate to revise the budget if it turns out to be unrealistic in retrospect, or if factors outside the control of the relevant manager occurred which made the original budget inappropriate.

■ Standards also may be revised prior to performing variance analysis. Operational variances describe variances calculated by comparing actual performance against a revised standard.

■ Traditional cost variances can be analysed into planning and operational as follows:
  • Price (rate) planning variance:
    (Actual quantity × Original standard price) − (Actual quantity × Revised standard price)
  • Operational price (rate) variance:
    (Actual quantity × Actual price) − (Actual quantity × Revised standard price)
  • Planning usage (efficiency) variance:
    (Revised SQ for actual output − Original SQ for actual output) × Original standard price
  • Operational usage (efficiency) variance:
    (Actual quantity − Revised SQ for actual output) × Original standard price.

■ The sales volume variance can also be analysed into a market volume (planning) variance and a market share (operational) variance. A revised budgeted sales quantity is found by multiplying the budgeted market share with the actual market size.
  • Market volume variance is then (Original budget quantity − Revised standard quantity) x Standard contribution per unit.
  • Market volume variance is (Revised standard quantity − Actual sales quantity) x Standard contribution per unit.

■ The use of standard costing and variance analysis aims at improving operational efficiency. Managers need to be aware of the potential adverse effects which variance analysis can have on the behaviour of those being appraised.

Session 13 Quiz
Estimated time: 15 minutes

1. State TWO general reasons budgets might be revised prior to performing variance analysis. (1)

2. Describe how the planning usage variance is calculated. (2.2.2)

3. State whether the "market share" variance is considered to be an operating or a planning variance. (2.4.1)

4. List FOUR advantages to updated standards and budgets in the variance analysis process. (2.5)

5. Describe THREE possible adverse consequences of using variance analysis as a management tool. (3.1)

Study Question Bank
Estimated time: 40 minutes

Priority		Estimated Time	Completed
Q24	Spike Co	40 minutes	

EXAMPLE SOLUTIONS

Solution 1—Budget Revisions

13-**15**

Budget revisions should be made in the case of the increase in fuel costs and the volcano ash—as these are clearly outside of the control of the management.

The lost revenue from the strike is less clear. On the one hand, the strike could be "blamed" on the management, for poor industrial relations. It would therefore be inappropriate to revise the budget, and management should be "blamed" for the loss of revenue during this period. On the other hand, it could be argued that it was outside management's control because unions called the strike.

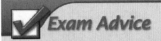

Exam Advice

Although the answer above may appear a little "woolly" in that it does not reach a definite conclusion, the real world often presents situations with no right answer. In F5 exams, the examiner wants both sides of the argument for questions of this nature rather than a quick conclusion.

Solution 2—Materials Price Variances

(a) Traditional price variance

	$
Actual materials at actual price	42,500
Actual materials at standard price (10,000 x 4)	40,000
Materials price variance (adverse)	2,500

(b) Planning and operational variances

Planning variance

	$
Actual materials at original standard price (10,000 x 4)	40,000
Actual materials at revised standard price (10,000 x 4.5)	45,000
Planning price variance (adverse)	5,000

Operational variance

	$
Actual materials at actual price	42,500
Actual materials at revised standard price (10,000 x 4.5)	45,000
Operational price variance (favourable)	2,500

(c) Comment on purchasing manager's performance

The price variance reflects to some extent the performance of the purchasing manager:

- If the purchasing manager is effective, he may be able to negotiate better prices.
- If price variances are adverse, however, this suggests that the manager is not managing to achieve the standard price, and is therefore not "doing a good job."

The traditional price variance is $2,500,000 adverse, suggesting that the purchasing manager has not performed well. However, this would not be a fair conclusion. The reason that the actual cost of materials was higher than the standard was that the market prices of Material X increased after the standard was set. This increase was outside of the manager's control, so he should not be held responsible. Therefore, the traditional variance does not fairly reflect the purchasing manager's performance.

The operational variance compares the performance against a standard that has been updated to reflect the change in the market price. It provides a more reliable indicator of performance. In this case, the operational price variance is favourable, which suggests that the purchasing manager has performed well. He has managed to obtain a price below the market price. Because this is more reliable, it can be said to be more fair.

Solution 3—Labour Efficiency Variances

(a) Traditional labour efficiency variance

	Kilos/Hours, etc
Actual hours worked	320
Standard hours for an actual output (1,000 x 0.25)	250
Difference	70
At standard rate per hour	$10
Labour efficiency variance (adverse)	$700

(b) Planning on operational efficiency variances

Planning efficiency variance

	Hours
Original standard hours for actual output	250
Revised standard hours for actual output (1,000 x 0.3)	300
Difference	50
At standard rate per hour	$10
Labour planning efficiency variance (adverse)	$500

Operational efficiency variance

	Hours
Actual hours worked	320
Revised standard hours for actual output	300
Difference	20
At standard rate per hour	$10
Labour operational efficiency variance (adverse)	$200

(c) Fairness of operational efficiency variance

The traditional efficiency variance is $700 adverse. This would reflect unfavourably on the factory manager as the actual factory hours were almost 30% more than the standard. It has been claimed, however, that the standard was overly optimistic. Using an inappropriate standard would certainly not be fair, so the traditional variance would not be a fair measure of performance.

The standard has been revised to make it more realistic. The operational variance compares the actual performance against the revised standard and should therefore be a fairer indicator of the performance of the factory manager. This is still adverse, but the actual hours worked are only 6.7% higher than the revised standard, so the situation is not as bad as indicated by the traditional variance.

Care must be taken when revising such standards, to ensure that the standard is not simply revised to hide poor performance. It would be necessary to challenge the assertion that the original standard was overly optimistic and to ascertain how the revised standard time of 0.3 per unit was reached.

Solution 4—Materials

(a) Traditional price and usage variances

	$
Price variance (2.50 − 3.00) 86,000	43,000 A
Usage variance (22,000 x 4 − 86,000) $2.50	5,000 F
Total variance	38,000 A

(b) Planning price and operational price variances

Planning variance

	$
Actual materials at original standard price (86,000 x 2.5)	215,000
Actual materials at revised standard price (86,000 x 2.8)	240,800
Planning price variance (adverse)	25,800*

Operational variance

	$
Actual materials at actual price (86,000 x 3)	258,000
Actual materials at revised standard price (86,000 x 2.8)	240,800
Operational price variance (adverse)	17,200*

*Commentary

*The sum ($25,800 + $17,200) equals the traditional price variance of $43,000.

(c) Planning usage and operational usage variances

Planning usage variance

	Kg
Original standard quantity for actual output (22,000 x 4)	88,000
Revised standard quantity for actual output (22,000 x 3.75)	82,500
Difference	5,500
At standard price per kg	$2.50
Materials planning usage variance (favourable)	$13,750*

Operational usage variance

	Kg
Actual quantity used	86,000
Revised standard quantity for actual output	82,500
Difference	3,500
At standard price per kg	$2.50
Materials operational usage variance (adverse)	$8,750*

*Commentary

*The sum ($13,750 − $8,750) equals the traditional usage variance of $5,000 favourable. This revised analysis still indicates that there is inefficiency on the part of the buying department and that there could be better use of materials.

Compare this with the traditional analysis which suggested a more serious inefficiency in buying (i.e. $43,000 adverse price variance) coupled with efficient use of materials.

Solution 5—Learning Curves and Variances

(a) **Labour rate variance**

	$
Actual labour hours × Actual rate	80
Actual labour hours × Standard rate (350/60) × $12	70
Labour rate variance (adverse)	10

Labour efficiency variance

	$
Actual labour hours × Standard rate	70
Standard hours for actual production × Standard rate (4 units × 100 minutes) × 12/60	80
Labour efficiency variance (favourable)	10

(b) **Re-calculated labour efficiency variance**

Actual labour hours × Standard rate	70
Standard hours for actual production × Standard rate (working) 324 minutes × $12/60	65
Labour efficiency variance (adverse)	5

Working—standard hours for actual production taking into account the learning rate of 90%.

Output (units)	Cumulative average time	Total time
1	100	100
2	90	180
4	81	324

Solution 6—Sales Planning and Operational Variances

(a) **Sales volume variance**

(1,850 − 1,795) $20 = $1,100 Favourable

(b) **Planning and operating sales volume variances table***

Market volume variance

	Units
Budgeted sales quantity	1,795
Revised budgeted quantity (37,500 × 5%)	1,875
Difference	80
× Standard contribution per unit	$20
Market volume variance	$1,600 (F)

Market share variance

	Units
Actual sales quantity	1,850
Revised budgeted quantity	1,875
Difference	25
× Standard contribution per unit	$20
Market share variance	$500 (A)

*The market volume variance is favourable, meaning that the actual market size was greater than expected. This is a planning variance and is outside of the control of Acme Co.

The market share variance is adverse because actual sales were below the budgeted market share of the actual market.

Performance Measurement

FOCUS

This session covers the following content from the *ACCA Study Guide.*

D. Performance Measurement and Control

4. Performance analysis in private sector organisations

a) Describe, calculate and interpret financial performance indicators (FPIs) for profitability, liquidity and risk in both manufacturing and service businesses. Suggest methods to improve these measures. ☐

b) Describe, calculate and interpret non-financial performance indicators (NFPIs) and suggest methods to improve the performance indicated. ☐

c) Analyse past performance and suggest ways for improving financial and non-financial performance. ☐

d) Explain the causes and problems created by short-termism and financial manipulation of results and suggest methods to encourage a long-term view. ☐

f) Discuss the difficulties of target setting in qualitative areas. ☐

Session 14 Guidance

■ **Note** that this session introduces ratio analysis of financial performance indicators as well as analysis of non-financial performance indicators. Remember that ratios and indicators are just tools to discover underlying business dynamics, rather than an end in themselves.

■ **Read** the article "Performance Measurement". This article relates to the question "Thatcher International Park", which is in Becker's Revision Question Bank.

(continued on next page)

VISUAL OVERVIEW

Objective: To understand the scope of performance measurement and to calculate and understand financial and non-financial performance indicators.

```
┌─────────────────────────────────────┐
│   OBJECTIVES OF PERFORMANCE          │
│         MEASUREMENT                  │
├─────────────────────────────────────┤
│  • Objectives of Performance         │
│    Measurement                       │
│  • The Performance Hierarchy         │
│  • Hierarchy of Objectives           │
└─────────────────────────────────────┘

┌─────────────────────────────────────┐
│   FINANCIAL PERFORMANCE              │
│     INDICATORS (FPIs)                │
├─────────────────────────────────────┤
│  • Introduction                      │
│  • Returns to Capital                │
│  • Profit Margins                    │
│  • Asset Turnover Ratios             │
│  • Liquidity Ratios                  │
│  • Gearing                           │
│  • Interest Cover                    │
│  • Exam Approach                     │
└─────────────────────────────────────┘

┌─────────────────────────────────────┐
│   NON-FINANCIAL PERFORMANCE          │
│     INDICATORS (NFPIs)               │
├─────────────────────────────────────┤
│  • Weaknesses of FPIs                │
│  • KPIs                              │
│  • Operational NFPIs                 │
│  • Advantages of NFPIs               │
│  • Ways to Improve                   │
│  • Target Setting                    │
└─────────────────────────────────────┘
```

Session 14 Guidance

■ **Understand** how performance measures cascade through a hierarchy of objectives (s.1).

■ **Know** financial performance indicators and understand their underlying meaning (s.2).

■ **Recognise** shortcomings of FPIs for determining underlying causes of poor financial performance, and the ways to improve financial performance by employing NFPIs (s.3).

1 Objectives of Performance Measurement

1.1 Main Objectives of Performance Measurement

As part of an organisation's corporate strategy planning, directors will define the organisation's objectives. These objectives may be organised into a hierarchy of objectives, the performance hierarchy.

Performance measurement aims to measure how successfully the organisation achieves its objectives. As such, performance indicators form part of the organisation's control system.

The main objectives of a performance measurement system are to:

- design measures which are consistent with the strategy for each level of the organisation;
- set objective, quantifiable targets based on those measures rather than subjective appraisal;
- develop reward schemes based on managers' performance against the targets; and
- judge managers fairly; i.e. on outcomes they control.

1.2 The Performance Hierarchy

The idea of the performance hierarchy was introduced in the session on budgeting. As a reminder, the objectives of an organisation are often based on a hierarchy—the performance hierarchy.

Typically the hierarchy consists of:

- Mission—the main reason for the existence of the organisation.
- Corporate objectives—more concrete objectives, stating what the mission means in practical terms to the primary stakeholder groups (e.g. to increase the market value of the company by more than a given percentage over the longer term).
- Subsidiary objectives—other objectives of the organisation may relate to other stakeholder groups (e.g. to reduce the amount of pollution by a given percentage).
- Unit objectives—these are objectives for the operating departments (units) of the organisation. They should contribute to the subsidiary and corporate objectives.

1.3 Hierarchy of Objectives

- Because there is a hierarchy of objectives, there will also be a hierarchy of performance measures.
- Performance targets and measures will be set at all levels within the organisation.
- In a well-designed system, these targets and measures will be consistent with the organisation's overall goals.

2 Financial Performance Indicators (FPIs)

2.1 Introduction

▓ Traditional performance measurement considered only financial measures. This was considered to be appropriate, because it was assumed that the primary objective of all organisations was to maximise shareholder wealth. Focusing on financial measures seemed a natural way to achieve this objective.

▓ Much of the material covered already in earlier sessions relates to FPIs, in particular:

- Budgeting
- Standard costing and variances
- Activity-based costing
- Specialist management accounting techniques.

▓ This section introduces some additional, widely used ratios used for financial performance evaluation.

2.2 Returns on Capital

Measures describing returns to the various providers of capital include:*

▓ Return on equity (ROE):

$$\text{Return on equity} = \frac{\text{Profit after tax}}{\text{Equity}} \times 100$$

▓ Return on capital employed (ROCE):

$$\text{Return on capital employed} = \frac{\text{Profit BEFORE interest and tax}}{\text{Share capital + reserves + long-term liabilities}} \times 100$$

Commentary

*In practice, variants of the ROCE formula may be used. What is important is to match the profit figure with the appropriate capital. If profit is after interest, it should be divided by equity. If profit is before interest, it should be divided by equity plus long-term debt, because that profit will be shared between providers of debt and equity finance.

2.2.1 Meaning of Return on Capital Employed

▓ Shows the return generated on the long-term capital invested in the firm. This can be compared with other companies in the same industry sector or to the company's cost of capital.

▓ Comparing companies in other sectors does not provide valid information. Service industries, for example, require less capital than manufacturing industries and will show a greater return on capital employed for each dollar of profit.

2.2.2 Methods to Improve Return on Capital Employed

✔ Invest in projects that generate a higher return on capital.

✗ Manipulate profits and capital employed by using different accounting policies.

✗ Delay investment in new plant and machinery or reduce investment on intangible assets. As the non-current assets become depreciated, their carrying amount (net book value) falls, reducing the capital employed, and therefore improving the return on capital. Such measures may harm the organisation in the longer term.

2.3   Profit Margins

Profit margins relate profit to revenue. Because there are many profit sub-totals in the income statement (gross profit, profit before interest and tax, etc.) there are many potential profit margins.

The most commonly used are the gross profit margin and the net profit margin.

2.3.1   Gross Profit Margin

Gross profit is the profit after deducting the costs of buying or making the products the company produces. It therefore reflects performance of the company's products.

$$\text{Gross profit margin} = \frac{\text{Gross profit}}{\text{Revenue}} \times 100$$

2.3.2   Meaning of Gross Profit Margin

A falling gross profit margin over time means:

- that either the selling price at which the company sells its goods is declining, or
- that the cost of making or buying those goods is increasing, but those increases cannot be passed onto customers.

In either case, a prolonged decline is a bad sign. It suggests that the products or services the company sells are losing popularity, and this puts into question the viability of the business.

Gross profit margins may also reflect an organisation's pricing strategy.

- Companies that use a premium pricing strategy are likely to have a high gross profit margin.
- Companies that aim to sell for a low price, to achieve a larger volume of sales, are likely to have a low gross profit margin.

2.3.3   Methods to Improve Gross Profit Margins

✔ Introduce new products that are popular with customers. These can be sold for a higher margin.

✔ Use **target costing** to reduce cost of sales.

✗ Reclassify direct expenses as administrative. Gross profit depends on the company's policy regarding what it considers direct expense versus administrative expense. Changes in such policies should be viewed with suspicion.

2.3.4   Net Profit Margin

Net profit describes "bottom line" profit after deducting all costs. Net profit margin shows overall profits as a percentage of revenue.

$$\text{Net profit margin} = \frac{\text{Net profit after tax}}{\text{Revenue}} \times 100$$

Definition

Target costing— subtracting a desired profit margin from a competitive market price to determine the maximum acceptable cost.

2.3.5 Meaning of Net Profit Margin

Net profit is sometimes referred to as "the bottom line", as it is profit after deducting all costs. The net profit margin shows overall profits as a percentage of revenue.

- Although this gives a broad indicator of the performance of the organisation, further analysis should consider that the causes of changes will need to be investigated.
- Net profit margin reflects the following three areas:

  1. The underlying popularity of the company's products and services (this is also reflected in the gross margin).

  2. The amount of control the company has over administrative-type expenses.

  3. Costs of debt financing. This will depend partly on whether the company has changed the amount of debt and partly on whether interest rates have changed.

2.3.6 Ways to Improve the Net Profit Margin

- ✔ Introduce new products that are popular with customers. These can be sold for a higher margin.
- ✔ Use target costing to reduce cost of sales.
- ✔ Increasing sales volume should increase net profit margins if a high portion of the company's costs are fixed (e.g. in a training company).
- ✔ Better control over administrative expenses (e.g. salaries).
- ✔ Using less debt finance.

2.4 Asset Turnover Ratio

The asset turnover ratio relates revenue to the amount of capital invested in the business:

$$\frac{\text{Sales}}{\text{Capital employed}}$$

It indicates whether or not the capital invested is appropriate, given the value of sales revenue. Excessive levels of capital invested will lead to a low turnover ratio.

The asset turnover ratio can be improved by:

- ✔ Selling non-current assets that are not being utilised fully.
- ✔ Recognising impairments and writing down the value of the assets.*
- ✔ Improving working capital management (e.g. by collecting receivables more quickly or reducing inventory levels through better inventory management).

*Arguably this is merely financial engineering as it does not improve actual performance.

2.4.1   Analysis of Return on Capital Employed

Return on capital employed ratio (see s.2.2) is the product of the operating profit margin and the asset turnover:

ROCE = Operating profit margin × Asset turnover

$$\frac{\text{Profit before interest and tax}}{\text{Capital employed}} = \frac{\text{Profit before interest and tax}}{\text{Sales}} \times \frac{\text{Sales}}{\text{Capital employed}}$$

This relationship can be used to provide insights into the ROCE for a particular business. For example, if a business is experiencing a decline in ROCE this could be due to:

✗   a decline in the asset turnover ratio;

✗   a fall in profit margin; or

✗   a decline in both ratios.

Finding out which of these factors gave rise to the decline will point the analyst in the right direction to find the underlying causes.

2.5   Liquidity Ratios

▓ Liquidity ratios measure the ability of the organisation to meet its liabilities as they become due (e.g. suppliers, interest on bank loans, overdrafts).

▓ Creditors could take legal action against a company that fails to pay when due, which, in the worst case, could lead to liquidating the company. Many profitable companies occasionally face liquidity problems.

▓ Operating cash flows represent the ultimate measure of liquidity. If the company generates positive operating cash flows sufficient to replace any non-current assets, then the company is less likely to experience liquidity problems.

2.5.1   Current Ratio

The current ratio measures the organisation's current assets in relation to current liabilities. A ratio less than 1 means current liabilities exceed current assets.

$$\text{Current ratio} = \frac{\text{Current assets (at period end)}}{\text{Current liabilities (at period end)}}$$

2.5.2 Quick Ratio (Acid Test Ratio)

Some analysts argue that inventory is not a liquid asset, so should not be considered a current asset.

$$\text{Quick ratio} = \frac{\text{Current assets} - \text{Inventory (at period end)}}{\text{Current liabilities (at period end)}}$$

■ It is sometimes referred to as the "acid test".*

■ The quick ratio is a more conservative version of the current ratio.

■ A low or declining ratio may indicate an inability to meet its liabilities as they come due. This could result from generating insufficient cash flows to pay its suppliers on time or large investments in non-current assets.*

*Literally, an acid test is a test to determine whether or not a metal is real gold.

*Commentary

*One international food retailer, which regularly reports a current ratio of about 0.3, illustrates the fallacy of using a single current ratio target to indicate satisfactory liquidity. The company in question has low inventory, as food only lasts a few days. It has few receivables, as most of its sales are for cash. It invests cash balances in non-current assets, so it holds low cash balances. The company does not pay its suppliers for three months, so it has large payables balances. Far from indicating liquidity problems, the company uses its suppliers as a free source of financing.

2.5.3 Ways to Increase Liquidity Ratios

✔ Use loans and equity to finance acquisition of non-current assets.

✔ Generate positive cash flows to repay short-term liabilities on time.

✗ Manipulate by year-end window dressing.

Example 1 Window Dressing

Extracts from the statement of financial position	
	$000
Receivables	900
Cash	500
Payables	1,000

Required:

(a) **Calculate the quick ratio.**

(b) **Re-calculate the ratio if $400,000 of payments are made just prior to the year end.**

2.6 Gearing

Gearing (or "leverage") measures the portion of a company's finance provided by debt. The advantage of debt is that it is a relatively cheap source of financing as:

- Providers of debt require a lower return than do providers of equity finance because they receive preferential repayment in the event of default and thus face less risk.

- Interest on debt is also a tax-deductible expense, which further reduces the cost of debt.

However, companies with too much debt (gearing) increase the risk of not being able to repay the interest and/or principal on the debt.

2.6.1 Gearing Ratios

Two gearing ratios are commonly used:*

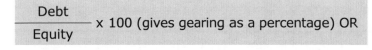

$$\frac{\text{Debt}}{\text{Equity}} \times 100 \text{ (gives gearing as a percentage) OR}$$

$$\frac{\text{Debt}}{\text{Equity plus debt}} \times 100$$

Commentary

*Gearing ratios measure the proportion of borrowed funds (which pay a fixed return) to equity capital (shareholders' funds) and provide information about a company's financial risk due to debt burden.

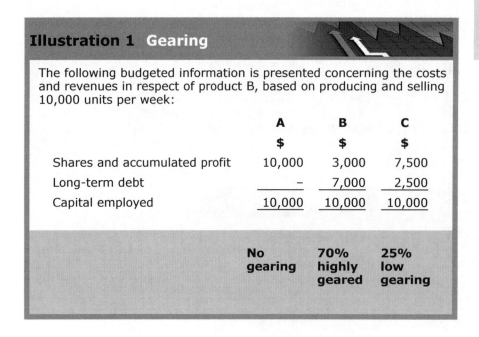

Illustration 1 Gearing

The following budgeted information is presented concerning the costs and revenues in respect of product B, based on producing and selling 10,000 units per week:

	A	B	C
	$	$	$
Shares and accumulated profit	10,000	3,000	7,500
Long-term debt	–	7,000	2,500
Capital employed	10,000	10,000	10,000
	No gearing	70% highly geared	25% low gearing

2.6.2 Meaning of Gearing

■ A gearing ratio in isolation means very little. It is only useful if the gearing of the organisation is compared with industry averages, or with other companies in the same business area to determine whether or not the gearing is too high.

■ In industries with stable profits, companies can sustain higher levels of gearing. High gearing ratios increase risk in companies in which profits fluctuate because a fall in profits may mean that the company cannot repay interest on its loans.

■ An increase in gearing over time may reflect changes in the level of debt deemed acceptable to the finance director. Alternatively, it may indicate that insufficient cash flows cause the company to borrow money to finance short-term operations.

2.7 Interest Cover

Shows the extent to which profit covers return on debt (interest).

Used by lenders to determine vulnerability of interest payments to a drop in profit.

$$\text{Interest cover} = \frac{\text{Profit before interest and tax}}{\text{Interest}}$$

2.8 Approach to Financial Performance Evaluation Exam Questions

2.8.1 Comments Not Calculations

In F5, few marks are available for simply calculating ratios in performance evaluation questions. Candidates need to show that they have the ability to comment on what the numbers and calculations show about how the organisation has performed.

2.8.2 Approach

Before writing anything, spend a few minutes reviewing and analysing the information. The following is a suggested approach to this planning time:

■ Review the "big picture"—look at revenue growth, profit growth and any other major trends visible in the data.

■ Calculate a limited number of ratios that you think are necessary to investigate further any trends identified in the analysis (e.g. if revenues have grown, but profits have not changed, it may be worth calculating gross profit margins to identify if this is the cause of the sluggish profits).

■ If capital is given, calculate return on capital employed as this can indicate how well the organisation provides a return on the capital invested.

■ Review the information given in the scenario and look for clues which might explain the trends. Information such as "the company operates in a competitive environment" might explain falling gross profit margins.

Having planned in this way, start to write your answer. Comment on each trend identified.

■ Comment means:

- State what happened (e.g. profits increased by 20% between quarter 1 and quarter 2).

- State why this happened using any relevant information provided in the scenario to help identify why (e.g. revenue increased by 10% and many of the company's costs are fixed, so this has led to a 20% rise in profits).

- Link this to other related items. For example, if depreciation rose significantly due to investment in new machinery, perhaps spending on repairs may have fallen.

- Express an opinion (e.g. an increase of profits of 20% is impressive given that the company is operating in a competitive environment).

It is a good idea to show any ratio calculations separately (e.g. in an appendix). This looks professional.

Example 2 Financial Performance Measurement

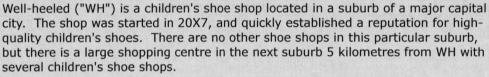

Well-heeled ("WH") is a children's shoe shop located in a suburb of a major capital city. The shop was started in 20X7, and quickly established a reputation for high-quality children's shoes. There are no other shoe shops in this particular suburb, but there is a large shopping centre in the next suburb 5 kilometres from WH with several children's shoe shops.

The retail space next door to WH became vacant at the start of 20Y0. Because this was also owned by the same landlord, WH decided to rent this space too, expanding the area of the shop from 40 square meters to 60.

The company employs one full-time shop assistant, and starting in 20Y0 employed an additional assistant to work on Saturdays. The owner of WH also works in the shop, but does not take a salary for her time.

The country in which WH is located was hit badly by an economic downturn in the first half of 20Y0, but started to recover in the second half of 20Y0. Inflation in 20X9 and 20Y0 was 2%.

The income statements for the years 20X9 and 20Y0 are presented below:

		20X9		20Y0
	$	$	$	$
Sales		180,000		240,000
Less: Cost of sales		120,000		168,000
Gross profit		60,000		72,000
Less expenses				
Staff Costs	20,000		30,000	
Rent	7,200		10,800	
Marketing	5,000		6,000	
Light and heat	1,000		1,200	
		33,200		48,000
Net profit		26,800		24,000

Required:

Assess the financial performance of the shop using the information above.

3 Non-financial Performance Indicators (NFPIs)

3.1 Financial Performance Indicators

3.1.1 Inherent Weaknesses

Traditional performance measurement relied almost exclusively on financial measures. However, since the 1980s, many companies recognised that there are inherent weaknesses in focusing only on financial factors.

■ FPIs may lead to excessive focus on cost reduction. Short-term cost reductions may be achieved at the expense of long-term performance due to the effect on staff morale, quality and other factors.

■ FPIs ignore the drivers of business success. The things which drive business success are:

● Quality
● Delivery
● Customer satisfaction
● After-sales service.

■ FPIs can be manipulated (e.g. using different accounting policies and "window dressing") to make the performance look better. Possible solutions to this are:

● to use profit growth over a number of years;
● to use non-financial performance measures that encourage managers to take account of the factors that drive success that may otherwise be sacrificed in the interests of increasing short-term profits.

Since the 1980s, therefore, many companies have started to develop non-financial performance indicators.

Because companies have a hierarchy of objectives, they also have a hierarchy of performance measures.

3.1.2 FPIs and Short-Termism

Many organisations use financial performance measures such as profit and ROCE. Managers are often given bonuses or better prospects of promotion if the organisation achieves these financial targets.*

Managers may therefore take a short-term view and concentrate their efforts on achieving the next set of financial targets, effectively ignoring the longer term. This short-termism in performance management is often referred to as myopia.
Myopia may exist for the following reasons:

■ Achieving a bonus now seems much more attractive than achieving a bonus in the future.

■ If managers are expecting to be promoted, or there is high management turnover, managers may take the view that future financial performance is not relevant to them, as they will be working somewhere else by then.

■ Shareholders may take a short-term view of performance and will be disappointed if the targets of the current period are not met.*

The examiner believes that organisations are obsessed with financial measures of performance, whereas NFPIs drive businesses forward in the long run. FPIs may measure success, but they do not ensure success.

*Failure to achieve them may adversely affect promotion prospects.

*This is particularly relevant to listed companies that fear failure of meeting quarterly earnings expectations of stock market investors.

There is nothing wrong with improving the current year's profits. However, some actions to improve financial performance in the current period will harm the business in the longer term. For example:

- Failing to invest in worthwhile projects (i.e. that would generate profits over a number of years) because:
  - they may reduce profits in the shorter term;
  - the initial investment in capital assets and increase in depreciation leads to a lower ROCE in the early years of a project.
- Failing to invest in "value building" activities (e.g. research and development, training, advertising and marketing) that may bring long-term benefits, but would lead to high costs in the current financial periods.*
- Cutting down on activities that lead to better quality of a product. In the long term this may lead to a loss of customers and therefore revenue.
- Reducing headcount, which may lead to a reduction in the quality of customer service.
- Recruitment freezes during economic downturns, which mean that the organisation does not develop the skills and knowledge needed to compete when the economic climate improves.*
- Salary freezes that may lead to increased staff turnover. High staff turnover can lead to the loss of "corporate knowledge", and high costs of recruiting and training new staff.

The use of NFPIs can mitigate this myopic behaviour in the following ways:

- Measures of the quality of a product or a service should ensure that managers do not cut back on these.
- Measures relating to staff satisfaction (e.g. staff turnover) should reduce cutbacks in staff-related expenditure.
- A more balanced view of performance should focus on the drivers of longer-term growth.

*Many such revenue expenses cannot be capitalised under financial reporting standards such as IAS 38.

*Similarly, cutbacks in training and development.

3.2 Key Performance Indicators

Many companies identify **critical success factors** (CSFs) at the strategic level.

- Organisations should only identify a small number of critical success factors.
- Key performance indicators (KPIs) measure how well an organisation meets its critical success factors.

Critical success factor—an outcome required by an organisation to achieve its mission.

Illustration 2 Key Performance Indicators

Vodafone Group plc, the British multinational mobile telephone operator, monitors the following key performance indicators on a quarterly basis:

- Vodafone live! active devices and 3G devices
- Active customers
- Average monthly revenue per user (ARPU)
- Non-voice services as a percentage of service revenues
- Customer churn
- Voice usage volumes.

3.3   Operational NFPIs

Having set NFPIs consistent with the organisation's strategic objectives, non-financial performance measures can be set at all levels of an organisation.

Example 3 Manufacturing NFPIs

Required:

Suggest some possible non-financial performance measures which might be used in a manufacturing organisation to measure the following attributes:

Attribute	NFPI
Product quality	
Product delivery	
Customer satisfaction	
After-sales service	

3.4   Advantages of NFPIs

✔ Usually easier to calculate than financial reports, so can be provided much more quickly (e.g. at the end of each shift).

✔ More flexible as organisations can come up with any measures appropriate to their objectives.

✔ Less easily manipulated than financial measures.

3.5   Ways to Improve Performance Indicated by Non-financial Indicators

3.5.1   Quality Indicators

Many organisations use quality improvement programmes to improve the measured quality of products or services. Such programmes normally include quality control and quality assurance:

✔ Quality control focuses on measuring the quality of the products and comparing this against a predetermined standard. Typically, this involves quality inspectors.

✔ Quality assurance means having procedures to ensure good quality. This might include redesigning processes, using better-quality materials and "quality meetings" during which staff members suggest ways to improve quality.

Example 4 Non-financial Performance

Ben's Grub Co (BG) operates a food takeaway and delivery service based in Homeland. Customers buy ready meals by either walking into one of BG's takeaway shops or by placing an order for home delivery by telephone or Internet. Home deliveries are delivered by motorcycle.

BG's mission is to provide excellent-quality food, by buying only the freshest products, and excellent service, by recruiting and retaining the best staff. Its meals are of good quality and aimed at busy middle-class professionals with high levels of disposable income.

A performance measurement report focusing on non-financial measures has been used for a number of years. The report for the last two years contains the following information, with industry average figures, where available:

	Year 1	Year 2	Industry average
% of orders delivered in 30 minutes	86%	81%	80%
Quality of meals—rating by independent reviewer (out of 10)	9	8	6
Average customer rating (out of 5)	4.3	3.7	3
Number of meals sold	62,000	70,000	
Number of online sales	18,000	27,000	
Number of website visits	400,000	450,000	
Number of new meals launched	3	5	
Number of complaints	500	760	
Staff turnover (Number of leavers ÷ Average headcount)	35%	30%	60%
Number of employees	20	22	

The industry average conversion rate (number of online sales as a percentage of website visits) is 4.5%.

Required

Assess the non-financial performance of BG for the last two years, based on the information provided.

3.5.2 Customer Service

Customer service is particularly important in service industries, but the level of after-sales service is also important in manufacturing industries. Ways to improve indicated performance include:

✔ Provide training to staff so they understand the importance of customer service.

✔ Provide incentives to staff (e.g. "employee of the month" rewards and prizes for good performance) to reward improvements in this area.

3.6 Target Setting in Qualitative Areas

■ The session on budgeting and standard costing dealt with problems inherent in setting financial targets. Most of the issues relating to setting financial targets also apply to qualitative areas. In qualitative areas, however, there may be additional complications.

3.6.1 Qualitative Areas of Performance

The most important qualitative areas of performance tend to be:

■ Quality of product or service

■ Customer satisfaction

■ Delivery

■ After-sales service.

These are the areas that organisations wish to measure using NFPIs.

3.6.2 Difficulties of Setting Targets for Qualitative Areas

When setting targets for qualitative areas, the following difficulties will be experienced:

✗ Identifying the drivers of improved performance. Rather than simply measuring customer satisfaction, for example, it is better to identify what our staff can actually do to achieve greater customer satisfaction, and then set targets based on these. It is often difficult to identify these drivers however, and some judgement will be required.

✗ Many qualitative factors cannot be measured. For example, how do you measure "friendliness of staff"?

✗ Staff behaviour in response to set targets. Staff will aim to achieve the targets but perhaps not in the expected manner.

Illustration 3 Call Centre

A call centre recently introduced a target of two minutes per call in an attempt to increase the number of calls handled. It discovered that staff hung up on customers after two minutes to avoid a variance.

✗ Setting the level of difficulty of the targets. Staff will become demotivated by excessively difficult targets, and will not improve performance based on excessively easy targets.

Summary

- Performance measurement attempts to identify how well an organisation achieves its stated objectives.

- An organisation can rank its objectives in a hierarchy from its mission, strategic objectives and critical success factors, down to lower level objectives designed to support strategic objectives.

- Traditional performance measurement systems focuses on financial measures. There are many different financial performance indicators. The most important categories are:

  - Interest cover
  - Profit margins
  - Return on capital
  - Asset turnover ratios
  - Liquidity ratios
  - Gearing ratios.

- Financial measures exclude important factors that drive the financial performance of an organisation. NFPIs should be used in addition to financial measures.

- NFPIs attempt to measure non-financial aspects of performance (e.g. quality, customer satisfaction and staff morale).

 ## Session 14 Quiz
Estimated time: 15 minutes

1. Identify the profit line which should be used when calculating return on capital employed, where capital employed means equity plus long-term liabilities. (2.2)
2. State THREE methods to improve gross profit margins. (2.3.3)
3. Describe the "quick ratio" calculation. (2.5.2)
4. State the interest cover ratio and explain its meaning. (2.7)
5. List the areas covered by non-financial performance indicators. (3.1)
6. Discuss difficulties of setting targets for qualitative areas. (3.6.2)

 ## Study Question Bank
Estimated time: 50 minutes

Priority		Estimated Time	Completed
Q25	Ties Only	**50 minutes**	

EXAMPLE SOLUTIONS

Solution 1—Window Dressing

(a)   Quick ratio $= \dfrac{\$1.4m}{\$1m} = 1.4:1$

(b)   Quick ratio $= \dfrac{\$1.4m - 0.4m}{\$1m - 0.4m} = \dfrac{\$1m}{\$0.6m} = 1.7:1$

Key Point

The quick ratio (and current ratio) can be manipulated by making a payment just prior to the year end to improve the reported liquidity position.

Solution 2—Financial Performance Measurement

Sales revenues increased by one third (33%) between 20X9 and 20Y0. This is impressive given that the shop is only 5 kilometres from a big shopping centre. It is also impressive given that the economy was in recession during the first half of 20Y0. The cause of the increase in sales could be due to increases in prices or increases in volume. Given the fall in the gross profit margin (see following), it would seem more likely that sales volumes have risen. This reflects the reputation that the shop is gaining locally for high-quality products.

Gross profit margins fell from 33.3% in 20X9 to 30% in 20Y0. This suggests that sales prices have fallen, or that cost increases from suppliers have not been passed on to customers. This is probably due to the fact that during a recession the business recognises that customers are more price conscious. Prices may also have been lowered to gain more customers, and so may be related to the increase in revenues. If gross margins continue to decline, this may cast doubt on the viability of the business in the long term. In this case, however, it seems more likely that the fall in margins will be a temporary phenomenon, caused by the recession.

Staff costs have increased by 50%. This is likely to be due to the employment of an additional shop assistant in 20Y0. Because the assistant works only on Saturdays, however, we would not expect that alone to account for a 50% increase. The existing shop assistant probably was given a pay rise; perhaps to compensate for being busier now that the shop has increased in size. Staff costs as a percentage of revenue have risen from 11.1% in 20X9 to 12.5% in 20Y0. The owners need to ensure that they do not let this cost continue to rise above the level of sales, or this will reduce profitability.

Rent also has increased, due to the larger space occupied. The cost per square metre has remained constant at $180 per square metre per year, which shows that the landlord has not increased the rent, possibly due to the recession. The 50% increase in space has not been matched by such a large increase in revenue, but it does leave the shop space to grow in future years.

Marketing has increased by 20%. Because the revenue has increase by 33.3% however, it seems that the marketing effort is producing good results.

Light and heat have increased by 20%. Given the 50% increase in the size of the shop, this is good. In practice, light and heat are items which are outside of the control of businesses, as the prices are set by large energy firms with little competition.

Net profit actually declined, in spite of the increase in revenues. Net profit margin was 10% in 20Y0 compared to 14.8% in 20X9. This fall in margins is mainly due to the fall in gross margins (had gross margin remained constant, profits would be $8,000 higher), and partly due to additional staff costs and rent. Hopefully gross margins may increase in future years as the economy recovers. The staff costs and rent should remain fairly constant in future years, allowing an increase in revenues to be achieved without an increase in such expenses.

Overall, the owners of the company would probably be disappointed that, in spite of a significant increase in revenues, profits actually fell. However, the business is in a good position to benefit from an economic recovery in 20Y1.

Solution 3—Manufacturing NFPIs

Attribute	NFPI
Product quality	■ Percentage of items rejected by quality control
	■ Number of items returned by customers
Product delivery	■ Percentage of customer orders delivered on time
	■ Waiting time from order to delivery
	■ Cycle time
Customer satisfaction	■ Number of customers returning
	■ Number of complaints
After-sales service	■ Waiting time
	■ Number of complaints
	■ Use of customer surveys to measure their satisfaction.

Solution 4—Non-financial Performance

BG aims to provide excellent service and excellent quality to busy middle-class professionals. Such customers probably pay a higher price, but expect an excellent level of quality for both food and service. It is essential therefore that BG keeps the quality level high, otherwise customers may be lost.

Delivery is an important aspect of quality of service and is measured by the percentage of orders delivered in 30 minutes. This has fallen from 86% in Year 1 to 81% in Year 2. This may be because more meals have been sold, putting additional pressure on the delivery staff. Although Year 2 delivery performance is still better than the industry average, this decline needs to be stopped. Management needs to investigate the reasons for the decline and take remedial action (e.g. hire additional motorbike drivers).

The quality of meals also has declined, according to an independent rating. In isolation, the decline of only 1 point (from 8 to 7) may not be a cause of great concern, as such ratings are very subjective and may depend on a number of factors. However, the decline in customer ratings from 4.3 to 3.7 appears to corroborate the suggestion that the quality of food has indeed declined. Both ratings are above the industry average, but this is to be expected given the focus on excellent quality. Management should spend time checking that the quality of the food is improved and try to find out why these ratings are declining.

The number of meals sold has increased by 12% (from 62,000 in Year 1 to 70,000 in Year 2). This appears to be due to the increase in online sales, which have increased by 9,000 (i.e. 50%). This suggests that more customers are being attracted by the website. It is likely that some existing customers are switching to online ordering from more traditional methods. The ability to order online is clearly an important tool for the business and it has done well to exploit this. The overall increase in sales is also a good sign; even if the quality of food and service has declined, this has not been reflected yet in the sales figures.

The number of website visits has increased by 11.1 % (from 400,000 to 450,000), which shows that the website is being discovered by more people. It is not stated whether any Web-marketing activities might have increased its visibility (e.g. paying search engines such as Google a fee for ensuring that Ben's Grub is listed towards the top of any search for "takeaway food" or having links placed on other websites).

The "conversion rate" is the number of online sales as a percentage of website visits. As this shows the percentage of visits that leads to a sale it is a measure of how well the website persuades visitors to place an order. In Year 1, the conversion rate was 4.5%, rising to 6% in Year 2. The Year 1 rate was the same as the industry average; the Year 2 rate shows an increase above this. This is a good sign that shows that the website is relatively good in encouraging potential customers to actually place an order.

The number of complaints has risen by 52%. As a percentage of meals sold, this was 0.8% in Year 1 and 1.1% in Year 2). Although the proportion of complaints appears to be low, the increase is a cause for concern. It could be related to the reduction in the percentage of meals delivered in less than 30 minutes or the apparent decline in the quality of meals. The number does not seem significantly large, so hopefully the situation can be remedied to avoid the loss of customers.

Staff turnover is well below industry averages in both years and has declined over the two years. This is a positive sign that staff members enjoy working for BG. It is particularly important in service industries that staff members are motivated, as any lack of motivation may lead to customers experiencing a poor level of service. Low staff turnover also means that costs of training new staff are reduced and that customers benefit from better service from experienced staff. BG has explicitly recognised the importance of staff in its mission statement (where it mentions that it wishes to recruit and retain the best staff) and it seems that the company is indeed managing to retain its staff.

There has been a slight increase in the number of employees from 20 in Year 1 to 22 in Year 2. Staff utilisation can be calculated by dividing the number of meals sold by the number of staff. This was 3,100 in Year 1 and rose slightly to 3,182 in Year 2. Although higher staff utilisation is good from a financial point of view, it should not be too high, as this may lead to staff being overworked and the quality of service declining. Given the other signs of a fall in the quality of service, management should give serious consideration to employing additional staff.

Overall, BG has had a successful year in terms of increased sales, particularly online sales. However, there are signs that the quality of service and the quality of food are starting to decline, so management must take action to ensure that this is stopped before customers are lost.

Further Aspects of Performance Analysis

FOCUS

This session covers the following content from the *ACCA Study Guide.*

D. Performance Measurement and Control

4. Performance analysis in private sector organisations

d) Explain the causes and problems created by short-termism and financial manipulation of results and suggest methods to encourage a long-term view. ☐

e) Explain and interpret the Balanced Scorecard, and the Building Block model proposed by Fitzgerald and Moon. ☐

6. Performance analysis in not-for-profit organisations and the public sector

a) Comment on the problems of having non-quantifiable objectives in performance management. ☐

b) Explain how performance could be measured in this sector. ☐

c) Comment on the problems of having multiple objectives in this sector. ☐

d) Outline Value for Money (VFM) as a public sector objective. ☐

7. External considerations and behavioural aspects

a) Explain the need to allow for external considerations in performance management, including stakeholders, market conditions and allowance for competitors. ☐

b) Suggest ways in which external considerations could be allowed for in performance management. ☐

c) Interpret performance in the light of external considerations. ☐

d) Identify and explain the behavioural aspects of performance management. ☐

e) Describe, calculate and interpret non-financial performance indicators (NFPIs) and suggest methods to improve the performance indicated. ☐

f) Discuss the difficulties of target setting in qualitative areas. ☐

g) Analyse past performance and suggest ways for improving financial and non-financial performance. ☐

h) Explain the causes and problems created by short-termism and financial manipulation of results and suggest methods to encourage a long term view. ☐

(continued on next page)

VISUAL OVERVIEW

Objective: To consider further aspects, potential benefits and problems of performance measurement systems.

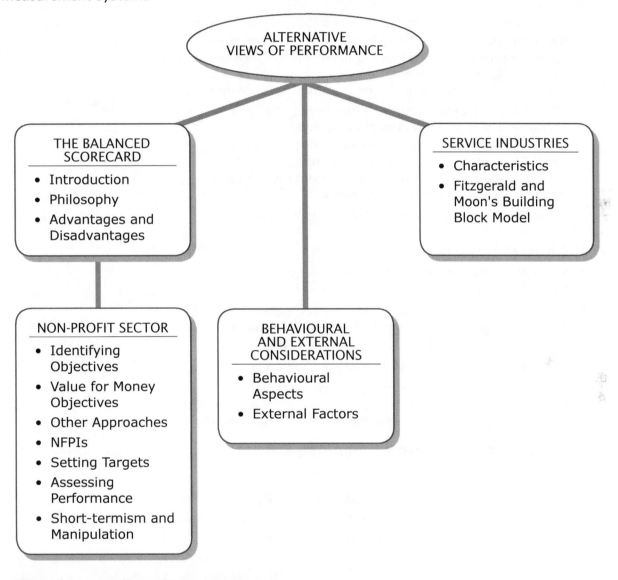

1 The Balanced Scorecard

1.1 Introduction

- *Session 14* examined the weaknesses inherent in relying exclusively on financial performance indicators (FPIs) and the benefits of using non-financial performance indicators (NFPIs) to supplement these.

- NFPIs became very popular during the 1980s. Two problems arose, however:

    ✗ Organisations often ignored financial performance entirely. This is clearly not appropriate when the objective of an organisation is to maximise the wealth of its shareholders.

    ✗ Organisations developed too many NFPIs, many of which conflicted, and this resulted in confusion.

- In response to these problems, Kaplan and Norton developed the balanced scorecard approach. The objective of the balanced scorecard is to provide top management with an integrated set of performance measures.

- The balanced scorecard looks at performance from four perspectives:

    1. Customer perspective—how do our customers see us?

    2. Internal business process perspective—at what must we excel?

    3. Learning and growth perspective—the company must continue to grow and change in the modern dynamic business environment.

    4. Financial perspective—how do we look to shareholders?

- The four perspectives should complement each other. If customers are happy, for example, this should lead to greater revenues and profits, which improve the financial perspective.

1.2 Balanced Scorecard Philosophy

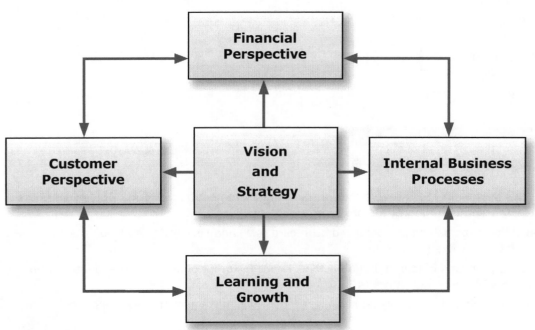

1.2.1 Setting Measures and Performance Targets

■ Within each of the four perspectives, management needs to identify:

1. Objectives—what are the main objectives?

2. Measures—how can the performance be measured against the objectives?

3. Targets—what targets should be set for each of the measures?

4. Initiatives—what actions could be taken to improve performance?

1.2.2 Leading and Lagging Indicators

■ Kaplan and Norton are interested in the cause and effect aspects of performance measurement. In this, they talk about leading and lagging indicators.

- **Lagging (downstream)** indicators show the effect of decisions long after they were made. The balanced scorecard refers to financial measures as a lagging indicator because that performance results from past decisions.

- **Leading (upstream)** indicators drive future financial performance. These are the non-financial performance indicators relating to customer, internal business processes and learning and growth.

1.2.3 Importance of Strategy

■ Kaplan and Norton also realised that companies chose many performance measures inconsistent with company strategy. The company should choose objectives for the four areas that reflect its mission and strategy, and measure appropriate results.

■ Many companies began to use the balanced scorecard not simply as a performance measurement tool, which was the original objective, but also as a tool to clarify and manage strategy.

1.3 Advantages and Disadvantages

✔ It leads to a wider view of the performance of an organisation rather than concentrating on the financial aspects of performance.

✔ It links performance measurement to the objectives of the organisation and therefore its strategy. This ensures that what is being measured is relevant to the strategy and objectives of the entire organisation.

✔ Using only a small number of KPIs ensures that management is able to concentrate on the most important aspects and not be confused by an excessive number of performance indicators.

✗ Introducing the balanced scorecard would require training and a change in culture. Managers and staff may initially be sceptical.

✗ Identifying the most appropriate measures may be difficult.

✗ The balanced scorecard focuses only on the needs of two stakeholders—owners and customers; it ignores the needs of other groups, such as employees.

Objective—a specific, measurable statement of what will be done to achieve goals within a defined time frame.*

Performance measure—a quantitative or qualitative characterisation of performance used to evaluate progress toward an objective.

*Although the terms *objectives* and *goals* are widely used interchangeably, a goal tends to be more of a longer-term aspiration.

Illustration 1 The Balanced Scorecard

Graham Morgan describes how the balanced scorecard approach might be used by the low-cost airlines in an ACCA Technical article *Performance Measures to Support Competitive Advantages*:

Objective	Measure
Business process perspective	
Punctuality	Adherence to schedule Percentage of flights on time
Avoidable delays	Analysis of late flights between avoidable and unavoidable
Effectiveness of direct selling	Enquiry/booking conversion rate
Innovation and growth	
Route network development	Time taken to breakeven load factor for new routes
Development of individuals	Number of routes withdrawn Expenditure on training Internal promotion rates
Customer perspective	
Customer satisfaction	Customer ratings
Customer complaints	Compensation payments
Customer loyalty	Repeat business Switching to other airlines
Convenience of airport	Average length of journey to airports
Financial perspective	
Profitability	Return on capital employed
Financial stability	Gearing
Utilisation	Load factors
Low costs	Average cost-per-seat kilometre

> **Exam Advice**
>
> Do not confuse goals (objectives) and performance measures in questions about the Balanced Scorecard.

2 Service Industries

2.1 Characteristics of Service Industries*

1. **Simultaneity** (also called inseparability)—production and consumption of the service happens at the same time.

2. **Perishability**—the inability to store the service. It must be provided when the customer wants it; it cannot be prepared in advance and stored in inventory.

3. **Heterogeneity** (i.e. lack of homogeneity), also called variability—unlike goods coming off a production line, which may all be identical, the quality of services will likely vary from service to service. For example, haircut quality depends on the hairdresser's talent, training, skill and disposition. This makes quality more difficult to measure.

4. **Intangibility**—there is no good with physical features produced (e.g. smell, touch, sound, visual representation, etc.) Customers can point to specific features of a product and indicate the physical characteristics that fill their value proposition. Customers cannot always point to some physical characteristic of a service to help the firm understand what they value.

>
> ***Commentary**
>
> *Four characteristics of services make their measurement of performance more difficult than goods.

2.2   Fitzgerald and Moon's Building Block Model

2.2.1   Purpose of the Model

Fitzgerald and Moon designed the Building Block model as a framework for service companies to use in designing a system of performance evaluation, linked to reward schemes for managers.

There are three "blocks"—dimensions, standards and rewards.

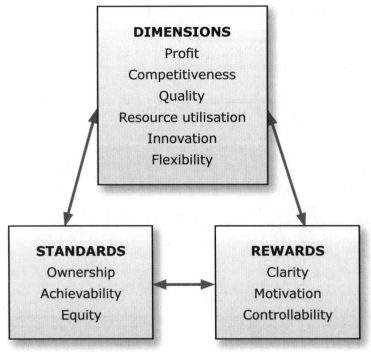

2.2.2   Dimensions

▨ Dimensions are the aspects of performance which must be measured. There are six dimensions in the Fitzgerald and Moon model. Organisations need to identify performance measures based on these six dimensions. (Similar to the four perspectives in the balanced scorecard model.)

▨ The six dimensions are:

   1. Financial performance

   2. Competitiveness

   3. Quality

   4. Resource utilisation

   5. Flexibility

   6. Innovation.

▨ Financial performance and competitiveness are referred to as results, while quality, resource utilisation, flexibility and innovation are described as the determinants. If the organisation performs well in the determinants, this will lead to good performance in the results.

Illustration 2   Car Dealer's Performance

Additional research by Fitzgerald discovered a car dealer in the UK that used the following methods of measuring performance:

- ▓ Financial performance: profitability by dealer.

- ▓ Competitiveness: market share and new car registrations by post code.

- ▓ Quality of service: mystery customer, post-transaction customer assessment.

- ▓ Resource utilisation: sales per employee.

2.2.3   Standards

- ▓ There are three principles that should be applied in setting targets for managers:

    1. **Ownership**—managers should take ownership of (believe in) the targets. Managers who participate in setting targets will be more likely to believe in them.

    2. **Achievability**—targets should be challenging but achievable; otherwise, managers will dismiss the targets rather than be motivated to achieve them. Owing to the principal-agent problem, those responsible for results will always push for easier targets.

    3. **Equity**—the organisation should maintain a realistic level of difficulty for its standards across all business areas.

2.2.4   Reward Schemes

Reward schemes may be linked to performance by paying managers bonuses if they achieve targets. Three principles apply:

1. **Clarity**—employees must understand the performance measurement scheme.

2. **Motivation**—bonuses should motivate staff to achieve the targets.

3. **Controllability**—managers' performance evaluations should only measure factors they control.

3   Non-profit Sector

3.1   Identifying Objectives

- ▓ The non-profit sector includes:

    - ● Public sector bodies such as schools and hospitals.

    - ● Not-for-profit organisations (NFP organisations) and non-governmental organisations (NGOs).*

- ▓ Objectives of NFP organisations are more difficult to measure because:

    - ✗ The objectives are difficult to quantify. How can a hospital's objective "to improve health in the area" be measured?

    - ✗ Many non-profit bodies have multiple stakeholders, each with potentially conflicting objectives.

***Commentary**

*NGOs may receive significant funding from government; NFP organisations typically raise funds from those interested in the organisations' goals.

▦ Consider a state-funded university as an example.

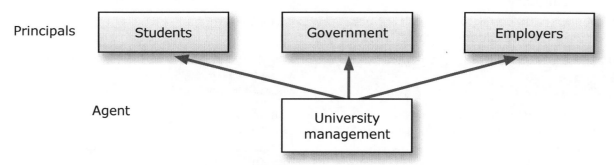

▦ University management is accountable to multiple stakeholders.

▦ However, stakeholder requirements may *conflict*:

  ● Students may desire small class sizes, large library, etc.

  ● Government wants to minimise costs per student.

▦ Designing a performance measurement system in which multiple and conflicting objectives exist is obviously very difficult. Management must rank its stakeholders and prioritise objectives accordingly.

3.2 Value for Money Objectives

The value for money (VFM) framework attempts to evaluate performance of non-profit and other non-commercial organisations. VFM focuses on how well the organisation has achieved its objectives given the funding it received.

▦ Three performance indicators measure VFM:*

  1. Economy (minimising inputs)

  2. Efficiency (maximising the output/input ratio)

  3. Effectiveness (achievement of objectives).

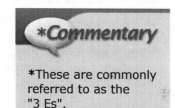

*These are commonly referred to as the "3 Es".

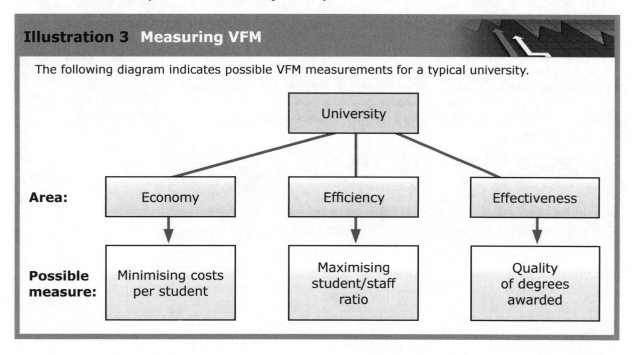

Illustration 3 Measuring VFM

The following diagram indicates possible VFM measurements for a typical university.

■ It is clear that high effectiveness may *conflict* with economy and efficiency.

■ Multiple and conflicting objectives also may exist due to the multiple stakeholders involved.

Example 1 NFP Objectives

Since the 1980s, there has been a considerable extension of management accounting into the public sector (e.g. hospitals and schools).

At the same time management accounting was being introduced into these areas, many governments were specifying objectives for the public services, for example:

> Hospitals—"to improve the standard of patient care".

> Schools—"to improve the quality of education".

Governments have also laid stress on the efficient use of resources in these areas.

Required:

Comment on the above objectives and assess how management accounting can contribute towards their achievement.

3.3   Non-Financial Performance Indicators (NFPIs)

NFPIs were introduced in *Session 14*. NFPIs are particularly useful in not-for-profit organisations for the following reasons:

■ The overall objectives of NFP organisations are normally non-financial in nature, so it does not make sense to judge their performance primarily using financial measures.

■ Commercial organisations generally have one overriding objective; to maximise the wealth of shareholders. However, NFP organisations, particularly in the public sector, have multiple objectives to reflect the needs of different stakeholders (e.g. different people will have different beliefs as to what they think a local council should provide).

■ It may be difficult to identify a cost unit in not-for-profit organisations (e.g. in a hospital that carries out many different types of procedure, there is no single appropriate unit of output). This makes financial performance measurement more difficult.

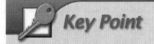

Key Point

Performance measurement requires a wider range of performance measures and many of these will be non-financial.

Example 2 Non-financial Performance Indicators

Suggest ONE non-financial performance indicators for each of the situations below. Explain why you think it would be a useful measure of performance:

1. The quality of education in a school.

2. The effectiveness of a charity that aims to reduce the effects of a particular illness on the population in a developing country.

3. The quality of clinical care in a hospital.

4. The effectiveness of the local police force in dealing with crime.

3.4   Setting Targets

Targets are often used to improve performance. Actual performance is then compared with the targets and management investigates when targets are missed.*

Setting qualitative targets (those relating to NFPIs) can be difficult in NFP organisations because:

✗   Determining the appropriate level of difficulty for the target is difficult. If too difficult, it may demotivate; if too easy, it will not challenge sufficiently.

✗   Meaningful targets need to take into account differences in the external environment. In schools, for example, exam results will be largely influenced by the demographics of the school. It may not be appropriate to set the same targets for all schools.

✗   Managers who are judged by the performance measures need to "buy into" the targets that have been set. Managers may be more willing to accept targets if they have been involved in setting them.

✗   Identifying measures for qualitative areas can be difficult enough, even before consideration of setting the target.

✗   Targets are often based on results rather than effort. In many organisations, the hard work of staff may not always be reflected in the results (e.g. mortality rates in hospitals may reflect many factors, not just the efforts of the medical staff).

*Similar to the concept of comparing financial performance against budgets or the use of standard costing and variance analysis.

3.5   Assessing Performance

Assessing performance in the NFP sector is similar to assessing performance in the commercial sector. However, it is important to take into account the objectives of the organisation. Performance is only meaningful when judged in the context of what the organisation wishes to achieve.

▤   Most NFP organisations do not exist to make profits so using traditional performance measures such as return on capital employed is meaningless.*

▤   Reducing costs may be good in the sense of increasing efficiency, but may also conflict with some of the non-financial objectives, especially if it means that the service provided to stakeholders is adversely affected.

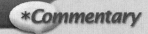

*Some NFP companies do exist to make profits, but these are then passed on to charitable causes rather than to shareholders. Examples include charity shops.

Example 3 Evaluation of Performance

Ayersome Leisure (AL) is a sports centre that is owned and managed by the council of Bigton. Its mission is "To promote healthy living in Bigton". The council has become increasingly concerned by the growing deficit generated by the centre as the council has to subsidise all such deficits.

The financial report of the centre for the last two financial years (most recent and prior) the budget for the most recent year are as follows:

	Prior $000	Most recent $000	Budget $000
Revenue	700	606	792
Less costs:			
Depreciation	25	25	25
Salaries	450	500	550
Maintenance	150	200	200
Other costs	124	75	125
Surplus(deficit)	(49)	(194)	(108)

The centre offers four sporting activities: Squash, Swimming, Gym and Badminton. The following information is available in respect of these for the most recent financial year:

	Squash	Swimming	Gym	Badminton
Hours open each day:	12	10	12	6
% utilisation				
Daytime	50	70	15	50
Evening	80	70	50	50
Revenue ($000)	101	203	252	50
Annual cost saving ($000)				
If activity is discontinued:	21	120	51	60

AL offers free access to all facilities to local schools to encourage sports development and to those over 60 years to promote healthy lifestyles. Free-access users comprise 30% of all users. It is estimated that 60% of these users would continue to use the facilities if they had to pay the standard charges for them. The remaining 40% would not use the facilities if free access were to be withdrawn.

With the exception of the avoidable costs identified (i.e. the annual cost savings if an activity is discontinued) all costs are general fixed overheads.

There has been a decline in evening users of both the gym and the swimming pool because a private health club opened during the year in Bigton. A former visitor to the club commented that he preferred the health club because even though it was much more expensive than AL, it attracted a more exclusive clientele.

Required:

(a) Evaluate the financial and non-financial performance of the sports centre for the most recent year.

(b) Suggest ways in which the financial performance of the centre could be improved in the future.

3.6 Short-Termism and Manipulation of Results

Performance measurement systems aim to ensure that the management and staff of an organisation work towards the goals of the organisation. The famous management writer Peter Drucker said "what gets measured gets done" meaning that if a particular area of performance is measured, management and staff are more likely to focus their efforts on doing it well. However, performance measurement systems can have certain problems—both in the NFP sector and in the commercial sector.

Two particular problems are:

✗ Short-termism—managers and staff focus on meeting only short-term targets (typically those set for the current financial year) and ignore the longer-term performance of the organisation.

✗ Manipulation of data—trying to make the reported results look better than they really are.

Short-termism can be a particular problem in the public sector because budgets are typically set by governments on an annual basis with no longer-term plans being set.

Short-termism may occur in both commercial and NFP organisations (see also s.4).

3.7 Other Approaches

In many countries, government has increased the use of performance measurement in the public sector in order to:

▓ Improve efficiency—thereby reducing government spending and tax.

▓ Increase transparency—so taxpayers can see what their taxes are being used for.

▓ Improve decision-making about the allocation of scarce resources—so that available finance is used where it will best achieve government's objectives.

Although the "3 Es" framework (above) is a cornerstone of many approaches to performance measurement, other commonly used approaches to performance measurement in the public sector include:

▓ Zero-based budgeting (see *Session 8,* s.3.5.7)

▓ Benchmarking—this is where the performance of a public sector organisation is compared to that of a "best-in-class" organisation. For example, the performance of a procurement department in a hospital may be compared against that of a commercial organisation.*

▓ League tables—these institutional rankings are used in areas such as health, policing and education. They help determine whether schools or hospitals are deemed to be "failing", whether police forces are tackling crime effectively and how students rate their university courses.*

*An appropriate metric to measure this performance might be the total cost of placing an order.

*Ranking schools by exam results may lead to poorer performing schools working harder to compete with better performing schools.

4 Behavioural and External Considerations

4.1 Behavioural Aspects of Performance Management

■ Performance management is the whole process of identifying the objectives of the organisation, setting targets, measuring performance against targets and taking action in an attempt to improve sub-standard performance.

■ Managers need to understand how performance measurement can affect employee behaviour.

4.1.1 Potential Benefits of Performance Measurement Systems

✔ Understanding organisational objectives (e.g. increased market share) and improved employee motivation to contribute towards achieving them. This should help goal congruence.

✔ Developing agreed measures of performance within the organisation (e.g. ROCE).

✔ Allowing comparison of different organisations (e.g. ratio analysis).

✔ Promoting accountability of the organisation to its stakeholders.

4.1.2 Potential Problems

✗ **Tunnel vision**—an obsession with maximising measured performance at the expense of non-measured performance. Staff may ignore important areas that are not measured.

✗ **Myopia** (short-sightedness)—maximising short-run performance at the expense of long-run success. For example, cutting back on staff training during recessions will leave the firm unprepared for growth when the economy improves.

✗ **Manipulation of data**—creative reporting (e.g. trying to classify all adverse variances as planning variances rather than operational variances).

✗ **Gaming**—e.g. building slack into budgets.

✗ **Incongruent goals**—managers do not share organisational goals. For example, if a manager is judged based on the ROCE of his division, he will reject projects which would reduce this, even if they might increase the company's overall return on capital employed.

4.1.3 Solutions to Potential Problems

✔ Involve staff at all levels in the design and implementation of the system.

✔ Encourage staff to take a long-term view (e.g. through company share option scheme).

✔ Ensure that the system of performance evaluation is "audited" by experts to identify problems.

✔ Review the system regularly.

✔ Audit data used in performance measurement to prevent/detect manipulation.

4.2   External Factors

Organisations do not exist in a vacuum, so performance measurement needs to consider external as well as internal factors.

4.2.1   Stakeholders

■ A stakeholder is defined as any person or group affected by an organisation.*

■ Ignoring stakeholder objectives may result in adverse implications for an organisation.

   ● If staff salaries are too low, for example, staff will become demotivated and good employees may leave the organisation.

   ● There also could be strikes. These factors could lead to poor customer service, which will ultimately affect the profits of the organisation.

■ Management needs to consider who are the most important stakeholders; consider what their objectives are; and identify ways to measure how these objectives are being met.

■ Staff surveys, for example, are a common method used to assess staff satisfaction.

Commentary

*Traditionally, performance measurement focused only on the owners' interests.

Illustration 4   Stakeholder Groups

The following are the most common stakeholder groups and ways they can affect an organisation's performance:

Group	Objectives
Employees	Satisfactory remuneration Good working conditions
Customers	Good-quality products
Suppliers	Long-term relationships Pay within agreed terms
General public	Potential employment Economic effect on region Environmental impact
Government	Compliance with law (e.g. environment)

4.2.2   Market Conditions and Competitors

■ An organisation's market conditions will affect its economic performance, and may affect different parts of the organisation in different ways. For example, performance analysis should consider market differences when comparing two divisions.

■ Competitor performance will directly affect organisational performance. Price competition within a market, for example, will likely lead to price cuts of the organisation's products and will have a financial impact.

■ Performance evaluations should consider factors that management could not control. This principle has been discussed in previous sessions on budgeting and variance analysis, so in summary:

- Performance evaluation should measure actual results against budgets revised to take account of factors not originally considered.

- Standards can be revised to take into account changes in the environment. For example, the sales volume variance can be split into a market volume and a market share variance.

■ Generally speaking, performance measurement should be flexible enough to take into account external factors.

Example 4 Stakeholder Views of Performance

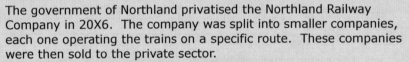

The government of Northland privatised the Northland Railway Company in 20X6. The company was split into smaller companies, each one operating the trains on a specific route. These companies were then sold to the private sector.

One of the private companies formed was the Great Suburban Railway Company, which provides passenger train services on a busy commuter route between the capital city of Bigton, and Smallton, a distance of 100 km.

Financial and other information relating to the Great Suburban Railway for three financial years are presented below.

	20X7	20X8	20X9
Revenue ($000)	30,000	32,000	35,000
Profit ($000)	(1,000)	2,000	5,000
Number of passenger journeys (000)	2,000	1,900	1,900
Number of employees	500	450	400
% of trains arriving on time	70%	72%	75%

Other information

The Great Suburban Railway is the only company licensed to operate services on the route between Bigton and Smallton.

The aims of privatising the trains were to stop the subsidy the government had previously paid to the train company and to increase the punctuality of services.

Since privatisation, passengers have complained that the number of carriages on each train has been reduced, leading to a shortage of seats during peak times.

Required:

Discuss the performance of the Great Suburban Railway from the perspective of:

(a) a shareholder;

(b) the government; and

(c) the population of Smallton.

Summary

- The balanced scorecard approach to performance measurement aims at ensuring that various performance measures support the overall strategy of the business.
- The balanced scorecard looks at performance from four perspectives—customer; internal processes; learning and growth; and financial.
- Performance measurement in the service sector is more difficult to measure than in manufacturing, due to:
  - Simultaneity
  - Perishability
  - Heterogeneity
  - Intangibility
- In the Fitzgerald and Moon Building Block model, performance in service businesses can be measured based on six dimensions:
  1. Financial performance
  2. Competitiveness
  3. Quality of service
  4. Resource utilisation
  5. Flexibility
  6. Innovation
- Performance measurement in non-profit organisations is more difficult due to:
  - difficulty in quantifying the objectives;
  - many stakeholders have interests in such organisations.
- Performance measurement in the non-profit sector is often based on the "3 Es" (i.e. economy, efficiency and effectiveness).

Session 15 Quiz
Estimated time: 15 minutes

1. List the FOUR perspectives from which the performance of an organisation is measured using the Balanced Scorecard. (1.1)

2. Identify the FOUR characteristics of service industries which make performance management and measurement more complex than for manufacturing organisations. (2.1)

3. List the SIX dimensions of measuring the performance of organisations in the service industry based on the Fitzgerald and Moon Building Block model. (2.2.1)

4. Give TWO reasons why measuring the performance of non-profit organisations may be more complex than measuring the performance of companies with a profit motive. (3.1)

5. Explain the meaning of the term efficiency in the context of the "3 Es" used for measuring the performance of organisations in the non-profit sector. (3.2)

Study Question Bank
Estimated time: 1 hour, 20 minutes

Priority		Estimated Time	Completed
Q26	Value for Money	40 minutes	
Q27	Eatwell Restaurant	40 minutes	

EXAMPLE SOLUTIONS

Solution 1—NFP Objectives

The objectives quoted in the question are too general to provide a mechanism for measuring whether the school or hospital has attained those objectives.

In spite of widely acknowledged difficulties measuring efficiency and effectiveness of not-for-profit (NFP) organisations, management accountants must help managers involved in decisions regarding the organisation's resources. This is especially so in the case of NFP organisations where, invariably, a significant proportion of the cost base is fixed.

■ Economy can be defined as: "The terms and conditions under which the authority acquires human and material resources. An economical operation acquires resources of the appropriate quality and provides a service to the appropriate standard at the lowest cost."

■ Effectiveness is defined as: "The extent to which a programme achieves its established goals or other intended effects."

■ Efficiency is defined as: "The relationship between goods or services produced and resources used to produce them. An efficient operation produces the maximum output for any given set of resource input; or it has minimum input for any given quantity and quality of services provided."

From the above definitions it can be seen that *efficiency* is the optimum of *economy* and *effectiveness* (i.e. the measure of output over input).

Consideration of the above "3 Es" provides a clear understanding as to what governments mean by "the efficient use of resources in these areas". The introduction of management accounting techniques within hospitals and schools has led managers to focus greater attention on the achievement of economy, efficiency and effectiveness.

The principal problem, which is typical of schools and hospitals, lies in the difficulty in measuring the output (i.e. effectiveness) of such organisations.

In acknowledging that non-financial objectives can be more subjective than financial objectives when deciding whether they have been achieved, management accountants need to ensure the definition of organisational objectives in a manner which facilitates the measurement of the extent to which "patient care" and "quality of education" have been achieved.

Measurable objectives having been established, the management accountant should proceed to develop performance indicators which will serve as measurements of effectiveness (i.e. the extent to which the prescribed objectives have been met).

The management accountant will need to ensure that the control systems capture the information which will be used to assess the effectiveness of the organisation, and that any deficiencies in this respect are remedied.

Solution 2—Non-financial Performance Indicators

Proposed indicator*	Why a useful measure
1. Quality of education in a school	
Exam results – % of pupils passing final exams	Exam results are a measure of how much the pupils have learned. Pass rates reflect how well the students have been taught.
% of pupils that achieve entry to University or higher education	One objective of schools is to enable talented students to achieve their potential and gain entry to a good university.
2. Effectiveness of charity in reducing effects of a disease	
Fall in number of cases of a disease reported each period	Shows a fall in the disease which may reflect the work of the charity.
Number of people inoculated against a disease	Reflects the work actually performed by the charity (although this may not measure very well how effective the results were).
3. Quality of clinical care in a hospital	
% of patients that are cured and not readmitted within 3 months	Shows % of cases where there was a positive outcome which reflects the level of clinical care given.
Waiting time for operation (time from referral by doctor until operation performed)	Long waiting time may be caused by poor level of clinical care in hospitals, delaying additional operations.
4. Effectiveness of local police force	
% of arrested criminals convicted	Reflects the ability of police to collect sufficient evidence to ensure criminals are convicted.

Solution 3—Evaluation of Performance

(a) Performance

The deficit for the most recent financial year is $194,000. This is almost four times that of the prior year and 80% higher than the budgeted deficit for the year. It is understandable that the council is concerned about this.

The main reason for failure to meet the budget is the decline in revenue which is most likely due to the opening of a new health club in Bigton, which has attracted some users away from a public sports centre. There is little that the management of AL can do about this as it would not be appropriate for a publicly-funded leisure centre to offer the same luxurious levels of service as a private health club. However, the existence of the competition and the expected decrease in revenue must be planned for in the future and costs reduced.

Salaries have increased by 11% compared to the prior year, although this is only half the budgeted increase. This is due to either increased staff numbers or increased salaries or both. Given the decline in revenues, management should not have increased the level of staffing.

Accessibility of the sports centre is good, with squash and gym being available 12 hours per day and swimming 10 hours per day. Badminton is only available for six hours per day, but this may reflect a lack of demand.

Utilisation of all activities is over 50% except for the gym, which has only 15% utilisation during the day, perhaps due to gym users being at work. Squash is particularly in demand with 80% utilisation in the evenings. The high utilisation rates mean that the centre is providing services that are valued by the community.

The provision of free facilities to the over 60s and schools may appear to be bad from a financial point of view, but ALs objective is to promote healthy living, not to make a profit. Of the 30% of users who enjoy free access 40% would not use the facilities if they had to pay for them, so it can be said that the sports centre does satisfy a social need in encouraging people to take exercise.

Overall, the financial performance is poor and the sports centre needs to find ways to reduce the deficit in future years. However, the sports centre is providing a good and valued service to the local community.

(b)   Improving Financial Performance

As noted in part (a), revenue fell considerably due to the opening of a private health club. The private club probably provides an exclusive service to its clients, while a publicly-owned sports centre has an objective of inclusivity. There is probably little that AL can do to win back the clients that prefer the exclusivity of a private club, so the fall in revenue has to be accepted. Improving financial performance therefore requires AL to focus on cost reductions.

Badminton is not a particularly popular activity. Revenue from badminton was $50,000. If Badminton were to be discontinued, costs of $60,000 would be avoided. Ceasing badminton would therefore save $10,000 a year.

Management may consider reducing staff costs. Reducing staff costs to prior year levels would save $50,000. Additional savings might be possible if staff levels are reduced during times of low utilisation (e.g. in the gym during the day when usage is only 15%).

While squash and swimming are available for 12 hours per day, it may be possible to reduce this availability during less busy times. Perhaps opening one hour later and closing one hour earlier could save costing without causing too much inconvenience to users.

Finally it is noted that 30%of users enjoy free access. If this were to be withdrawn, 60% of these would continue to use the facilities. This means revenue would increase by approximately $109,000 (30% × 606,000 × 60%). However, withdrawing free access may go against AL's stated mission. As a compromise, perhaps free access to over 60s could be "means tested" (i.e. over 60s on low incomes would continue to enjoy free access, but those on higher incomes would have to pay).

Solution 4—Stakeholder Views of Performance

(a) From the perspective of shareholders

Shareholders will be pleased with the performance since privatisation. Revenues have increased by 16.67% from 20X7 to 20X9, which is good for a business such as railways in which demand is likely to be limited. The reason for the increase would appear to be higher ticket prices, as the number of passenger journeys (volume) actually fell during the period.

While the company recorded a loss in 20X7, the first year after privatisation, it made a good profit in 20X8 and 20X9. In fact, profits have actually risen by more than revenue in absolute terms. This shows that the company has reduced costs at the same time that revenues have increased. Net profit margin rose from 6.25% in 20X8 to 14.2% in 20X9.

It appears that the company has performed well from the perspective of shareholders.

(b) The government

The government will be pleased that it no longer has to subsidise the railway generally, and will be pleased that the company appears to be surviving in the private sector.

Another objective of privatisation was to increase the punctuality of trains. The Great Suburban Railway has improved punctuality, measured as the percentage of trains arriving on time, from 70% to 75% from between 20X7 and 20X9, so some progress has been made. However, 25% of trains are still late, and the government (and passengers) will not be pleased with this.

(c) The population of Smallton

The main objective for the people of Smallton likely is to have a reliable train service to the capital which charges reasonable prices.

Punctuality has already been discussed, and it is likely that passengers would be happy with the increase in the percentage of trains arriving on time, although they would hope for further improvements in this area.

One area that customers are unlikely to be pleased about is the apparent increase in ticket prices. Dividing total revenue by number of passenger journeys, the average ticket per journey has risen from $15 in 20X7 to $18.42 in 20X9, an increase of 22%. This is a large increase, and is not likely to be popular unless accompanied by better service in some way.

Customers are also complaining about the reduced number of carriages, leaving people without a seat during peak times. So it does not appear that passengers are experiencing better service.

The number of passengers has fallen by 5% between 20X7 and 20X9. This is likely to be due to the increase in prices. People may be finding alternative ways to travel to the capital (such as by bus) or reducing their journeys.

Overall, the people of Smallton are not likely to be happy with the performance of the privatised company.

Divisional Performance Evaluation

FOCUS

This session covers the following content from the *ACCA Study Guide.*

D. Performance Measurement and Control
5. Divisional performance and transfer pricing
c) Explain the meaning of, and calculate, Return on Investment (ROI) and Residual Income (RI), and discuss their shortcomings.
d) Compare divisional performance and recognise the problems of doing so.

Session 16 Guidance

- **Comprehend** that assessing divisional performance is similar to assessing organisational performance and that the financial and non-financial measures covered in earlier sessions are relevant for divisions too.
- **Understand** the two important principles with respect to divisional performance evaluation: goal congruence and the controllability principle (s.2).
- **Recognise** that the nature of the division (cost centre, profit centre, etc) determines which measures may or may not be appropriate in assessing its performance (s.2.2.2).

(continued on next page)

VISUAL OVERVIEW

Objective: To describe and apply performance measures in a divisional organisation structure.

```
DECENTRALISATION
• Benefits
• Problems
• Conditions
  for Successful
  Decentralization

DIVISIONAL PERFORMANCE
EVALUATION
• Measurement Characteristics
• Possible Measures
• Controllable and Traceable Profit

RETURN ON INVESTMENT (ROI)
• Calculations
• Components of Capital
• Advantages
• Disadvantages

RESIDUAL INCOME (RI)
• Calculations
• Advantages
• Disadvantages
```

Session 16 Guidance

■ **Know** the benefits and weaknesses of and calculations for return on investment (s.3) and residual income (s.4).

■ **Read** the article "Decentralisation and the Need for Performance Measurement".

1 Decentralisation

Definition

Decentralisation—delegation of authority to make decisions.

■ **Decentralisation** requires the creation of autonomous business units or divisions to align responsibility with decentralised authority.

■ These units can be:
- cost centres;
- profit centres; and
- investment centres.

1.1 Benefits

✔ Senior management can concentrate on *strategy*—delegating routine decisions frees senior management for long-term corporate planning.

✔ Faster decision-making—divisional managers are "on the spot" and can react quickly to changes.

✔ Better decision-making—specialist managers are likely to understand their part of the business better than senior management.

✔ Motivation—divisional managers are given responsibility and status and may increase effort.

✔ Training and career progression—divisional managers acquire skills and experience which may prepare them for senior management (e.g. managers may be "rotated" between divisions).

✔ Tax advantages—locating divisions in certain areas which enjoy tax incentives or government grants.

1.2 Problems

✗ Lack of goal congruence—risk that divisional managers will make decisions *not* consistent with overall organisational objectives.

✗ Increased information requirements—reporting systems must be introduced to monitor divisional performance.

✗ Lost economies of scale—costs may rise through duplication of common activities. A central purchasing department may achieve better prices and lower overall overhead than divisional purchasing departments.

✗ Loss of central control—top management loses control to divisional managers. Conflict may occur if top management disagrees with the decisions of divisional managers.

1.3   Conditions for Successful Decentralisation

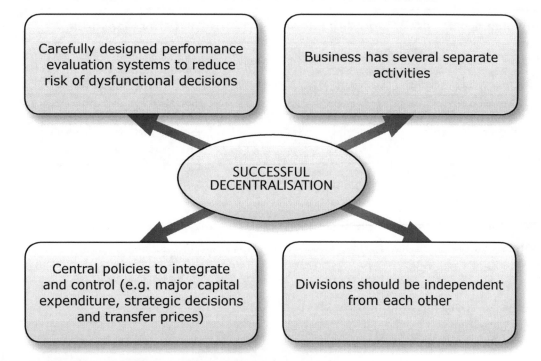

2   Divisional Performance Evaluation

Senior management retains responsibility to measure and monitor divisional performance and divisional managers.

2.1   Measurement Characteristics

- **Goal congruence**—performance measures should encourage decisions consistent with company objectives.
- **Timeliness**—performance reporting must be fast enough to allow any required corrective action.
- **Controllability**—evaluation should assess only divisions and divisional managers on performance under their control.

2.2   Possible Measures

- The measures used will depend on the type of business unit monitored.
- Focusing on one key measure of performance opens the door to gaming the system, myopia and a variety of other problems associated with inadequate performance measurement. Therefore, senior managers should evaluate divisional performance based on a range of measures—a *balanced scorecard* approach.
- The range of measures could include:
  - variance analysis—care must be taken in identifying the controllability and responsibility for each variance;
  - ratio analysis;
  - return on investment;
  - residual income; and
  - non-financial measures.

2.2.1   Ratio Analysis

Profitability Measures	Liquidity Measures	Other Measures

• Net profit margin
• Gross profit margin
• Contribution margin
• Expenses as percentage of sales
	• Current ratio
	• Quick ratio
	• Receivables days
	• Payables days
	• Inventory turnover
		• Contribution per key factor/limited resource
		• Sales per employee
		• Industry specific cost-related ratios such as:
		  —transport cost per km
		  —overheads per chargeable hour

2.2.2   Non-financial Measures

■ Staff turnover (also days lost through absenteeism)

■ New customers gained

■ Proportion of repeat bookings

■ Orders received

■ Set-up times (also customer waiting times)

■ New products developed

■ % Returns

■ % Rejects/reworks (also number of complaints received)

■ On-time deliveries

■ Client contact hours

■ Training time per employee.

2.2.3   Measures by Division

Division Type	Possible Measure
Cost centre	**Financial** Cost variances Costs per unit produced **Non-financial** Labour turnover
Profit centre	As above, plus: **Financial** Controllable profit (if assessing manager) Traceable profit (if assessing division) Sales variances Profit margins Contribution margins **Non-financial** Customer returns
Investment centre	As above, plus: **Financial** Return on investment Residual income Liquidity ratios: • Current ratio • Receivables days **Non-financial** Number of new products developed

2.3   Controllable and Traceable Profit

	$	$
External sales		x
Internal sales		x
		x
Variable costs *Controllable by manager*	x	
Fixed costs	x	
		(x)
Controllable Profit		x
Divisional costs outside manager's control		(x)
Traceable Profit		x
Allocated head-office costs		(x)
Divisional net profit		x

- **Controllable profit** should be used to assess the *manager's* performance.
- **Traceable profit** should be used to assess the *division's* performance.

3   Return on Investment (ROI)

Definition

Return on investment (ROI)—a return on capital employed which compares income with the operational assets used to generate that income.*

*Commentary

*Profit is before interest and tax because interest is affected by financing decisions and tax is an appropriation.

3.1   Calculations

3.1.1   For Assessing Manager

$$ROI = \frac{\text{Controllable profit}}{\text{Capital employed}} \times 100$$

3.1.2   For Assessing Division

$$ROI = \frac{\text{Traceable profit}}{\text{Capital employed}} \times 100$$

3.2 Components of Capital

Investment in capital usually has two components:

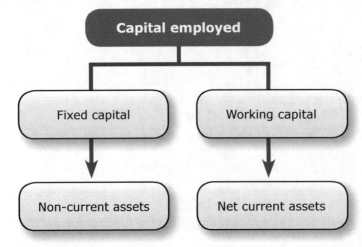

*Commentary

*Analysts advise shareholders whether to buy or sell the company's shares. Therefore, they influence the market value of the company.

- ROI is basically the divisional version of company ROCE often used by analysts.*

- ROI is a measure of divisional performance. It is *not* an investment appraisal method. In practice, however, divisional managers often use ROI for investment appraisal.

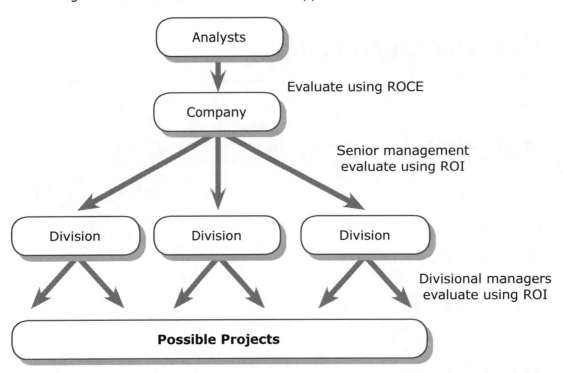

- If divisional managers choose projects with high ROI, then the division's ROI should be high. The head office will favourably assess the manager.

- *But* an ROI hurdle alone may *not* promote reliable decisions on a firm-wide basis.

Example 1 ROI

The managers of Division X and Division Y are evaluated using return on investment (ROI) as the main measure of divisional performance. Each manager is evaluating a potential investment project for his or her respective departments.

Details of the potential projects, along with information about existing departmental ROI, is provided below:

	Division X	Division Y
Controllable investment in possible project	$100,000	$100,000
Controllable profit from possible project	$16,000	$11,000
Current division ROI	18%	9%
Company cost of capital	13%	

Required:

(a) Determine whether the divisional managers would accept the project available to their respective divisions.

(b) Comment on whether each manager's decision is congruent with the main objective of the organisation, which is to maximise the wealth of its shareholders.

Solution

(a)

	Accept	Reject
Division X		
Division Y		

(b) Comment:

3.3 Advantages

✔ Relative measure—easy to compare divisions.

✔ Similar to ROCE used externally by analysts.

✔ Focuses attention on scarce capital resources.

✔ Encourages reduction in non-essential investment by:
- selling off unused fixed assets; and
- minimising the investment in working capital.

✔ Easily understood percentages (especially by non-financial managers).

3.4 Disadvantages

✗ Risk of dysfunctional decision-making (*Example 1*).

✗ Definition of capital employed is subjective.

   For example, should non-current assets be valued using:

   (a) carrying amount (i.e. net book value);

   (b) historical cost; or

   (c) replacement cost?

   Should leased assets and intangible assets be included?

✗ If net book value is used, ROI will become inflated over time because of depreciation.

✗ Risk of *window-dressing*; boosting reported ROI by:
- under investing; and/or
- cutting discretionary costs (particularly if ROI is linked to bonus systems).

4 Residual Income

Definition

Residual income (RI)—pre-tax profit less imputed interest charge for capital invested.

4.1 Calculations

4.1.1 For Assessing Manager

	$
Controllable profit	x
Imputed interest charge	(x)
Residual income	x

4.1.2 For Assessing Division

	$
Traceable profit	x
Imputed interest charge	(x)
Residual income	x

4.1.3 Imputed Interest

▨ Imputed interest is notional interest charged on the division by the head office.

> Imputed interest = Capital employed × Interest rate

▨ The company's cost of capital is often used as the basis for the interest rate.

Example 2 Residual Income

Continuing from *Example 1*. The method of evaluating the performance of divisional managers has changed from return on investment to residual income.

The two divisional managers are considering the investment projects considered in *Example 1*:

	Division X	Division Y
Controllable investment in possible project	$100,000	$100,000
Controllable profit from possible project	$16,000	$11,000
Current division ROI	18%	9%
Company cost of capital	13%	

Required:

(a) What decision will the manager of each division make?

(b) Is the decision-making goal congruent?

Solution

(a)

	Division X	Division Y
Controllable profit		
Imputed interest		
Residual income		

The manager of Division X will _____ the project.

The manager of Division Y will _____ the project.

(b) Goal congruent?

4.2   Advantages

✔ As an *absolute* measure it gives more reliable decision-making than ROI.

✔ A risk-adjusted cost of capital can be used to reflect different risk positions of different divisions.

4.3   Disadvantages

✗ Definition of capital employed.

✗ Effect of depreciation.

✗ Window dressing.

} As per ROI

✗ Difficult to compare divisions of different sizes.

✗ Less easily understood than a percentage.

Example 3 RI

A divisional manager is evaluated by the head office using RI and therefore uses RI to appraise projects.

Company cost of capital = 10%

New project details: Investment $600,000
3-year life
No residual value
Annual cash inflow $500,000.

Required:

Calculate RI for each of the three years. Use net book value at the start of each year as capital employed.

Solution

	Year		
	(1) $000	(2) $000	(3) $000
Cash flow			
Depreciation			
Profit			
NBV			
Imputed interest			
Profit − interest = residual income			

Session 16

Summary

- Decentralisation allows senior managers to focus on strategy rather than operations.

- It promotes faster and better decision-making, and may better motivate divisional managers.

- It may, however, result in loss of central control, incongruence of goals and strategies, and increased information requirements.

- Divisional performance measures should be congruent, timely and controllable by the divisional manager.

- Controllable profit will measure profit as if calculated using only costs under the manager's control. From controllable profit, the organisation can determine profits traceable to the division by subtracting divisional costs outside the manager's control.

- ROI in the context of measuring divisional returns will equal either controllable (manager) or traceable (divisional) profit divided by capital employed. Profit will be profit before interest or tax.

- Divisional ROI will increase as the manager approves projects with greater project ROI.

- Residual income equals controllable profit after an imputed interest charge. Incongruent decisions also can be minimised when a firm accepts projects with positive residual income.

- The major drawback of the residual income approach is measuring returns from divisions of different sizes.

- Definition of capital employed, effects of depreciation on measured assets, and window dressing affect both ROI and residual income.

Session 16 Quiz
Estimated time: 30 minutes

1. Define goal congruence. (2.1)

2. Describe the controllability principle. (2.1)

3. True or false? Return on investment is not an appropriate measure of the performance of a cost centre. (2.2)

4. State the profit figure which should be taken to assess the performance of a divisional manager. (2.3)

5. State whether residual income is a "relative" measure or an "absolute" measure. (4.2)

6. True or false? Residual income is consistent with maximising shareholder wealth. (4.2)

Study Question Bank
Estimated time: 40 minutes

Priority		Estimated Time	Completed
Q28	Brace Co	40 minutes	

EXAMPLE SOLUTIONS

Solution 1—ROI

(a)

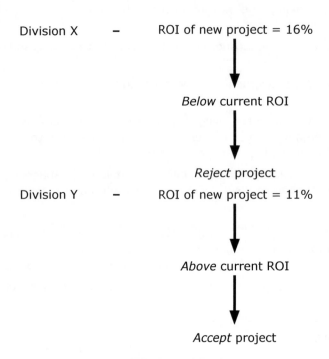

Division X — ROI of new project = 16%

Below current ROI

Reject project

Division Y — ROI of new project = 11%

Above current ROI

Accept project

(b)

The new project available to Division X has an ROI above the cost of capital and should probably be *accepted*.

The new project available to Division Y has an ROI *below* the cost of capital and should probably be *rejected*.

The divisional managers are making decisions in their own best interests, *not* in the company's best interests.

Lack of good congruence.*

> ***Commentary**
>
> *Maximising shareholders' wealth is achieved by investing in projects in which the return on those projects is higher than the cost of capital required to finance them.

Solution 2—Residual Income

(a)

	Division X	Division Y
Controllable profit	16,000	11,000
Imputed interest	(13,000)	(13,000)
Residual income	3,000	(2,000)

The manager of Division X will __*accept*__ the project.

The manager of Division Y will __*reject*__ the project.

(b) Goal congruent?

Yes

Solution 3—RI

	Year		
	(1) **$000**	**(2)** **$000**	**(3)** **$000**
Cash flow	500	500	500
Depreciation	(200)	(200)	(200)
Profit	300	300	300
NBV	600	400	200
Imputed interest	60	40	20
Profit − interest = residual income	240	260	280

Transfer Pricing

FOCUS

This session covers the following content from the *ACCA Study Guide.*

D. Performance Measurement and Control

5. Divisional performance and transfer pricing

a) Explain and illustrate the basis for setting a transfer price using variable cost, full cost and the principles behind allowing for intermediate markets.

b) Explain how transfer prices can distort the performance assessment of divisions and decisions made.

Session 17 Guidance

Understand that, although transfer pricing may appear to be a complicated topic, the opportunity cost approach to transfer pricing is based on the following:

- The minimum transfer price acceptable to the selling division is that which covers the marginal (variable) cost plus the opportunity cost of making the goods or services to be transferred.
- The maximum transfer price acceptable to the buying division would be the lower of: the external market price (if this exists) and the net revenue to the buying division of selling the ultimate product. Net revenue means the final selling price minus the costs incurred in the buying division (s.2).

(continued on next page)

VISUAL OVERVIEW

Objective: To describe and assess the effect of transfer prices on divisional performance evaluation.

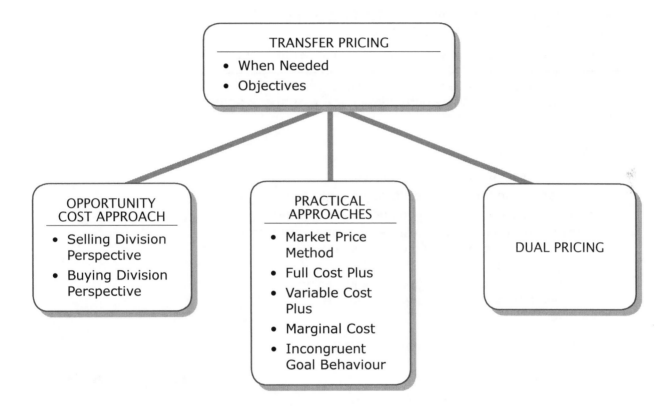

■ **Read** the article "Transfer Pricing".

■ **Recognise** the alternative presented by various practical approaches to determining selling and buying prices, along with the advantages and disadvantages of each (s.3).

■ **Understand** the mechanics and advantages of dual pricing as an optimal transfer pricing method (s.4).

1 Transfer Pricing

Definition

Transfer price—the price at which one division transfers goods or services to another division within a company or from one subsidiary to another within a group.

An earlier session described methods of setting prices for goods and services between independent parties.

In divisionalised organisations, the output of one department may form the input for another department. For the purpose of preparing management accounts for the two departments, which reflects the work performed by both divisions, a **transfer pricing system** is required.

1.1 When Needed

■ A transfer pricing policy is needed when:
  - an organisation has been decentralised into divisions; and
  - inter-divisional trading of goods or services occurs.
■ Transfers between divisions must be recorded in monetary terms as revenue for supplying divisions and costs for receiving divisions.
■ Transfer pricing is more than just a bookkeeping exercise. It can have a large effect on the behaviour of divisional managers.

1.2 Objectives of Transfer Pricing

1.2.1 Goal Congruence

■ Transfer prices should encourage divisional managers to make decisions in the best interests of the organisation as a whole.
■ Any divisionalised organisation faces a risk of dysfunctional decision-making. Where inter-divisional trading occurs, this risk is particularly high.
■ Achievement of goal congruence must be the *primary objective* of a transfer pricing system.*

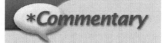

*Commentary

*Senior management must design a transfer pricing system that encourages divisional managers to make good decisions.

Illustration 1 Goal Congruence

ABC Consulting has offices in several major cities in Eastern Europe. Sometimes consultants in one office work on projects for other offices. The transfer price charged is $1,100 per day of consulting.

The managing director of the Kiev office of ABC Consulting discovered that he could hire reliable consultants on a freelance basis for $500 per day. On a recent project, in July, he used the services of a local freelance consultant for five days, paying $2,500 in total. "I've saved the Kiev office $3,000!" he declared triumphantly at the end of the week.

During the week in question, the Moscow office of ABC Consulting had a free consultant who could have done the work the freelance consultant was hired to do. This consultant earns a fixed salary, so the additional cost to the company of this consultant working on the project in Kiev would have been a flight ticket of $500 and accommodation of $500 in total.

The decision of the managing director of the Kiev office to hire the freelance consultant cost ABC an additional $1,500 (the fee paid to the freelance consultant of $2,500 less the savings on travel and accommodation of $1,000).

This is an example of goal incongruence. The managing director of the Kiev office made a decision that was good for the Kiev office, but not good for the overall group. The reason for this was that the internal transfer price was too high.

1.2.2 Divisional Autonomy

■ Divisional managers should be free to make their own decisions. A transfer pricing system should help eliminate the head office *telling* divisions what to do.*

1.2.3 Divisional Performance Evaluation

■ Transfer prices should be "fair" and allow an objective assessment of divisional performance.

■ There is likely to be *conflict* between these objectives.

*Autonomy should improve the motivation of divisional managers.

Goal congruence must take priority.

2 Opportunity Cost Approach

2.1 Supplying Division Perspective

■ The selling division will accept a minimum transfer price equal to:

Marginal (variable cost) + Opportunity cost

■ The opportunity cost is usually the lost contribution from external sales, either of:
  • the product subject to the transfer price; or
  • other products which the supplying division makes.

2.1.1   Scenario 1—Opportunity Cost Is Zero

When to use:

| No external market **or** | **and** | No production |
| External market but spare capacity | | constraints |

In this situation, opportunity cost is zero because internal transfers do not reduce contribution from external sales.

Example 1   No Opportunity Cost

Division Buy requires some components for its electronic games console. Division Sell has some spare capacity and could make the components for a variable cost of $60 each.

Required:

(a) Calculate the minimum transfer price acceptable to Division Sell.

(b) State what will happen if Division Buy can buy externally for $55.

(c) Conclude whether the actions of Division Buy and Division Sell in part (b) lead to goal congruence.

2.1.2   Scenario 2—Opportunity Cost Arises*

When to use:

External market exists **and**
Supplying division operates at full capacity

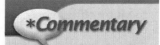

*Commentary

*An opportunity cost arises when an internal sale sacrifices an external sale.

Example 2   With Opportunity Cost

Division Red makes Product Y and Product Z. The maximum capacity of the factory is 5,000 units per month in total. This capacity can be used to make either 5,000 units of Product Y or 5,000 units of Product Z, or any combination of the two.

	Y	Z
Selling price	$12	$16
Variable cost	$9	$11
Extra cost if sold externally	$1	$1
Contribution	$2	$4

Required:

(a) Determine which product Division Red would make and what would be the monthly contribution of the division.

(b) Division Blue has asked Division Red to supply 1,000 units of Product Y per month. **Determine the minimum transfer price which would be acceptable to Division Red.**

(c) Division Blue now informs Division Red that it can buy product Y from an external supplier for $11 per unit and is not prepared to accept a price above this from Division Red.

Explain what would happen if both divisions were given autonomy to make their own decisions. Comment on whether this benefits the company as a whole.

2.2 Buying Division Perspective

- The maximum transfer price acceptable to the buying division will be the lower of:
  - the external market price (if an external market exists); or
  - the net revenue of the buying division.
- The net revenue of the buying division means the ultimate selling price of the goods/ services sold by the buying division, less the cost of those goods incurred by the buying division.

Illustration 2 Maximum Transfer Price

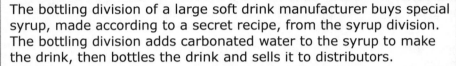

The bottling division of a large soft drink manufacturer buys special syrup, made according to a secret recipe, from the syrup division. The bottling division adds carbonated water to the syrup to make the drink, then bottles the drink and sells it to distributors.

Each bottle is sold for 50 cents. The bottling division has calculated that the costs of making the drink and bottling it (excluding the cost of buying the syrup) are 20 cents per bottle. The net revenue of the bottling division is therefore 30 cents per bottle.

If the syrup division were to propose a transfer price in excess of 30 cents per bottle for the syrup, the bottling division would incur a loss.

Example 3 Alternative Transfer Prices

Division I is an intermediate division. It supplies a special chemical to division F, the final division. Division I has spare capacity.

Output of the chemical is limited. Variable cost per kg is $500. No external market for the chemical exists.

Division F processes the chemical into the final product. Each unit of the final product requires 1 kg of the chemical. Demand for the final product exceeds production.

Selling price per unit of the final product is $1,000. The further processing cost per unit in Division F is $200.

Required:

(a) **Calculate the maximum price Division F will be prepared to pay for one kg of the chemical.**

(b) **Calculate the minimum price Division I will accept for 1 kilo of the chemical.**

(c) **Comment on the performance evaluation issues if:**
(i) **a transfer price of $500 is used**
(ii) **a transfer price of $800 is used.**

(d) **Suggest an alternative transfer price which would lead to a fairer evaluation of the performance of the two divisions.**

---

3 Practical Approaches

3.1 Market Price Method

▓ May be used if buying and selling divisions can buy/sell *externally* at market price.

▓ However, the market price might need to be *adjusted* downwards if internal sales incur lower costs than external sales (e.g. due to lower delivery costs).

Advantages	Disadvantages
✔ *Optimal* for goal congruence if the selling division is at *full capacity*.	✗ Only possible if a perfectly competitive external market exists.
✔ Encourages efficiency—the supplying division must compete with external competition.	✗ Market prices may fluctuate.

3.2 Full Cost Plus

▓ The supplying division charges full absorption cost plus a mark-up.

▓ *Standard* costs should be used rather than actual to avoid selling divisions transferring inefficiencies to buying divisions.

Advantages	Disadvantages
✔ Easy to calculate if standard costing system exists.	✗ The fixed costs of the selling division become the variable costs of the buying division—may lead to dysfunctional decisions.
✔ Covers all costs of the selling division.	
✔ May approximate to market price.	✗ If the selling division has *spare capacity* it may lead to dysfunctional decisions.
	✗ Mark-up is arbitrary.

3.3 Variable Cost Plus

▓ Similar to above—dysfunctional if spare capacity exists.

3.4 Marginal Cost

Marginal cost = Variable cost + Any incremental fixed costs e.g. stepped costs

Advantage	Disadvantage
✔ *Optimal* for goal congruence when: • the selling division has *spare capacity*; or • no external market exists.	✗ May be difficult to calculate (variable cost is often used as an approximation).

3.5   Incongruent Goal Behaviour

✗   All the practical approaches suffer from the potential problem that the transfer price may lead to behaviour that is not congruent with overall firm goals. The selling division may set a price too high for the buying division, leading the buying division to buy externally or forgo production.

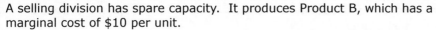

Illustration 3   Lack of Goal Congruence

A selling division has spare capacity. It produces Product B, which has a marginal cost of $10 per unit.

Another division within the company used Product B in its production. The selling division can provide all of the supplies required by the buying division within its spare capacity. The buying division can also obtain supplies of Product B externally for $15 per unit.

If a transfer price is set higher than $15 per unit using any of the practical methods described above, then the buying division will buy externally.

This leads to an extra cost to the company overall of $5 per unit of product B because Product B could be produced internally by the selling division for $10 per unit.

4   Dual Pricing

Dual pricing is sometimes used in situations where there is no transfer price that would be acceptable to both the buying division and the selling division, so in the absence of intervention by the head office, the two divisions would not trade with each other.

The head office may wish both divisions to trade for non-financial reasons and may therefore use a system of dual pricing to encourage them to do so.

Dual pricing works as follows:

■   A higher price is used when calculating the revenue of the selling division for goods supplied to the buying division.

■   A lower price is used when calculating the costs in the buying division for the goods supplied to it by the selling division.

■   The head office absorbs the difference between the two as a head office overhead.

Summary

■ Transfer pricing occurs between a selling division and a buying division in the same company, or between subsidiaries in the same group. Transfer pricing can affect divisional managers' behaviour.

■ Appropriate transfer pricing aligns divisional goals with an organisation's strategic objectives while allowing an objective assessment of divisional performance.

■ A division with no external market or ample spare capacity has zero opportunity cost because transfers do not reduce contribution from external sales. Its marginal cost would serve as an appropriate transfer price.

■ A division with an external market or no spare capacity would lose external sales by an internal transfer. Its marginal cost plus the lost contribution would serve as an appropriate transfer price.

■ Practical approaches all suffer from the potential problem of incongruent divisional and overall corporate goals.

  ● Market price method optimises overall corporate objectives when a selling division operates at full capacity and has an external market.

  ● Full cost plus method uses standard costs plus a mark-up, but mark-up is arbitrary and the method may lead to dysfunctional decisions where spare capacity exists.

  ● Variable cost plus is similar but uses standard variable rather than full costs. It is not suitable when fixed costs represent a high proportion of total costs.

  ● Marginal costs (variable plus incremental fixed costs) represent an optimal outcome for the overall company where no external market exists or the selling division has spare capacity.

■ Dual pricing solves the problem of goal incongruence as the head office absorbs the difference in prices charged by the selling division and paid by the buying division while still allowing appropriate assessment of each division manager's performance.

Session 17 Quiz
Estimated time: 15 minutes

1. List THREE goals of transfer pricing. (1.2)
2. Discuss TWO scenarios for transfer pricing from the supply division perspective. (2.1)
3. Describe the advantages and disadvantages of the market price method of transfer pricing. (3.1)
4. State the purpose of using standard variable or full costs rather than actual costs in a transfer pricing scheme. (3.2, 3.3)
5. Describe dual pricing and why it presents an optimal alternative to other transfer pricing schemes. (4)

Study Question Bank
Estimated time: 1 hour, 10 minutes

Priority		Estimated Time	Mastery
Q29	Able & Baker	40 minutes	
Q30	Wash Co	30 minutes	

EXAMPLE SOLUTIONS

Solution 1—No Opportunity Cost

(a)   **Minimum transfer price** = Marginal cost + Opportunity Cost = $60 + $0 = $60.

Opportunity cost is $0 because the 500 units needed could be produced within the spare capacity of Division Sell.

(b)   **External price $55**

Division Buy will buy externally. No transfer takes place.

(c)   **Conclusion**

Both divisions are acting in the company's overall best interests. By buying externally for $55, Division Buy is saving the company $5 per component, since the cost to the company of making the components is $60.

Solution 2—With Opportunity Cost

(a)   Division Red would clearly make Product Z, as this generates the highest contribution per unit. Total contribution would therefore be $20,000 per month ($5,000 x 4).

(b)   The minimum transfer price acceptable to Division Red for Product Y is:

	$
Marginal (variable) cost	9
Opportunity cost	4
Minimum transfer price	13

The opportunity cost is the lost contribution per unit from selling Product Z.

(c)   Division Red would refuse to sell for less than $13, so Division Blue would buy externally for $11 per unit.

Both divisions are acting in a way that is good for the organisation as a whole. Although the variable cost to the company of making Product Y is only $9, the opportunity cost of $4 is a real cost.

The cost to Division Red of producing Product Y, and therefore the cost to the company as a whole, is $13 per unit. By buying externally for $11, Division Blue is saving the company $2 per unit.

Solution 3—Alternative Transfer Prices

(a)   Maximum transfer price to Division F = Net revenue

	$
Selling price	1,000
Further processing costs in Division F	(200)
Net revenue	800

The net revenue of $800 per kilo represents the maximum that Division F would be prepared to pay to Division I for the chemical. If the price exceeds this, then Division F will incur a loss.

(b)   Minimum price acceptable to Division I

	$
Marginal (variable) cost per kilo	500
Opportunity cost	0
Minimum transfer price	500

(c)   Performance evaluation

(i) If the minimum transfer price of $500 is used, then Division I will make no profit.

(ii) If the maximum transfer price of $800 is used, then Division F makes no profit.

(d)   Alternative transfer price

Any transfer price between $500 and $800 per kilo should be acceptable to both parties. Without any further information about the nature of the production process and how much effort is made by the two divisions, it is difficult to make a judgement about what would be a "fair" transfer price.

One suggestion might be to set a transfer price that is the mid-point between the minimum and the maximum. This would be a price of $650 per kilo. If this were the case, both divisions could share the profits equally.

Performance Management Information Systems

FOCUS

This session covers the following content from the *ACCA Study Guide.*

D. Performance Measurement and Control

1. Performance management information systems

a) Identify the accounting information requirements and describe the different types of information systems used for strategic planning, management control and operational control and decision-making. ☐

b) Define and identify the main characteristics of transaction processing systems; management information systems; executive information systems; and enterprise resource planning systems. ☐

c) Define and discuss the merits of, and potential problems with, open and closed systems with regard to the needs of performance management. ☐

2. Sources of management information

a) Identify the principal internal and external sources of management accounting information. ☐

b) Demonstrate how these principal sources of management information might be used for control purposes. ☐

c) Identify and discuss the direct data capture and process costs of management accounting information. ☐

d) Identify and discuss the indirect costs of producing information. ☐

e) Discuss the limitations of using externally generated information; ☐

3. Management reports

a) Discuss the principal controls required in generating and distributing internal information. ☐

b) Discuss the procedures that may be necessary to ensure security of highly confidential information that is not for external consumption. ☐

Session 18 Guidance

■ **Understand** how Anthony's model relates to the different levels of performance management information systems (s.1).

■ **Recognise** the sources of management information and how companies use it to control organisation outcomes (s.2).

(continued on next page)

VISUAL OVERVIEW

Objective: To describe the factors which should be taken into account when designing performance measurement systems.

PERFORMANCE MANAGEMENT INFORMATION

- Anthony's Model
- Modern Information Technology
- Systems Theory

SOURCES OF MANAGEMENT INFORMATION

- Principal Sources
- Use of Information in Control
- Direct Costs of Information
- Indirect Costs of Information
- Limitations of External Data

MANAGEMENT REPORTS

- Controls
- Confidential Information

Session 18 Guidance

■ **Know** the types of information and controls on them (s.3).

1 Performance Management Information Systems

Definition

Information systems—consist of people, procedures and possibly computer hardware and software, working together to collect, store, process and communicate information.

■ The use of Information Technology (IT) is widespread in modern **information systems**, and IT can support all levels of management.*

■ Performance management information systems provide the information required to assist management in the following areas:

- **Planning:** setting the long-term strategic direction of the organisation, as well as planning for the medium and short term.

- **Control** of the organisation: management needs to monitor how the organisation is actually performing against the plan, and take actions to correct any significant deviations away from the plan.

- **Decision-making:** managers need to make decisions at many different levels. The information systems should provide them with the information to do this.

■ The development of modern information systems means that many organisations now use a single information system to provide all the information to manage the different aspects of a business. The boundary between "performance management information systems" and "other information systems" is becoming increasingly blurred and irrelevant.

*Commentary

*An information system does not simply mean a computerised application. Manual information systems have existed since evolution. The use of smoke signals by tribes to warn of the approach of enemies is a type of information system.

1.1 Anthony's Model

Robert Anthony described three levels of management within an organisation:

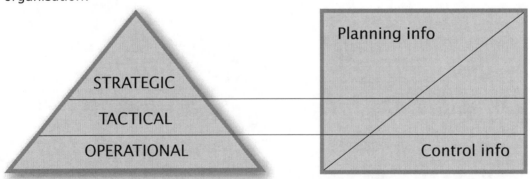

1.1.1   Strategic Planning

■ This is the highest level of management in an organisation, and it is normally carried out by the board of directors or an equivalent body. This level of management concerns itself with setting goals and objectives for the organisation over the long term.*

■ This may include the following:

- Deciding which products or markets to be in.
- Investment decisions.
- Planning for environmental changes.
- Identifying the competitive advantage of the organisation.

*Longer-term timescale—this could be a period of many years.

1.1.2   Tactical Management

■ Tactical management, or management control, usually is carried out by a middle level of management. It involves taking the strategic plan and making it happen. The time for planning is normally one year. Tactical management includes the following tasks:

- Ensuring that resources are obtained and used effectively and efficiently in accomplishing the objectives of the organisation.
- Implementing the strategic decisions, often by way of a long-term plan.
- Preparing annual budgets, and comparing actual results with budgets on a monthly basis.
- Recruiting staff.

1.1.3   Operational Management

■ Operational management focuses on day-to-day running of the business, and operational managers will be responsible for departments within an organisation. Operational managers are involved in:

- Routine planning such as staff rotas (schedules).
- Programmed decisions based on internal, transaction-based information (e.g. ordering inventory when inventory levels fall to reorder levels).

Example 1   Planning and Control

Vacation Lodge runs a chain of three-star hotels throughout the world. The company's head office is in New York, where the executive and non-executive directors are based.

Each hotel has a management team headed by a general manager. The other members of the management team are the financial controller, the rooms division manager, the food and beverage manager, the sales and marketing manager, and the head of security.

Each hotel has a restaurant manager, who manages the staff in the restaurants, including the chefs in the kitchen.

Required:

Describe the types of plans which will be prepared by the directors, the management teams and the restaurant manager. For each plan, describe control measures which can be used to see how well the plan is being achieved.

1.1.4 Strategic Planning and Control Information

■ Information for strategic planning normally:

- Addresses objectives at a high level, not detailed (e.g. a summarised statement of profit or loss for the entire organisation).
- Includes much external information.
- Addresses ad hoc information needed one time only for special projects, rather than on a regular basis.
- Will contain forecasts covering a longer time horizon.

■ Examples of information for strategic planning include the following:

- Economic and market forecasts
- Analysis of competitors

■ Examples of strategic control information are:

- Profits by business segment
- External factors influencing the organisation
- Present and potential market studies
- Investment appraisal

1.1.5 Tactical Planning and Control Information

■ Information to support tactical planning, on the other hand, will:

- Contain more detailed information (e.g. detailed statements of profit or loss analysing revenue and costs by division, or product).
- Be mainly internal, although some external information may be used.
- Be provided regularly (e.g. monthly analysis of revenues compared with budgets and variance analysis).
- Contain forecasts over periods up to 12 months.

■ The most obvious example of information used for tactical planning is the annual budget.

■ Examples of tactical control measures include:

- Analysis of sales by product/customer/geographical location.
- Inventory levels.
- Cash flow projections.

1.1.6 Operational Planning and Control Information

■ Operational planning normally requires transaction-based data. This is almost entirely internal, covering short-term periods.

■ Examples of operational control measures include:

- Variances (e.g. materials and labour)
- Receivables/payable levels
- Payroll details
- Customer complaints
- Output records.

1.2   Modern Information Technology

The introduction of Information Technology into the workplace has changed the work of the management accountant. This section looks at some common types of IT systems.

1.2.1   Transactions Processing Systems (TPS)

A TPS collects and stores data about transactions and may include controls. A transaction takes place when goods or services are exchanged for some form of payment. For example:

- Purchasing an airline ticket from an airline's website.
- Buying groceries from a supermarket. The transaction is recorded when the cashier records the sale in the cash register, typically using a bar-code reader.*
- Withdrawing cash from a bank ATM.
- Receiving inventory into the warehouse of a factory.

Transactions processing systems use one of two approaches to process the data:

1. **Batch processing**—individual transactions of the same type are collected (into "batches") and stored for later (periodic) input to the computer. Processing proceeds in discrete "runs". Payroll transactions are often processed using batch processing:

   - information about new joiners, leavers, hours worked, etc is collected during a particular period;
   - payroll calculations are made at the end of the period (e.g. a week or a month).
   - ✔ Batch processing is easier to control as data can be checked and validated before processing.

2. Real time systems processing—transactions are processed immediately as they occur.

   - ✔ This has the obvious advantage that information in the system is always up-to-date.
   - ✘ The disadvantage is that it can be difficult to control and the risk of errors is greater.

A TPS will include controls to ensure that the information entered into the system is valid and that the processes are accurate. This is important; otherwise, the information that is generated by the system will not be reliable.

IT allows much of the transaction processing to be performed automatically, with limited human input.

*Payment is also taken at this point.

Illustration 1 EPOS

The TPS in a supermarket may include the use of an electronic point of sale (EPOS) system, where the goods are scanned by the cashier using a bar-code reader when the customer is checking out. It may also use an electronic data interchange (EDI) system that enables the supermarket's system to communicate with the suppliers' systems. The following transactions cycle occurs:

1. Customer proceeds to checkout and cashier scans the bar code on the products to calculate the amount payable.

2. Inventory database is updated to reflect the sale of goods.

3. Customer presents credit or debit card—this is scanned and the payment transferred from the customer account to the supermarkets bank account. Alternatively, the customer pays in cash and the system records a cash receipt.

4. At the end of the shift, the cashier counts the cash in the cash register and compares this to the system's record of how much cash there should be.

5. Re-order level is reached for an item of inventory.

6. EDI is used to automatically place an order with suppliers.

7. When an order is ready, the supplier informs the retailer that goods have been sent (also through EDI).

8. Bar codes on goods can be used to track them during delivery.

9. When received, bar codes are read and the retailer's systems updated (e.g. inventory control, purchases and payables). Supplier may also be informed that the goods have been received (through EDI).

10. Supplier sends purchase invoice to retailer (through EDI).

11. Invoice details checked by the retailer's system and agreed to information already on database.

12. Payment authorised and then made by EDI authorising the retailer's bank to allow a transfer of funds to the supplier's bank.

13. Retailer's database updated to record payment and settlement of the liability.

1.2.2 Management Information Systems (MIS)

 Definition

Management information systems—systems which convert data from internal and external sources into information used by management to enable them to make decisions. Management accounting systems compose that part of the system which provides management accounting information.

An MIS is therefore any system for:

■ obtaining data;

■ processing it to produce useful information; and

■ distributing this to the relevant managers or members of staff.

Information from an information system is used for three purposes:

1. **Planning**—deciding what the organisation (or that part of the organisation under the control of a particular manager) will do.

2. **Controlling**—ensuring that the organisation stays on course to meet its plan.*

3. **Decision-making**—deciding between different courses of action (e.g. whether or not to develop a new product).

*Variance analysis is an example of a control system.

Example 2 Information

Suggest examples of information that would be required from an information system for each of the following:

(a) A market trader working in a fruit market

(b) Materials purchasing department in a factory.

Information systems come in many different shapes and sizes. For example:

- In a small, owner-managed organisation, the MIS will be informal; the owner will obtain most of the information that he needs:
  - from discussions with the staff; and
  - by observing what is happening.

- In larger organisations, specially designed information systems will be needed. The growth of IT has led to organisations taking a more formal approach to designing the information systems that they need.*

*Accounting systems were among the first information systems to be formally developed within organisations.

Especially in larger organisations, care should be taken to plan the needs of an information system before it is developed, to avoid the risk of the following problems:

✗ Poor communication of information to appropriate personnel.

✗ Bad decisions being made because of inaccurate data.

✗ Information is provided late.

Various types of management information systems are discussed in more detail below, including:

- Executive information systems (EIS)
- Enterprise resource planning systems (ERP)
- Decision support systems (DSS)
- Business intelligence systems.

1.2.3 Executive Information System (EIS)

Definition

Executive information system—a management information system designed to assist the decision-making of senior management of an organisation by providing summarised information from both internal and external sources relevant to meeting the strategic goals of the organisation. It is a specific type of decision support system.

▓ An EIS typically provides senior management with high-level information about the performance of the company. This information may come by accessing the central database, using reporting tools.

▓ The systems may also be linked to external data sources (e.g. financial information from Internet sites).

▓ Diagrams and charts often accompany numerical data. Many such systems have "drill down" facilities whereby clicking on a number in a report will provide more detailed analysis.

▓ An EIS often allows users to design the layout of reports relevant for them. This overcomes the problem experienced in many information systems whereby senior managers receive standard reports on a monthly basis which are not relevant to their concerns.

1.2.4 Enterprise Resource Planning Systems (ERP)

Definition

Enterprise resource planning system—a software system which provides a seamless flow of information across an entire organisation using a shared database.

▓ In the early days of computerised information systems, it was common for different departments (e.g. accounting and sales) to have separate systems. There was little sharing of information across an organisation.

▓ An ERP system aims to provide the needs of more than one department, and typically the whole organisation.

▓ The "modules" which may be found in an ERP system typically include the following:*

  ● Accounting and financial
  ● Inventory control
  ● Supply chain management
  ● Material requirement planning (MRP)
  ● Customer relationship management (CRM).

***Commentary**

*Examples of ERP software providers include SAP, Sage and Lawson.

▓ Implications of the introduction of an ERP system for the management accountant include:

  ● A reduction in gathering and processing routine information. In a supermarket, for example, sales are recorded when barcodes are scanned at the checkouts.

  ● A change in the work of the management accountant, who can now spend more time as a business advisor because the system automates many routine tasks he once performed.

1.2.5 Decision Support Systems (DSS)

▓ Decision support systems assist in complex decision-making. Such systems typically analyse large amounts of data and provide information about the likely outcome of decisions based on rules and assumptions programmed into the system.

▓ These systems automate tasks at the strategic and tactical levels of management.

▓ Decision support systems do not require judgement and can therefore be programmed.

▓ A simple example of a decision support system is a financial
model in Excel, which calculates the net present value of
a potential investment. Users can change variables in the
model, and do what-if analysis to help decide whether to go
ahead with an investment.

Illustration 2 Decision Support System

A car insurance company sells policies through its central call centre.
Potential customers call the call centre and are offered a premium
for their car insurance. If they are satisfied with the offer, they can
accept it and pay over the phone using credit cards.

The insurance premium offered depends on many factors, such as
the age and gender of the customer, the postal address and whether
or not the customer has any history of accidents or speeding fines.

The staff in the call centre use a decision support system to enter all
the relevant data about the customer. Once all the data have been
entered, the system calculates the premium.

▓ Decision support systems do not have to be as complex as the
illustration. A forecasting model in Excel, whereby variables
such as economic growth can be changed, would also be
described as a decision support system.

1.2.6 Business Intelligence Systems

▓ This term describes systems used to identify trends and
relationships in large volumes of data. This can then be used,
for example, to identify ways to increase sales.

▓ The trends which Business Intelligence Systems are used to
identify are typically:

● Which of the organisation's customers are most profitable?

● What opportunities exist for cross-selling products?

● How can more effective marketing campaigns be used?

● Which sales channels are the most effective for which
products?

▓ Business intelligence systems make use of data mining, a
process whereby vast quantities of data are interrogated to
identify trends.

1.2.7 Systems and Anthony's Model

The different systems described above can be matched to
different levels of management described in Anthony's model
as follows:

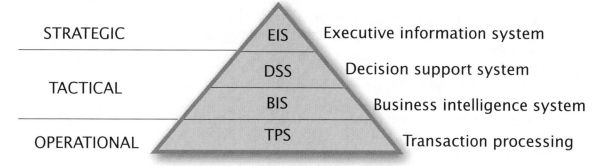

STRATEGIC	EIS	Executive information system
TACTICAL	DSS	Decision support system
	BIS	Business intelligence system
OPERATIONAL	TPS	Transaction processing

1.3   Systems Theory

1.3.1   Systems

A system takes input, processes it and produces output. For example, an air-conditioning system takes warm air and cools it. A management accounting system takes raw data (the input) and processes this to form useful information for management (the output).

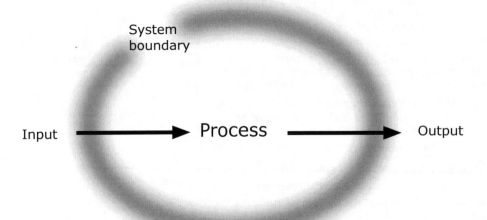

System boundary

Input ⟶ **Process** ⟶ Output

- A system has a boundary, which defines where the system exists. The boundary may be physical (e.g. in an air-conditioning system), or virtual (e.g. a management accounting system).

- The *environment* exists outside the system.

- Many disciplines, such as physics and biology, use systems theory. Management accountants are interested in the business as a system.

1.3.2   Open Systems

- Open systems react to the environment around them. They take inputs from the environment and put outputs back into the environment.

- As the environment around it changes, a system will also adapt if it is to survive. The human body, for example, is a very complex system. When it is hot, the body sweats to keep itself at the required temperature. If it did not, it would overheat, leading to illness and possibly even death.

- A successful business will react to its environment:

  - In the short term, businesses react to demand from customers. If demand is rising, production will rise to meet demand.

  - In the longer term, the organisation will react to changes in consumer tastes and attitudes and attempt to provide new products and services.

  - If businesses fail to react to changes in customer tastes and demands, then they will lose customers and eventually become bankrupt.

- The design of an MIS system should provide external information which enables the organisation to react to the environment.

1.3.3 Advantages and Disadvantages of Open Systems

✔ Open systems take account of the environment and adapt to the environment. This means that they are more likely to survive.

✔ Open systems receive feedback from the environment and use this to change and prosper.*

✗ The environment poses a source of risk to the system. For example, an IT system that is linked to the Internet is subject to the risk of hackers and viruses.

1.3.4 Closed Systems

▥ Closed systems do not interact with their environment. In practice, totally closed systems are rare. An example of a truly closed system would be an experiment which takes place in a vacuum, or a country which does not trade with other countries.

▥ Closed organisations will be internally focused. Production may be based on what the organisation can produce rather than on what the customer actually wants. This may lead to surplus inventory of finished goods, for example.

▥ If the organisation does not anticipate changes in customer needs, it will not be able to succeed in the long run.

1.3.5 Advantages and Disadvantages of Closed Systems

✔ Closed systems are protected from harmful influences outside the system, because they take nothing from the environment.

✔ Closed systems may include a closed feedback loop that allows the system to monitor itself.

✗ Because closed systems do not take anything from the environment, they can only remain stable or decline.

1.3.6 Relevance of Systems Theory to Performance Management

▥ The performance management system of an organisation is a type of system. Accordingly, it must be able to change with the environment around it—as the organisation grows, demands on the system will change. If the system cannot react to these changes, it will be necessary to design a new system.

▥ As the business environment changes, types of performance management systems also change. New management accounting techniques such as ABC have been developed to help organisations become more competitive.

*Commentary

*For example, in a budgetary control system, feedback is actual performance against the budget. If costs are too high, the system can be changed to ensure that the budget is met.

2 Sources of Management Information

2.1 Principal Sources

2.1.1 Internal

■ The principal internal sources of management information from within the organisation are:

- **Accounting system**—provides information on costs and revenues, and can provide sophisticated information such as the cost of a product using ABC.
- **Inventory system**—contains information about movements in and out of inventory.
- **Payroll system**—contains information about employee costs by department.
- **Purchase processing system**—contains information about suppliers (invoices, addresses, key personnel, costs and invoices received).
- **Sales processing system**—contains detailed information about all customers' purchases and preferences. In retail businesses, many customers use loyalty cards so, whenever they buy from the company, the sales system records information about who is buying what.
- **Qualitative information systems** (e.g. customer satisfaction)—aggregates customer surveys or other qualitative data.

■ Although these systems have a primary purpose, the information they hold could be interrogated and used to provide other useful management information. For example, information in the sales processing system could be used to analyse sales by customer or by product for marketing purposes.

2.1.2 External

■ External information is likely to be used for strategic purposes. As indicated previously, this includes information about competitors, markets, the economy and so on.

■ **Primary information** is where tailored information is provided to meet an organisation's need, such as:

- market research into new products; or
- obtaining information about prices charged by competitors.

■ **Secondary information** is data produced for general use, such as:

- government statistics;
- country reports produced by consulting firms; and
- business directories which contain detailed information about the activities of other organisations.

■ Trade magazines or other similar publications may provide useful information about external factors affecting a business.

2.1.3 Intranets

- An intranet is a private internal network within an organisation. The aim of an intranet is to allow the sharing of information throughout the organisation.

- Controls should exist to ensure that employees only have access to information that is relevant to their function. It would be inappropriate, for example, if all employees have access to the human resources files.

- An intranet also may be connected to the Internet, allowing external sources of information to be obtained.

2.1.4 Internet

- The Internet is a useful source of information. The following may prove helpful:
  - Competitors' websites.
  - Online newspapers with access to back copies.
- Online databases may contain useful information, such as the names and addresses of potential customers.

2.2 Use of Information in Control

- Refer back to the previous section for a detailed discussion of Anthony's model and the different levels of management and their style.

- Senior managers are more involved in long-term planning and control of the organisation. Control concerns high-level information (e.g. actual profits for a period by division, market share, etc). Senior management compares this information with the long-term plan and takes action if the plan is not being achieved.

- Tactical managers are interested in running the organisation efficiently. They will be interested in more detailed, usually internal, information. Comparison of actual costs and revenues against budget will be one of the major pieces of information used for control. Monitoring quality also will be important.

- Operational managers would be interested in detailed transactional information from all the sub-systems (e.g. the inventory system).

2.3 Direct Costs of Information

- The most significant costs associated with a management accounting information system can be classified as:
  - Design and implementation costs. This includes the costs of system design and testing, hardware, software, installation and training. External consultants may perform many of these activities, but there may be considerable staff overtime costs, too.
  - Day-to-day running costs (including staff costs of accounting staff, maintaining and repairing hardware).
  - Storage costs (including costs of hardware, such as servers).

2.3.1 Direct Data Capture Costs

■ These are the costs of getting the data into the system in the first place. Direct data capture methods include:

- Use of bar codes and scanners in supermarkets—cheaper and accurate

- Keyboard entry—more expensive and subject to errors.

■ The costs of data capture include the costs of staff entering the data, in addition to the capital costs of the computer equipment.

2.3.2 Processing

■ Processing means converting the data into useful information. Processing includes:

- Filtering

- Summarising

- Analysing

- Reporting

■ The costs of processing include the costs of setting up the information system and the salaries of the operators of the system.

■ There also may be costs involved in auditing the information in the system.

2.4 Indirect Costs of Information

■ The indirect costs involved in producing information by establishing and maintaining an information system include:

- Capital costs
- One-off revenue costs
- Costs associated with external sources.

2.4.1 Capital Costs

■ Purchase of hardware and software

■ Purchase and construction of buildings

■ Infrastructure (e.g. air conditioning, fire systems)

■ Network and communication systems

■ Support equipment (e.g. desks, chairs, cabinets, fireproof storage).

2.4.2 One-Off Revenue Costs

■ Such costs would be incurred on specific projects to develop new systems:

- Feasibility study (research, report writing, etc.)

- Project team costs (salaries, support, administration, travel)

- Analysing, designing, developing and testing of system

- Installation (e.g. hardware and software) and changeover (e.g. conversion of data)

- Correcting errors (e.g. due to poor design or implementation, may be very costly)

- Producing documentation (e.g. technical and user manuals)

- Training users

- Redundancy/early retirement of staff

- Recruitment of staff with relevant experience to run systems.

2.4.3 Costs Associated With External Sources

■ An external market research or similar organisation may develop information for the organisation, possibly at considerable cost:

- Fees paid to the research company.
- Costs of the research—such as giving rewards to consumers for completing questionnaires.

■ The costs of secondary sources of information are generally lower than the costs of primary:

- subscriptions to online databases and business directories;
- subscription fees to newspapers, including archiving services;
- costs of Internet access; or
- time the staff uses to obtain the information.

2.5 Limitations of External Data

■ The use of external data has limitations compared to internally generated data:

✗ It may not exactly match the requirements of the organisation, as it was not specifically designed for the organisation.

✗ Much useful data will be unavailable (e.g. the practices adopted by competitors).

✗ Because the information is external, it is likely to be available to competitors, too.

3 Management Reports

3.1 Controls

3.1.1 Purpose of Controls

■ Controls and procedures over the distribution and generation of internal information need to be in place to ensure the following:

- Reports are only prepared when the benefits of the report exceed the cost of producing it.
- Reports should only be sent to relevant managers. There is a danger of "information overload" if certain managers are copied on every report, with the result that they will not read any of them.
- Information is not duplicated.
- Only relevant information is included in the report.

3.1.2 Types of Control

■ The format of reports should be agreed in advance.

■ Distribution lists should be provided for all reports.

3.2 Confidential Information

3.2.1 Security

 **Definition**

Information security—protects the interests of those relying on information (and the information systems and communications which deliver the information) from harm resulting from hacking, operational error, sabotage and other threats.

Security—protection of the system from harm.

Privacy—restriction of knowledge to authorised persons.

Security and privacy are very closely related, and it is often difficult to determine whether a particular risk relates to security or privacy. What is clear, however, is that security relates to the whole of the system whereas privacy only relates to the data held within the system.

3.2.2 General Security Controls

■ Training all staff in computer security procedures:
- Attitude of mind (e.g. integrity, carefulness, security aware).
- Strong security culture within the organisation.

■ Staffing arrangements:
- Authorisation for access and change routines to programs.
- Segregation of duties (programmers should not have access to live programs).
- Thorough vetting of job applicants before being employed.
- Sensitive staff banned from premises when sacked (and security passes withdrawn/disabled).
- Risk analysis on sensitive staff (e.g. to identify low morale, poor motivation, potential "grudge" bearers).

■ Physical access controls:
- Security guards
- Time controls (e.g. only allowed access between certain times)
- Electronic door locks (PIN, card or bio-data entry).

3.2.3 Logical Access Controls

■ The logical access system is the system of facilities developed and maintained to protect data or software from the potential threats of unauthorised access. Controls may include:
- Physical access controls (see previous)
- System passwords (see following)
- Usage logs (usually computer generated)
- Storage of back-up disks and drives in secure locations
- On-site and off-site
- Use of heat resistant safes.

3.2.4 Passwords

■ **Password** characters should be alpha, numeric, upper and lower case and, preferably, the password should be non-sensible (i.e. not a normal word) but not too difficult so as to make it impossible to remember (hence the conundrum).

 **Definition**

Password—a sequence of characters known only to the user and which allows access to a computer system (or part thereof).

- In some very secure systems, passwords must have a special character (*, &, #, @, etc).

- Passwords should be changed regularly and not connected with the user (e.g. birthday, address) or written down (under the keyboard or a stick-it pad on the VDU).

- Passwords for access to different functions should not be the same (e.g. a password for general access to the system should not be the same as that for access to the payroll).

- Each access level of a password-protected program should be protected with a different password.

- Attributes for each password should be established (e.g. read only, read and write, valid for x number of entries, valid until a given date or event, etc).

- Passwords should never be divulged or readable from the VDU as entered (i.e. an asterisk or dot should be visible rather than the actual character typed).

- The company policy on passwords should be documented and made available to all members of staff.

- Unlimited attempts at using a password should be blocked by high-risk systems. For example, only three attempts are allowed at ATMs, after which the cash card is "swallowed" by the system and not returned.

3.2.5   Hacking

- **Hacking** originally described unauthorised activity by individuals who saw systems security as a challenge and wished to show that they could breach the security in place. The term now describes stealing (also includes reading) or changing data or any other aspect of a system (e.g. changing programs, adding additional routines).

> **Definition**
>
> **Hacking**—deliberate unauthorised access to a system and the data within that system.

- Most people consider hacking to be an external threat (e.g. via the Internet). However, the majority of hacking is carried out internally by employees.

- Hacking usually takes one of two forms:

1. **Authorisation attack**—password cracking using computer programs which work through dictionaries and other sources to generate passwords for repeated sending to the system until the right password is found.

2. **Trapdoor/backdoor attacks**—utilising existing weakness within the program code of the system. Sometimes these are deliberately programmed into the system by the programmer who, for example, can bypass the password system at a later date.

3.2.6   Prevention of Hacking

- Measures include:
  - Physical security
  - Logical security
  - System logs and audit trails
  - Sentinels ("watchdog" programs which check for unusual activity)
  - Data encryption
  - Strong quality control and risk analysis procedures in developing programs and websites.

▦ Many of the alterations made to organisations' websites, for example, are due to poor programming and security features of the Web pages and sites which allow access to the system behind the Web pages.

3.2.7 Encryption

▦ The principle of encryption is to make any intelligible data unintelligible—which can then be read only by using the decryption key.

▦ This process prevents unauthorised access to, or understanding of, for example, the data being transmitted or stored.

▦ It involves an algorithm (the operation itself) and a key (a secret numerical code usually consisting of a large number of letters, numbers and symbols).

▦ In order to be read, the message must be unscrambled (decrypted) by using a matching key.

▦ Helps protect critical information (e.g. credit card details) and addressees the problems of authentication and integrity (once the credit card details have been unscrambled by the receiver, however, they may be subject to hacking).

3.2.8 Software Audit Trail

Definition

Audit trail—record of significant data about each transaction.

▦ A software **audit trail** could include, for example, user and terminal identifications, the time and date of the transaction, transaction type (e.g. despatch), quantities and values, and cross-references to related transactions (e.g. invoice).

▦ The software audit trail records information about online transactions so the transaction and its path (both backward and forward) can be inspected and verified by third parties (e.g. internal auditors, system analysts).

3.2.9 Testing Systems Security

▦ It is of no use to have security systems in place unless they work—and are known to work. Using in-house staff to test the system may be one option, but they may have a vested interest in the system.

▦ Many external organisations (e.g. major accountancy practices and consultancies) offer "attack and penetration" services to their clients (i.e. they attempt to physically and logically enter the computer system).

▦ Physical will cover, for example, attempted access to the surroundings of the computer system and into the computer room.

▦ Logical will cover attempting to penetrate the system directly through dial-up connections, tapping external data lines and gaining access codes and other information (often simply by asking).

Summary

- Anthony described three levels of management: strategic, tactical and operational.

- An MIS is a combination of people, procedures, computer hardware and software, for recording and processing data and converting it into useful information for management. These include:

  - ERP systems which can be used by all functions within the organisation and include a central shared database.

  - EIS which provide high-level information to senior management and typically include reporting tools and drill-down facilities.

  - DSS which support programmed decisions by analysing a large number of variables.

  - Transaction processing systems such as inventory recording systems.

- Systems theory describes the concept of a system, whereby inputs to the system are processed to produce outputs. Open systems react to their environment and closed systems do not. Business should be an open system in order to process stimulus from its operating environment.

- Controls must exist over management reports to ensure that:

  - The benefits of producing the report exceed the costs of producing it.

  - Reports are only distributed to relevant personnel.

  - Information is not duplicated.

- Procedures must exist to ensure the security of confidential data. Such procedures typically include:

  - Personnel controls to ensure only trustworthy people are recruited.

  - Physical controls to prevent unauthorised access to confidential data.

  - Passwords to prevent unauthorised access to systems.

  - System logs and other monitoring programmes to detect suspicious activities.

  - Firewalls to prevent external access to the systems.

Session 18 Quiz
Estimated time: 15 minutes

1. State FOUR examples of strategic control information. (1.1.4)
2. State THREE tactical control measures and THREE operational control measures. (1.1.5, 1.1.6)
3. Describe common types of IT systems. (1.2)
4. List SIX internal sources of management information within an organisation. (2.1)
5. Suggest limitations of using external data compared to internally generated data. (2.5)
6. Describe the purpose of controls and procedures over the distribution of internal information. (3.1.1)
7. Suggest measures to prevent hacking. (3.2.6)

Study Question Bank
Estimated time: 30 minutes

Priority		Estimated Time	Completed
Q31	Hotelco	30 minutes	

EXAMPLE SOLUTIONS

Solution 1—Planning and Control

The following is not an exhaustive list of the plans and controls—any other reasonable plans and controls are also relevant.

	Plans	**Controls**
Board of directors	Five-year financial plan New hotel openings	Actual profits v plan monitoring progress
Management team	Annual budget Staff head count	Compare actual against budget Occupancy rates Actual v plan
Restaurant manager	Menus Staff rotas	Food wasted Staff attendance

Solution 2—Information

Market Trader

The market trader will need to have some forecasts of demand for each type of fruit on a particular day. This will probably be based on experience and "gut feeling" rather than on any formal information.

The trader will also need to know what prices customers are willing to pay and what prices competitors are charging.

How much cash has been taken each day. This will be ascertained by counting cash.

The information systems used by a market trader are therefore very informal, based on observation.

Materials Purchasing Department

The materials purchasing department will need to know the following information:

- Existing quantities of all materials in the warehouse.
- Expected use during the forthcoming period. This will be based on production schedules and bills of materials for each product that is made.
- Information about economic order quantities to ensure that purchasing decisions minimise the costs of holding and ordering inventory.

Index

U

V

W

Y

Z

ACCA

F5 PERFORMANCE MANAGEMENT

STUDY QUESTION BANK

For Examinations from September 2017 to June 2018

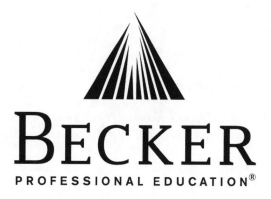

Acknowledgement

Past ACCA examination questions are the copyright of the Association of Chartered Certified Accountants and ha7ve been reproduced by kind permission.

CONTENTS

Question 1 GADGET CO

Gadget Co produces three products, A, B and C, all made from the same material. Until now, it has used traditional absorption costing using labour hours to allocate overheads to its products.

The company is now considering an activity based costing system in the hope that it will improve profitability. Information for the three products for the last year is as follows:

	A	B	C
Production and sales volumes (units)	15,000	12,000	18,000
Selling price per unit	$7.50	$12	$13
Raw material usage (kg) per unit	2	3	4
Direct labour hours per unit	0·1	0·15	0·2
Machine hours per unit	0·5	0·7	0·9
Number of production runs per annum	16	12	8
Number of purchase orders per annum	24	28	42
Number of deliveries to retailers per annum	48	30	62

The price for raw materials remained constant throughout the year at $1·20 per kg. Similarly, the direct labour cost for the whole workforce was $14·80 per hour. The annual overhead costs have been analysed by activity as follows:

	$
Machine set up costs	26,550
Machine running costs	66,400
Procurement costs	48,000
Delivery costs	54,320

Required:

(a) Calculate the full cost per unit for products A, B and C under traditional absorption costing, using direct labour hours as the basis for apportionment.   (5 marks)

(b) Calculate the full cost per unit of each product using activity based costing.   (9 marks)

(c) Using the information given and your calculation from (a) and (b) above, explain how activity based costing may help Gadget Co improve the profitability of each product.
(6 marks)

(20 marks)

Question 2 FLOPRO

(a) Flopro makes and sells two products A and B, each of which passes through the same automated production operations. The following estimated information is available for period 1:

    (i)   Product unit data:

	A	B
Selling price per unit ($)	60	70
Direct material cost ($)	2	40
Variable production overhead cost ($)	28	4
Overall hours per product unit (hours)	0·25	0·15

    (ii)   Budgeted production/sales of products A and B are 120,000 units and 45,000 units respectively. The selling prices per unit for A and B are $60 and $70 respectively.

(iii)   Maximum demand for each product is 20% above the budgeted sales levels.

(iv)   Total fixed production overhead cost is $1,470,000. This is absorbed by products A and B at an average rate per hour based on the estimated production levels.

One of the production operations has a maximum capacity of 3,075 hours that has been identified as a bottleneck that limits the overall production/sales of products A and B. The bottleneck hours required per product unit for products A and B are 0·02 and 0·015 respectively.

Required:

Calculate the mix (units) of products A and B that will maximise net profit and the value ($) of the maximum net profit.   (8 marks)

(b)   The bottleneck situation detailed in **(a)** still applies. Flopro has decided to determine the profit maximising mix of products A and B based on the throughput accounting principle of maximising the throughput return per production hour of the bottleneck resource. This may be measured as: *Throughput return per production hour = (selling price – material cost)/bottleneck hours per unit.*

All other information detailed in **(a)** still applies, except that the variable overhead cost as per **(a)** is now considered to be fixed for the short/intermediate term, based on the value ($) which applied to budgeted production/sales.

Required:

(i)   **Calculate the mix (units) of products A and B that will maximise net profit and the value of that net profit.**   (8 marks)

(ii)   **Calculate the throughput accounting ratio for product B which is calculated as: *throughput return per hour of bottleneck resource for product B/overall total overhead cost per hour of bottleneck resource.***   (3 marks)

(iii)   **Comment on the interpretation of throughput accounting ratios and their use as a control device. You should refer to the ratio for product B in your answer.**   (6 marks)

(25 marks)

Question 3 LITTLE CHEMICAL CO

The Little Chemical Co (LCC) manufactures a small range of speciality chemicals for use in the agriculture industry. Recently the company received a large fine because some of the chemical discharges produce emissions of sulphur dioxide into the atmosphere in excess of permitted standards. As a result of the fine, the company has received bad publicity and lost many of its customers.

The managing director of LCC has told the other directors that the company needs to manage the impact of its operations on the environment more carefully. He has also heard that environmental management accounting is becoming more common and wishes to know what this is. He states "Our existing management accounts tell us nothing about our environmental costs or about the amount of emissions and other pollution that we produce. We need this information so we can manage them."

(a)   **Explain why the management of environmental costs is becoming increasingly important to organisations such as LCC.**   (4 marks)

(b) Explain the meaning of the term environmental management accounting, and illustrate how it can help LCC to improve the management of its environmental activities.
(6 marks)

(10 marks)

Question 4 SCOVET

Scovet Co has identified a market for a new product D for which the following estimated information is available:

(1) Sales revenue for the years 20X2, 20X3 and 20X4 of $6m, $7m and $6m respectively. No sales are expected after 20X4. The unit selling price will be $10 throughout the period.

(2) Contribution to sales percentage of 60% for each year.

(3) Product specific fixed costs in the years 20X2, 20X3 and 20X4 of $2.5m, $2.2m and $1.8m respectively.

(4) Capital investment of $4.5m on 1 January 20X2 with nil residual value at 31 December 20X4.

Note: Ignore taxation and the time value of money.

Required:

(a) Calculate the total profit of product D over its life.
(4 marks)

(b) Calculate the cost per unit of product D, which includes absorption of all product specific costs over the life of the product.
(3 marks)

(7 marks)

Question 5 PARSER CO

The managing director of Parser Co, a small business, is considering undertaking a one-off contract and has asked her inexperienced accountant to advise on what costs are likely to be incurred so that she can price at a profit. The following schedule has been prepared:

Costs for special order

	Notes	$
Direct wages	1	28,500
Supervisor costs	2	11,500
General overheads	3	4,000
Machine depreciation	4	2,300
Machine overheads	5	18,000
Materials	6	34,000
		98,300

Notes

(1)   Direct wages comprise the wages of two employees, particularly skilled in the labour process for this job, who could be transferred from another department to undertake work on the special order. They are fully occupied in their usual department and sub-contracting staff would have to be bought-in to undertake the work left behind. Subcontracting costs would be $32,000 for the period of the work. Different subcontractors who are skilled in the special order techniques are available to work on the special order and their costs would amount to $31,300.

(2)   A supervisor would have to work on the special order. The cost of $11,500 is comprised of $8,000 normal payments plus $3,500 additional bonus for working on the special order. Normal payments refer to the fixed salary of the supervisor. In addition, the supervisor would lose incentive payments in his normal work amounting to $2,500. It is not anticipated that any replacement costs relating to the supervisor's work on other jobs would arise.

(3)   General overheads comprise an apportionment of $3,000 plus an estimate of $1,000 incremental overheads.

(4)   Machine depreciation represents the normal period cost based on the duration of the contract. It is anticipated that $500 will be incurred in additional machine maintenance costs.

(5)   Machine overheads (for running costs such as electricity) are charged at $3 per hour. It is estimated that 6000 hours will be needed for the special order. The machine has 4000 hours available capacity. The further 2000 hours required will mean an existing job is taken off the machine resulting in a lost contribution of $2 per hour.

(6)   Materials represent the purchase costs of 7,500 kg bought some time ago. The materials are no longer used and are unlikely to be wanted in the future except on the special order. The complete Inventory of materials (amounting to 10,000 kg), or part thereof, could be sold for $4·20 per kg. The replacement cost of material used would be $33,375.

Because the business does not have adequate funds to finance the special order, a bank overdraft amounting to $20,000 would be required for the project duration of three months. The overdraft would be repaid at the end of the period. The company uses a cost of capital of 20% to appraise projects. The bank's overdraft rate is 18%.

The managing director has heard that, for special orders such as this, relevant costing should be used that also incorporates opportunity costs. She has approached you to create a revised costing schedule based on relevant costing principles.

Required:

(a)   Briefly explain what is meant by opportunity cost.   (2 marks)

(b)   Adjust the schedule prepared by the accountant to a relevant cost basis, incorporating appropriate opportunity costs.   (11 marks)

(13 marks)

Question 6 SNIFF CO

Sniff Co manufactures and sells its standard perfume by blending a secret formula of aromatic oils with diluted alcohol. The oils are produced by another company following a lengthy process and are very expensive. The standard perfume is highly branded and successfully sold at a price of $39.98 per 100 millilitres (ml).

Sniff Co is considering processing some of the perfume further by adding a hormone to appeal to members of the opposite sex. The hormone to be added will be different for the male and female perfumes. Adding hormones to perfumes is not universally accepted as a good idea as some people have health concerns. On the other hand, market research carried out suggests that a premium could be charged for perfume that can "promise" the attraction of a suitor. The market research has cost $3,000.

Data has been prepared for the costs and revenues expected for the following month (a test month) assuming that a part of the company's output will be further processed by adding the hormones.

The output selected for further processing is 1,000 litres, about a tenth of the company's normal monthly output. Of this, 99% is made up of diluted alcohol, which costs $20 per litre. The rest is a blend of aromatic oils costing $18,000 per litre. The labour required to produce 1,000 litres of the basic perfume before any further processing is 2,000 hours at a cost of $15 per hour.

Of the output selected for further processing, 200 litres (20%) will be for male customers and 2 litres of hormone costing $7,750 per litre will then be added. The remaining 800 litres (80%) will be for female customers and 8 litres of hormone will be added, costing $12,000 per litre. In both cases the adding of the hormone adds to the overall volume of the product as there is no resulting processing loss.

Sniff Co has sufficient existing machinery to carry out the test processing.

The new processes will be supervised by one of the more experienced supervisors currently employed by Sniff Co. His current annual salary is $35,000 and it is expected that he will spend 10% of his time working on the hormone adding process during the test month. This will be split evenly between the male and female versions of the product.

Extra labour will be required to further process the perfume, with an extra 500 hours for the male version and 700 extra hours for the female version of the hormone-added product. Labour is currently fully employed, making the standard product. New labour with the required skills will not be available at short notice.

Sniff Co allocates fixed overhead at the rate of $25 per labour hour to all products for the purposes of reporting profits.

The sales prices that could be achieved as a one-off monthly promotion are:

–   Male version: $75.00 per 100 ml;
–   Female version: $59.50 per 100 ml.

Required:

(a)   **Outline the financial and other factors that Sniff Co should consider when making a further processing decision.**

     Note: No calculations are required.   (4 marks)

(b)   **Assess whether or not Sniff Co should further process the perfume. You should provide separate calculations for the male and the female versions of the perfume.**
                                                                                                     (14 marks)

(c)   Calculate the selling price per 100 ml for the female version of the product that would ensure further processing would break even in the test month.   (2 marks)

(20 marks)

Question 7 A TO C CO

A to C Co manufactures three products, A, B, and C.   The contribution per unit of each of these products is as follows:

Product	A	B	C
	$	$	$
Selling price	10	20	30
Less			
Materials cost	(6.2)	(7.6)	(20.4)
Direct labour	(2.0)	(8.0)	(3.0)
Variable overhead	(1)	(3)	(3)
Contribution per unit	0.8	1.4	3.6

Total fixed costs are $9,000 per month

Budgeted production and estimated maximum demand for each product for the following month are as follows:

Product	A	B	C
	Units	*Units*	*Units*
Budgeted sales	4,000	2,000	4,000
Maximum demand	4,100	4,600	4,100

Required:

(a)   Calculate monthly break-even revenue assuming that sales of the three products are made in the budgeted mix.   (2 marks)

(b)   Draw a profit volume chart, showing two lines:

   (i)   On the assumption that sales of all products are made using the budgeted mix of products.   (2 marks)

   (ii)   On the assumption that sales of the product with the highest contribution to sales ratio are made first, followed by the product with the second highest, and so on, with sales of each product being made up until maximum demand.   (6 marks)

(10 marks)

Question 8 BVX

BVX manufactures three garden furniture products – chairs, benches and tables. The budgeted unit cost and resource requirements of each of these items are detailed below:

	Chair $	Bench $	Table $
Timber cost	5.00	15.00	10.00
Direct labour cost	4.00	10.00	8.00
Variable overhead cost	3.00	7.50	6.00
Fixed overhead cost	4.50	11.25	9.00
	16.50	43.75	33.00
Budgeted volumes per annum	4,000	2,000	1,500

- These volumes are believed to equal the market demand for these products.
- Fixed overhead costs are attributed to the three products on the basis of direct labour hours.
- The labour rate is $4.00 per hour.
- The cost of the timber is $2.00 per square metre.

The products are made from a specialist timber. A memo from the purchasing manager advises you that because of a problem with the supplier, it is to be assumed that this specialist timber is limited in supply to 20,000 square metres per annum.

The sales director has already accepted an order for 500 chairs, 100 benches and 150 tables which if not supplied would incur a financial penalty of $2,000. These quantities are included in the market demand estimates above.

The selling prices of the three products are:

    Chair $20
    Bench $50
    Table $40

Required:

(a)   **Determine the optimum production plan and state the net profit that this should yield per annum.** (6 marks)

(b)   **Calculate and explain the maximum price which should be paid per square metre in order to obtain extra supplies of the timber.** (4 marks)

(10 marks)

Question 9 OPTIMAL PRODUCTION PLAN

A company uses linear programming to establish an optimal production plan in order to maximise profit. The company finds that for the next year materials and labour are likely to be in short supply. Details of the company's products are as follows:

	A $	B $
Materials (at $2 per kg)	6	8
Labour (at $6 per hour)	30	18
Variable overheads (at $1 per hour)	5	3
Variable cost	41	29
Selling price	50	52
Contribution	9	23

There are only 30,000 kg of materials and 36,000 labour hours available. The company also has an agreement to supply 1,000 units of product A which must be met.

Required:

(a)   **Formulate the objective function and constraint equations for this problem.**   (4 marks)

(b)   **Plot the constraints on a suitable graph and determine the optimal production plan.**
(6 marks)

(10 marks)

Question 10 TABULAR APPROACH

A company manufactures a single product, product Y. It has documented levels of demand at certain selling prices for this product as follows:

Demand	Selling price per unit	Cost per unit
Units	$	$
1,100	48	22
1,200	46	21
1,300	45	20
1,400	42	19

Required:

Using a tabular approach calculate the marginal revenues and marginal costs for product Y at the different levels of demand, and so determine the selling price at which the company profits are maximised.

(10 marks)

Question 11 ALBANY

Albany has recently spent some time on researching and developing a new product for which they are trying to establish a suitable price. Previously they have used cost plus 20% to set the selling price.

The standard cost per unit has been estimated as follows:

Direct materials	$	
Material 1	10	(4 kg at $2·50/kg)
Material 2	7	(1 kg at $7/kg)
Direct labour	13	(2 hours at $6·50/hour)
Fixed overheads	7	(2 hours at $3·50/hour)
	37	

Required:

(a) **Using the standard costs calculate two different cost plus prices using two different bases and explain an advantage and disadvantage of each method.** **(6 marks)**

(b) **Give two other possible pricing strategies that could be adopted and describe the impact of each one on the price of the product.** **(4 marks)**

(10 marks)

Question 12 SHIFTERS HAULAGE

Shifters Haulage (SH) is considering changing some of the vans it uses to transport crates for customers. New vans come in three sizes; small, medium and large. SH is unsure about which type to buy. The capacity is 100 crates for the small van, 150 for the medium van and 200 for the large van.

Demand for crates varies and can be either 120 or 190 crates per period, with the probability of the higher demand figure being 0.6.

The sale price per crate is $10 and the variable cost $4 per crate for all van sizes subject to the fact that if the capacity of the van is greater than the demand for crates in a period then the variable cost will be lower by 10% to allow for the fact that the vans will be partly empty when transporting crates.

SH is concerned that if the demand for crates exceeds the capacity of the vans then customers will have to be turned away. SH estimates that in this case goodwill of $100 would be charged against profits per period to allow for lost future sales regardless of the number of customers that are turned away.

Depreciation charged would be $200 per period for the small, $300 for the medium and $400 for the large van.

SH has in the past been very aggressive in decision-making, pursuing rapid growth strategies. However, managers have recently grown more cautious as the business has become more competitive.

Required:

(a) **Prepare a profits table showing the SIX possible profit figures per period.** **(9 marks)**

(b) **Using your profit table from (b) above discuss which type of van SH should buy taking into consideration the possible risk attitudes of the managers.** **(5 marks)**

(c) **Suggest three methods that businesses can use to reduce the uncertainty that exists in their decision making.** **(6 marks)**

(20 marks)

Question 13 DECISION TREES

An oil company has recently acquired rights in a certain area to conduct surveys and geological test drillings that may lead to lifting oil where it is found in commercially exploitable quantities.

The area is already considered to have good potential for finding oil in commercial quantities. At the outset the company has the choice to conduct further geological tests or to carry out a drilling programme immediately. On the known conditions, the company estimates that there is a 70% chance of further tests indicating that a significant amount of oil is present.

Whether the tests show the possibility of oil or not, or even if no tests are undertaken at all, the company could still pursue its drilling programme or alternatively consider selling its rights to drill in the area.

Thereafter, however, if it carries out the drilling programme, the likelihood of final success or failure in the search for oil is considered dependent on the foregoing stages. Thus:

(i)   If the tests indicated that oil was present, the expectation of success in drilling is given as 80%.

(ii)   If the tests indicated that there was insufficient oil present, then the expectation of success in drilling is given as 20%.

(iii)   If no tests have been carried out at all, the expectation of finding commercially viable quantities of oil is given as 55%.

Costs and revenues have been estimated for all possible outcomes and the net present value of each is given below:

Outcome	Net present value $m
Geological testing	(10)
Drilling cost	(50)
Success in finding oil	150
Sale of exploitation rights:	
Tests indicate oil is present	65
Tests indicate "no oil"	15
Without geological tests	40

Required:

(a)   **Prepare a decision tree diagram to represent the above information.**   (8 marks)

(b)   **For the management of the company, calculate its best course of action.**   (7 marks)

(c)   **Explain the value of decision trees in providing management with guidance for decision-making. Illustrate examples of any situations where you consider their use would be of benefit.**   (5 marks)

(20 marks)

Question 14 BRT CO

BRT Co makes a range of glassware ornaments. The marketing plan for 20X1 is based on the three products that have proved most popular in the past: Dog, Bunny and Cat. The expected sales for each product and selling price are as follows:

	Dog	Bunny	Cat
Sales	10,000	20,000	5,000
Price	$10	$5	$20

The following are direct costs of manufacturing each ornament:

	Dog	Bunny	Cat
Materials			
Silicates @ $2/kg	5.0 kgs	6.0 kgs	7.0 kgs
Recycled glass @ $0.10/kg	1.2 kgs	1.3 kgs	1.4 kgs
Labour			
Blowers @ $2/hour	30 mins	45 mins	60 mins
Finishing and packing @ $3/hour	30 mins	30 mins	60 mins

Opening inventory levels are as follows:

Dog	2,000 units
Bunny	2,000 units
Cat	1,000 units
Recycled glass	1,000 kgs
Silicates	23,500 kgs

The required closing inventory levels for finished products are

Dog	1,000
Bunny	2,000
Cat	500

There must also be sufficient closing raw materials inventory to cope with a level of production equivalent to 20% of the 2011 demand.

Required:

Prepare the following budgets:

(a)	Sales budget;	(4 marks)
(b)	Production budget (in numbers of Dog, Bunny and Cat);	(5 marks)
(c)	Materials usage budget (for recycled glass and silicates in kgs);	(3 marks)
(d)	Materials purchases budget (in quantities and $s);	(4 marks)
(e)	Labour budget (in hours and $s).	(4 marks)

(20 marks)

Question 15 ZERO-BASED BUDGETING

Some commentators argue that: "With continuing pressure to control costs and maintain efficiency, the time has come for all public sector organisations to embrace zero-based budgeting. There is no longer a place for incremental budgeting in any organisation, particularly public sector ones, where zero-based budgeting is far more suitable anyway."

Required:

(a) Discuss the particular difficulties encountered when budgeting in public sector organisations compared with budgeting in private sector organisations, drawing comparisons between the two types of organisations. (5 marks)

(b) Explain the terms "incremental budgeting" and "zero-based budgeting". (4 marks)

(c) State the main stages involved in preparing zero-based budgets. (3 marks)

(d) Discuss the view that "there is no longer a place for incremental budgeting in any organisation, particularly public sector ones", highlighting any drawbacks of zero-based budgeting that need to be considered. (8 marks)

(20 marks)

Question 16 PC CO

You have recently been appointed as an assistant management accountant in a large company, PC Co. When you meet the production manager, you overhear him speaking to one of his staff, saying:

"Budgeting is a waste of time. I don't see the point of it. It tells us what we can't afford but it doesn't keep us from buying it. It simply makes us invent new ways of manipulating figures. If all levels of management aren't involved in the setting of the budget, they might as well not bother preparing one."

Required:

(a) Identify and explain SIX objectives of a budgetary control system. (9 marks)

(b) Discuss the concept of a participative style of budgeting in terms of the six objectives identified in part (a). (11 marks)

(20 marks)

Question 17 TOMKINS CO

Tomkins Co is engaged in the production of electronic musical instruments. The management accountant wishes to prepare a flexible budget for 20X1. He obtains the following information from a summary of electricity cost as related to direct labour hours for 20X0:

Month	Electricity cost $	Direct labour hours
May	1,548	297
June	1,667	350
July	1,405	241
August	1,534	280
September	1,600	274
October	1,600	266
November	1,613	285
December	1,635	301

Required:

Using the above data, estimate and using the high low method:

(i) the annual fixed element of electricity cost;
(ii) the variable element per hour of direct labour.

(5 marks)

Question 18 ALEX CO

Alex Co makes specialist computer equipment for the space exploration industry. It recently introduced a new product, the electroscope. This has to be assembled by hand and the process is very labour intensive.

A budget was set for the product of 50 hours per unit, based on the time taken to make the first unit. The first unit was produced in November Actual output and productive labour hours used for the first six months were as follows:

Month	Number of batches made and sold	Labour time taken
November	1	50
December	1	33
January	2	55
February	4	91
March	8	160
April	16	320

The management accountant was surprised that the actual production time was below the flexed budget every month after November. He realised that he had not taken into account the learning curve when he set the budget.

Required:

(a)   **Estimate the learning rate for the period.**   (5 marks)

(b)   **Determine when the steady state was reached.**   (5 marks)

                                                                                                         (10 marks)

Question 19 MERMUS CO

Mermus Co is comparing budget and actual data for the last three months.

	Budget $	Budget $	Actual $	Actual $
Sales		950,000		922,500
Cost of sales				
Raw materials	133,000		130,500	
Direct labour	152,000		153,000	
Variable production overheads	100,700		96,300	
Fixed production overheads	125,400		115,300	
		511,100		495,100
		438,900		427,400

The budget was prepared on the basis of 95,000 units produced and sold, but actual production and sales for the three-month period were 90,000 units.

Mermus uses standard costing and absorbs fixed production overheads on a machine hour basis. A total of 28,500 standard machine hours were budgeted. A total of 27,200 machine hours were actually used in the three-month period.

Required:

(a)   Prepare a revised budget at the new level of activity using a flexible budgeting approach.   (4 marks)

(b)   Calculate the following:

    (i)   Raw material total cost variance;
    (ii)   Direct labour total cost variance;
    (iii)   Fixed overhead efficiency variance;
    (iv)   Fixed overhead capacity variance;
    (v)   Fixed overhead expenditure variance.   (8 marks)

(c)   Suggest possible explanations for the following variances:

    (i)   Raw materials total cost variance;
    (ii)   Fixed overhead efficiency variance;
    (iii)   Fixed overhead expenditure variance.   (6 marks)

(d)   Explain three key purposes of a budgeting system.   (7 marks)

                                                                                                                                       (25 marks)

Question 20 PORTLAND CO

Portland Co manufactures one product from a standard grade of material. The standard cost card indicates the following:

		$
Material	6 kgs @ $1.60	9.60
Labour	3 hours @ $4	12.00
Variable overhead	3 hours @ $1.70	5.10
Fixed overhead	3 hours @ $3	9.00
Standard cost per unit		35.70
Standard selling price		40.00
Standard profit per unit		4.30

Budgeted production and sales for week 1	1,100 units

Actual results for the week were as follows:

Production		1,000 units

		$
Materials	6,500 kgs @ $1.50	9,750
Labour	3,100 hours worked and paid	12,500
Variable overhead		5,200
Fixed overhead		9,800
		37,250
Sales	1,000 units @ $39	39,000
Actual profit		1,750

Required:

Calculate relevant variances in as much detail as the information allows.

(10 marks)

Question 21 MILBAO CO

Milbao Co makes and sells three types of electronic game for which the following budget/standard information and actual information is available for a four-week period:

Model	Budget sales (units)	Standard unit data Selling price $	Variable cost $	Actual sales (units)
Superb	30,000	100	40	36,000
Excellent	50,000	80	25	42,000
Good	20,000	70	22	18,000

Budgeted fixed costs are $2,500,000 for the four-week period. Budgeted fixed costs should be charged to product units at an overall budgeted average cost per unit where it is relevant to do so.

Required:

(a)   Calculate the sales volume variance for each model and in total for the four-week period where (i) contribution and (ii) net profit is used as the variance valuation base.

(6 marks)

(b)   Calculate the TOTAL sales quantity and sales mix variances for Milbao Co for the four-week period, using contribution as the valuation base. (Variances for individual models are not required.)

(4 marks)

(10 marks)

Question 22 PAN-OCEAN CHEMICALS

Pan-Ocean Chemicals has one product that requires inputs from three types of material to produce batches of product Synthon. Standard cost details for a single batch are shown below:

Material type	Materials Standard Kgs	Materials Standard price per Kg ($)	Labour Standard hours	Labour Standard rate per hour ($)
S1	8	0·3	1	5·00
S2	5	0·5		
S3	3	0·4		

A standard loss of 10% of input is expected. Actual production was 15,408 kgs for the previous week. Details of the materials used were:

Actual material used (kg)

S1	8,284
S2	7,535
S3	3,334

Total labour cost for the week was $6,916 for 1,235 hours worked.

Required:

(a) **Calculate:**

(i)   **Total material mix, yield and usage variances;**   (10 marks)
(ii)   **Labour rate and efficiency variances.**   (2 marks)

(b) **Explain why the sum of the mix variances for materials measured in kg should be zero.**

(2 marks)

(14 marks)

Question 23 DENZEL CO

Denzel makes and sells a single product. The company budgeted to make and sell 120,000 units in November. The standard cost of labour for the product was as follows:

Labour 1.25 hours @ $12 per hour

Actual output for November was 122,000 units. Labour cost for the month was as follows:

	$
Labour (158,600 hours @ $12.6)	1,998,360

Prior to calculation of variances, it has been decided to revise the standard cost retrospectively, to take account of the following, which are considered to be outside of the control of the managers whose performance is evaluated based on variances:

(1)   A 3% increase in the labour rate to $13 per hour- due to negotiations with unions that were concluded after the initial standard had been set.

(2)   The standard for labour use had anticipated that the company would buy a new machine which would lead to a 10% decrease in labour hours. Instead of buying a new machine, existing machines had been improved, so a more appropriate standard is considered to be 1.4 hours per unit.

Required:

(a) **Prepare a statement reconciling the standard labour cost of actual output (based on the original standard) with the actual cost. The reconciliation should show the total planning variance and the total operating variance.** (4 marks)

(b) **Analyse the planning variance into labour usage planning variance and labour price planning variance.** (4 marks)

(c) **Discuss the principles that should be applied in deciding whether or not a standard should be revised.** (5 marks)

(d) **Discuss the factors to be considered in deciding whether a variance should be investigated.** (5 marks)

(18 marks)

Question 24 SPIKE CO

Spike Co manufactures and sells good quality leather bound diaries. Each year it budgets for its profits, including detailed budgets for sales, materials and labour. If appropriate, the departmental managers are allowed to revise their budgets for planning errors.

In recent months, the managing director has become concerned about the frequency of budget revisions. At a recent board meeting he said, "There seems little point budgeting any more. Every time we have a problem the budgets are revised to leave me looking at a favourable operational variance report and at the same time a lot less profit than promised."

Required:

(a)   **Describe the circumstances when a budget revision should be allowed and when it should be refused.** (4 marks)

(b)   Two specific situations have recently arisen, for which budget revisions were sought:

Materials

A local material supplier was forced into liquidation. Spike's buyer managed to find another supplier, 150 miles away at short notice. This second supplier charged more for the material and a supplementary delivery charge on top. The buyer agreed to both the price and the delivery charge without negotiation. "I had no choice", the buyer said, "The production manager was pushing me very hard to find any solution possible!" Two months later, another, more competitive, local supplier was found.

A budget revision is being sought for the two months where higher prices had to be paid.

Labour

During the early part of the year, problems had been experienced with the quality of work being produced by the support staff in the labour force. The departmental manager had complained in his board report that his team were "unreliable, inflexible and just not up to the job".

It was therefore decided, after discussion of the board report, that something had to be done. The company changed its policy so as to recruit only top graduates from good quality universities. This has had the effect of pushing up the costs involved but increasing productivity in relation to that element of the labour force.

The support staff departmental manager has requested a budget revision to cover the extra costs involved following the change of policy.

Required:

Discuss each request for a budget revision, putting what you see as both sides of the argument and reach a conclusion as to whether a budget revision should be allowed.
(6 marks)

(c)   The market for leather bound diaries has been shrinking as the electronic versions become more widely available and easier to use. Spike has produced the following data relating to leather bound diary sales for the year to date:

Budget
Sales volume	180,000 units
Sales price	$17.00 per unit
Standard contribution	$7.00 per unit

The total market for diaries in this period was estimated in the budget to be 1.8m units. In fact, the actual total market shrank to 1.6 million units for the period under review.

Actual results for the same period

Sales volume	176,000 units
Sales price	$16.40 per unit

Required:

(i)	Calculate the total sales price and total sales volume variance.	(2 marks)
(ii)	Calculate market size and market share variances.	(4 marks)
(iii)	Comment on the sales performance of the business.	(4 marks)

(20 marks)

Question 25 TIES ONLY CO

Ties Only Co is a new business, selling high quality imported men's ties via the Internet. The managers, who also own the company, are young and inexperienced but they are prepared to take risks. They are confident that importing quality ties and selling via a website will be successful and that the business will grow quickly. This is despite the well-recognised fact that selling clothing is a very competitive business.

They were prepared for a loss-making start and decided to pay themselves modest salaries (included in administration expenses in Table 1 below) and pay no dividends for the foreseeable future.

The owners are so convinced that growth will quickly follow that they have invested enough money in website server development to ensure that the server can handle the very high levels of predicted growth. All website development costs were written off as incurred in the internal management accounts that are shown below in Table 1.

Significant expenditure on marketing was incurred in the first two quarters to launch both the website and new products. It is not expected that marketing expenditure will continue to be as high in the future.

Customers can buy a variety of styles, patterns and colours of ties at different prices.

The business's trading results for the first two quarters of trade are shown below in table 1.

Table 1

	Quarter 1		Quarter 2	
	$	$	$	$
Sales		420,000		680,000
Less: Cost of Sales		(201,600)		(340,680)
Gross Profit		218,400		339,320
Less: Expenses				
Website development	120,000		90,000	
Administration	100,500		150,640	
Distribution	20,763		33,320	
Launch marketing	60,000		40,800	
Other variable expenses	50,000		80,000	
Total expenses		(351,263)		(394,760)
Loss for quarter		(132,863)		(55,440)

Required:

(a)   **Assess the financial performance of the business during its first two quarters using only the data in Table 1 above.**   (12 marks)

(b)   **Briefly consider whether the losses made by the business in the first two quarters are a true reflection of the current and likely future performance of the business.**   (4 marks)

(c)   The owners are well aware of the importance of non-financial indicators of success and therefore have identified a small number of measures to focus on. These are measured monthly and then combined to produce a quarterly management report.

The data for the first two quarters management reports is shown below:

Table 2

	Quarter 1	Quarter 2
Website hits[1]	690,789	863,492
Number of ties sold	27,631	38,857
On time delivery	95%	89%
Sales returns	12%	18%
System downtime	2%	4%

The industry average conversion rate for website hits to number of ties sold is 3·2%. The industry average sales return rate for internet-based clothing sales is 13%.

Required:

Comment on each of the non-financial data in Table 2 above taking into account, where appropriate, the industry averages provided, providing your assessment of the performance of the business.   (9 marks)

(25 marks)

Question 26 VALUE FOR MONEY

(a)   **Outline the meaning of the phrase "Value for Money" and explain how the concepts underpinning it may be used to evaluate organisational performance.**   (12 marks)

(b)   **Evaluate the following four measures, which have been suggested by a working party as published performance indicators of a publicly funded and operated fire-fighting and rescue service:**

(i)   **Annual cost of the service;**
(ii)   **Cost per emergency call-out;**
(iii)   **Average response time to arrive at incident;**
(iv)   **Fire deaths per thousand head of population.**   (8 marks)

(20 marks)

---

[1] A website hit is automatically counted each time a visitor to the website opens the home page of Ties Only Co.

Question 27 EATWELL RESTAURANT

The owners of Eatwell Restaurant have diversified business interests and operate in a wide range of commercial areas. Since buying the restaurant in 201V they have carefully recorded the data below:

Recorded Data for Eatwell Restaurant (201W – 201Z)

	201W	201X	201Y	201Z
Total meals served	3,750	5,100	6,200	6,700
Regular customers attending weekly	5	11	15	26
Number of items on offer per day	4	4	7	9
Reported cases of food poisoning	4	5	7	7
Special theme evenings introduced	0	3	9	13
Annual operating hours with no customers	380	307	187	126
Proposals submitted to cater for special events	10	17	29	38
Contracts won to cater for special events	2	5	15	25
Complimentary letters from satisfied customers	0	4	3	6
Average number of customers at peak times	18	23	37	39
Average service delay at peak times (minutes)	32	47	15	35
Maximum seating capacity	25	25	40	40
Weekly opening hours	36	36	40	36
Written complaints received	8	12	14	14
Idle time	570	540	465	187
New meals introduced during the year	16	8	27	11
Financial data	$	$	$	$
Average customer spend on wine	3	4	4	7
Total revenue	83,000	124,500	137,000	185,000
Revenue from special events	2,000	13,000	25,000	55,000
Profit	11,600	21,400	43,700	57,200
Value of food wasted in preparation	1,700	1,900	3,600	1,450
Total revenue of all restaurants in locality	895,000	1,234,000	980,000	1,056,000

Required:

(a)   **Assess the overall performance of the business using Fitzgerald and Moon's dimensions of performance.**   (14 marks)

(b)   **Identify any additional information that you would consider of assistance in assessing the performance of Eatwell Restaurant in comparison with another restaurant. Give reasons for your selection and explain how they would relate to the key performance area categories used in (a).**   (6 marks)

(20 marks)

Question 28 BRACE CO

(a)   Brace Co is an electronics company specialising in the manufacture of home audio equipment. Historically, the company has used solely financial performance measures to assess the performance of the company as a whole. The company's Managing Director has recently heard of the "balanced scorecard approach" and is keen to learn more.

Required:

Describe the balanced scorecard approach to performance measurement.   (10 marks)

(b)   Brace Co is split into two divisions, A and B, each with their own cost and revenue streams. Each of the divisions is managed by a divisional manager who has the power to make all investment decisions within the division. The cost of capital for both divisions is 12%. Historically, investment decisions have been made by calculating the return on investment (ROI) of any opportunities and at present, the return on investment of each division is 16%.

A new manager who has recently been appointed in division A has argued that using residual income (RI) to make investment decisions would result in "better goal congruence" throughout the company.

Each division is currently considering the following separate investments:

	Project for Division A	*Project for Division B*
Capital required for investment	$82·8 million	$40·6 million
Sales generated by investment	$44·6 million	$21·8 million
Net profit margin	28%	33%

The company is seeking to maximise shareholder wealth.

Required:

Calculate both the return on investment and residual income of the new investment for each of the two divisions. Comment on these results, taking into consideration the manager's views about residual income.   (10 marks)

(20 marks)

Question 29 ABLE & BAKER

(a)   The transfer pricing system operated by a divisional company has the potential to make a significant contribution towards the achievement of corporate financial objectives.

Required:

State the potential benefits of operating a transfer pricing system within a divisionalised company.   (5 marks)

(b)   A company operates two divisions, Able and Baker. Able manufactures two products X and Y. Product X is sold to external customers for $42 per unit. The only outlet for product Y is Baker.

Baker supplies an external market and can obtain its semi-finished supplies (product Y) from either Able or an external source. Baker currently has the opportunity to purchase product Y from an external supplier for $38 per unit. The capacity of division Able is measured in units of output, irrespective of whether product X, Y or a combination of both are being manufactured. The associated product costs are as follows:

	X	Y
Variable costs per unit	32	35
Fixed overheads per unit	5	5
Total unit costs	37	40

Required:

Using the above information, provide advice on the determination of an appropriate transfer price for the sale of product Y from division Able to division Baker under the following conditions:

(i)   **When division Able has spare capacity and limited external demand for product X;**   (3 marks)

(ii)   **When division Able is operating at full capacity with unsatisfied external demand for product X.**   (4 marks)

(c)   The design of an information system to support transfer-pricing decision-making necessitates the inclusion of specific data.

Identify the data that needs to be collected and how you would expect it to be used.
                                                                                (6 marks)

                                                                                (18 marks)

Question 30 WASH CO

Wash Co assembles and sells two types of washing machines – the Spin (S) and the Rinse (R). The company has two divisions: the assembly division, and the retail division.

The company's policy is to transfer the machines from the assembly division to the retail division at full cost plus 10%. This has resulted in internal transfer prices, when S and R are being transferred to the retail division, of $220·17 and $241·69 respectively. The retail division currently sells S to the general public for $320 per machine and R for $260 per machine. Assume it incurs no other costs except for the transfer price.

The retail division's manager is convinced that, if he could obtain R at a lower cost and therefore reduce the external selling price from $260 to $230 per unit, he could significantly increase sales of R, which would be beneficial to both divisions. He has questioned the fact that the overhead costs are allocated to the products on the basis of labour hours; he thinks it should be done using machine hours or even activity based costing.

You have obtained the following information for the last month from the assembly division:

	Product S	Product R
Production and sales (units)	3,200	5,450
Materials cost	$117	$95
Labour cost (at $12 per hour)	$6	$9
Machine hours (per unit)	2	1
Total no. of production runs	30	12
Total no. of purchase orders	82	64
Total no. of deliveries to retail division	64	80

Overhead costs:	$
Machine set-up costs	306,435
Machine maintenance costs	415,105
Ordering costs	11,680
Delivery costs	144,400
	———
Total	877,620
	———

Required:

(a) **Using traditional absorption costing, calculate new transfer prices for S and R if machine hours are used as a basis for absorption rather than labour hours.**

Note: round all workings to 2 decimal places. (3 marks)

(b) **Using activity based costing to allocate the overheads, recalculate the transfer prices for S and R.**

Note: round all workings to 2 decimal places. (8 marks)

(c) **Calculate last month's profit for each division, showing it both for each product and in total, if activity based costing is used.** (4 marks)

(15 marks)

Question 31 HOTELCO

Hotelco owns and runs 35 hotels in the UK, some catering mainly for tourists and holidaymakers, other servicing business travellers. In addition to providing accommodation, each hotel has a bar and restaurant which are open to both residents and non-residents.

Until now the company's accounts department, based at its head office, has produced an annual balance sheet and profit and loss account, but has not been required to produce any periodic management accounts.

The directors of Hotelco are concerned that the company's profitability is declining. They have therefore decided to introduce a management information system that will enable them to monitor the performance of individual hotels.

They propose to install a microcomputer in each hotel, networked to head office. Relevant data will be input by the accountant at each hotel, enabling reports to be generated for each hotel individually and for the company as a whole.

Required:

Describe the reports that should be generated by Hotelco's management information system. Your answer should include the information to be contained in each report and why this would be relevant to management in monitoring performance.

(12 marks)

Answer 1 GADGET CO

(a) **Traditional absorption costing**

Total annual overhead costs:	$
Machine set up costs	26,550
Machine running costs	66,400
Procurement costs	48,000
Delivery costs	54,320
	195,270

Overhead absorption rate:

	A	B	C	Total
Production volumes	15,000	12,000	18,000	
Labour hours per unit	0·1	0·15	0·2	
Total labour hours	1,500	1,800	3,600	6,900

Therefore, overhead absorption rate = $195,270 ÷ 6,900 = $28·30 per hour.

Cost per unit

	A	B	C
	$	$	$
Raw materials ($1·20 × 2:3:4 kg)	2·4	3·6	4·8
Direct labour ($14·80 × 0·1:0·15:0·2 hours)	1·48	2·22	2·96
Overhead ($28·30 × 0·1:0·15:0·2 hours)	2·83	4·25	5·66
Full cost per unit	6·71	10·07	13·42

(b) **Activity based costing**

Cost drivers

Cost pools	$	Cost driver
Machine set up costs	26,550	36 production runs (16 + 12 + 8)
Machine running costs	66,400	32,100 machine hours (7,500 + 8,400 + 16,200)
Procurement costs	48,000	94 purchase orders (24 + 28 + 42)
Delivery costs	54,320	140 deliveries (48 + 30 + 62)
	195,270	

Cost per machine set up	$26,550 ÷ 36 = $737·50
Cost per machine hour	$66,400 ÷ 32,100 = $2·0685
Cost per order	$48,000 ÷ 94 = $510·6383
Cost per delivery	$54,320 ÷ 140 = $388

Allocation of overheads to each product:

	A $	B $	C $	Total $
Machine set up costs	11,800	8,850	5,900	26,550
Machine running costs	15,514	17,375	33,510	66,400
Procurement costs	12,255	14,298	21,447	48,000
Delivery costs	18,624	11,640	24,056	54,320
	58,193	52,163	84,913	195,270
Number of units produced	15,000	12,000	18,000	
	$	$	$	
Overhead cost per unit	3·88	4·35	4·72	

Total cost per unit	A $	B $	C $
Materials	2·4	3·6	4·8
Labour	1·48	2·22	2·96
Overheads	3·88	4·35	4·72
	7·76	10·17	12·48

(c) **How ABC may improve profitability**

When comparing the full unit costs for each of the products under absorption costing as compared to ABC, the following observations can be made:

Product A

The unit cost for product A is 16% higher under ABC as opposed to traditional absorption costing. Under ABC, it is $7·76 per unit compared to $6·71 under traditional costing. This is particularly significant given that the selling price for product A is $7·50 per unit. This means that when the activities that give rise to the overhead costs for product A are taken into account, product A is actually making a loss. If the company wants to improve profitability it should look to either increase the selling price of product A or somehow reduce the costs. Delivery costs are also high, with 48 deliveries a year being made for product A. Maybe the company could seek further efficiencies here. Also, machine set up costs are higher for product A than for any of the other products, due to the larger number of production runs. The reason for this needs to be identified and, if possible, the number of production runs needs to be reduced.

Product B

The difference between the activity based cost for B as opposed to the traditional cost is quite small, being only $0·10. Since the selling price for B is $12, product B is clearly profitable whichever method of overhead allocation is used. ABC does not really identify any areas for concern here.

Product C

The unit cost for C is 7% lower under ABC when compared to traditional costing. More importantly, while C looks like it is making a loss under traditional costing, ABS tells a different story. The selling price for C is $13 per unit and, under ABC, it costs $12·48 per unit. Under traditional absorption costing, C is making a loss of $0·42 per unit. Identifying the reason for the differences in C, it is apparent that the number of production runs required to produce C is relatively low compared to the volumes produced. This leads to a lower apportionment of the machine set up costs to C than would be given under traditional absorption costing. Similarly, the number of product tests carried out on C is low relative to its volume.

ABC is therefore very useful in identifying that C is actually more profitable than A, because of the reasons identified above. The company needs to look at the efficiency that seems to be achieved with C (low number of production runs less testing) and see whether any changes can be made to A, to bring it more in line with C. Of course, this may not be possible, in which case the company may consider whether it wishes to continue to produce A and whether it could sell higher volumes of C.

Answer 2 FLOPRO

(a)   **Optimum product mix**

The contribution per product unit (selling price – variable cost) may be calculated as:

$$A = \$60 - (2 + 28) = \$30$$
$$B = \$70 - (40 + 4) = \$26$$

	A	B
Contribution per unit	$30	$26
Bottleneck hours per unit	0·02	0·015
Contribution per bottleneck hour	$1,500	$1,733
Ranking	②	①

Therefore produce and sell product B up to its maximum demand and then product A with the remaining capacity:

Maximum demand of product B (45,000 × 120%)	54,000 units
Bottleneck hours required for B (54,000 × 0·015)	810 hours
Bottleneck hours available for A (3,075 – 810)	2,265 hours
Output of product A which is possible (2,265 ÷ 0·02)	113,250 units

Maximum net profit:

		$
Contribution product A	113,250 × $30	3,397,500
Contribution product B	54,000 × $26	1,404,000
Total contribution		4,801,500
Less: Fixed overhead cost:		1,470,000
Net profit		3,331,500

(b)   **Throughput accounting**

(i)   *Product mix to maximise net profit*

Throughput per unit is calculated as selling price – direct material cost:

$$A = \$60 - 2 = \$58$$
$$B = \$70 - 40 = \$30$$

	A	B
Throughput per unit	$58	$30
Bottleneck hours per unit	0·02	0·015
Throughput return per bottleneck hour	$2,900	$2,000

Flopro should sell product A up to its maximum demand and then product B using the remaining capacity.

Maximum demand of product A (120,000 × 120%)	144,000 units
Bottleneck hours required for A (144,000 × 0·02)	2,880 hours
Bottleneck hours available for B (3,075 – 2,880)	195 hours
Output of product B which is possible (195 ÷ 0·015)	13,000 units

Maximum net profit:

	$000
Throughput return product A 144,000 × ($60 – 2)	8,352
Throughput return product B 13,000 × ($70 – 40)	390
Total throughput return	8,742
Less: Overhead cost:	
Variable based on budget (120,000 × $28 + 45,000 × $4)	(3,540)
Fixed	(1,470)
Net profit	3,732

(ii)   *Throughput accounting ratio for product B*

$$\text{Throughput accounting ratio} = \frac{\text{Throughput return per hour of bottleneck}}{\text{Total overhead cost per hour of bottleneck}}$$

Throughput return per hour of bottleneck for product B was calculated in part (i) as $2,000.

Total overhead cost per hour of bottleneck:

Total overhead costs: (3,540,000 + 1,470,000)	$5,010,000
Total hours of bottleneck:	3,075
⇒Total overhead cost per hour of bottleneck (5,010,000 ÷ 3075)	$1629.27

$$\text{Throughput accounting ratio} = \frac{2,000}{1,629.27} = 1.2275$$

(iii)   *Interpretation*

Where throughput accounting principles are applied, a product is worth producing and selling if its throughput return per bottleneck hour is greater than the production cost per throughput hour. This may be measured by the throughput accounting ratio. Where the ratio is less than 1·00, return exceeds cost and the focus should be on improving the size of the ratio.

Efforts may be made to improve the position for each product and in total by focusing on areas such as

■   Improved throughput ($) per unit by increasing selling price or reducing material cost per unit. Product B has a very high material element ($40 per unit)

■   Improving the throughput ($) per unit by reducing the time required on the bottleneck resource. Reducing the time for product B from 0·015 hours to 0·01 hours through methods change would improve its ratio.

■   Improving the overall position by reducing the cost of spare capacity. This may be achieved by operational re-design aimed at reducing or eliminating the impact of any bottlenecks.

The throughput ratio for product B is 1·2275 which is greater than 1·00 and therefore acceptable. Its ratio is considerably less than that of product A, which is 1·780 ($2,900 ÷ $1,629·27). The product ratio may be used as a basis for the monitoring of trend, by product and in total.

Answer 3 LITTLE CHEMICAL CO

(a)   **Why the management of environmental costs is becoming increasingly important**

There are three main reasons why the management of environmental costs is becoming increasingly important:

(1)   Increasing awareness of environmental issues means that organisations are expected to behave in an environmentally friendly way. LCC has recently experienced a loss of customers due to its own poor reputation.

(2)   Environmental costs account for a huge portion of costs for many industrial companies such as LCC. In addition to fines, there are image costs, such as the loss of customers that LCC experienced due to excessive pollution. There may also be costs of compliance – such as measuring emissions to ensure they are within legal limits. Management needs to be aware of such costs in order to manage them.

(3)   There may be benefits associated with better environmental behaviour – such as cost savings if action is taken to reduce waste.

(b)   **Environmental management accounting**

The managing director of LCC has complained that the existing management accounts do not provide management with an accurate view of environmental costs. As a result of this, management make decisions that are bad for the environment and bad for the organisation's profits. In the case of LCC, for example, more information is needed about the current level of emissions and the costs and benefits of reducing these.

Environmental management accounting (EMA) means providing information to management to help them to manage the environmental costs and activities.

EMA does not provide only financial information. The United Nations Division for Sustainable Development distinguishes between:

■   Physical information such as the use, flows and destinies of energy, water and materials, including waste.

■   Monetary information on environment related costs, earning and savings.

EMA makes use of management accounting techniques such as activity-based costing (ABC) and life cycle costing, which can be used to manage environmental costs more effectively. In ABC, for example, the drivers that cause environmental costs to be incurred can be identified. Managers can then take steps to reduce the use of the drivers, so that the environmental costs are reduced without reducing output.

EMA would help the managers at LCC to better understand the impact of their activities on the environment. Physical information about the amount of emissions generated could be provided so managers can monitor these and find ways to reduce them. In addition, financial information about the costs and benefits of environmental programs could assist in decision making about investments in new equipment that would help to reduce the pollution.

Tutorial note: *This topic will not be examined numerically.*

Answer 4 SCOVET CO

(a)   Profit over the life of the product

	1 Jan. 20X2 $m	31 Dec. 20X2 $m	31 Dec. 20X3 $m	31 Dec. 20X4 $m
Initial investment	–4.5			
Contribution (at 60%)	3.6	4.2	3.6	
Fixed costs		–2.5	–2.2	–1.8
Net cash flow	–4.5	1.1	2.0	1.8

Net cash flow and therefore profit 0.4 million.

Hence product D is viable on financial grounds since it generates positive profit over its life.

(b)   Cost per unit

	$
Variable cost per unit ($10 × 0.4)	4.00
Fixed cost per unit (W)	5.79
Total cost per unit	9.79

WORKING

	$m
Initial investment	4.5
Fixed costs:	
20X2	2.5
20X3	2.2
20X4	1.8
Total product specific fixed costs	11.0
Budgeted sales units (millions)	1.9
Budgeted fixed cost per unit ($)	5.79

	$m
Budgeted sales units: Total revenue over the life of the product	19
Budgeted units (at $10 per unit)	1.9

Answer 5 PARSER CO

(a) **Opportunity cost**

Opportunity costs represent the value of the loss or sacrifice when choosing between scarce alternatives. Lack of scarcity implies zero opportunity cost.

(b) **Revised costs for special order**

	Notes	$
Subcontractor costs	1	31,300
Supervisor costs	2	1,000
General overheads	3	1,000
Machine maintenance	4	500
Machine overheads	5	22,000
Materials	6	31,500
Interest costs	7	900
		88,200

Notes:

(1) The choice lies between the two subcontractor costs that have to be employed because of the shortage of existing labour. The minimum cost is to have subcontractors employed who are skilled in the special process.

(2) Only the difference between the bonus and the incentive payment represents an additional cost that arises due to the special order. Fixed salary costs do not change.

(3) Only incremental costs are relevant.

(4) Depreciation is a period cost and is not related to the special order. Additional maintenance costs are relevant.

(5) The relevant costs are the variable overheads ($3 × 6,000 hours) that will be incurred, plus the displacement costs of $2 × 2,000 hours making a total of $22,000.

(6) Since the materials are no longer used the replacement cost is irrelevant. The historic cost of $34,000 is a sunk cost. The relevant cost is the lost sale value of the inventory used in the special order which is: 7,500 kg × $4·20 per kg = $31,500.

(7) Full opportunity costing will also allow for imputed interest costs on the incremental loan. The correct interest rate is the overdraft rate since this represents the incremental cost the company will pay. Simple interest charges for three months are therefore: $(^3/_{12}) × \$20,000 × 18\% = \$900$.

Answer 6 SNIFF CO

(a) **Financial and other factors to consider in further processing decision**

- **Incremental revenue.** The new perfume, once further processed, should generate a higher price and the extra revenue is clearly relevant to the decision.

- **Incremental costs.** A decision to further process can involve more materials and labour. Care must be taken to only include those costs that change as a result of the decision and therefore sunk costs should be ignored.

Sunk costs would include, for example, fixed overheads already incurred before the further process decision was taken. The shortage of labour means that its "true" cost will be higher and need to be included.

- **Impact on sales volumes.** Sniff is selling a "highly branded" product. Existing customers may well be happy with the existing product. If the further processing changes the existing product too much, sales and loyalty could be affected.

- **Impact on reputation.** As is mentioned in the question, adding hormones to a product is not universally popular. Many groups exist around the world that protest against the use of hormones in products. This association could damage sniff.

- Potential legal cases being brought regarding allergic reactions to hormones.

(b)   **Further processing decision**

Production costs for 1,000 litres of the standard perfume

		$
Aromatic oils	10 litres × $18,000	180,000
Diluted alcohol	990 litres × $20	19,800
Material cost		199,800
Labour	2,000 hours × $15	30,000
Total		229,800
Cost per litre		229·80
Sales price per litre		399·80

Lost contribution per hour of labour used on new products
($399,800 − $199,800) ÷ 2,000 hours = $100 per hour.

Incremental costs

	Male		Female	
		$		$
Hormone	2 litre × $7,750	15,500	8 litre × $12,000	96,000
Supervisor	Sunk cost	0	Sunk cost	0
Labour	500 hours × $100	50,000	700 hours × $100	70,000
Fixed cost	Sunk cost	0	Sunk cost	0
Market research	Sunk cost	0	Sunk cost	0
Total		65,500		166,000

Incremental revenues

	Male		Female	
		$		$
Standard	200 litre × $399.80	79,960	800 litre × $399.80	319,840
Hormone added	202 litre × $750	151,500	808 litre × $595	480,760
Incremental revenue		71,540		160,920
Net benefit/(cost)		6,040		(5,080)

The Male version of the product is worth further processing in that the extra revenue exceeds the extra cost by $6,040.

The Female version of the product is not worth further processing in that the extra cost exceeds the extra revenue by $5,080.

In both cases the numbers appear small. Indeed, the benefit of $6,040 may not be enough to persuade management to take the risk of damaging the brand and the reputation of the business. To put this figure into context: the normal output generates a contribution of $170 per litre and on normal output of about 10,000 litres this represents a monthly contribution of around $1.7m (after allowing for labour costs).

Future production decisions are a different matter. If the product proves popular, however, Sniff might expect a significant increase in overall volumes. If Sniff could exploit this and resolve its current shortage of labour then more contribution could be created. It is worth noting that resolving its labour shortage would substantially reduce the labour cost allocated to the hormone added project. Equally, the prices charged for a one off experimental promotion might be different to the prices that can be secured in the long run.

(c)   **Selling price per 100 ml for female version of product**

The selling price charged would have to cover the incremental costs of $166,000. For 808 litres that would mean the price would have to be:

$$\frac{(\$166,000 + \$319,840)}{808 \text{ ltrs}} = \$601.29 \text{ per litre}$$

or about $60.13 per 100 ml.

This represents an increase of only 1.05% on the price given and so clearly there may be scope for further consideration of this proposal.

Answer 7 A TO C CO

(a)   **Calculation of monthly break even revenue**

Using the formula: Break even revenue $= \dfrac{\text{Fixed cost}}{\text{Weighted average C/S ratio}} = \dfrac{\$9,000}{0.102} = \$88,236$

WORKING

Weighted average C/S ratio $= \dfrac{\text{Budgeted total contribution}}{\text{Budgeted total revenue}}$

Product	A	B	C	Total
Budgeted sales (units)	4,000	2,000	4,000	
Selling price per unit	10	20	30	
Budgeted revenue	40,000	40,000	120,000	200,000
Contribution per unit	0.8	1.4	3.6	
Budgeted contribution	3,200	2,800	14,400	20,400
C/S ratio	0.08	0.07	0.12	0.102

Weighted average C/S ratio is therefore 0.102.

Tutorial note: *The C/S ratios of the individual products are not required to calculate the weighted average C/S ratio. However, they are needed for the next part of the question.*

(b) **Profit volume charts**

See the chart on the next page. The X-axis shows total revenue; the Y-axis profit.

(i) *Sales in standard product mix*

In order to draw this line it is sufficient to know only two points, and to draw a straight line between them:

When revenue = 0, loss = total fixed cost, = $9,000.

When revenue is as per budget, it is $200,000 (see part (c) above). Profit at this point is total contribution less fixed costs, being $20,400 – $9,000 = $11,400.

(ii) *Products sold in order of C/S ratio*

In this situation it is assumed that product C would be sold first, as it has the highest C/S ratio. Sales of product C would be made up until maximum demand for product C is reached, after which sales of product A would start, up to maximum demand for product A, and finally sales of product C.

The Profit volume chart will be multi gradient, as the gradient depends on the C/S ratio of the product. In order to draw the chart, it is necessary to calculate revenue and profit at each of the following points:

- Zero revenue;
- Maximum sales of Product C only;
- Maximum sales of Product C and Product A;
- Maximum sales of all three products.

	Sales revenue	Contribution	Fixed cost	Profit
Zero revenue	0	0	(9,000)	(9,000)
Sell 4,100 units of C	123,000	14,760	(9,000)	5,760
Sell 4,100 units of A and C	164,000	18,040	(9,000)	9,040
Sell 4,100 units of A and C and 4,600 units of B	256,000	24,480	(9,000)	15,480

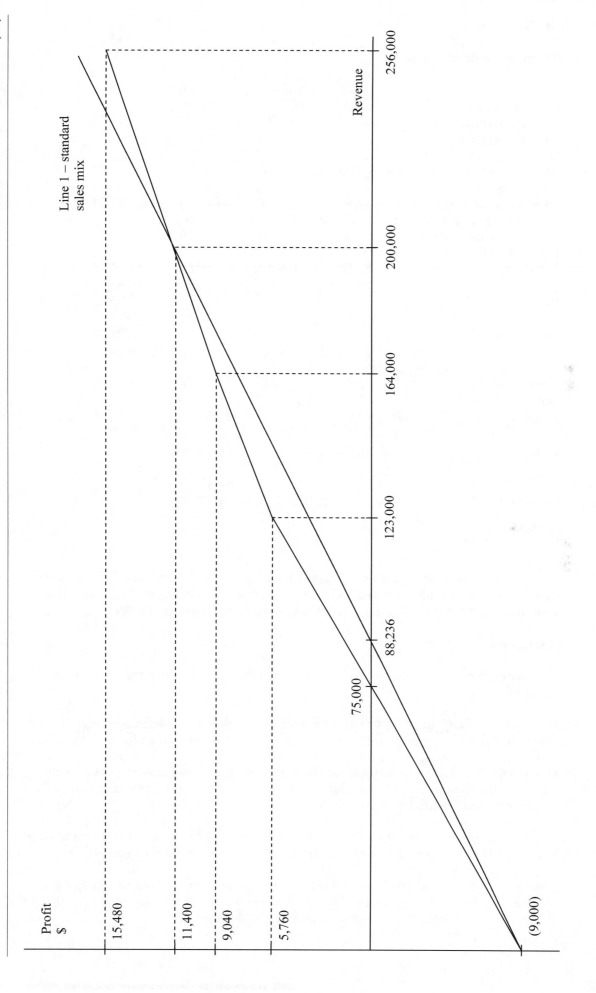

Answer 8 BVX

(a)   Optimum production plan

	Chair	Bench	Table	Total
Contribution/unit	$8.00	$17.50	$16.00	
Timber/unit (m²)	2.5	7.5	5	
Contribution/m²	$3.20	$2.33	$3.20	
Ranking	1st	3rd	1st	
Minimum units to avoid penalty	500	100	150	
Timber required for minimum units (m²)	1,250	750	750	2,750
Number of units to maximum demand/production resources	3,500	233	1,350	
Timber used for production above minimum units	8,750	1,747.5	6,750	17,247.5
Timber used				19,997.5
Timber available				20,000
Total number of units to be produced	4,000	333	1,500	

Contribution from:		$
Chairs	4,000 × $8.00	32,000.00
Benches	333 × $17.50	5,827.50
Tables	1,500 × $16.00	24,000.00
		61,827.50
Fixed costs		54,000.00
Profit		7,827.50

Since the optimum plan includes production of sufficient quantities of each item to meet the order comprising the minimum demand, and production of the most profitable items already meets the maximum demand, there is no need to consider the financial penalty.

(b)   Maximum price

The maximum price which should be paid for the timber, a scarce resource, is also known as its shadow price.

The shadow price is the price at which the purchaser makes a nil contribution from its use. Therefore it is necessary to consider the use of any additional timber acquired.

The present situation is that demand for chairs and tables is fully satisfied from the existing resources, but there is some unsatisfied demand for benches. Thus any additional timber would be used to manufacture more benches.

Based on the current input cost of $2.00 per m^2 each m2 of timber earns a contribution of $2.33. Thus the maximum price to be paid is the sum of these values; $4.33 per m^2.

However, there is no benefit in obtaining more timber than can be used to satisfy the total demand for benches, so this shadow – price of $4.33 per m2 only applies for up to 12,500 m^2 of timber. Thereafter there is no use for the timber, so its shadow price is nil.

Answer 9 OPTIMAL PRODUCTION PLAN

(a)   **Objective function and constraints**

Objective is to maximise profit:
Let a = the number of units of A to be produced
Let b = the number of units of B to be produced
Objective function: 9a + 23b

Constraints:
Non-negativity	$b \geq 0$
Restriction on A	$a \geq 1{,}000$
Materials	$3a + 4b \leq 30{,}000$
Labour	$5a + 3b \leq 36{,}000$

(b)   **Graphical solution**

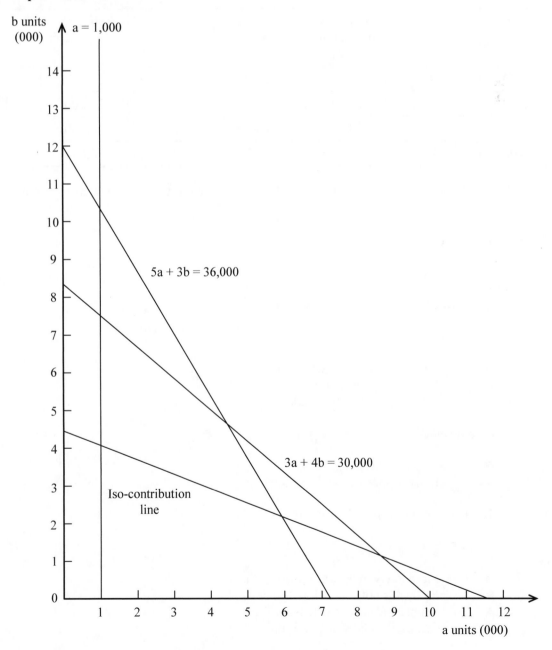

Optimal point is the intersection of the lines:

a = 1,000; and
materials constraint 3a + 4b = 30,000.

(3 × 1,000) + 4b = 30,000
3,000 + 4b = 30,000 therefore 4b = 30,000 – 3,000 giving 4b = 27,000
so b = 27,000 ÷ 4,000 therefore b= 6,750 units

The optimal production plan is to make 1,000 units of A and 6,750 units of B.

Answer 10 TABULAR APPROACH

Demand	Selling price per unit	Total revenue	Marginal revenue	Cost per unit	Total cost	Marginal cost
Units	$	$	$	$	$	$
		= units × unit selling price			= units × cost per unit	
1,100	48	52,800	52,800	22	24,200	24,200
1,200	46	55,200	2,400	21	25,200	1,000
1,300	45	58,500	3,300	20	26,000	800
1,400	42	58,800	300	19	26,600	600

MR ≥ MC at 1,300 units, therefore profits will be maximised at this point which is a selling price of $45.

Answer 11 ALBANY

(a)   **Cost plus prices**

Marginal cost plus = $30 × 120% = $36

Advantage

■   Simple and easy to calculate.
■   Focuses on contribution.
■   Can easily adjust the mark-up

Disadvantage

■   May not cover fixed costs.
■   Ignores price/demand relationship

Total cost plus = $37 × 120% = $44·40

Advantage

■   More likely to ensure a profit is made.
■   Product is not sold below full cost.
■   Simple and easy to calculate.
■   Can easily adjust the mark-up.

Disadvantage

- Fixed costs need to be allocated to the cost unit which may be ambiguous.
- Ignores price/demand relationship.

(b) **Possible pricing strategies**

Any two of the following:

- Price skimming – tends to lead to a high price initially, useful if the product is completely new.

- Penetration pricing – go to market with a low price initially to gain market share.

- Price discrimination – use two different prices in two different markets if there are barriers between the markets (e.g. age, time and location).

- Premium pricing – charging a higher price than the competitors as the product can be differentiated.

- Cost plus pricing – leads to a price that will cover costs although care needs to be taken with regard to marginal cost plus to ensure that the plus is large enough to cover fixed costs.

- Market price – leads to an acceptable price but one which may vary.

- Price to maximise profits although a demand function will need to be established – leads to an optimal price but may not affect the market price.

Answer 12 SHIFTERS HAULAGE

(a) **Profit calculations**

	Small van	Medium van	Large van
Capacity	100	150	200
Low Demand (120)	300 ^{W1}	468 ^{W3}	368 ^{W5}
High Demand (190)	300 ^{W2}	500 ^{W4}	816 ^{W6}

WORKINGS

	W1	W2	W3	W4	W5	W6
Sales	1,000	1,000	1,200	1,500	1,200	1,900
Variable cost	(400)	(400)	(480)	(600)	(480)	(760)
Goodwill	(100)	(100)		(100)		
VC adjustment			48		48	76
Depreciation	(200)	(200)	(300)	(300)	(400)	(400)
Profit	300	300	468	500	368	816

(b) **Van purchase decision**

The type of van to buy depends on the risk attitude of the investor. If they were optimistic about the future then the maximax criteria would suggest that they choose the large van as this has the potentially greatest profit. If they are more pessimistic, then they would focus on the minimum expected returns and choose the medium van, as the worst possible result is $468, which is better than the other options. As the business managers are becoming more cautious they may prefer a maximin criterion.

Expected values could be calculated thus:

Small van	$300
Medium van ($468 × 0.4) + ($500 × 0.6)	$487
Large van ($368 × 0.4) + ($816 × 0.6)	$637

Given SH is considering replacing a number of vans you could argue that an EV approach has merit (not being a one-off decision – assuming individual booking sizes are independent of each other).

The final decision lies with the managers, but given their cautiousness, a medium-sized van would seem the logical choice. The small van could never be the correct choice.

(c)   **Methods of uncertainty reduction**

Market research

This can be desk-based (secondary) or field-based (primary). Desk-based is cheap but can lack focus. Field-based research is better in that you can target your customers and your product area, but can be time consuming and expensive. The Internet is bringing down the cost and speeding up this type of research, email is being used to gather information quickly on the promise of free gifts etc.

Simulation

Computer models can be built to simulate real life scenarios. The model will predict what range of returns an investor could expect from a given decision without having risked any actual cash. The models use random number tables to generate possible values for the uncertainty the business is subject to. Again, computer technology is assisting in bringing down the cost of such risk analysis.

Sensitivity analysis

This can be used to assess the range of values that would still give the investor a positive return. The uncertainty may still be there, but the affect that it has on the investor's returns will be better understood. Sensitivity calculates the % change required in individual values before a change of decision results. If only a (say) 2% change is required in selling price before losses result an investor may think twice before proceeding. Risk is therefore better understood.

Calculation of worst and best case figures

An investor will often be interested in range. It enables a better understanding of risk. An accountant could calculate the worst-case scenario, including poor demand and high costs whilst being sensible about it. He could also calculate best-case scenarios including good sales and minimum running costs. This analysis can often reassure an investor. The production of a probability distribution to show an investor the range of possible results is also useful to explain risks involved. A calculation of standard deviation is also possible.

Answer 13 DECISION TREES

(a) **Diagram**

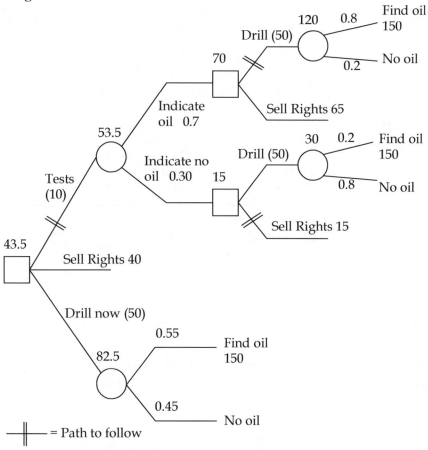

(b) **Best course of action**

The company should undertake geological tests. If the tests indicate that oil is present then a drilling programme should be carried out. However, if the tests indicate that there is no oil then the company should sell the drilling rights.

This strategy will maximise expected returns at $43.5m.

(c) **Value of decision trees**

The main value of a decision tree is that it maps out clearly all the decisions and uncertain events and exactly how they are interrelated. They are especially beneficial where the outcome of one decision affects another decision. For example in the above, the probability of eventual success changes depending on the test outcomes. The analysis is made clearer by annotating the tree with probabilities, cash flows, and expected values so that the optimum decisions (based on expected values) can be clearly seen.

However, drawing a tree diagram is only one way of undertaking a decision. It is based on the concept of expected value and as such suffers from the limitations of this technique. For example, in this example, if the test drilling proves positive, the tree indicated the company should drill, as opposed to selling the rights. But if it does there is a 20% chance of it losing $50 million. A risk-averse company may well decide to accept the safer option and sell the rights and settle for $65 million.

Answer 14 BRT CO

(a)   **Sales budget**

	Dog	Bunny	Cat	Total
Units (000)	10	20	5	35
Unit selling price	$10	$5	$20	
Sales revenue ($000)	$100	$100	$100	$300

(b)   **Production budget**

	Dog	Bunny	Cat	Total
Sales	10,000	20,000	5,000	35,000
Closing inventory	1,000	2,000	500	3,500
	11,000	22,000	5,500	38,500
Opening inventory	(2,000)	(2,000)	(1,000)	(5,000)
Production	9,000	20,000	4,500	33,500

(c)   **Materials usage (kg)**

	Dog	Bunny	Cat	Total
Silicates	45,000	120,000	31,500	196,500
Recycled glass	10,800	26,000	6,300	43,100

(d)   **Materials purchases**

	Silicates kg	Silicates $	Recycled glass kg	Recycled glass $
Usage	196,500	393,000	43,100	4,310
Closing inventory (W)	41,000	82,000	9,000	900
	237,500	475,000	52,100	5,210
Opening inventory	(23,500)	(47,000)	(1,000)	(100)
Purchases	214,000	428,000	51,100	5,110

(e)   **Labour utilisation budget – hours**

	Blowers	Finishing and packing	Total
Dog (9,000)	4,500	4,500	9,000
Bunny (20,000)	15,000	10,000	25,000
Cat (4,500)	4,500	4,500	9,000
	24,000	19,000	43,000
Hourly rate	$2	$3	
Total cost	$48,000	$57,000	$105,000

WORKING

	kg
Silicates	
20% × 10,000 × 5	10,000
20% × 20,000 × 6	24,000
20% × 5,000 × 7	7,000
	41,000
Recycled glass	
20% × 10,000 × 1.2	2,400
20% × 20,000 × 1.3	5,200
20% × 5,000 × 1.4	1,400
	9,000

Answer 15 ZERO-BASED BUDGETING

(a) **Difficulties in the public sector**

In the public sector, the objectives of the organisation are more difficult to define in a quantifiable way than the objectives of a private company. For example, a private company's objectives may be to maximise profit. The meeting of this objective can then be set out in the budget by aiming for a percentage increase in sales and perhaps the cutting of various costs. If, on the other hand, the public sector organisation is a hospital, for example, then the objectives may be largely qualitative, such as ensuring that all outpatients are given an appointment within eight weeks of being referred to the hospital. This is difficult to define in a quantifiable way, and how it is actually achieved is even more difficult to define.

This leads onto the next reason why budgeting is so difficult in public sector organisations. Just as objectives are difficult to define quantifiably, so too are the organisation's outputs. In a private company the output can be measured in terms of sales revenue. There is a direct relationship between the expenditure that needs to be incurred i.e. needs to be input in order to achieve the desired level of output. In a hospital, on the other hand, it is difficult to define a quantifiable relationship between inputs and outputs. What is easier to compare is the relationship between how much cash is available for a particular area and how much cash is actually needed. Therefore, budgeting naturally focuses on inputs alone, rather than the relationship between inputs and outputs.

Finally, public sector organisations are always under pressure to show that they are offering good value for money, i.e. providing a service that is economical, efficient and effective. Therefore, they must achieve the desired results with the minimum use of resources. This, in itself, makes the budgeting process more difficult.

(b) **Incremental and zero-based budgeting (ZBB)**

"Incremental budgeting" is the term used to describe the process whereby a budget is prepared using a previous period's budget or actual performance as a base, with incremental amounts then being added for the new budget period.

"Zero-based budgeting", on the other hand, refers to a budgeting process which starts from a base of zero, with no reference being made to the prior period's budget or performance. Every department function is reviewed comprehensively, with all expenditure requiring approval, rather than just the incremental expenditure requiring approval.

(c)   **Stages in ZBB**

(1)   Activities are identified by managers. These activities are then described in what is called a "decision package". This decision package is prepared at the base level, representing the minimum level of service or support needed to achieve the organisation's objectives. Further incremental packages may then be prepared to reflect a higher level of service or support.

(2)   Management will then rank all the packages in the order of decreasing benefits to the organisation. This will help management decide what to spend and where to spend it.

(3)   The resources are then allocated based on order of priority up to the spending level.

(d)   **No longer a place for incremental budgeting**

The view that there is no longer a place for incremental budgeting in any organisation is a rather extreme view. It is known for encouraging slack and wasteful spending, hence the comment that it is particularly unsuitable for public sector organisations, where cash cutbacks are being made. However, to say that there is no place for it at all is to ignore the drawbacks of ZBB. These should not be ignored as they can make ZBB implausible in some organisations or departments. They are as follows:

■   Departmental managers will not have the skills necessary to construct decision packages. They will need training for this and training takes time and money.

■   In a large organisation, the number of activities will be so large that the amount of paperwork generated from ZBB will be unmanageable.

■   Ranking the packages can be difficult, since many activities cannot be compared on the basis of purely quantitative measures. Qualitative factors need to be incorporated but this is difficult.

■   The process of identifying decision packages, determining their purpose, costs and benefits is massively time consuming and therefore costly.

■   Since decisions are made at budget time, managers may feel unable to react to changes that occur during the year. This could have a detrimental effect on the business if it fails to react to emerging opportunities and threats.

It could be argued that ZBB is more suitable for public sector than for private sector organisations. This is because:

■   it is far easier to put activities into decision packages in organisations which undertake set definable activities. Local government, for example, have set activities including the provision of housing, schools and local transport;

■   it is far more suited to costs that are discretionary in nature or for support activities. Such costs can be found mostly in not for profit organisations or the public sector, or in the service department of commercial operations.

Since ZBB requires all costs to be justified, it would seem inappropriate to use it for the entire budgeting process in a commercial organisation. Why take so much time and resources justifying costs that must be incurred in order to meet basic production needs? It makes no sense to use such a long-winded process for costs where no discretion can be exercised anyway. Incremental budgeting is, by its nature, quick and easy to do and easily understood. These factors should not be ignored.

In conclusion, whilst ZBB is more suited to public sector organisations, and is more likely to make cost savings in hard times such as these, its drawbacks should not be overlooked.

Answer 16 PC CO

(a)   **Objectives of a budgetary control system**

To compel planning

Budgeting makes sure that managers plan for the future, producing detailed plans in order to ensure the implementation of the company's long term plan. Budgeting makes managers look at the year ahead and consider the changes in conditions that might take place and how to respond to those changes in conditions.

To co-ordinate activities

Budgeting is a method of bringing together the activities of all the different departments into a common plan. If an advertising campaign is due to take place in a company in three months' time, for example, it is important that the production department know about the expected increase in sales so that they can scale up production accordingly. Each different department may have its own ideas about what is good for the organisation. For example, the purchasing department may want to order in bulk in order to obtain bulk quantity discounts, but the accounts department may want to order in smaller quantities so as to preserve cash flow.

To communicate activities

Through the budget, top management communicates its expectations to lower level management. Each department has a part to play in achieving the desired results of the company, and the annual budget is the means of formalising these expectations. The whole process of budget setting, whereby information is shared between departments, facilitates this communication process.

To motivate managers to perform well

The budget provides a basis for assessing how well managers and employees are performing. In this sense, it can be motivational. However, if the budget is imposed from the top, with little or no participation from lower level management and employees, it can have a seriously demotivating effect. (This is discussed further in (b).)

To establish a system of control

Expenditure within any organisation needs to be controlled and the budget facilitates this. Actual results are compared to expected results, and the reasons for any significant, unexpected differences are investigated. Sometimes the reasons are within the control of the departmental manager and he must be held accountable; at other times, they are not.

To evaluate performance

Often, managers and employees will be awarded bonuses based on achieving budgeted results. This makes more sense than evaluating performance by simply comparing the current year to the previous year. The future may be expected to be very different than the past as economic conditions change. Also, events happen that may not be expected to reoccur. For example, if weather conditions are particularly wet one year, a company making and selling umbrellas would be expected to make higher than usual sales. It would not be fair to assess managers against these historical sales levels in future years, where weather conditions are more normal.

Tutorial note: *Only six objectives were required. Other objectives that could be explained are:*

To delegate authority to budget holders: A formal budget permits budget holders to make financial decisions within the specified limits agreed (i.e. to incur expenditure on behalf of the organisation).

To ensure achievement of the management's objectives: Objectives are set not only for the organisation as a whole but also for individual targets. The budget helps to work out how these objectives can be achieved.

(b)   **Participative budgeting**

"Participative budgeting" refers to a budgeting process where there is some level of involvement from subordinates within the organisation, rather than budgets simply being set by the top level of management.

There are various views about whether participative budgeting is more effective than other styles.

Extent to which participative budgeting helps to achieve objectives

To compel planning

Participative budgeting will compel planning. Although participation can take many forms, often it will take the form of bottom-up budgeting, whereby the participation starts at the lowest level of management and goes all the way up to the top. If this is the case, then planning is taking place at many levels, and should be more accurate than if it simply takes place at a high level, by individuals who are not familiar with the day to day needs of the business.

To co-ordinate activities

Co-ordination of activities may become more time consuming if a participative style of budgeting is used. This is because, not only does there need to be co-ordination between departments but there also has to be co-ordination between the different levels of management within each department. The process should be cumbersome but also effective, with everyone knowing exactly what the plan is.

To communicate activities

Communication will be particularly effective with participative budgeting, although how effective depends on the extent of the participation. If all levels of management are involved, from the bottom up, then all levels of management know what the plan is. However, the plan may change as different departments' budgets are reviewed together and the overall budgeted profit compared to the top level management's expectations. Hence, it may be the case that those people involved in the initial budgets (i.e. lower level management) have to deal with their budgets being changed.

To motivate managers to perform well

If managers play a part in setting the budget, they are more likely to think that the figures included in them are realistic. Therefore, they are more likely to try their best to achieve them. However, it may be that managers have built budgetary slack into their budgets, in an attempt to make themselves look good. Therefore, managers could end up performing less well than they would do had tougher targets been set by their superiors.

To establish a system of control

In terms of establishing a system of control, it is largely irrelevant whether the budget setting process is a participative one or not. What is important is that actual results are compared to expected, and differences are investigated. This should happen irrespective of the budget setting process. Having said that, control is only really effective if the budgeted figures are sound. As stated above, whilst they are more likely to be realistic if a participative style of budgeting is used, the system is open to abuse in the form of budgetary slack.

To evaluate performance

Managers will be appraised by comparing the results that they have achieved to the budgeted results. A participative budget will be an effective tool for this provided that participation is real rather than pseudo and provided that the managers have not built slack into their figures, which has gone uncorrected.

Tutorial note: *The main difficulty with discursive questions such as this are that candidates write poorly structure answers that often bear little relevance to the question asked. It is important to spend time thinking and planning before writing an answer. Things to consider when planning are:*

- *What are the instruction verbs in the question?*
- *What does the examiner want me to do?*
- *What theoretical knowledge do I have that might be relevant here?*
- *What facts (if any) are given in the scenario that might be relevant?*
- *How should I structure my answer?*

The instruction verbs in (a) are "identify and explain". "Identify" simply requires a statement but "explain" calls for reasoning. So for each objectives of budgeting stated it is necessary to explain why it is relevant or important.

In (b) the instruction verb was "discuss". This requires an opinion that is supported by facts and logical reasoning. Here, a discussion about how participative (or bottom up) budgeting might help (or hinder) each of the objectives identified in (a) was called for.

The examiner often complains about poorly structured answers to discursive questions. Many candidates simply write a "sea of words" with no paragraph breaks and no apparent logic to the flow of comments. A planned and structured answer will "stand out from the crowd". Here, an obvious structure would be a paragraph for each of the objectives, with a clear sub heading (neatly underlined with a rule in the paper-based exam).

Finally, think before you write. Make sure you answer the question the examiner asked; not the question that you wished had been asked.

Answer 17 TOMKINS CO

Variable and fixed costs using the high-low method

Maximum labour hours = 350, cost $1,667
Minimum labour hours = 241, cost $1,405
An increase of 209 hours gives a cost increase of $262.

Variable cost $= \dfrac{\$267}{109} = \$2.40$ per labour hour

Using the maximum activity level:
Fixed cost per month = $1,667 – (350 × $2.40) = $827
Therefore, annual fixed cost = $827 × 12 = $9,924

Answer 18 ALEX CO

(a)   **Estimation of learning rate**

Month		Cumulative output	Cumulative hours	Cumulative average hours per unit	Comment
November	1	50		50.0	
December	2	(50 + 33) 83		41.5	83% of Nov
January	4	(83 + 55) 138		34.5	83% of Dec
February	8	(138 + 91) 229		28.6	83% of Jan
March	16	(229 + 160) 389		24.3	85% of Feb
April	32	(389 + 320) 709		22.15	91.1%

Estimated learning rate is 83%. As cumulative output doubles, cumulative average time consistently falls to 83% of the previous cumulative average time. However, the reduction appears to become less starting in March, suggesting that a steady state is reached after that.

(b)   **Estimate of when steady state starts**

The steady state is reached when no further improvement in time is taken (i.e. the incremental time per unit no longer falls). This seems to occur at the beginning of March, since the incremental time of all units in March is 20 and this does not fall further in April.

Month	Output	Incremental hours	Incremental hours per unit
November	1	50	50
December	1	33	33
January	2	55	27.5
February	4	91	22.8
March	8	160	20
April	16	320	20

Answer 19 MERMUS CO

(a)   **Revised budget using flexible budgeting**

The flexed budget will be based on the actual activity level of 90,000 units.

	$	$
Sales: $950,000 × $^{90}/_{95}$		900,000
Cost of sales		
Raw materials: 133,000 × $^{90}/_{95}$	126,000	
Direct labour: 152,000 × $^{90}/_{95}$	144,000	
Variable production overheads: 100,700 × $^{90}/_{95}$	95,400	
Fixed production overheads:	125,400	
	————	490,800
		409,200

(b)   **Variance calculations**

Raw materials cost total variance = 126,000 – 130,500 = $4,500 (Adverse)
Direct labour cost total variance = 144,000 – 153,000 = $9,000 (Adverse)

Fixed overhead absorption rate = 125,400/28,500 = $4.40 per machine hour.
Standard machine hours for actual production = 28,500 × $^{90}/_{95}$ = 27,000 hours.

Standard fixed overhead (actual production) = 27,000 × 4.4 = $118,800
Fixed overhead absorbed on actual hours = 27,200 × 4.4 = $119,680
Fixed overhead efficiency variance = 118,800 – 119,680 = 880 (Adverse)

Fixed overhead absorbed on actual hours = 27,200 × 4.4 = $119,680
Fixed overhead absorbed on budgeted hours = 28,500 × 4.4 = $125,400
Fixed overhead capacity variance = 119,680 – 125,400 = $5,720 (Adverse)

Budgeted overhead expenditure = $125,400
Actual overhead expenditure = $115,300
Fixed overhead expenditure variance = 125,400 – 115,300 = $10,100 (Favourable)

(c)   **Variance explanations**

Raw materials cost variance

The budgeted raw material cost for production of 95,000 units was $1.40 per unit (133,000/95,000) but the actual raw material cost for production of 90,000 units was $1.45 per unit (130,500/90,000). The raw material cost per unit may have increased either because more raw materials per unit were used than budgeted, or because the price per unit of raw material was higher than budgeted. Calculation of the raw material price and usage sub-variances would indicate where further explanation should be sought.

Fixed overhead efficiency variance

The fixed overhead efficiency variance measures the extent to which more or less standard hours were used for the actual production than budgeted. In this case, a total of 27,200 machine hours were actually used, when only 27,000 standard machine hours should have been used. The difference may be due to poorer production planning than expected or to machine breakdowns.

Fixed overhead expenditure variance

The fixed overhead expenditure variance measures the extent to which budgeted fixed overhead differs from actual fixed overhead. Here, actual fixed overhead is $10,100 less than budgeted. This could be due to an error in forecasting fixed production overheads such as rent and power costs, or to a decrease in fixed production overheads, such as changing to a cheaper cleaning contractor.

(d)   **Purposes of a budgeting system**

Key purposes of a budgeting system that could be discussed include planning, co-ordination, communication, control, motivation and performance evaluation. Students were required only to discuss three key purposes.

Planning

One of the key purposes of a budgeting system is to require planning to occur. Strategic planning covers several years but a budget represents a financial plan covering a shorter period (i.e. a budget is an operational plan). Planning helps an organisation to anticipate key changes in the business environment that could potentially impact on business activities and to prepare appropriate responses. Planning also ensures that the budgeted activities of the organisation will support the achievement of the organisation's objectives.

Co-ordination

Many organisations undertake a number of activities, which need to be co-ordinated, if the organisation is to meet its objectives. The budgeting system facilitates this co-ordination since organisational activities and the links between them are thoroughly investigated during budget preparation, and the overall coherence between the budgeted activities is reviewed before senior managers agree the master budget. Without the framework of the budgeting system, individual managers may be tempted to make decisions that are not optimal in terms of achieving organisational objectives.

Communication

The budgeting system facilitates communication both vertically (e.g. between senior and junior managers) and horizontally (e.g. between different organisational functions). Vertical communication enables senior managers to ensure that employees at all levels understand organisational objectives. Communication also occurs at all stages of the budgetary control process (e.g. during budget preparation and investigation of period-end variances).

Control

One of the most important purposes of a budgeting system is to facilitate cost control through the comparison of budgeted costs and actual costs. Variances between budgeted and actual costs can be investigated in order to determine the reason why actual performance has differed from what was planned. Corrective action can be introduced if necessary in order to ensure that organisational objectives are achieved. A budgeting system also facilitates management by exception, whereby only significant differences between planned and actual activity are investigated.

Motivation

The budgeting system can influence the behaviour of managers and employees, and may motivate them to improve their performance if the target represented by the budget is set at an appropriate level. An inappropriate target has the potential to be de-motivating, however, and a key factor here is the degree of participation in the budget-setting process. It has been shown that an appropriate degree of participation can have a positive motivational effect.

Performance evaluation

Managerial performance is often evaluated by the extent to which budgetary targets for which individual managers are responsible have been achieved. Managerial rewards such as bonuses or performance-related pay can also be linked to achievement of budgetary targets. Managers can also use the budget to evaluate their own performance and clarify how close they are to meeting agreed performance targets.

Answer 20 PORTLAND CO

(1)   **Sales volume variance**

	Units
Actual sales	1,000
Budgeted sales	1,100
Variance (units)	100
× standard profit per unit	$4.3
Sales volume variance (Adverse/"A")	$430

(2) Sales price variance

	$
Actual sales × actual price	39,000
Actual sales × standard price (1,000 × $40)	40,000
	___
Sales price variance (A)	1,000
	___

(3) Materials price variance

	$
Actual materials purchased at actual price	9,750
Actual materials at standard price (6,500 × $1.6)	10,400
	___
Materials price variance (Favourable/"F")	650
	___

(4) Materials usage variance

	Kgs
Actual materials used	6,500
Standard quantity for actual output (1,000 units × 6)	6,000
	___
Variance (kgs)	500
× standard cost per kg	$1.6
	___
Material usage variance (A)	$800
	___

(5) Labour rate variance

	$
Hours paid at actual rate	12,500
Hours paid at standard rate (3,100 × $4)	12,400
	___
Labour rate variance (A)	100
	___

(6) Labour efficiency variance

	Hours
Hours worked	3,100
Standard hours for actual output (1,000 units × 3)	3,000
	___
Efficiency variance (hours)	100
Standard cost per hour	$4
	___
Labour efficiency variance (A)	$400
	___

(7) Variable overhead rate variance

	$
Actual variable overhead cost	5,200
Labour hours worked × standard variable overhead absorption rate per hour (3,100 × $1.7)	5,270
	___
Variable overhead rate variance (F)	70
	___

(8) **Variable overhead efficiency variance**

	Hours
Hours worked	3,100
Standard hours for actual output (1,000 units × 3)	3,000
Efficiency variance hours	100
Standard variable overhead rate per hour	$1.7
Labour efficiency variance (A)	$170

(9) **Fixed overhead expenditure variance**

	$
Actual fixed cost	9,800
Budgeted fixed cost (1,100 units × $9)	9,900
Fixed overhead expenditure variance (F)	100

(10) **Fixed overhead volume variance**

	Units
Actual output	1,000
Budgeted output	1,100
Volume variance (units)	100
× standard fixed overhead cost per unit	$9
Volume variance (A)	$900

(11) **Fixed overhead capacity variance**

	Hours
Hours worked	3,100
Budgeted labour hours (1,100 units × 3 hours)	3,300
Capacity variance hours	200
Standard fixed overhead absorption rate per hour	$3
Capacity variance (A)	$600

(12) **Fixed overhead efficiency variance**

	Hours
Hours worked	3,100
Standard hours for actual output (1,000 units × 3 hours)	3,000
Efficiency variance hours	100
Standard fixed overhead absorption rate per hour	$3
Fixed overhead efficiency variance (A)	$300

Tutorial note: *The fixed overhead capacity and efficiency variances provide a further analysis of the fixed overhead volume variance.*

Answer 21 MILBAO CO

(a)   **Sales volume variances**

(i)   *Contribution basis*

	Superb	Excellent	Good
Actual sales (units)	36,000	42,000	18,000
Budget sales (units)	30,000	50,000	20,000
Difference	6,000	(8,000)	(2,000)
Contribution ($)	60	55	48
Variance	360,000 F	(440,000) A	(96,000) A

(ii)   *Net profit basis*

	Superb	Excellent	Good
Actual sales (units)	36,000	42,000	18,000
Budget sales (units)	30,000	50,000	20,000
Difference	6,000	(8,000)	(2,000)
Profit ($)	35	30	23
Variance	210,000 F	(240,000) A	(46,000) A

(b)   **Total sales quantity and sales mix variances**

Sales mix variance

Product	Actual sales (units)	Actual sales in budgeted mix (units)	Difference (units)	Standard contribution $	Sales mix variance $
Superb	36,000	28,800 (30%)	7,200	60	432,000
Excellent	42,000	48,000 (50%)	(6,000)	55	(330,000)
Good	18,000	19,200 (20%)	(1,200)	48	(57,600)
	96,000	96,000	0		44,400 Fav

Sales quantity variance

Product	Actual sales in budgeted mix (units)	Budgeted sales (units)	Difference (units)	Standard margin $	Sales quantity variance $
Excellent	28,800	30,000	(1,200)	60	(72,000)
Superb	48,000	50,000	(2,000)	55	(110,000)
Good	19,200	20,000	(800)	48	(38,400)
	96,000	100,000	(4,000)		(220,400) Adv

Answer 22 PAN-OCEAN CHEMICALS

(a)   **Variances**

(i)   *Materials*

Mix variance

Standard cost per batch:

S1:	$8 \times 0.3 =$	2.4
S2:	$5 \times 0.5 =$	2.5
S3:	$3 \times 0.4 =$	1.2
		6.1 for 16kg

Actual usage in standard mix:

S1	$9,576.5$
S2	$5,985.3$
S3	$3,591.3$
Total	$19,153.0$

Standard cost of input per kg $= 6.1 \div 16 = \$0.38125$
Input in standard mix $= 19,153 \times 0.31825 = \$7,302.1$

Mix variance: $7,586.3 - 7,302.1 = \$284.2A$.

Alternative calculation

	Actual usage in standard mix	Actual usage	Variance kg	Standard cost $	Variance $
S1	$9,576.5$	$8,284$	$1,292.5\ F$	0.30	$387.8\ F$
S2	$5,985.3$	$7,535$	$1,549.7\ A$	0.50	$774.9\ A$
S3	$3,591.2$	$3,334$	$257.2\ F$	0.40	$102.9\ F$
Total	$19,153.0$	$19,153$			$284.2\ A$

Yield variance

Standard output $= 90\% \times 19,153 = 17,237.7$ kgs

A standard input per batch of 16kg of materials should yield: $90\% \times 16 = 14.4$kg of output. Therefore, the standard cost per kg of output is $(1 \div 14.4) \times 6.1 = \$0.42361$.

The yield variance $= 0.42361(17,237.7 - 15,408.1) = \$775.1A$.

Usage variance

Usage variance = 775·1A + 284·2A = 1,059·3A

Proof of usage variance: actual production of 15,408kgs required input of $(^{10}/_9 \times 15,408)$ = 17,120 kgs which, in standard proportions, is:

S1	8,560	0·30	2,568
S2	5,350	0·50	2,675
S3	3,210	0·40	1,284
Total	17,120		6,527 (or 15,408 × 0·42361 = 6,527)

Actual proportions:

S1	8,284	0·30	2,485·2
S2	7,535	0·50	3,767·5
S3	3,334	0·40	1,333·6
Total	19,153		7,586·3

Variance = 6,527 – 7,586·3 = 1,059·3A

(ii)   Labour

Standard labour cost = \$5 ÷ 14·4 = \$0·3472 per kg

Rate variance: 6,916 – (1,235 × 5) = \$741A

Efficiency variance = (1,235 × 5) – (15,408 × 0·3472) = \$825A

Total variance = 6,916 – (15,408 × 0·3472) = 825A + 741A = \$1,566A.

(b)   Mix variances

The total mix variance measured in quantity is zero since the expected mix is based on the total quantity actually used and hence the difference between total expected and total actual is nil.

Answer 23 DENZEL CO

(a)   Comparison of standard labour cost with actual labour cost

	$
Standard cost of actual output based on original standard	
(122,000 units × 1.25 hours × \$12 per hour)	1,830,000
Planning variance (balancing figure)	390,400 (A)
Revised standard cost of actual output	
(122,000 units × 1.4 hours × \$13 per hour)	2,220,400
Operating variance (balancing figure)	222,040 (F)
Actual labour cost	1,998,360

(b)   **Planning variances**

Usage variance

	$
Actual output × original standard time per unit × original standard rate (122,000 × 1.25 hours × $12)	1,830,000
Actual output × revised standard time per unit × original standard rate (122,000 × 1.4 hours × $12)	2,049,600
Planning usage variance	219,600 (A)

Price variance

	$
Actual output × revised standard time per unit × original standard rate	2,049,600
Actual output × revised standard time per unit × revised standard rate (122,000 × 1.4 hour × $13)	2,220,400
Planning price variance	170,800 (A)

Tutorial note: *The sum of the planning price variance and the planning usage variance is $390,400, which is the total planning variance obtained in part (a).*

(c)   **Principles of revising standards**

Variance analysis is used to assess the performance of various managers involved in the purchasing and production process. Their performance is compared to a target, the standard cost, and any differences between actual and standard will be considered to be the responsibility of the manager.

The controllability principle is that managers should only be judged on things they have control over. Where standards turn out to be unrealistic, due to changes that are outside of the control of the managers, they do not reflect accurately the performance of the managers. Standards should therefore be revised for uncontrollable factors before variance analysis is performed.

The risk of revising variances is that managers may be tempted to include inefficiencies in the revised standard to reduce any adverse variances, which may be due to internal factors. Variances should not be revised to include internal, controllable factors or inefficiencies.

In practice, there is likely to be some discussion of whether a change should be included in the revision of a variance or not. It is important therefore that all revisions are authorised by a senior, independent body, such as a budget committee before being used for variance analysis. This should ensure that changes made are fair and reasonable.

(d)   **Variance investigation**

Tutorial note: *The following factors could be discussed.*

Size

Larger cost savings are likely to arise from taking action to correct large variances and a policy could be established of investigating all variances above a given size. Size can be linked to the underlying variable in percentage terms as a test of significance: for example, a policy could be established to investigate all variances of 5% or more.

Adverse or favourable

It is natural to concentrate on adverse variances in order to bring business operations back in line with budget. However, whether a variance is adverse or favourable should not influence the decision to investigate. The reasons for favourable variances should also be sought, since they may indicate the presence of budgetary slack or suggest ways in which the budgeting process could be improved. Favourable variances may also indicate areas where the budget is easy to achieve, suggesting that the motivational effect of a budget could be improved by introducing more demanding targets.

Cost versus benefits

If the expected cost of investigating a variance is likely to exceed any benefits expected to arise from its correction, it may be decided not to investigate.

Historic pattern of variances

A variance that is unusual when compared to historic patterns of variances may be considered worthy of investigation. Statistical tests of significance may be used to highlight such variances.

Reliability and quality of data

If data is aggregated or if the quality of the measuring and recording system is not as high as would be liked, there may be uncertainty about the benefits to arise from investigation of variances.

Answer 24 SPIKE CO

(a)   **Budget revisions**

A budget forms the basis of many performance management systems. Once set, it can be compared to the actual results of an organisation to assess performance. A change to the budget can be allowed in some circumstances but these must be carefully controlled if abuse is to be prevented.

Allow budget revisions when something has happened that is beyond the control of the organisation that renders the original budget inappropriate for use as a performance management tool.

Senior management who should attempt to take an objective and independent view should approve these adjustments.

Disallow budget revisions for operational issues. Any item that is in the operational control of an organisation should not be adjusted.

This type of decision is often complicated and each case should be viewed on its merits.

The direction of any variance (adverse or favourable) is not relevant in this decision.

(b)   **Budget revision requests**

Materials

Arguments in favour of allowing a revision:

■   The nature of the problem is outside the control of the organisation. The supplier went in to liquidation; it is doubtful that Spike could have expected this or prevented it from happening.

■   The buyer, knowing that budget revisions are common, is likely to see the liquidation as outside his control and hence expect a revision to be allowed. He may see it as unjust if this is not the case and this can be demoralising.

Arguments against allowing a budget revision:

■   There is evidence that the buyer panicked a little in response to the liquidation. He may have accepted the first offer that became available (without negotiation) and therefore incurred more cost than was necessary.

■   A cheaper, more local supplier may well have been available, so it could be argued that the extra delivery cost need not have been incurred. This could be said to have been an operational error.

Conclusion: The cause of this problem (liquidation) is outside the control of the organisation and is the prime cause of the overspending. Urgent problems need urgent solutions and a buyer should not be penalised in this case. A budget revision should be allowed.

Labour

Argument in favour of allowing a revision: The board made this decision, not the departmental manager. It could be argued that the extra cost on the department's budget is outside their control.

Arguments against allowing a budget revision:

■   This decision is entirely within the control of the organisation as a whole. As such, it would fall under the definition of an operational decision. It is not usual to allow a revision in these circumstances.

■   It is stated in the question that the departmental manager complained in his board report that the staff level needed improving. It appears that he got his wish and the board could be said to have merely approved the change.

■   The department will have benefited from the productivity increases that may have resulted in the change of policy. If the department takes the benefit then perhaps they should take the increased costs as well.

Conclusion: This is primarily an operational decision that the departmental manager agreed with and indeed suggested in his board report. No budget revision should be allowed.

An alternative view is that the board made the final decision and as such the policy change was outside the direct control of the departmental manager. In this case a budget revision would be allowed.

(c) **Sales variances**

(i) *Total sales variances*

Sales price variance = (Actual SP – Standard SP) × Actual sales volume
= (16.40 – 17.00) × 176,000
= $105,600 (Adverse)

Sales volume variance = (Actual sales volume – Budget sales volume) × std. contribution
= (176,000 – 180,000) × 7
= $28,000 (Adverse)

(ii) *Market size and share variances*

Market size variance = (Revised sales volume – budget sales volume) × std. contribution
= (160,000 – 180,000) × 7
= $140,000 (Adverse)

Market share variance = (Actual sales volume – revised sales volume) × std. contribution
= (176,000 – 160,000) × 7
= $112,000 (Favourable)

(iii) *Comment on sales performance*

Sales price: The biggest issue seems to be the decision to reduce the sales price from $17.00 down to $16.40. This "lost" $105,600 of revenue on sales made compared to the standard price.

It seems likely that the business is under pressure on sales due to the increased popularity of electronic diaries. As such, they may have felt that they had to reduce prices to sustain sales at even the level they achieved.

Volume: The analysis of sales volume into market size and share shows the usefulness of planning and operational variances. Overall, the sales level of the business is down by 4,000 units, losing the business $28,000 of contribution or profit. This calculation does not in itself explain how the sales department of the business has performed.

In the face of a shrinking market they seem to have performed well. The revised level of sales (allowing for the shrinking market) is 160,000 units and the business managed to beat this level comfortably by selling 176,000 units in the period.

As mentioned above, the reducing price could have contributed to the maintenance of the sales level. Additionally, the improved quality of support staff may have helped maintain the sales level. Equally the actions of competitors are relevant to how the business has performed. If competitors have been active then merely maintaining sales could be seen as an achievement.

Spike should be concerned that its market is shrinking.

Answer 25 TIES ONLY CO

(a)   **Financial performance**

Sales growth

Ties Only has had an excellent start to their business. From a standing start they have made $420,000 of sales and then grown that figure by over 61% to $680,000 in the following quarter. This is impressive particularly given that the clothing industry is very competitive. Equally it is often the case that new businesses make slow starts, this does not look to be the case here.

Gross profit

The gross profit for the business is 52% for quarter 1 and 50% for quarter 2. Comparable industry data is not provided so firm conclusions cannot be drawn. However, gross profit has reduced by 2% in just one quarter. This is potentially serious and should not be allowed to continue.

The cause of this fall is unclear, price pressure from competitors is possible, who may be responding to the good start made by the business. If Ties Only were reducing its prices, this would reflect on the gross profit margin produced.

It could also be that the supply side cost figures are rising disproportionately. As the business has grown so quickly, it may have had to resort to sourcing extra new supplies at short notice incurring higher purchase or shipping costs. These could all reduce gross margins achieved.

Website development

Website costs are being written off as incurred to the management accounting profit and loss account. They should be seen as an investment in the future and unlikely to continue in the long term. Website development has been made with the future in mind; future website costs may be expected to be lower than at present. Taking this into consideration the loss made by the business does not look as serious as it first appears.

Administration costs

These are 23·9% of sales in quarter 1 and only 22·1% of sales in quarter 2. This could be good cost control, impressive given the youth and inexperience of the management team.

Also any fixed costs included in the cost (directors' salaries are included) will be spread over greater volume. This would also reduce the percentage of cost against sales figure. This is an example of a business gaining critical mass. The bigger it gets the more it is able to absorb costs. Ties Only may have some way to go in this regard, gaining a much greater size than at present.

Distribution costs

This is a relatively minor cost that again appears under control. Distribution costs are likely to be mainly variable (postage) and indeed the proportion of this cost to sales is constant at 4·9%.

Launch marketing

Another cost that although in this profit and loss account is unlikely to continue at this level. Once the "launch" is complete this cost will be replaced by more general marketing of the website. Launch marketing will be more expensive than general marketing and so the profits of the business will improve over time. This is another good sign that the results of the first two quarters are not as bad as they seem.

Other costs

Another cost that appears under control in that it seems to have simply varied with volume.

(b) **Reflection of future performance**

Although the business has lost over $188,000 in the first two quarters of its life, this is not as disastrous as it looks. The reasons for this view are:

■ New businesses rarely breakeven within six months of launch;

■ The profits are after charging the whole of the website development costs, these costs will not be incurred in the future;

■ Launch marketing is also deducted from the profits. This cost will not continue at such a high level in the future.

The major threat concerns the fall in gross profit percentage that should be investigated.

The owners should be relatively pleased with the start that they have made. They are moving in the right direction and without website development and launch marketing they made a profit of $47,137 in quarter 1 and $75,360 in quarter 2.

If sales continue to grow at the rate seen thus far, then the business (given its ability to control costs) is well placed to return significant profits in the future.

The current profit (or loss) of a business does not always indicate a business's future performance.

(c) **Non-financial indicators of success**

Website hits

This is a very impressive start. A new business can often find it difficult to make an impression in the market. Growth in hits is 25% between the two quarters. If this continued over a year the final quarter hits would be over 1·3m hits. The Internet enables new businesses to impact the market quickly.

Number of ties sold

The conversion rates are 4% for quarter 1 and 4·5% for quarter 2. Both these figures may seem low but are ahead of the industry average data. (Industry acquired data must be carefully applied, although in this case the data seems consistent.) It appears that the business has a product that the market is interested in. Ties Only is indeed looking competitive.

Average price achieved for the ties:

Quarter 1: $\dfrac{\$420,000}{27,631}$ = $15·20 per tie

Quarter 2: $\dfrac{\$680,000}{38,857}$ = $17·50 per tie

This suggests that the fall in gross profit has little to do with the sales price for the ties. The problem of the falling gross profit must lie elsewhere.

On time delivery

Clearly the business is beginning to struggle with delivery. As it expands, its systems and resources will become stretched. Customers' expectations will be governed by the terms on the website, but if expectations are not met then customers may not return. More attention will have to be placed on the delivery problem.

Sales returns

Returns are clearly common in this industry. Presumably, ties have to be seen and indeed worn before customers accept them as suitable. The concern here is that the business's return rate has jumped up in quarter 2 and is now well above the average for the industry. In other words, performance is worsening and below that of the competitors. If the business is under pressure on delivery (as shown by the lateness of delivery) it could be that errors are being made. If wrong goods are sent out then disappointed customers will return them.

The alternative view is that the quality of the product is not what is suggested by the website. If the quality is poor then unhappy customers could well return the products.

This is clearly concerning and an investigation is needed.

System down time

System down time is to be avoided by Internet based sellers as much as possible. If the system is down then customers cannot access the site. This could easily lead to lost sales at that time and cause customers not to try again at later dates. Downtime could be caused by insufficient investment at the development stage or the site being is under pressure due to peaking volumes. This second explanation is more likely in this case (as money was invested to build the server to a high specification).

The down time percentage has risen alarmingly and this is concerning. Figures for the average percentage down time achieved by comparable systems are needed to be able to comment further.

The owners are likely to be disappointed given the level of initial investment they have already made. A discussion with the website developers may well be warranted.

Summary

This new business is doing well. It is growing rapidly and ignoring non-recurring costs is profitable. It needs to focus on delivery accuracy, speed and quality of product. It also needs to focus on a remedy for the falling gross profit margin.

WORKINGS

(1)   Gross profit

Quarter 1:   Quarter 2:

$$\frac{218,400}{420,000} = 52\%$$ $$\frac{339,320}{680,000} = 50\%$$

(2)   Website conversion rates

Quarter 1:   Quarter 2:

$$\frac{27,631}{690,789} = 4\%$$ $$\frac{38,857}{863,492} = 4\cdot5\%$$

(3)   Website hits growth

Between quarter 1 and quarter 2 the growth in website hits has been:

$$\frac{863,492}{690,789} = 1\cdot25 = 25\%$$

Answer 26 VALUE FOR MONEY

(a)   Meaning of VFM

Interested parties need to be able to make judgements about the performance of the organisation with which they are concerned. Commercial organisations can usually be evaluated by a range of profitability and other financial measures that are suitable for organisations that are subject to competitive pressures in terms of their markets and funding requirements.

In organisations that operate in a monopoly situation or do not charge for the goods or services that they provide such measures are either inappropriate or impossible to calculate. Alternative measures of performance have been developed over time to evaluate such organisations and these have given rise to the general concept of value for money.

VFM is usually assessed through three groupings of performance indicators which are used to measure economy, efficiency and effectiveness. These are often referred to as the "3 Es".

Economy is concerned with the amount of resources that an organisation has used in its operations; put bluntly the question is "how much did it cost?" It should be noted that economy is primarily concerned only with inputs, without reference to either quantity or quality of outputs.

Efficiency is concerned with the relationship between the resources used and the output of goods and services. It follows that the outcome of this measure can be affected by changing either the inputs and/or outputs. Thus such measures are equivalent to, say, the cost of a unit produced in a factory. Often, though, the measure to use is not so clear-cut and so a range of effectiveness measures is often used in response to this problem.

Effectiveness is about the achievement of intended results; are the policy objectives being achieved? Thus effectiveness measures are concerned only with outputs, regardless of inputs. Since they are concerned with objectives and goals they are often "soft" measures rather than those that can be objectively quantified. Again a range of measures is usually appropriate.

In summary, economy is concerned with inputs, effectiveness with outputs and efficiency with the relationship between the two.

In order to use VFM to evaluate performance it is necessary to use all of the three types of measures and to take an overview based upon the results. Such performance indicators give an insight into performance when used comparatively, both within and between organisations.

An example of the relationship between the three types of measure may be useful to illustrate the points:

Imagine one was attempting to evaluate the performance of a hospital. A measure of economy may be "cost per member of staff". Changing the relative grades of staff employed can clearly change this ratio. Moving towards lower grades of staff will reduce the ratio but may not be in the interest of patients.

A measure of effectiveness may be "length of waiting list for surgery". No doubt waiting times could be reduced if more resources were made available.

A measure of efficiency may be "cost per hip-replacement operation". This measure can be affected either by reducing the cost of the hip-replacement team or by the team replacing more hips within a given cost.

(b)   Evaluation of measures

(i)   Annual cost of service

This is a measure of economy since it is based on inputs. Whilst a low cost may be favourable in terms of public funding requirements, it may not produce a generally acceptable level of service.

(ii)   Cost per call-out

This is measure of efficiency since it links inputs to outputs. Managers in the service could work to improve this ratio by cost reduction measures and by affecting, where possible, the services they can provide thus maximising call-outs relative to the fixed costs.

(iii)   Average response time to arrive at incident

This is a measure of effectiveness in that responding to calls for help is the output of the organisation. Response times could be improved with more resources, for example more fire stations, vehicles and personnel.

(iv)   Fire deaths per thousand head of population

Again, a measure of effectiveness since reducing casualties would certainly figure in the policy objectives. Managers could influence this ratio through a variety of measures, both critical and preventative.

In general terms such measures are only useful when taken together since manipulation of, or response to, one will usually affect others. In this case more measures should probably be developed to attempt to evaluate the service.

One of the key qualitative characteristics of published accounting information is comparability and this is relevant to the considerations of the working party. As for all performance indicators, users may be expected to make comparisons between organisations.

Because of this, it would be useful if there were consensus in respect of standard methods of calculating and presenting these performance indicators across relevant organisations. If standardisation cannot be achieved then individual organisations could increase the usefulness of their performance with indicators by stating the methods of calculation that they have used.

Benchmarking against the most successful organisations would also give meaningful context to the figures and help both internal and external users of such published information in making informed assessments on an entity's performance.

Answer 27 EATWELL RESTAURANT

(a)　　**Overall business performance**

Tutorial note: According to Fitzgerald and Moon the performance can be categorised into the key areas of financial, competitiveness, resource utilisation, quality of service and innovation/flexibility.

Financial

- Continuous turnover growth with a 123% increase over the period.
- Annual compound growth rate.
- An even faster growth in profit – approximate fivefold increase.
- Profits growing faster than revenue create an increasing net profit margin from 14% in 201W to 30.9% in 201Z. This may have arisen from improved resource utilisation (see below) resulting in a gradual decrease in the ratio of fixed costs to revenues.

Competitiveness

This is concerned with market share and growing new business areas.

Market share is measured by the rate of restaurant turnover to the turnover of all restaurants in the locality. This commences with 9.2% in 201W and continually increases to 17.5% in 201Z. There is also a rapid growth in the proposals submitted for new events (10 to 38), and even more significantly, is the faster growth in contracts won. The success rate increases from 20% in 201W to 66% in 201Z. The restaurant is therefore competing increasingly successfully in this developing business area. The restaurant is becoming increasingly price competitive.

Quality of service

The increasing number of regular customers would suggest that many customers are satisfied with the total package that the restaurant offers. This may be partly due to service quality or other factors such as price competitiveness. The growth in complaints, complimentary letters, reported cases of food poisoning and the service delivery data would suggest rather a mixed situation. It is difficult to provide a definitive comment regarding the quality of service over the period, especially as the number of customers nearly doubled over the period. Even additional calculations, such as those involving key service quality data per 100 customers would not provide the basis for an overall conclusive comment.

Innovation/Flexibility

The restaurant has fared quite well in this respect considering:

- the increase in the number of dishes on offer;
- the introduction of theme evenings;
- the development of the catering activities for special events.

The restaurant is prepared to try new dishes although the extent of its experimentation varies considerably from year to year. Also, the fluctuating and somewhat unsatisfactory service delays suggest that they are not managing to flex their resources adequately to meet peak demand levels.

Resource utilisation

The business activity level continually increased over the period (meals served) with a decline in non-productive time and the hours of operation with no customers. All these suggest an improvement in resource utilisation. We do not know whether the increase in seating capacity in 201Y arose from extending the floor area available or from the provision of more seating within a constant space. Although this capacity increase permitted more customers to be fed at peak times, it did result in a fluctuation in the annual number of meals served at each seat, 150 (201W), 204 (201X), 155 (201Y), 167 (201Z). A brief attempt was made in 201Y to extend the opening hours and increase the hourly utilisation of the premises.

(b)   **Additional information to assess performance**

Financial

- The value of assets required to generate the profits – to calculate the ROCE.

- Details of cost categories (e.g. labour, food overheads – to assess comparative financial ratios).

- Did the increase in capacity in 201Y require additional capital investment – to assess the marginal returns?

- The level of business risk inherent in alternative business and the associated expected return.

Competitiveness

- National trends in restaurant attendance and revenues provide broader comparisons.
- Data on/customer surveys of restaurants in targeted customer groups.

Quality of service

- To assess various intangible factors (e.g. politeness of staff, atmosphere and décor, responsiveness to customer requests).

- Food writers or expert ratings.

Innovation/Flexibility

- Staff training and the potential for multi-skilled activities to provide greater operational flexibility.

- The ability to cope with non-standard requests (e.g. special dietary needs and respond to customer needs).

Resource utilisation

- Data on employee numbers would facilitate the calculation of business activity per employee.

- Data on floor area per customer.

Answer 28 BRACE CO

(a)   **Balanced scorecard**

The balanced scorecard is a strategic management technique for communicating and evaluating the achievement of the strategy and mission of an organisation. It comprises an integrated framework of financial and non-financial performance measures that aim to clarify, communicate and manage strategy implementation. It translates an organisation's strategy into objectives and performance measurements for the following four perspectives:

Financial perspective

The financial perspective considers how the organisation appears to shareholders. How can it create value for its shareholders? Kaplan and Norton, who developed the balanced scorecard, identified three core financial themes that will drive the business strategy: revenue growth and mix, cost reduction and asset utilisation.

Customer perspective

The customer perspective considers how the organisation appears to customers. The organisation should ask: "to achieve our vision, how should we appear to our customers?"

The customer perspective should identify the customer and market segments in which the business units will compete. There is a strong link between the customer perspective and the revenue objectives in the financial perspective. If customer objectives are achieved, revenue objectives should be too.

Internal perspective

The internal perspective requires the organisation to ask: "what must we excel at to achieve our financial and customer objectives?" It must identify the internal business processes that are critical to the implementation of the organisation's strategy. Kaplan and Norton identify a generic process value chain consisting of three processes; the innovation process, the operations process and the post-sales process.

Learning and growth perspective

The learning and growth perspective requires the organisation to ask whether it can continue to improve and create value.

If an organisation is to continue having loyal, satisfied customers and make good use of its resources, it must keep learning and developing. It is critical that an organisation continues to invest in its infrastructure (i.e. people, systems and organisational procedures) in order to provide the capabilities that will help the other three perspectives to be accomplished.

(b)   **Divisional performance**

ROI

Division A
Net profit = $44·6m × 28% = $12·488m
ROI = $12·488m ÷ $82·8m = 15·08%

Division B
Net profit = $21·8m × 33% = $7·194m
ROI = $7·194m ÷ $40·6m = 17·72%

Residual income

Division A
Divisional profit = $12·488m
Capital employed = $82·8m
Imputed interest charge = $82·8m × 12% = 9·936m
Residual income = $12·488m – $9·936m = $2·552m.

Division B
Divisional profit = $7·194m
Capital employed = $40·6m
Imputed interest charge = $40·6m × 12% = $4·872m
Residual income = $7·194 – $4·872 = $2·322m.

Comments

If a decision about whether to proceed with the investments is made based on ROI, it is possible that the manager of Division A will reject the proposal whereas the manager of Division B will accept the proposal. This is because each division currently has a ROI of 16% and since the Division A investment only has a ROI of 15·08%, it would bring the division's overall ROI down to less than its current level. On the other hand, since the Division B investment is higher than its current 16%, the investment would bring the division's overall ROI up.

Considering what would actually be best for Brace as a whole; both investments have a healthy return and should therefore be accepted. Hence, the fact that ROI had been used as a decision-making tool has led to a lack of goal congruence between Division A and the company as whole. This backs up what the new manager of Division A is saying. If residual income was used in the decision-making process, both proposals would be accepted by the divisions since both have a healthy RI. In this case, RI helps the divisions to make decisions that are in line with the best interests of Brace. This also supports the new manager's view.

It is important to note, however, that each of the methods has numerous advantages and disadvantages that have not been considered here.

Answer 29 ABLE & BAKER

(a)   **Potential benefits**

- Achieving global/corporate profit optimality;

- Goal congruence between divisions and group;

- Fostering divisional autonomy and local decision making;

- The measurement of divisional financial performance via the generation of a recognised income figure;

- The provision of "pricing signals" that induce decisions to improve corporate profitability.

(b) **Transfer price**

(i) *Spare capacity*

When division Able has spare capacity the incremental cost to the company of producing Y is $35. The cost of the external supply is $38. Therefore it is cheaper for the company if division Able supplies Y. The transfer price should be fixed at a price above $35, to provide an incentive for Able to supply and generate a contribution towards the recovery of fixed costs and below $38 to encourage Baker to buy. The price should be set so that both divisions, acting independently and in their own interests, choose to trade at the set price.

(ii) *Full capacity*

The situation now requires a consideration of the opportunity cost of diverting resources away from the supply of external customers. For every additional unit of Y produced and supplied to Baker, Able will have to sacrifice indirectly $10 in lost contribution from external sales ($42 – $32). So the relevant cost of making a unit of Y in these circumstances is $35 plus $10 i.e. $45. $45 represents the "real" cost of supplying division Baker with one unit of product Y. It is therefore better for the company to purchase product Y from the external supplier for $38. This can be ensured by fixing the transfer price of Y above $38, to discourage Baker from buying it from Able. At a price of $40, Baker would not choose to buy from Able, and it would not be in the interest of Able to sell to the other division.

(c) **Data to be collected**

- Unit variable costs to identify the incremental costs of producing the different products and services;

- Sales prices in the external market to assess potential contribution towards overheads and profit;

- Current and maximum capacity levels to ascertain the opportunity cost of lost sales;

- The limiting factors that are constraining the capacity so that the managers can take appropriate action to expand capacity;

- The value of the shadow prices so that the managers can evaluate whether it is worthwhile to acquire specific resources;

- The availability and prices of obtaining supplies from external suppliers (for make or buy decisions).

Answer 30 WASH CO

(a) **Transfer price using machine hours**

Total overhead costs = $877,620
Total machine hours = $(3,200 \times 2) + (5,450) \times 1 = 11,850$
Overhead absorption rate = $877,620 ÷ 11,850 = $74·06
Overhead cost for S = $2 \times \$74·06 = \$148·12$ and for R = $1 \times \$74·06 = \$74·06$.

	Product S	Product R
	$	$
Materials cost	117.00	95.00
Labour cost (at $12 per hour)	6 .00	9.00
Overhead costs	148·12	74·06
Total cost	271·12	178·06
10% mark-up	27·11	17·81
Transfer price using machine hours	298·23	195·87

(b)   **Transfer price using ABC**

Machine set up costs: driver = number of production runs.
30 + 12 = 42.
Therefore cost per set up = $306,435 ÷ 42 = $7,296·07

Machine maintenance costs: driver = machine hours: 11,850 (S = 6,400; R = 5,450)
$415,105 ÷ 11,850 = $35·03

Ordering costs: driver = number of purchase orders
82 + 64 = 146.
Therefore cost per order = $11,680 ÷ 146 = $80

Delivery costs: driver = number of deliveries.
64 + 80 = 144.
Therefore cost per delivery = $144,400 ÷ 144 = $1,002·78

Allocation of overheads to each product

	Product S	Product R	Total
	$	$	$
Machine set-up costs	218,882	87,553	306,435
Machine maintenance costs	224,192	190,913	415,106
Ordering costs	6,560	5,120	11,680
Delivery costs	64,178	80,222	144,400
Total overheads allocated	513,812	363,808	877,620
Number of units produced	3,200	5,450	8,650
	$	$	
Overhead cost per unit	160·57	66·75	
Transfer price per unit:			
Materials cost	117.00	95.00	
Labour cost	6.00	9.00	
Overhead costs	160·57	66·75	
Total cost	283·57	170·75	
Add 10% mark up	28·36	17·08	
Transfer price under ABC	311·93	187·83	

(c) **Profit allocation**

Using ABC transfer price from part (b):

Assembly division	Product S	Product R	Total
Production and sales	3,200	5,450	
	$	$	
10% mark up	28·36	17·08	
Profit	90,752	93,086	183,838

Retail division	Product S	Product R	Total
Production and sales	3,200	5,450	
	$	$	
Selling price	320	260	
Cost price	(311·93)	(187·83)	
Profit per unit	8·07	72·17	
Total profit	25,824	393,327	419,151

Answer 31 HOTELCO

A well-designed management information system should provide relevant, accurate and timely information to all levels of management. Hence the introduction of a new system should not only allow the directors to monitor performance, but may actively help to address the issue of declining profits by providing greater feedback to tactical and operational managers.

(a) **Periodic reports**

The computerisation of hotel records and the on-line link to head office allow the latter to acquire and assimilate large volumes of data rapidly. This would permit monthly financial statements to be produced for each hotel in time for directors to review them and action their findings whilst the implications are still relevant.

The statements should comprise balance sheet, cash flow and profit and loss account, and would enable directors to gain an overview of the effects of local management decisions and the effectiveness of corporate policy on a regional basis.

These periodic reports should include comparative data in addition to actual data. Figures could be included for budget/previous periods/industry data. Variances could be reported.

(b) **Demand reports**

The new system should also be capable of producing a range of reports on demand such that senior management can assess high risk aspects of the business as required (i.e. monthly or more frequently if desired).

(i) *Room occupancy report*

This report would detail what percentage of a hotel's available rooms was occupied and by utilising information from registration cards should split this figure between business and non-business users.

Incorporating room charge-out rates into the same report would enable management to:

- assess the accuracy of revenues from room letting;

- identify if variations in regional rates have a significant impact on occupancy rates and overall profitability;

- identify any trends in business/non-business usage and the opportunity for differential pricing and attracting more guests.

Room rates should also be compared to a centralised master file of approved rates and discounts to ensure hotel managers are not offering rooms at below cost in an attempt to attract business.

To ensure all income from rooms let is recorded, the room occupancy report should compare rooms for which income has been recorded to a housekeeper's report of rooms cleaned.

(ii)   Bad debts report

This report should highlight all debts more than (say) 60 days overdue.

Bad debts could be a major contributor to declining profits, particularly if the hotels catering for business travellers are taking block corporate bookings.

As an additional control to ensure that all reported bookings are genuine, this report should also include a comparison of revenues with a direct room cost such as laundry bills.

(iii)   Restaurant sales report

This should compare total revenues from the restaurant to the number of bills raised and occupancy rate, thereby allowing the directors to ascertain if unduly preferential arrangements are being allowed by some of their hotels.

Differentiation should also be made between billings to non-residents, as this will enable attention to be focused on this separate revenue source. This is important if the restaurant is not being operated at capacity such that non-residents could be a useful source of income.

(iv)   Bar sales report

Total billing should be compared as for restaurant sales, but without the division between residents and non-residents, as the latter would be difficult to obtain in view of the large number of cash transactions.

(v)   Restaurant and bar inventory report

Physical control over bar and restaurant inventory is difficult to maintain and losses represent a potentially significant restriction on profits.

An head office official should attend a physical count at each hotel. The quantities should then be the benchmark for subsequent movements and be "enforced" by random spot checks.

The inventory report should compare the verified figure as adjusted for subsequent purchases and sales to occupancy rate and highlight significant percentage variation from preceding months (i.e. indicating pilferage and misappropriation). The overall inventory holding of each hotel should be compared to inventory turnover to ensure the former does not represent an excessive usage of working capital.

(vi)   Cash availability report

Many of the bar and restaurant takings of each hotel will be in cash; like inventory, this is easily susceptible to misappropriation.

The head office directors will require a report that summarises the cash takings and receipts, and makes a comparison between hotels making allowances for differences in the number and type of resident (e.g. business users may utilise corporate client cards rather than their own cash).

(vii)   Wages report

Given that wages, often casual wages, represent a significant item of cash expenditure for hotels and one which can be directly related to revenue, a report should be produced detailing the number of waged staff per week and their wages.

This could then be compared to revenue reports to identify any significant departures from the expected relationship. This may indicate general inefficiency capable of improvement or fraud.

(c)   Error/exception reports

A unique feature of computerised systems is their ability to sift through large volumes of data and extract only those figures of significance to users.

These exception reports should be produced automatically to highlight matters such as:

- hotel revenue falling below budget (e.g. by more than 10%);
- group cash reserves/funding requirements exceeding available limits;
- hotels giving rooms below the approved room rates.

ABOUT BECKER PROFESSIONAL EDUCATION

Becker Professional Education provides a single solution
for students and professionals looking to advance their
careers and achieve success in:

- Accounting

- International Financial Reporting

- Project Management

- Continuing Professional Education

- Healthcare

For more information on how Becker Professional Education can
support you in your career, visit www.becker.com/acca.

Becker Professional Education
is an ACCA approved content provider

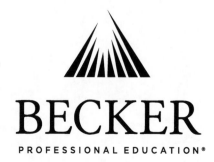